T0255896

Lecture Notes in Computer Science　14619

Founding Editors

Gerhard Goos
Juris Hartmanis

The series Lecture Notes in Computer Science (LNCS), including its subseries Lecture Notes in Artificial Intelligence (LNAI) and Lecture Notes in Bioinformatics (LNBI), has established itself as a medium for the publication of new developments in computer science and information technology research, teaching, and education.

LNCS enjoys close cooperation with the computer science R & D community, the series counts many renowned academics among its volume editors and paper authors, and collaborates with prestigious societies. Its mission is to serve this international community by providing an invaluable service, mainly focused on the publication of conference and workshop proceedings and postproceedings. LNCS commenced publication in 1973.

Xiaofeng Meng · Xueying Zhang · Danhuai Guo ·
Di Hu · Bolong Zheng · Chunju Zhang
Editors

Spatial Data and Intelligence

5th China Conference, SpatialDI 2024
Nanjing, China, April 25–27, 2024
Proceedings

 Springer

Editors
Xiaofeng Meng
Renmin University of China
Beijing, China

Danhuai Guo
Beijing University of Chemical Technology
Beijing, China

Bolong Zheng
Huazhong University of Science
and Technology
Wuhan, China

Xueying Zhang
Nanjing Normal University
Nanjing, China

Di Hu
Nanjing Normal University
Nanjing, China

Chunju Zhang
Hefei University of Technology
Hefei, China

ISSN 0302-9743 ISSN 1611-3349 (electronic)
Lecture Notes in Computer Science
ISBN 978-981-97-2965-4 ISBN 978-981-97-2966-1 (eBook)
https://doi.org/10.1007/978-981-97-2966-1

Preface

This volume contains the papers from the 5th Spatial Data Intelligence China Conference (SpatialDI 2024), which was held at Novotel Nanjing East Suning, Nanjing, during April 25–27, 2024.

SpatialDI 2024 was sponsored by the ACM SIGSPATIAL China Branch and the ACM SIGMOD China Branch, organized by Nanjing Normal University, and co-organized by Chinese Professionals in Geographic Information Sciences (CPGIS), the Modeling Geographical Systems Commission of the International Geographical Union (IGU-MGSC), Jiangsu Society of Remote Sensing and Geographic Information Systems, Jiangsu Provincial Society of Surveying, Mapping and Geographic Information, and the Yangtze River Delta Science Data Center of the National Earth System Science Data Center.

SpatialDI mainly aims to address the opportunities and challenges brought about by the convergence of computer science, geographical information science, AI, and beyond. The main topics of SpatialDI 2024 included generative AI and spatial data intelligence, spatiotemporal knowledge graphs and large geographic models, digital twins and smart cities, government spatiotemporal big data and data governance, emergency disaster reduction and sustainable development, spatial humanities and social geography computing, spatiotemporal data management and analysis, and intelligent processing and analysis of remote sensing images; the conference also included the ACM China SIGSPATIAL Rising Star and Doctoral Dissertation Award Forum.

This year, the conference received 95 submissions. Each submission was reviewed by at least three reviewers selected from the Program Committee in a single-blind process. Based on the reviewers' reports, 25 papers were finally accepted for presentation at the conference. The acceptance rate was 26%.

In addition to the regular papers, the conference featured a number of invited talks. Qingquan Li of Shenzhen University, China, delivered a talk entitled "Spatial Data Intelligence Empowers Dual-Carbon New Technology". Jiong Xie of Alibaba Cloud Database and Storage Laboratory, China, addressed "Physical World Full-Space Data Processing Accelerator". Gao Cong of Nanyang Technological University, Singapore, spoke about "Geospatial Entity Representation: a Step towards a Foundational Model of Cities".

The proceedings editors wish to thank our keynote and invited speakers and all the reviewers for their contributions. We also thank Springer for their trust and for publishing the proceedings of SpatialDI 2024.

April 2024

Xiaofeng Meng
Xueying Zhang
Danhuai Guo
Di Hu
Bolong Zheng
Chunju Zhang

Organization

Honorary Chairs

Jian Lv   Fellow of Chinese Academy of Sciences, Nanjing University, China

Chenghu Zhou   Fellow of Chinese Academy of Sciences, Institute of Geographic Sciences and Natural Resources Research, Chinese Academy of Sciences, China

Steering Committee

Xiaofeng Meng   Renmin University of China, China

Yunjun Gao   Zhejiang University, China

Yu Liu   Peking University, China

Guangzhong Sun   University of Science and Technology of China, China

Huayi Wu   Wuhan University, China

Xing Xie   Microsoft Research Asia, China

General Co-chairs

Linwang Yuan   Nanjing Normal University, China

Zhiming Ding   Institute of Software, Chinese Academy of Sciences, China

Tao Pei   Institute of Geographic Sciences and Natural Resources, Chinese Academy of Sciences, China

Program Co-chairs

Xueying Zhang   Nanjing Normal University, China

Danhuai Guo   Beijing University of Chemical Technology, China

| Zhipeng Gui | Wuhan University, China |
| Longbiao Chen | Xiamen University, China |

Local Organizing Co-chairs

Weihua Dong	Beijing Normal University, China
Jianqiu Xu	Nanjing University of Aeronautics and Astronautics, China
Di Hu	Nanjing Normal University, China

Publicity Co-chairs

| Peiquan Jin | University of Science and Technology of China, China |
| Hao Wu | Central China Normal University, China |

Proceedings Co-chairs

| Bolong Zheng | Huazhong University of Science and Technology, China |
| Chunju Zhang | Hefei University of Technology, China |

Sponsorship Co-chairs

| Qingfeng Guan | China University of Geosciences (Wuhan), China |
| Liang Wu | Zondy Cyber Group, China |

Industry Co-chairs

| Guanjie Zheng | Shanghai Jiao Tong University, China |
| Xiaoping Du | Institute of Aerospace Information Innovation, Chinese Academy of Sciences, China |

Special Forum Co-chairs

Feng Zhang   Zhejiang University, China
Chao Chen   Chongqing University, China

Paper Selection Co-chairs

Yang Yue   Shenzhen University, China
Lizhen Wang   Yunnan University, China

Overseas Liaison Co-chairs

Xinyue Ye   Texas A&M University, USA
Fusheng Wang   State University of New York at Stony Brook, USA

Registration Co-chair

Na Ren   Nanjing Normal University, China

Contents

Spatiotemporal Data Prediction

Remote Sensing Data Classification

Applications of Spatiotemporal Data Mining

Spatiotemporal Data Analysis

Multi-view Contrastive Clustering with Clustering Guidance and Adaptive Auto-encoders

Bingchen Guo[1], Bing Kong[1(✉)], Lihua Zhou[1], Hongmei Chen[1], and Chongming Bao[2]

[1] School of Information Science and Engineering, Yunnan University, Kunming 650091, Yunnan, People's Republic of China
kongbing@ynu.edu.cn
[2] National Pilot School of Software, Yunnan University, Kunming 650091, Yunnan, People's Republic of China

Abstract. Graph-based clustering plays an important role in the clustering area. However, in general clustering tasks, the graph structure of data does not exist, so the strategy for constructing the graph is crucial for the performance of the subsequent tasks. In the subsequent comparison task, existing methods fail to consider the class information and will introduce false-negative samples in the random negative sampling, causing poor performance. To this end, we propose a multi-view comparison clustering framework based on clustering guidance and adaptive encoder. First, the graph is constructed adaptively according to the generative perspective of the graphs. The adaptive process is designed to induce the model to exploit the high-level information behind data and utilize the non-Euclidean structure. Then, representations can be optimized by aligning with clustered class information, and simultaneously, the optimized representations can promote clustering, leading to more powerful representations and clustering results. Extensive experiments on five datasets demonstrate that our method achieves new state-of-the-art results on clustering tasks.

Keywords: Multi-view Clustering · Self-supervised Learning · Contrastive Learning · Representation Learning

1 Introduction

With the development of information collection and processing technologies, multi-view data [1] with multiple features are ubiquitous in various application domains. The significant difference between multi-view clustering [2] and single-view clustering is that the former requires extracting shared valuable representations from multiple views. In order to fully exploit the topological and node attribute information of graph data, graph neural network [3] (GNN) methods have been developed in recent years. Compared with autoencoders [4] (AEs), GNNs have powerful nonlinear feature extraction capabilities, and the extracted features can be directly applied to the downstream tasks of clustering. Graph Convolutional Network [5] (GCN) methods define convolution operations

X. Meng et al. (Eds.): SpatialDI 2024, LNCS 14619, pp. 3–14, 2024.
https://doi.org/10.1007/978-981-97-2966-1_1

on graph data for feature extraction. Motivated by the great success of autoencoders, methods based on graph autoencoder [6] (GAE) networks extract deep embeddings in a self-training manner. Multi-view clustering methods based on generalized Bayesian networks [7] mine the key information required for clustering by extracting the deep representations of each view and fusing them into a coherent representation that fully takes into account the complementary information between views. Despite the remarkable performance, there are two problems that need to be solved for existing multi-view clustering methods:

(1) How to go about better constructing the graph structure of the data [8]?
(2) The clustering process is unsupervised [9], what approach should be taken to supervise the operation of the model?

In order to solve these problems, this paper presents a multi-view clustering model MAAC with clustering guidance and adaptive encoder. The model better integrates the attribute information and structural information of the samples, and after obtaining the low-dimensional representations of each view simply mixes and then projects them to obtain the shared representations, and then utilizes the clustering results to guide the comparison learning. Specifically, an initial graph of the data is first constructed according to the differences of the data sets, and the graph is reconstructed according to the reconstruction loss and L2 regularization to obtain a better graph representation. In the subsequent comparison task, the clustering results are used to act as pseudo-labels to iteratively optimize the clustering objective in order to fully explore the correlation between the representation learning and clustering tasks.

Overall, the contributions of this paper are summarized as follows:

1. A multi-view clustering model (MAAC) is proposed, which can construct the graph structure adaptively by means of an adaptive encoder. Additionally, clustreing guidance module is utilized to iteratively optimize the clustering objective. Making the generated low-dimensional representation more cluster-oriented.
2. Utilizing the step size and distance between nodes to capture the correlation between nodes more accurately, and combines local structure maintenance to avoid the representation collapse problem. Enable more reasonable aggregation of neighboring nodes.
3. Clustering guidance module to guide comparison learning, the predictive labels generated during model iteration are used to backward supervise the model, so that the problem of false negative samples in comparison learning can be alleviated, thus improving the clustering performance.

2   Related Work

2.1   Multi-view Clustering

The basic idea of multiview clustering is to explore the consistency and complementary information embedded in multiview data and learn a clustering partition that fits all views. Thanks to the powerful representation capability of GCNs, a wide range of researchers have explored deep clustering methods that use GCNs to extract both graph structure and node information. Kipf [5] et al. use GCNs as an encoder to aggregate attribute information of neighboring nodes and form feature representations, and then use inner product decoders to reconstruct the graph's adjacency matrices, and Xie [10] et al. allow the model to learn a more favorable node representations for subsequent clustering tasks.

Considering that the representation collapse problem of GCNs is not better mitigated, Li [11] et al. propose an adaptive graph encoder network model, which aims to induce the model to take full advantage of the high-level information behind the data and utilize the non-Euclidean structure through an adaptive process. With the introduction of adaptive node weights and adaptive neighborhood size, it can be applied to different types of data with good robustness.

2.2 Contrastive Learning

Contrast learning is one of the unsupervised methods that have developed rapidly in recent years. Contrast learning aims to group positive sample pairs and exclude negative sample pairs, where positive sample pairs represent different augmented views of a graph. Negative pairs are the enlarged views of other graphs. Federici [12] et al. investigate the relationship between contrast learning and multi-view learning from information bottleneck theory. In this way, contrast learning can help to learn a more robust representation of data features. Meanwhile, Tsai [13] et al. combine contrast learning and multi-view learning, which can further improve the learning effect. In addition, there are some works that explore the effect of applying contrast methods on multiple perspectives and find that this can help extract consistent information. Ke [14] proposed a contrast mixture model (CONAN) that maximizes consistent information across perspectives and discards task-irrelevant information through a common representation from the perspective of an information bottleneck. Specifically, comparison methods pull positive samples together while pushing negative samples apart, so the quality of the positive and negative samples determines the performance of the comparison method. Specifically, SCAGC [15] and GDCL [16] improve the quality of negative samples by randomly selecting samples from different clusters.

3   The Framework of MAAC Network

In this section, we provide a detailed description of our proposed method, MAAC, which overall framework is presented in Fig. 1. The framework comprises three main modules: the adaptive auto-encoder module, the contrastive fusion module, and the cluster guidance module. The first module utilizes Euclidean distance to combine sample and neighbor information. The second module focuses on enhancing sample discrimination. Finally, the self-supervised module integrates representation learning and clustering tasks into a single step, enabling them to work in tandem and reinforce each other.

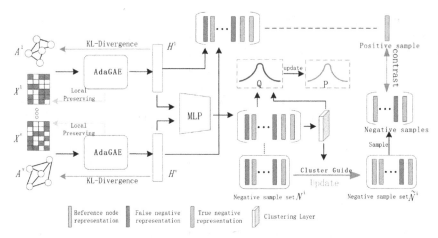

Fig. 1. MAAC model architecture diagram

3.1 Adaptive Graph Auto-encoder

In order to fully exploit the correlation between nodes in the graph and allow the network to extract low-dimensional representations that are more suitable for downstream tasks, a graph adaptive encoder strategy is used by introducing the weights of nodes, the size of neighborhoods, in order to learn the representation H.

Graph Generation for Probability Distributions. In general clustering scenarios, links between two nodes frequently do not exist. Therefore, we need to construct a weighted graph via some scheme.The underlying connectivity distribution of node v_i is represented by the conditional probability $p(v|v_i)$. Since $p(v_j|v_i) \geq 0$, the probabilities can be considered as effective weights. And in general $p(v_j|v_i) \neq p(v_i|v_j)$. Thus, the construction of the weighted graph is equivalent to finding the underlying connectivity distribution. If $p(v_i|v_j)$ is larger, then v_i and v_j are said to be similar. After obtaining the connectivity distribution, by converting the directed graph to an undirected graph by

$$W_{ij} = (p(v_i|v_j) + p(v_j|v_i))/2 \text{ such that } \sum_{j=1}^{n} p(v_j|v_i) = 1, \text{effect is shown in Fig. 2.}$$

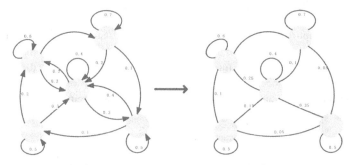

Fig. 2. Tectonic map of connectivity distribution

Based on the above definition, give the definition of $p(v_j|v_i)$:

$$p(v_j|v_i) = \frac{(d_{i.}^{(k+1)} - d_{ij})_+}{\sum_{v=1}^{k} d_{i.}^{(k+1)} - d_{i.}^{(v)}} \tag{1}$$

where $d_{i.}^{(k+1)}$ denotes the k + 1st value of the Euclidean distance from node v_i to all other nodes and d_{ij} denotes the Euclidean distance between nodes v_i to v_j. is used to calculate the strength of the relationship between user i and other users.

Auto-encoder for Weighted Graph. Encoder: we can simply set $\tilde{A} = W$ and $\hat{A} = \tilde{D}^{-\frac{1}{2}}\tilde{A}D^{-\frac{1}{2}}$. The encoder consists of multiple GCN layers and aims to transform raw features to latent features with the constructed graph structure. Specifically, the potential features generated by layer m are defined as:

$$H = \varphi_m(\hat{A}\varphi_{m-1}(...\varphi_1(\hat{A}XW_1)...)W_m) \tag{2}$$

Decoder: we aim to recover the connectivity distribution $p(v|v_i)$ based on Euclidean distances, instead of reconstructing the weight matrix $\tilde{A}$ via inner-products. Firstly, the distance of the latent feature H is calculated by $\hat{d}_{ij} = ||H_i - H_j||_2^2$. Secondly, the connectivity distribution is reconstructed by a normalization step.

$$q(v_j|v_i) = \frac{\exp(-\hat{d}_{ij})}{\sum_{j=1}^{n} \exp(-\hat{d}_{ij})} \tag{3}$$

Inputting $-\hat{d}_{ij}$ into the SoftMax layer, when $\hat{d}_{ij}$ is smaller, $q(v_j|v_i)$ is larger. In other. words, the similarity is measured by Euclidean distances rather than inner-products, which are usually used in GAE. To measure the difference between two distributions, Kullback-Leibler (KL) Divergence is therefore utilized and the objective function is defined as:

$$\min_{q(\cdot|v_i)} KL(p||q) \Leftrightarrow \min_{q(\cdot|v_i)} \sum_{i,j=1}^{n} p(v_j|v_i) \log \frac{1}{q(v_j|v_i)} \tag{4}$$

In order to prevent the problem of representation collapse, regular term is introduced here to ensure the sparsity of node connections, and the total loss is shown below:

$$\min_{q,H} \sum_{i,j=1}^{n} p(v_j|v_i) \log \frac{1}{q(v_j|v_i)} + \alpha tr(B\tilde{L}B^T) \tag{5}$$

α is a tradeoff parameter that balance the cross entropy term and local consistency penalty term.

3.2 Contrastive Fusion

After obtaining the low-dimensional representations of each view, in order to explore the view-consistent high-level information embedded in each H^v, here we use the contrastive fusion module:

$$Z = MLP([H^1; H^2; ...; H^v]) \tag{6}$$

where $MLP(\bullet)$ is a sub-network consisting of several fully connected layers. Z is the public representation we need. When maximizing the mutual information between Z and H^v, rather than simply adding H^v, Z can capture the intrinsic information of each view. Thus, we introduce cosine similarity to compute the similarity between Z and H^v with the following formula:

$$L_{con\_loss} = -\sum_{j=1}^{n} \log \frac{\exp(sim(z_j, h_j^v))}{\sum_{k=1}^{2N} 1_{[k \neq i]} \exp(sim(z_j, h_j^v))} \tag{7}$$

z_j represents the j-th sample in z and h_j^v represents the j-th sample in H^v. The above formula improves the discriminative power of the samples by maximizing the lower bound of mutual information. However, this framework fails to consider the class information, leading to less discriminative representations. Thus, we introduce a clustering layer into this framework and jointly optimize it with graph representations to alleviate these problems.

3.3 Graph Clustering

In order to obtain more accurate clustering results (pseudo-labels) and discriminative representations, the clustering loss L_{clu} is utilized to optimize both clustering and contrast learning. L_{clu} is defined as the KL scatter computed between the distributions P and Q, where Q is the distribution of soft labels as measured by the t-student scores, and P is the target distribution derived from Q. The KL scatter is then computed as a function of the t-student scores, and P is the target distribution:

$$L_{CLU} = KL(P||Q) = \sum_i \sum_j p_{ij} \log \frac{p_{ij}}{q_{ij}} \tag{8}$$

where i denotes the i-th node in and j denotes the j-th cluster.

$$q_{ij} = \frac{\left(1 + ||z_i - \mu_j||^2\right)^{-1}}{\sum_j \left(1 + ||z_i - \mu_j||^2\right)^{-1}} \tag{9}$$

where z_i is the feature vector obtained after the sample i is compressed by the encoder and dimensionality reduction, and μ_j is the clustering center of the j-th clusters, and $||\cdot||$ denoting the Euclidean distance. The target distribution P is of the following form:

$$p_{ij} = \frac{q_{ij}^2 / \sum_i q_{ij}}{\sum_j \left(q_{ij}^2 / \sum_i q_{ij}\right)} \tag{10}$$

$\sum_i q_{ij}$ is the clustering frequency, in the target distribution P. By minimizing the KL divergence loss between the target distribution Q and the distribution P, the clustering module learns a better representation of the clustering task.

$$L = \beta \sum_{i=1}^{n} L_{con\_loss} + L_{clu} \tag{11}$$

where β is a hyperparameter used to control the trade-off between the two terms. Furthermore, during training, the target distribution P is used as a base fact soft label, but also depends on the predicted soft label. Therefore, to avoid instability, one should not update P in each iteration, which is updated every T iterations according to Eq. 12. And given the learning rate lr, the clustering is updated by backpropagation:

$$\mu_j = \mu_j - \frac{lr}{n} \sum_{v_i \in V} \frac{\partial L_{clu}}{\partial \mu_j} \tag{12}$$

In this way, representations can be optimized by aligning with the clustering results, and simultaneously, the optimized representations can promote clustering, leading to more powerful results.

3.4 Clustering Guidance Strategy

After we obtain the clustering results, we can randomly select negative samples from clusters which are different from the positive samples' cluster. In this way, as a supervisory signals, the clustering results can be utilized to effectively decrease the false negative samples in the negative sampling process. In the absence of labels, existing graphical comparison learning methods obtain negative samples by randomly sampling from the set $N_i = \{v_m\}(m \neq i)$. This results in the presence of several false negative samples, as shown in Fig. 3. The ideal negative sample set for v_i can be obtained when nodes with same labels as v_i are removed from N_i. However, since ground-truth labels are unavailable, the pseudo labels is alternatively used to decrease the false-negative samples, which can alleviate the negative effect of false negative points. Specifically, the pseudo-labels generated by the clustering layer are denoted as $Y_p = \{y_i\}_{i=1}^n$. Then, to decrease the false negative samples in N_i, we remove the nodes with the same pseudo-label as node v_i from N_i and denote the new negative sample node set as $\tilde{N}_i$:

$$\tilde{N}_i = \{v_m\}(y_m \neq y_i) \tag{13}$$

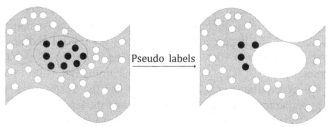

● Node with different true label from v_i ○ Node with same true label as v_i

Fig. 3. Clustering Guide Effect Diagram

4 Experiments

In this section, we conduct experiments on five benchmark datasets and evaluate the clustering performance compared to existing benchmark methods. This section reports the datasets, evaluation metrics and analysis of the experimental results. In addition, we perform ablation studies and parameter sensitivity analysis.

4.1 Datasets and Evaluation Measure

In order to verify the performance of MAAC. We select five datasets, including text dataset: 3Sources, image dataset: Ccv, LandUse-21, Hw2sources image and text dataset: Voc, and the statistical information of these five benchmark datasets is shown in Table 1. The clustering performance is measured using two standard evaluation matrices. Clustering Accuracy (ACC) and Normalized Mutual Information (NMI), where a higher value indicates better performance.

Table 1. Dataset description

dataset	views	samples	clusters	dimension
3Sources	3	169	6	3560/3601/3068
Landuse	3	2100	21	20/59/40
Voc	2	5649	20	512/399
Ccv	3	6773	20	5000/5000/4000
Hw2sources	2	2000	10	76/240

4.2 Implementation Details

We implemented MAAC on PyTorch running on CentOS Linux 7 with an Nvidia 3090 GPU and 24 GB memory. Adam optimization was used to train the model. For Voc, we set the learning rate to le-3, the dimension m of the low-order representation learned by the encoder is 256, and the hyperparameter is set to {1, 1}. For Landuse, we set m to 128 and the hyperparameter is {0.1, 0.1}, the learning rate to le−3. For Hw2sources, the hyperparameter is {0.05, 0.1}, m is 32 and the learning rate is set to le−2. The m of Ccv is 40, the hyperparameter is {0.01, 0.001} and the learning rate is le−3, For 3Sources, the hyperparameter is {1, 0.6}, m is 256 and the learning rate is set to le−3. we trained MAAC 50 times and reported the operation results of the average results. The comparison algorithms were downloaded from the author's home page or GitHub, and the experimental results were averaged through multiple experiments with the parameters suggested in the paper.

4.3 Baselines

In order to evaluate the clustering performance, spectral clustering and 9 multi-view clustering algorithms are selected as baseline for comparison. The algorithms are described as follows: Spectral clustering is one of the most classic traditional clustering methods. Two representative contrastive methods, i.e., CONAN, CMEGC. Two representative subspace methods, i.e., RMSL, SCMC, learn the relationships between samples by building a self-representation layer. Representative deep clustering methods, i.e., AE2-NETS, learn the potential embedment by the deep way and implement clustering algorithms. SMC, SMVSC and CAGL are three graph methods and AMGL is a graph fusion method.

4.4 Results

Table 2 reports the clustering performance of all compared methods on six benchmarks. From these results, we can conclude that 1) As can be seen from the table, the MAAC algorithm outperforms most of the baseline algorithms. For example, in the HW dataset, the algorithm proposed in this paper outperforms the suboptimal SMC by 1.3% and 0.7% in the ACC and NMI metrics, respectively. It also achieves good results in the Ccv and Landuer datasets, indicating the effectiveness of the model; 2) Comparing the methods, SMCGC algorithm outperforms the comparison algorithms CONAN and CMEGC in all the experimental metrics of the datasets, because these methods do not take into account the problem of false negative samples in constructing the negative samples, whereas MAAC model effectively avoids the problem of false negative samples in the comparative learning through the clustering guidance module. Improved clustering accuracy; 3) Graph approach, the three algorithms SMC, SMVSC and CAGL take a graph approach

Table 2. Clustering results on 5 datasets

dataset	3Sources	Voc	Ccv	Landuse	Hw2sources
Metrics	ACC NMI	ACC NMI	ACC NMI	ACC NMI	ACC NMI
SC-best	35.9 10.9	43.2 33.4	9.3 7.4	24.8 26.1	79.3 76.4
Ae2-Nets	51.3 40.7	57.1 57.1	9.2 4.1	20.9 23.5	93.8 88.4
AMGL	45.6 72.8	56.9 63.0	15.5 8.9	23.5 26.4	94.1 88.8
Conan	80.6 72.8	62.1 62.1	12.4 5.3	25.6 27.1	88.2 80.5
SMVSC	78.8 70.6	64.3 63.4	11.1 13.9	26.3 29.6	94.3 88.9
SMC	82.6 78.3	65.8 63.5	11.4 14.5	27.1 31.5	96.2 91.7
CMGEC	76.5 67.3	59.5 55.2	19.6 16.5	26.9 30.8	85.6 78.3
RMSL	53.1 49.3	47.7 44.8	21.5 15.7	25.7 28.6	80.3 72.7
SCMC	83.9 74.6	64.5 60.1	21.2 16.0	26.7 32.4	89.9 80.5
CAGL	88.3 79.8	64.6 63.7	**21.9** 17.0	27.5 **33.0**	94.9 89.1
Ours	**88.6 82.1**	**65.7 68.3**	21.4 **17.5**	**27.9** 32.8	**92.4**

to the data. A smoother node representation is obtained. But the graph approach cannot correct the wrong links between samples caused by low-level relationships and cannot utilize the high-level information behind the data. And when using graph encoder, the representation collapse occurs. MAAC algorithm captures the structural information of the nodes better by adaptive graph encoder, and effectively avoids the problem of representation collapse by L2 regularization; 4) Autoencoder methods, AE2-NETs, RMSL, SCMC only go for the attribute information of the nodes without considering the correlation information between the nodes, so even if these methods fully exploit the consistency and complementarity information of the multiview data they lead to sub-optimal results due to the influence of the dataset in their results.

4.5 Ablation Experiment

The importance of the mutual information supervision module and pseudo-labeling techniques in MAAC is demonstrated through ablation experiments to further show the effectiveness of the MAAC model. A framework consisting of graph encoder and KL scatter as the main parts is firstly used as the baseline (AK) as it is a main framework for the MAAC model to be trained. AK-AG, AK-CG and AK-AG-CG are denoted as the methods with the addition of adaptive encoder, clustering guidance and both, respectively.

From Table 3, it can be seen that AK-AG and AK-CG have higher metrics than AK on all four datasets. This indicates that the adaptive encoder and clustering guidance modules enhance the clustering results. However, the effect of adding the adaptive encoder on the 3Sources dataset decreases instead, mainly because clustering clusters are very unevenly distributed, which leads to the graph in the process of constructing the generated low-dimensional representations of the clusters with fewer nodes will have similar properties to the clusters with more nodes, which is not easy to carry out the subsequent work, thus affecting the clustering results. On the Hw and 3Sources dataset, since the initialized clustering results of the dataset are high, the effect is improved the most after the clustering guidance module, which indicates that the clustering guidance module can correct the sampling bias in the comparative learning, making the samples become more clearly distinguishable from each other, and effectively mitigating the problem of oversmoothing due to the over-similarity between samples.

Table 3. Ablation Experiment.

	AK	AK-AG	AK-CG	AK-AG-CG
3Sources	75.2	73.0	80.6	**88.6**
Landuse-21	20.3	26.1	25.1	**27.9**
Voc	57.9	63.2	60.8	**65.7**
Ccv	18.9	18.9	14.5	**21.4**
Hw	74.5	93.2	82.5	**97.5**

4.6   Cluster Visualization

In order to verify the effectiveness of MAAC more intuitively, CONAN, LMVSC, RMSL and MAAC are visualized on the Voc dataset using t-Distributed Stochastic Neighbor Embedding (t-SNE) algorithm. The corresponding visualization results are exhibited in Fig. 4. As shown in sub-figure (a), the distribution of the original data is denser and the clusters are more confusing with each other. Among them, different colors indicate different clusters. The results show that MAAC has a clearer structure and can better reveal the intrinsic clustering structure among the data. Subgraph (b), subgraph (c) and subgraph (d) achieved good results, but there are still some overlaps between clusters and some points are wrongly assigned to other clusters. And pulling apart the clusters between different classes, the boundary of each color is not clear, which leads them not to distinguish similar nodes of different classes well. MAAC has a clearer structure with more clustered samples between clusters, and there are clear contours between different clusters, which can better reveal the intrinsic clustering structure between the data.

(a)RAW   (b)RMSL   (c)LMVSC   (d)CONAN   (e)MAAC

Fig. 4. Visualization of Voc

5   Conclusion

In this paper, we first use Adaptive Auto-encoders to obtain better graphical structure, then use contrasitive fusion to enhance the discriminant ability of samples, and finally use a clustering guidance strategy to guide the operation of the model. The clustering task, ablation study, parameter sensitivity analysis and clustering visualization analysis on 5 datasets fully demonstrate the validity and superiority of MAAC model in clustering performance. In addition. In the process of collecting multi-view data in the real world, there will be deficiencies. How to effectively carry out clustering task in the missing data will also be our next research focus.

Acknowledgments. This research is supported by the National Natural Science Foundation of China (62062066, 61762090, 61966036 and 62276227), Yunnan Fundamental Research Projects (202201AS070015), Yunnan Key Laboratory of Intelligent Systems and Computing (202205AG070003), Yunnan Provincial Reserve Program for Young and Middle-aged Academic and Technical Leaders(202205AC160033).

References

1. Xu, C., Tao, D., Xu, C.: A survey on multi-view learning (2013). https://doi.org/10.48550/arXiv.1304.5634
2. Nie, F., Li, J., Li, X.: Self-weighted multiview clustering with multiple graphs. In: IJCAI, pp. 2564–2570. Melbourne (2017)
3. Scarselli, F., Gori, M., Tsoi, A.C., Hagenbuchner, M., Monfardini, G.: The graph neural network model. IEEE Trans. Neural Netw. **20**, 61 (2009)
4. Vincent, P., Larochelle, H., Bengio, Y., Manzagol, P.-A.: Extracting and composing robust features with denoising autoencoders. In: Proceedings of the 25th International Conference on Machine learning, pp. 1096–1103. Finland (2008)
5. Kipf, T.N., Welling, M.: Semi-supervised classification with graph convolutional networks (2016)
6. Kipf, T.N., Welling, M.: Variational Graph Auto-encoders (2016)
7. Wang, W., Arora, R., Livescu, K., Bilmes, J.: On deep multi-view representation learning. In: International Conference on Machine Learning, pp. 1083–1092. PMLR (2015)
8. Tiao, L., Elinas, P., Nguyen, H., Bonilla, E.V.: Variational graph convolutional networks. In: Proceedings of the Graph Representation Learning Workshop (2016)
9. Yang, X., et al.: Cluster-guided contrastive graph clustering network (2023). https://doi.org/10.48550/arXiv.2301.01098
10. Xie, J., Girshick, R., Farhadi, A.: Unsupervised deep embedding for clustering analysis. In: International Conference on Machine Learning, pp. 478–487. PMLR, Hawai (2016)
11. Li, X., Zhang, H., Zhang, R.: Adaptive graph auto-encoder for general data clustering (2020)
12. Tian, Y., Krishnan, D., Isola, P.: Contrastive multiview coding. In: Vedaldi, A., Bischof, H., Brox, T., Frahm, J.-M. (eds.) ECCV 2020. LNCS, vol. 12356, pp. 776–794. Springer, Cham (2020). https://doi.org/10.1007/978-3-030-58621-8_45
13. Tsai, Y.-H.H., et al.: Self-supervised learning from a multi-view perspective. https://doi.org/10.48550/arXiv.2006.05576
14. Ke, G., Hong, Z., Zeng, Z., Liu, Z., Sun, Y., Xie, Y.: CONAN: contrastive fusion networks for multi-view clustering. In: 2021 IEEE International Conference on Big Data (Big Data), pp. 653–660. IEEE, Orlando (2020)
15. Xia, W., Gao, Q., Yang, M., Gao, X.: Self-supervised contrastive attributed graph clustering (2021)
16. Zhao, H., Yang, X., Wang, Z., Yang, E., Deng, C.: Graph debiased contrastive learning with joint representation clustering. In: International Joint Conference on Artificial Intelligence. Montreal (2021)

Cloud-Edge Collaborative Continual Adaptation for ITS Object Detection

Zhanbiao Lian[1,2], Manying Lv[1,2], Xinrun Xu[1,2], Zhiming Ding[2], Meiling Zhu[2], Yurong Wu[1,2(✉)], and Jin Yan[1,2(✉)]

[1] University of Chinese Academy of Sciences, Beijing 100049, China
{lianzhanbiao21,lvmanying21,xuxinrun20,wuyurong20,
yvette.yan}@mails.ucas.ac.cn
[2] Chinese Academy of Sciences, Institute of Software, Beijing 100190, China
{zhiming,meiling}@iscas.ac.cn

Abstract. In the field of Intelligent Transportation Systems (ITS), the challenge of performance degradation in lightweight object detection models on edge devices is significant. This issue primarily arises from environmental changes and shifts in data distribution. The problem is twofold: the limited computational capacity of edge devices, which hinders timely model updates, and the inherent limitations in the generalization capabilities of lightweight models. While large-scale models may have superior generalization, their deployment at the edge is impractical due to computational constraints. To address this challenge, we propose a cloud-edge collaborative continual adaptation learning framework, specifically designed for the DETR model family, aimed at enhancing the generalization ability of lightweight edge models. This framework uses visual prompts to collect and upload data from the edge, which helps to fine-tune cloud-based models for improved target domain generalization. The refined knowledge is then distilled back into the edge models, enabling continuous adaptation to diverse and dynamic conditions. The effectiveness of this approach has been validated through extensive experiments on two datasets for traffic object detection in dynamic environments. The results indicate that our learning method outperforms existing techniques in continual adaptation and cloud-edge collaboration, highlighting its potential in addressing the challenges posed by dynamic environmental changes in ITS.

Keywords: Traffic object detection · continual adaptation · Cloud-Edge Collaboration

1 Introduction

Real-time video reasoning, crucial for intelligent traffic surveillance, heavily relies on object detection technologies [23]. Although cloud-based systems, like Microsoft Azure [12], employ complex, generalized deep neural network (DNN)

Z. Lian and M. Lv—have contributed equally to this work.

© The Author(s), under exclusive license to Springer Nature Singapore Pte Ltd. 2024
X. Meng et al. (Eds.): SpatialDI 2024, LNCS 14619, pp. 15–27, 2024.
https://doi.org/10.1007/978-981-97-2966-1_2

models, they face challenges with excessive data transmission over wide area networks (WAN), leading to performance degradation from data compression methods like frame filtering [10] and resolution reduction [4] under limited bandwidth. Conversely, edge-based DNN inference, which processes data on local devices, offers faster feedback but is limited by the computational resources of these devices, necessitating the use of simpler, lightweight models. While these models are energy-efficient, they struggle with generalizability and accuracy in varying real-time traffic conditions, leading to data drift issues, such as models trained in sunny conditions underperforming in adverse weather [13].

Domain adaptation enables model generalization from source to target domains but is computationally demanding, challenging for online execution on edge devices [11]. Research is increasingly focusing on cloud-edge collaborative computing to leverage cloud's computational power and edge's low latency, optimizing real-time traffic detection. Yet, creating an adaptive traffic detection architecture via cloud-edge collaboration faces hurdles, notably model adaptation efficiency. Cloud models' high parameter count makes fine-tuning for the target domain computationally intensive [11], a task complicated by constant traffic changes requiring ongoing model adjustments. Moreover, retraining with new data risks catastrophic forgetting [14].

To address real-world environmental changes in edge models, we propose a novel cloud-edge collaborative continual adaptation framework, depicted in Fig. 1. This framework involves edge devices sampling data from new target domains and uploading it to the cloud, where the cloud generalizes this data to new domains and imparts the learned knowledge to lightweight edge models.

Specifically, we introduce a cloud-edge collaborative Intelligent Transportation System (ITS) object detection framework tailored for the DETR family, the forefront in object detection technology [25]. Our approach utilizes a visual prompt-based update strategy in the cloud and a knowledge distillation update strategy on the edge. To mitigate communication bandwidth issues, a domain discriminator filters out context-specific samples, minimizing bandwidth requirements. For leveraging the large model's superior generalization, we apply domain query-based feature adversarial learning to adapt the large teacher model to the target domain. Knowledge from the large model is then distilled to the lightweight student model within the DETR family. Ultimately, the updated student model and visual prompt generator are deployed to the edge for real-world adaptability.

In summary, our key contributions are as follows:

1. We present a traffic object detection framework that utilizes cloud-edge collaboration, augmented with adaptive online learning.
2. We develop an unsupervised domain adaptation algorithm for updating cloud models, which leverages visual prompts and domain queries.
3. We introduces a knowledge distillation algorithm specifically tailored for DETR family models, aimed at updating edge models.
4. We conduct experiments on two real-world traffic datasets to evaluate our method, and the results show that our method outperforms the current state-of-the-art methods.

2   Related Works

Intelligent Traffic Object Detection. In the latest research within the intelligent traffic object detection domain,In 2023, a new algorithm for multi-scale traffic object detection was introduced, which is based on an improved YOLOv5s model. This method significantly enhances the accuracy of detecting small traffic targets by incorporating a detection head specifically designed for extremely small objects [9]. In 2022, an exploration into the performance of road vehicle detection utilizing drone-captured imagery was conducted, evaluating the effectiveness of mainstream deep learning technologies, such as the RetinaNet framework [16].

Cloud-Edge Collaborative Object Detection. The primary goal of cloud-edge collaboration techniques is to optimise the synergy between cloud and edge computing, thereby enhancing their computational capabilities and efficiency. Recent methodologies have explored different strategies for distributing computational tasks between the cloud and the edge. Study such as those in [2,3] have investigated offloading computational tasks to the cloud to augment the limited computational capabilities of edge devices. While these approaches have improved computational efficiency somewhat, they fall short of fully exploiting the potential for deep collaboration between cloud and edge computing. More comprehensive studies, such as AMS [8] and DCCL [21], have gone deeper, considering not only collaboration but also optimising resource allocation and task scheduling. However, these methods also have limitations, particularly in adapting to the dynamically changing data distributions in real-world scenarios, which calls into question their adaptability and flexibility.

3   Preliminaries

3.1   Definition

Domain: We define a domain D as a dataset in which all samples follow the same distribution, i.e., $\mathcal{D} = \{(x_i, y_i)_{i=1}^N\}(x \in \mathcal{X}, y \in \mathcal{Y}, \mathcal{X} \sim \mathcal{P})$, where N represents the size of the domain. The label space $\mathcal{Y}$ may be empty, indicating the absence of label data. $\mathcal{X} \sim \mathcal{P}$ signifies that the sample space follows the distribution $\mathcal{P}$.

3.2   Problem Statement

Given a lightweight model f_{edge} deployed on a edge device, we aim to maintain a certain performance level across a set of continuously changing target domains $\{\mathcal{D}_{t1}, \mathcal{D}_{t2}, ..., \mathcal{D}_{tT}\}$, while working with limited bandwidth resources. The target domains can have arbitrary data distributions.

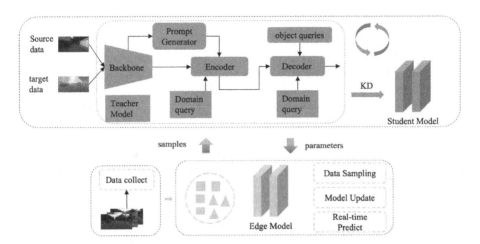

Fig. 1. The overview of the cloud-edge collaboration framework

4 The Framework for Continual Adaptation in Traffic Object Detection Based on Cloud-Edge Collaboration

In this section, we present a detailed exposition of our newly developed framework explicitly designed for updating cloud-edge collaboration models within the DETR family. The framework is structured around two core components as shown in Fig. 1:

- **Cloud Component: Dynamic Domain Adaptation.** Our approach employs a large-scale teacher model with an extensive parameter set, denoted as f_{tea}, located in the cloud. This model consistently gathers data from edge devices, enhancing its ability to generalize. To better adapt to unlabeled target domains, we integrate domain query-based adversarial learning, crucial for isolating domain-independent features. Additionally, we deploy a visual prompt generator, aimed at increasing model adaptation efficiency. This generator significantly bolsters the model's performance in target domain scenarios, while maintaining a low computational overhead.
- **Edge Component: Efficient Model Synchronization.** We deploy a lightweight model on edge, referred to as f_{edge}. To facilitate efficient knowledge transfer, we clone f_{edge} to create a lightweight student model, denoted as f_{stu}, which acts as the recipient of the teacher's knowledge. The knowledge acquired from f_{tea} is then transferred to f_{stu} using the knowledge distillation technique. In order to accelerate the acquisition of novel insights into teacher models, we have devised a relationship-based knowledge distillation loss specifically tailored to the characteristics of the DETR family of models.

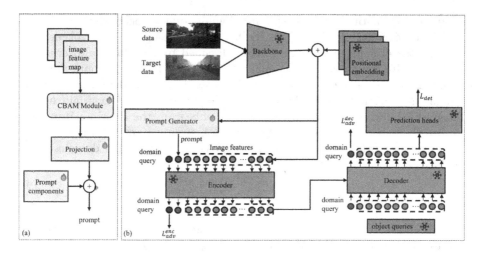

Fig. 2. Domain Adaptation for Cloud Models using Visual Prompts and Domain Queries

4.1   Cloud Component: Dynamic Domain Adaptation

Inspired by insights from [22], we design a visual prompt generator adept at generating effective visual prompts from unlabeled images. Recognizing the need for model adaptation to the target domain of unlabeled data, we incorporate the Deep Quality Feature Alignment (DQFA) mechanism, borrowed from the SFA framework [19]. This DQFA mechanism extracts and harmonizes global-level contextual features from images or object proposals, ensuring coherent data understanding. The schematic representation of our model is illustrated in Fig. 2.

Visual Prompt Generator. Previous work [5,7] has demonstrated that learnable visual prompts can provide flexibility to pre-trained models. However, current prompts, such as input tokens or pixel-level perturbations, are black boxes with limited learning capabilities and cannot reliably explore compelling knowledge benefiting object detection. Therefore, we propose designing information-rich prompts capturing multi-scale spatial priors and task-shared knowledge. To achieve this, as shown in Fig. 2 (a), we propose a lightweight visual prompt generator VPG. It contains a CBAM [20] module extracting local features of interest for input image feature map $X \in R^{H \times W \times C}$, where H, W, C denotes feature map size and number of channels respectively. There is then a projection layer mapping the new feature map to vector $q \in R^{1 \times D_p}$ where D_p is the prompt dimension. Inspired by coda-prompt [17], for the model to fully benefit from expanded parameters, we provide a set of learnable visual prompt components $VP \in R^{D_p \times M}$ where M is the number of components. The final prompt p is obtained through weighted summation of the attention mechanism as:

$$p = softmax(q \cdot VP^T) \cdot VP \tag{1}$$

Model Adaptation. We incorporate domain query tokens into both the encoder and decoder modules of our model. The two global feature tokens generated by the domain queries are further classified by two domain discriminators. These discriminators aim to make the extracted features more domain-specific and distinguishable, counter to the cross-domain model's goal of learning domain-invariant features. Therefore, we employ domain adversarial training with gradient reversal layers to reverse gradients from the discriminators and optimize the detection model for extracting domain-invariant features.

The encoder calculation form with added visual prompt and domain query is as follows.

$$[p_i, d_i^{enc}, E_i] = L_i^{enc}([p_{i-1}, d_{i-1}^{enc}, E_{i-1}]) \tag{2}$$

$$y_{d^{enc}} = head(d_N^{enc}) \tag{3}$$

where p_i and d_i represent the domain query token and the aggregated prompt features computed by the i-th Encoder layer, respectively. E_i represent the image feature tokens. The head is a domain discriminator. Similar to encoder, the decoder calculation form with domain query is as follows.

$$[d_i^{dec}, O_i] = L_i^{dec}([d_{i-1}^{dec}, O_{i-1}]) \tag{4}$$

$$y_{d^{dec}} = head(d_N^{dec}) \tag{5}$$

where O_i represent the object queries in DETR.

The adversarial learning loss consists of two parts: the encoder and the decoder. The encoder part is calculated as:

$$\mathcal{L}_{enc}^{DQFA}(f) = \mathbb{E}_{f \in \mathcal{D}_{src}} \log D(f) + \mathbb{E}_{f \in \mathcal{D}_{tgt}} \log(1 - D(f)) \tag{6}$$

Among them, $\mathcal{D}$ represents the domain discriminator. If the prediction result is source domain data, it is 0, and the target domain data is 1. The decoder part is similar to the encoder. Finally, the total adversarial learning loss is obtained as:

$$\mathcal{L}_{adv} = \lambda_1 \mathcal{L}_{enc}^{DQFA}(f) + \lambda_2 \mathcal{L}_{dec}^{DQFA}(g) \tag{7}$$

The overall loss is defined as:

$$\mathcal{L}_{all} = \mathcal{L}_{det}(I_{src}, y_{src}) - \mathcal{L}_{adv} \tag{8}$$

where L_{det} and L_{adv} represent the detection loss and feature adversarial loss respectively. I_{src} and y_{src} represent the source domain image and its label. During the model adaptation phase, it is crucial to freeze the remaining components of the model and only make updates to the visual prompt generator VPG. As shown in Fig. 2.

4.2   Edge Component: Efficient Model Synchronization

Our model adopts the architecture of the DETR family model and integrates visual prompts to enhance generalization. Due to its specific structure, traditional knowledge distillation methods may no longer apply. Therefore, combined with previous works, we designed a new knowledge distillation paradigm as shown in Fig. 3.

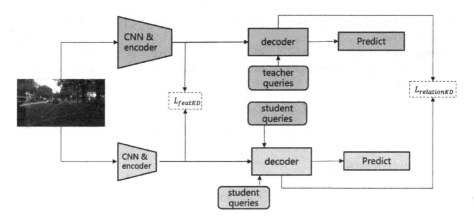

Fig. 3. Knowledge Distillation for Models on Edge

Feature-Level Knowledge Extraction: we use a general formulation of the loss function for feature distillation:

$$\mathcal{L}_{\text{featKD}} = \sum_{i=1}^{M} \sum_{k=1}^{c} \frac{A_k}{MHWc} \left\| \psi_i \odot \left(\boldsymbol{X}^T - \phi\left(\boldsymbol{X}^S \right) \right) \right\|_2^2 \tag{9}$$

where $X^T \in \mathbb{R}^{H \times W \times c}$ and $X^S \in \mathbb{R}^{H \times W \times c^S}$ denote the feature representations produced by the teacher and student models, respectively. H and W denote the height and width of the feature, and c is the channel number of the teacher's feature. ϕ is a learnable dimension adaptation layer designed to transform the student's feature dimension c^S into c. $\odot$ represents the Hadamard product of two matrices. $L(\cdot)$ indicates any loss function, such as the l2-norm distance, l1-norm distance, or maximum mean discrepancy loss. A_k is the channel attention weight computed by softmax($\cdot$), and $\psi_k \in \mathbb{R}^{H \times W}$ denotes a soft mask for the selection of knowledgeable regions in each channel, computed by calculating the similarity matrix between query embeddings and feature representations.

$$\psi_k = X^T \cdot Q_i^T \tag{10}$$

where Q_i^T is the k-th object query of the teacher model.

Instance-Level Relation Distillation: We reconceptualize the decoder output, positing the transformer's facilitation of global information access for each query and provision for each output to encapsulate information about other outputs suggests potential significance in learning interrelationships among outputs. To calculate relation distillation loss $L_{relationKD}$, we organize the student model decoder output into two undirected graphs. Each output serves as a vertex, with edge weight determined by cosine similarity. We employ graph convolutional networks (GCN) to process these constructed graphs, enabling computation of similarity between the student and teacher model outputs, thus generating the distillation loss.

Besides the distillation loss, for the optimization of the student model, we also use the pseudo labels generated by teacher model as supervision. The overall loss is as follows:

$$
\begin{aligned}
L_{stu} &= L_{Det} + L_{KD} \\
&= L_{Det} + L_{featKD} + L_{relationKD}
\end{aligned}
\tag{11}
$$

5   Experiments

In this section, we perform various experiments on two real traffic datasets to compare our proposed algorithmic framework with the baseline algorithm.

5.1   Datasets

We evaluate the method proposed in this study on two datasets, Bellevue Traffic and UA-DETRAC. The Bellevue Traffic Video Dataset consists of approximately 101 h of 1280×720 30 Hz videos taken from five traffic intersections in the City of Bellevue, Washington. All videos were captured in September 2017 from real traffic cameras mounted on poles. It consists primarily of daytime and nighttime. The UA-DETRAC dataset was mainly taken at road overpasses in Beijing and Tianjin (Beijing-Tianjin-Hebei scenario). Vehicles are divided into four categories, i.e., cars, buses, vans and other vehicles. Weather conditions are divided into four categories, i.e., cloudy, nighttime, sunny and rainy.

5.2   Experimental Settings

The proposed framework is developed in Golang, with roles such as video sources, edge devices, and the cloud implemented as independent processes that communicate via the Google Remote Procedure Call protocol. For DNN inference and model tuning, MMDetection, an object detection framework, is employed. Default configuration files from MMDetection specify most hyperparameters for retraining and inference, with the exception of training epochs, which are set to 40. We use Deformable DETR [24] as the basic model, with ResNet-101 as the backbone for the cloud and ResNet-18 as the backbone for the edge. edge devices utilize Sophon SM5 for inference, while the cloud relies on Nvidia GeForce RTX3090 GPUs. The evaluation metric used is mAP@0.5(%).

5.3   Methods for Comparison

- **Source-only** [1]. Source-only tests the performance of a model trained on the source domain across different target domains, without additional training on these target domains.
- **Pseudo-label** [15]. Pseudo-label uses pseudo labels, generated by a teacher model, to supervise the learning of a student model.

- **CoTTA** [18]. CoTTA is an attractive approach for the continual test-time adaptation (CTTA). CoTTA mitigate error accumulation and catastrophic forgetting with weighted averaging, data augmented averaging, and random recovery neurons.
- **AMS** [8]. AMS is a cloud engagement approach. To solve the resource limitations of the edge model, AMS performs distillation in the cloud and then transmits the model's parameters to the edge. The teacher network will not be updated.
- **DCC** [6]. DCC is the first to utilize visual prompts for model updates, but the chosen prompts are pixel dots lacking semantic properties.

5.4   Experimental Results

Table 1. Continual Adaptation capability on UA-DETRAC

Time	t									→		
Frames Group	1	2	3	4	5	6	7	8	9	10	Mean	Gain
Source-only	55.5	50.4	57.3	56.2	59.3	54.4	45.3	48.2	43.5	55.4	52.6	/
CoTTA	56.7	52.5	58.7	57.3	60.7	54.4	47.7	49.4	46.4	56.3	54.0	+1.4
Pseudo-Label	57.9	53.7	59.5	59.6	61.4	57.3	48.9	49.9	49.3	57.9	55.5	+2.9
AMS	58.6	55.0	59.0	61.2	62.2	62.7	50.2	52.1	52.7	58.4	57.2	+4.6
DCC	61.1	58.3	**62.7**	64.2	**67.7**	68.8	67.8	59.2	56.3	62.0	62.8	+10.2
Ours	**63.9**	**64.5**	59.3	**65.1**	64.5	**70.3**	**70.6**	**64.1**	**59.5**	**66.1**	**64.8**	**+12.2**

Table 2. Continual Adaptation capability on Bellevue Traffic

Time	t									→		
Frames Group	1	2	3	4	5	6	7	8	9	10	Mean	Gain
Source-only	62.5	49.4	57.3	56.2	67.3	64.4	60.3	57.2	54.5	50.4	57.9	/
CoTTA	62.7	49.5	57.7	57.3	67.7	64.4	64.7	58.4	57.4	54.3	59.4	+2.5
Pseudo-Label	62.9	50.7	58.5	58.6	70.4	67.3	63.9	59.9	61.3	57.9	61.1	+3.2
AMS	63.6	50.0	59.0	60.2	70.2	67.7	64.2	61.1	63.7	58.4	62.6	+4.7
DCC	63.1	52.3	**59.7**	**61.2**	71.7	68.8	67.8	65.2	63.3	64.0	63.7	+5.8
Ours	**63.9**	**54.5**	59.3	61.1	**72.5**	**70.3**	**69.6**	**67.1**	**64.5**	**65.1**	**66.5**	**+7.6**

Overall Performance. We compared our method to various baseline techniques across two datasets. Table 1 illustrates our method's performance on the UA-DETRAC dataset, while Table 2 presents results from the Bellevue Traffic Video Dataset. Our method surpassed others, an advantage attributable to two primary factors. Initially, Source-only approaches train the model singularly with source domain data, neglecting the dynamic nature of actual traffic. Conversely, methods like Pseudo-label, CoTTA, and AMS involve model updates but rely on a large cloud model to refine a smaller edge model, disregarding continuous

Table 3. Continual Adaptation capability on Bellevue Traffic with repeat environment

Time	t ⟶								Mean	Gain
Frames Group	day1	day2	night1	night2	day1	day2	night1	night2	Mean	Gain
Source-only	62.5	59.4	55.3	56.2	62.5	59.4	55.3	56.2	58.4	/
CoTTA	62.7	62.5	57.7	57.3	62.7	61.4	56.7	57.4	59.8	+1.4
Pseudo-Label	62.9	60.7	57.5	58.6	61.4	60.3	58.9	58.9	59.9	+1.5
AMS	63.6	60.0	59.0	60.2	64.2	61.7	60.2	61.1	61.2	+2.8
DCC	63.1	62.3	61.7	61.2	64.7	63.8	**62.8**	62.2	62.7	+4.3
Ours	**63.9**	**63.5**	**62.3**	**63.1**	**65.5**	**65.3**	62.5	**63.1**	**63.7**	**+5.3**

Table 4. Ablation Study on Bellevue Traffic

	Pseudo-Label	VPA	KD	Mean	Gain
1				57.9	/
2	✓			61.1	+3.3
3	✓	✓		63.3	+5.4
4	✓	✓	✓	65.5	+7.6

Table 5. Ablation Study on Bellevue Traffic for KD

	Pseudo-Label	featureKD	relationKD	Mean	Gain
1	✓			63.3	+5.4
2	✓	✓		64.5	+6.6
3	✓	✓	✓	65.5	+7.6

cloud model enhancements. Furthermore, the DCC method, despite updating the cloud model with a visual prompt, restricts diversity by reusing identical prompts for the same sample set. It directly fine-tunes the edge model with high-quality pseudo-labels from the updated cloud model, risking overfitting. In contrast, our approach introduces a novel DETR family of models and an instance-level visual prompt generator. This design significantly enhances edge model generalization by using cloud model-guided knowledge distillation for edge model updates, ensuring adaptive cloud model updates, and applying a consistent visual prompt generator on the edge model for improved generalization.

Performance Improvement for Avoiding Catastrophic Forgetting. The traffic environment in the real world is constantly changing and has the potential for recurring scenes to reappear. For instance, day and night alternate in a 24-hour day. It is challenging to avoid catastrophic forgetting when updating models. Based on the analysis above, we randomly selected two daytime videos and two nighttime videos. We repeated these four videos twice and conducted experiments to evaluate whether our method copes with catastrophic forgetting. Table 3 shows the detection results for each video. Most previous methods have not addressed the problem of catastrophic forgetting well. When faced with the same domain, the detection results in the second round are all degraded differently compared to the first round. However, both DCC and our method address the issue of catastrophic forgetting to some extent, and the detection results for each scenario in the second occurrence are better than those in the first occurrence.

Ablation Study. To ascertain the precise influence of the visual prompt adaptation and knowledge distillation modules on model performance, we conducted a series of ablation studies. As detailed in Table 4, the visual prompt adaptation module led to a 2.1% enhancement in performance over the baseline model. This increment underscores the efficacy of visual prompt adaptation in refining the model's comprehension of visual data. Moreover, incorporating the complete knowledge distillation strategy further elevated model performance by an additional 4.3%. This significant improvement underscores the crucial role of knowledge distillation in optimizing model efficacy.

To further examine the impact of various losses in knowledge distillation on the effectiveness of the transferred knowledge, we evaluate the model's performance with different distillation losses, as outlined in Table 5. Initially, we employed a no-knowledge distillation approach, using only the teacher model's inferences for fine-tuning the student model. Subsequently, we integrated feature distillation and relational distillation into the workflow, sequentially. The results indicate that both types of distillation losses enhance the model's final performance to different extents: feature distillation leads to an approximate 1.2% improvement, and relational distillation results in about a 1.0% increase. These findings underscore the individual and cumulative benefits of employing diverse distillation losses to optimize knowledge transfer in models.

6   Conclusion

We present a cloud-edge collaborative framework that enhances object detection in ITS. The framework combines the low-latency benefits of edge computing with the advanced computational capabilities of the cloud. The text introduces a new framework that uses unsupervised domain adaptation and knowledge distillation to enable continual model adaptation in dynamically changing environments. The proposed methods effectively address challenges such as performance degradation and catastrophic forgetting. The research has made significant contributions to the field of cloud-edge collaboration through the adaptive learning architecture, unsupervised domain adaptation algorithm, and knowledge distillation strategy for the DETR family of models. These advancements offer promising avenues for future exploration and development.

Acknowledgments. This work is supported by National Key R & D Program of China (No. 2022YFF0503900) and Key R & D Program of Shandong Province (No. 2021CXGC010104).

References

1. Carion, N., Massa, F., Synnaeve, G., Usunier, N., Kirillov, A., Zagoruyko, S.: End-to-end object detection with transformers. In: Vedaldi, A., Bischof, H., Brox, T., Frahm, J.-M. (eds.) ECCV 2020. LNCS, vol. 12346, pp. 213–229. Springer, Cham (2020). https://doi.org/10.1007/978-3-030-58452-8_13
2. Chinchali, S., et al.: Network offloading policies for cloud robotics: a learning-based approach. Autonomous Robots, Autonomous Robots (2019)
3. Crankshaw, D., Wang, X., Zhou, G., Franklin, M.J., Gonzalez, J.E., Stoica, I.: Clipper: a {Low-Latency} online prediction serving system. In: 14th USENIX Symposium on Networked Systems Design and Implementation (NSDI 17), pp. 613–627 (2017)
4. Du, K., et al.: Server-driven video streaming for deep learning inference. In: Proceedings of the Annual Conference of the ACM Special Interest Group on Data Communication on the Applications, Technologies, Architectures, and Protocols for Computer Communication, pp. 557–570 (2020)
5. Gan, Y., et al.: Decorate the newcomers: visual domain prompt for continual test time adaptation. In: Proceedings of the AAAI Conference on Artificial Intelligence, vol. 37, pp. 7595–7603 (2023)
6. Gan, Y., et al.: Cloud-device collaborative adaptation to continual changing environments in the real-world. In: Proceedings of the IEEE/CVF Conference on Computer Vision and Pattern Recognition, pp. 12157–12166 (2023)
7. Jia, M., et al.: Visual prompt tuning. In: Avidan, S., Brostow, G., Cissé, M., Farinella, G.M., Hassner, T. (eds.) ECCV 2022. LNCS, vol. 13693, pp. 709–727. Springer, Cham (2022). https://doi.org/10.1007/978-3-031-19827-4_41
8. Khani, M., Hamadanian, P., Nasr-Esfahany, A., Alizadeh, M.: Real-time video inference on edge devices via adaptive model streaming. In: Proceedings of the IEEE/CVF International Conference on Computer Vision, pp. 4572–4582 (2021)
9. Li, A., Sun, S., Zhang, Z., Feng, M., Wu, C., Li, W.: A multi-scale traffic object detection algorithm for road scenes based on improved yolov5. Electronics **12**(4), 878 (2023)
10. Li, Y., Padmanabhan, A., Zhao, P., Wang, Y., Xu, G.H., Netravali, R.: Reducto: on-camera filtering for resource-efficient real-time video analytics. In: Proceedings of the Annual Conference of the ACM Special Interest Group on Data Communication on the Applications, Technologies, Architectures, and Protocols for Computer Communication, pp. 359–376 (2020)
11. Liu, X., et al.: P-tuning: prompt tuning can be comparable to fine-tuning across scales and tasks. In: Proceedings of the 60th Annual Meeting of the Association for Computational Linguistics (Volume 2: Short Papers), pp. 61–68 (2022)
12. Madhuri, T., Sowjanya, P.: Microsoft azure v/s amazon AWS cloud services: a comparative study. Int. J. Innov. Res. Sci. Eng. Technol. **5**(3), 3904–3907 (2016)
13. Maltoni, D., Lomonaco, V.: Continuous learning in single-incremental-task scenarios. Neural Netw. **116**, 56–73 (2019)
14. McCloskey, M., Cohen, N.J.: Catastrophic interference in connectionist networks: the sequential learning problem. In: Psychology of Learning and Motivation, vol. 24, pp. 109–165. Elsevier (1989)

15. Pseudo-Label, D.H.L.: The simple and efficient semi-supervised learning method for deep neural networks. In: ICML 2013 Workshop: Challenges in Representation Learning, pp. 1–6 (2013)
16. Shao, M., Fang, Y., Guo, L., Xue, Q.: Research on yolov5 vehicle object detection algorithm based on attention mechanism. In: 2022 3rd International Conference on Big Data, Artificial Intelligence and Internet of Things Engineering (ICBAIE), pp. 609–612. IEEE (2022)
17. Smith, J.S., et al.: Coda-prompt: continual decomposed attention-based prompting for rehearsal-free continual learning. In: Proceedings of the IEEE/CVF Conference on Computer Vision and Pattern Recognition, pp. 11909–11919 (2023)
18. Wang, Q., Fink, O., Van Gool, L., Dai, D.: Continual test-time domain adaptation. In: Proceedings of the IEEE/CVF Conference on Computer Vision and Pattern Recognition, pp. 7201–7211 (2022)
19. Wang, W., et al.: Exploring sequence feature alignment for domain adaptive detection transformers. In: Proceedings of the 29th ACM International Conference on Multimedia, pp. 1730–1738 (2021)
20. Woo, S., Park, J., Lee, J.Y., Kweon, I.S.: CBAM: convolutional block attention module. In: Proceedings of the European Conference on Computer Vision (ECCV), pp. 3–19 (2018)
21. Yao, J., Wang, F., Jia, K., Han, B., Zhou, J., Yang, H.: Device-cloud collaborative learning for recommendation. In: Proceedings of the 27th ACM SIGKDD Conference on Knowledge Discovery & Data Mining, pp. 3865–3874 (2021)
22. Zhang, X., Gu, S.S., Matsuo, Y., Iwasawa, Y.: Domain prompt learning for efficiently adapting clip to unseen domains. Trans. Japanese Soc. Artif. Intell. **38**(6), B–MC2_1 (2023)
23. Zhao, P., et al.: Neural pruning search for real-time object detection of autonomous vehicles. In: 2021 58th ACM/IEEE Design Automation Conference (DAC), pp. 835–840. IEEE (2021)
24. Zhu, X., Su, W., Lu, L., Li, B., Wang, X., Dai, J.: Deformable DETR: deformable transformers for end-to-end object detection. In: International Conference on Learning Representations (2020)
25. Zong, Z., Song, G., Liu, Y.: DETRs with collaborative hybrid assignments training. In: Proceedings of the IEEE/CVF International Conference on Computer Vision, pp. 6748–6758 (2023)

Understanding Spatial Dependency Among Spatial Interactions

Yong Gao[1]([✉]) [iD], Haohan Meng[1], Tao Pei[2] [iD], and Yu Liu[1] [iD]

[1] Institute of Remote Sensing and Geographic Information System,
School of Earth and Space Sciences, Peking University, Beijing 100871, China
{gaoyong,menghh}@pku.edu.cn, liuyu@urban.pku.edu.cn
[2] State Key Laboratory of Resources and Environmental Information System,
Institute of Geographical Sciences and Natural Resources Research,
Chinese Academy of Sciences, Beijing 100101, China
peit@lreis.ac.cn

Abstract. Spatial dependency exhibits special regularities in spatial interactions. Measuring spatial dependency among spatial interactions can help discover interesting interaction patterns and clusters. Although some metrics have been set up, it is still unclear what potentially affects the presence of spatial dependency among spatial interactions. Thus, we propose an analytical framework to better understand spatial dependency among spatial interactions. First, we define spatial weight matrix for spatial interactions, and then extend Moran's I and LISA to spatial interactions. Second, we test factors such as first-order spatial autocorrelation and distance decay effect that influence the degree of spatial dependency among spatial interactions. Third, we construct a spatial econometric model for spatial interaction to demonstrate the significance of spatial dependency. The proposed analytical framework is applied in synthetic data and Beijing taxi flows. Results show that the spatial dependency among spatial interactions is positively correlated to the first-order spatial autocorrelation, which is affected by the distance decay effect under a gravity model. Incorporating spatial dependency into a spatial econometric interaction model can also improve its performance.

Keywords: Spatial interaction · Spatial autocorrelation · Taxi flows · Distance decay

1 Introduction

Spatial dependency refers to the the propensity for nearby locations to influence each other and to possess similar attributes [2], which can be measured by the degree of spatial autocorrelation. The presence of spatial autocorrelation not only indicates notable patterns of observed variables [13], but also violates the

Supported by the National Natural Science Foundation of China (grant no. 41971331).

independence assumption in classical statistics and regression [1]. Understanding spatial dependency is crucial to spatial analysis and modeling. Recently, there is a growing interest in the spatial dependency among spatial interactions. Spatial interaction, usually embodied in the form of spatial flows, is generally defined as the movement and interchange processes of people, goods and information among different geographical locations [11,25,33]. Spatial interactions that are geographically close to each other tend to be more related. Adjacent origins (or destinations) have similar levels of supplies (or demands), and neighboring pairs of origin-destination have similar choice processes [31], all of which lead to the situation that nearby spatial interactions have similar interaction strengths. Recent studies have also demonstrated the existence of spatial dependency among spatial interactions [29,36,38].

Some indices have been proposed for measuring spatial autocorrelation, but they are designed for point and areal data and cannot be applied to spatial interactions directly. Points and polygons are considered as first-order variables which can be abstracted as a mapping from geographical units P to attribute values V as $f : P \to V$. Spatial interactions are second-order variables as a mapping $f : P \times P \to V$ [21] since a flow contains an origin and a corresponding destination. Then we refer to its autocorrelation as second-order spatial autocorrelation. The classical spatial dependency measurements should be specifically tailored for spatial interactions.

Some attempts on measuring spatial dependency of spatial interactions have been made. They can be divided into four categories from a methodological perspective. Spatial statistics form the first category. Liu et al. [20] extended both global and local Moran's I statistics to vectors to measure spatial autocorrelation quantitatively. For collective flows aggregated by specific spatial regions, some extended Moran's I, Geary's C and LISA statistics have been developed to identify the global and local spatial autocorrelation patterns [3,4,26,27,30]. Some researchers extended Ripley's K-function and L-function to describe the spatial association and proximity of flows [9,14,15,28,35,37]. The second approach is spatial data clustering. If positive spatial autocorrelation exists, clusters of high values can be detected. Lu and Thill [22] constructed a method to evaluate vector autocorrelation qualitatively by assessing the closeness among points of each paired set. Zhu and Guo [38] presented a hierarchical clustering method to analyse flow patterns. Tao and Thill [29] proposed flowAMOEBA to identify regions of high-intensity spatial interactions. The third approach is eigenvector spatial filtering [5–7,32]. The main idea is to decompose a dependent variable (spatial interaction intensity) into a spatial component and a nonspatial component. The spatial component is determined by the spectral decomposition of the transformed spatial weights matrix, and the spatial autocorrelation among spatial interactions is accounted. The last category is spatial econometric interaction modeling. Fischer and Griffith [10] modeled spatial autocorrelation among flow residuals by introducing a spatial error structure of the origin and destination autoregressive dependency. A family of spatial econometric interaction models were also constructed [17].

These methods either focus on spatial autocorrelation patterns of spatial interactions or deal with model misspecification. Deep understanding of spatial dependency among spatial interactions is lacking, and the potential factors that influence the second-order spatial autocorrelation are still unknown. It is necessary to extend Moran's I to spatial interactions, where the key is defining spatial weight matrix and intensity similarity. The influencing factors should also be tested to understand the origin of second-order spatial autocorrelation, especially the nodal attractions and distance decay effect.

2   Methodological Framework

To better understand spatial dependency among spatial interactions, we propose an analytical framework, as shown in Fig. 1. This framework consists of three analytical modules. First, we define spatial weight matrix for spatial interactions, so their spatial autocorrelation can be measured by extending Moran's I and LISA index. Second, we explore factors that affect second-order spatial autocorrelation by exploring the relationship between second-order and first-order spatial autocorrelation. Third, we construct a spatial econometric interaction model that cooperates spatial dependency to prevent model misspecification.

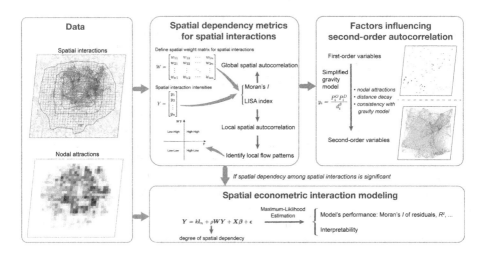

Fig. 1. The analytical framework.

2.1   Spatial Dependency Metrics for Spatial Interactions

Spatial interaction, which is usually embodied in the form of flow, describes the relationship between two places. A place can be a discrete point or an area where the origin or destination of a single movement is located, and the relationship is denoted by the interaction intensity that is measured by the OD count. A flow F_i is represented as a tuple $(u_i^O, v_i^O, u_i^D, v_i^D, y_i)$. Its intensity y_i indicates the connection strength between the corresponding origin and destination areas whose center coordinates are (u_i^O, v_i^O) and (u_i^D, v_i^D) respectively. Although spatial interaction and flow can replace each other, we tend to use spatial interaction in general contexts and flow in specific examples in this paper. The distance between two flows F_i and F_j can be computed by four-dimensional Euclidean distance with the following equation:

$$DF_{ij} = \sqrt{(u_i^O - u_j^O)^2 + (v_i^O - v_j^O)^2 + (u_i^D - u_j^D)^2 + (v_i^D - v_j^D)^2} \qquad (1)$$

Then, the spatial weight of two flows is defined as follows:

$$w_{ij} = \begin{cases} DF_{ij}^{-\alpha}, & i \neq j \ \text{ and } \ DF_{ij} \leq \delta \\ 0, & i = j \ \text{ or } \ DF_{ij} > \delta \end{cases} \qquad (2)$$

where δ is the distance threshold. α is a positive exponent concerned with distance decay effect, which usually ranges from 1 to 2 for flows at intra-urban scale [12,16,19] but smaller at inter-urban scale [34]. Binary spatial weights can also be defined through the contiguity of origin and destination places. Finally, row standardization is carried out, so all weights are scaled between 0 and 1.

The global spatial autocorrelation measurement for spatial interactions is defined as Eq. (3) by extending Moran's I, and the local measurement is as Eq. (4),

$$I = \frac{n}{\sum\limits_{i=1}^{n}\sum\limits_{j=1}^{n} w_{ij}} \frac{\sum\limits_{i=1}^{n}\sum\limits_{j=1}^{n} w_{ij}(y_i - \overline{y})(y_j - \overline{y})}{\sum\limits_{i=1}^{n}(y_i - \overline{y})^2} \qquad (3)$$

$$I_i = \frac{(y_i - \overline{y}) \sum\limits_{j=1}^{n} w_{ij}(y_j - \overline{y})}{\sum\limits_{i=1}^{n}(y_i - \overline{y})^2/n} \qquad (4)$$

where n is the number of total flows, w_{ij} denotes the spatial weight between two flows F_i and F_j, y_i is the intensity of F_i, and $\overline{y}$ is the average intensity of all flows. These two equations have the same form as the original Moran's I and I_i respectively, but their spatial weights are different. Since flows are second-order variables, these measurements can be called second-order indices, which are the counterparts of first-order indices for traditional first-order variables.

Since flows are second-order variables whose intensities do not follow a normal distribution, the distribution theory of first-order indices under the normalization assumption can not be used for second-order variables. By analogy with random permutation processes developed by [23,24], we can derive the expectation and variance of second-order Moran's I and I_i under the assumption of no spatial dependency. The expectation and variance of second-order indices are the same as those of first-order measurements under the randomization assumption. When n is not small, the second-order Moran's I follows an approximately normal distribution whatever the underlying distribution of flow intensities [8]. Therefore, we can get p-value from the standard normal distribution to evaluate whether the difference between observed spatial pattern and complete spatial randomness is statistically significant.

2.2 Factors Influencing Second-Order Spatial Autocorrelation

We are curious about potential factors that influence the second-order spatial autocorrelation. Thinking about the conditions that make spatial interactions occur, we assume that spatial interactions follow the gravity model as

$$y_i = \frac{P_i^O P_i^D}{d_i^\beta} \tag{5}$$

where y_i is the intensity of the spatial interaction F_i from i^O to i^D, P_i^O and P_i^D are the attractions of locations i^O and i^D respectively, d_i is the Euclidean distance between i^O and i^D, and β is the distance decay coefficient. According to the gravity model, we intuitively believe that the spatial autocorrelation of nodal attractions (first-order spatial autocorrelation) has an effect on second-order spatial autocorrelation. If nodal attractions show positive spatial autocorrelation, then adjacent origins (or destinations) have similar levels of supplies (or demands). Neighboring pairs of origin-destination have approximately equivalent distance decay effects. These lead to the situation that nearby spatial interactions have similar intensities. Moreover, the strength of distance decay effect affects the absolute intensities of interactions. If distance is a strong deterrent, most spatial interactions, especially those with long lengths, will have small intensities. It narrows the relative difference among spatial interaction intensities and contributes to the positive second-order spatial autocorrelation.

To verify the above inferences, we conduct experiments using synthetic data. Firstly, without loss of generality, the locations of first-order data are generated by a Poisson point process, and their attractions are simulated from a normal distribution. Secondly, their attractions are permuted to produce first-order data with different spatial autocorrelation. For the sake of generality, the first-order data with zero autocorrelation, positive autocorrelation and negative autocorrelation are generated one hundred times respectively. Thirdly, spatial interactions are generated using the gravity model (Eq. (5)) based on the above first-order variables. Finally, we measure the first-order spatial autocorrelation and the second-order spatial autocorrelation respectively, and explore the relationship between them under different conditions.

2.3 Spatial Econometric Interaction Modeling

Spatial dependency has important implications for modeling spatial interactions. Ignoring spatial dependency causes problems for traditional spatial regression [1].

Therefore, we construct a spatial lag model (SLM), as shown in Eq. (6), which takes the spatial dependency among spatial interaction intensities into account, as an application of measuring spatial dependency.

$$\boldsymbol{Y} = k\boldsymbol{l}_n + \rho\boldsymbol{W}\boldsymbol{Y} + \boldsymbol{X}\boldsymbol{\beta} + \boldsymbol{\epsilon} \tag{6}$$

$\boldsymbol{Y}$ denotes an $n\times 1$ vector consisting of intensities of observed spatial interactions. ρ denotes the degree of spatial dependency among spatial interactions. $\boldsymbol{W}$ is an $n \times n$ spatial weight matrix describing the arrangement of the observed spatial interactions, which can be constructed according to the methods in Sect. 2.1.1. $\boldsymbol{l}_n$ is an $n\times 1$ vector of ones associated with the constant term parameter k. $\boldsymbol{X}$ denotes an $n \times m$ matrix of exogenous first-order explanatory variables with the associated parameter $\boldsymbol{\beta}$ contained in an $m\times 1$ vector. $\boldsymbol{\epsilon} = (\epsilon_1, ..., \epsilon_n)^T$ is a vector of disturbance terms, where ϵ_i are independently and identically distributed error terms for all i with zero mean and variance σ^2.

We evaluate the performance of the model from perspectives of Moran's I of residuals, log likelihood and adjusted R^2. ρ is a key parameter that reflects the uniqueness of spatial econometric models, and also embodies the meaning of measuring spatial dependency.

3   Experiments and Results

3.1   Research Area and Data

The area within the 5th Ring Road in Beijing, China is chosen as the study area, which is divided in to $1\,\mathrm{km} \times 1\,\mathrm{km}$ grids, as shown in Fig. 2.

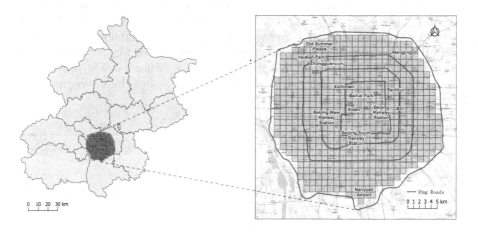

Fig. 2. Study area and research units.

The flows used in this study come from taxi trips in Beijing for 5 consecutive days from March 13 (Monday) to March 17 (Friday) in 2017. Each trip record contains the latitudes, longitudes and time stamps of pick-up and drop-off points. After filtering invalid records, we obtain 1,260,839 taxi ODs. Then intersected with those grids, taxi ODs are aggregated into taxi flows, and the flow intensity between two grids is determined by the number of the corresponding taxi ODs. Finally, there are 129,724 aggregated taxi flows in all 608 grids. The population data with a resolution of 250 m come from mobile phone positioning data in Beijing, 2018. It is provided by China Unicom that is one of the leading telecommunication operators in China.

3.2 Measuring Spatial Dependency Among Spatial Interactions

We create two sets of synthetic flow data, as shown in Fig. 3, to test the proposed spatial autocorrelation measurements. The space is discretized into a finite set of regular 1 km×1 km grids. The flow between two grids is represented by an arrow curve, and the number next to the flow represents its intensity. We construct a spatial weight matrix using Eq. (2) with $\alpha = 2$ and $\delta = 3$ km. In Fig. 3(a), the global Moran's I of flows is 0.990 with z-score $= 4.13$, which indicates positive spatial autocorrelation at the 0.01 significance level. The global Moran's I of flows in Fig. 3(b) is -0.386 with z-score $= -0.89$, implying negative spatial autocorrealtion but not significant. In fact, we can also visually identify such patterns in this figure. We also measure the spatial autocorrelation of this data by employing a binary spatial weight matrix based on rook contiguity. The global Moran indices of flows are 0.999 ($p = 0.01$) and -0.505 (not significant) respectively, which are consistent with the former results. The extended Moran's I of spatial interactions is effective regardless of the form of spatial weight matrix. Furthermore, we use the same synthetic flows to examine the extended local Moran's I. Results show that local Moran indices of flows in Fig. 3(a) are all positive at the 0.01 significance level after Sidak correction. In the left part of Fig. 3(a), each flow has larger intensity than average and so do their neighbors. These flows form a cluster of high intensity. Similarly, the right part of Fig. 3(a) constitutes a cluster of low-intensity flows. Local Moran indices of flows in Fig. 3(b) are all negative but not statistically significant. The local associations recognized by our methods are consistent with the truth.

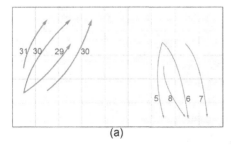 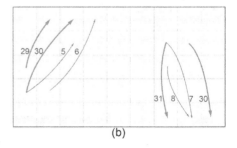

(a)   (b)

Fig. 3. Synthetic flows.

For taxi flows in Beijing, We construct a spatial weight matrix using Eq. (2). α is set to 1.5 because distance decay coefficient of power law function usually ranges from 1 to 2 [20]. δ is set to 3 km because it is distant enough to distinguish two flows. The global Moran's I of taxi flows is 0.420 at the 0.001 significance level, indicating significant positive spatial dependency. We can find this pattern intuitively from the intensity distribution of taxi flows, as shown in Fig. 4(a). We also measure the spatial dependency using rook contiguity weight matrix and get a similar result. The local patterns of taxi flows are identified by the extended local Moran's I, as plotted in Fig. 4(b). CBD, Sanlitun, Wangjing, Beijing Railway Station and Xizhimen are popular origins and destinations of high-high flow clusters. Most taxi flows under such pattern have short lengths of about two kilometers, indicating the distance decay effect on taxi travels. High-low outliers usually have long distances and are associated with transportation hubs such as railway stations and airports. Low-high outliers usually have adjacent origins or adjacent destinations to high-high clusters, such as Weigongcun to Xizhimen and Siyuanqiao to Sanlitun. These flows may be overlooked in general spatial analysis because of low intensities, but they can be identified by the second-order LISA. Low-low clusters are dispersed throughout the study area, and the lengths of such flows are relatively longer, mostly over ten kilometers.

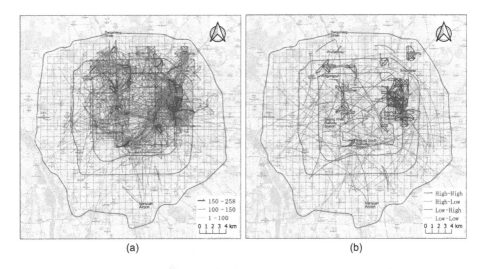

(a)   (b)

Fig. 4. Taxi flows in Beijing. (a) Intensity distribution. (b) Local spatial patterns.

3.3 Exploring Factors Influencing Second-Order Spatial Autocorrelation

According to the inferences in Sect. 2.2, we create synthetic data which is shown in Fig. 5 and measure the second-order spatial autocorrelation under different first-order spatial autocorrelation and distance decay effects. Different situations of first-order spatial autocorrelation are generated by the permutations of nodal attractions. The distance decay effect is controlled by setting various distance decay coefficients β. Studies have shown that distance decay coefficient usually ranges from 1 to 2 for spatial interactions at intra-urban scale [12, 16, 19] but smaller at inter-urban scale [34]. In order to include extreme cases, the distance decay coefficient β ranges from 0 to 2.5 in our experiments.

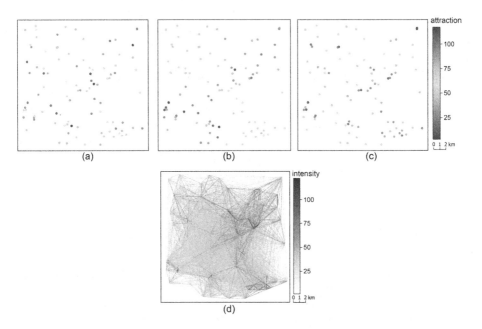

Fig. 5. Synthetic first-order data and second-order data. (a)-(c) Synthetic first-order data with zero, positive and negative autocorrelation, respectively. (d) Spatial interactions generated by gravity model using first-order data in Fig. 5(b).

The indices of second-order spatial autocorrelation are calculated and then plotted together with first-order spatial autocorrelation in scatter diagrams. For first-order spatial autocorrelation, the spatial weight is defined by $w_{kl} = d_{kl}^{-1.5}$, where d_{kl} is the Euclidean distance between two points k and l. If the distance exceeds 3 km, the corresponding weight would be set to zero. For second-order spatial autocorrelation, the spatial weight matrix is constructed by Eq. (2), where $\alpha = 1.5$ and $\delta = 3$ km. As shown in Fig. 6, the horizontal and vertical axes of the scatter plot represent the global autocorrelation indexes of the first-order and second-order variables, respectively. The green, blue and red points in scatter plots indicate the positive, none, and negative first-order spatial autocorrelation, respectively.

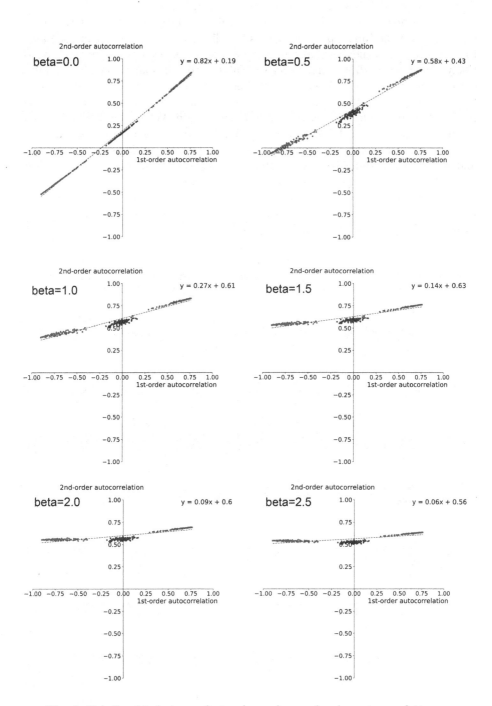

Fig. 6. Relationship between first-order and second-order autocorrelation.

Results show that the slope of the fitted line is always positive but the slope decreases and the intercept increases as the distance decay coefficient increases from 0 to 2.5. It indicates that the second-order spatial autocorrelation is positively correlated with the first-order spatial autocorrelation. When the distance decay effect increases, this correlation becomes weaker. Extremely, if the distance decay coefficient equals to 0, the second-order spatial autocorrelation is only related to the first-order spatial autocorrelation. When the distance decay coefficient ranges from 0.5 to 1.5, the spatial dependency among spatial interactions are simultaneously affected by both nodal attractions (first-order variables) and distance according to gravity model. When the distance decay coefficient reaches 2.0 and greater, long-distance interactions approach zero. All spatial interactions have almost equal intensities so the global spatial dependency is remarkable. Then, positive second-order spatial autocorrelation does not necessarily require positive first-order spatial autocorrelation.

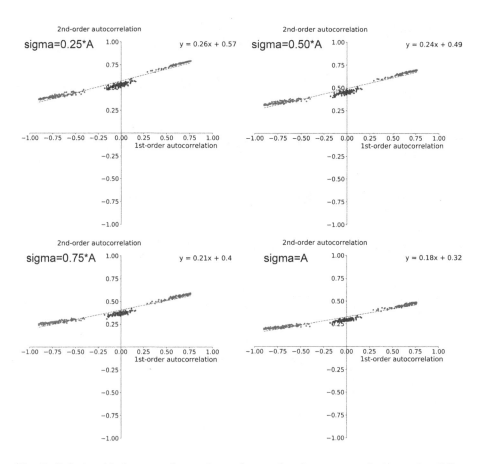

Fig. 7. Relationship between first-order and second-order autocorrelation under different levels of random noise.

Nevertheless, the gravity model is a relatively strict constraint. In real world, spatial interactions do not always conform to the gravity model perfectly. In order to simulate this situation, we add random noise when generating spatial interactions. The random noise follows a normal distribution with a mean of zero and standard deviation of σ. Figure 7 shows the scatter plots of first-order and second-order spatial autocorrelation under different levels of random noise. As the noise get stronger, the slope of the fitting line and the intercept decline simultaneously. Noise masks the intrinsic spatial pattern of spatial interactions, so the degree of second-order spatial autocorrelation is weakened. Therefore, goodness of fit of gravity model also influences the transmission from first-order spatial autocorrelation to second-order spatial autocorrelation.

Moreover, we investigate the influence of these factors by Beijing taxi flows. The nodal attractions in the gravity model are represented by the population as shown in Fig. 8(a). The distance decay coefficient β is solved by the slope of least square regression in its logarithmic form [18]. Results show that the distance decay coefficient β is 1.12 with $R^2 = 0.34$. The low R^2 suggests that Beijing taxi flows do not match gravity model perfectly. The global Moran's I of first-order variables is 0.658 which is significant at 0.001 level, and the global Moran's I of second-order variable is 0.420 as presented in Sect. 3.2. The first-order spatial autocorrelation is strong, but not adequately transmitted to the second-order spatial autocorrelation because of distance decay effect. The imperfect fit of the taxi flows to the gravity model is also another reason for the relatively weak second-order spatial autocorrelation.

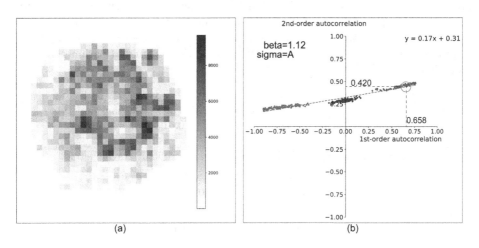

(a)   (b)

Fig. 8. Synthetic second-order data approaching real Beijing taxi flows. (a) Population distribution. (b) First-order and second-order spatial autocorrelation of synthetic data.

In addition, we create synthetic second-order data to approach the real situation of Beijing taxi flows. The synthetic first-order data remain unchanged, but the distance decay coefficient of the gravity model is set to 1.12 which is consistent with the real distance decay coefficient of taxi flows. When generating flows, random noise with standard deviation equals the average intensity of Beijing taxi flows (denoted by A) has also been added, so as to approximate the situation that Beijing taxi flows do not match gravity model perfectly. Results are shown in Fig. 8(b). We can find the corresponding part of the real situation of Beijing taxi flows whose first-order spatial autocorrelation index is 0.658 and second-order spatial autocorrelation index is 0.420 in the simulation experiment, as indicated by the yellow circle. Our inferences about the transmission from first-order spatial autocorrelation to second-order spatial autocorrelation hold true in both synthetic and real data.

3.4   Modeling Spatial Interactions Incorporating Spatial Dependency

To illustrate the application of measuring spatial dependency, we construct a spatial lag model (Eq. (6)) that takes the spatial dependency among flow intensities into account. The log-additive gravity model ((7)), which has been the workhorse model of spatial interactions for a long time, is chosen as the baseline model.

$$\ln y_i = \ln k + a \ln P_i^O + b \ln P_i^D + c \ln d_i \tag{7}$$

The sample data of dependent variable are the 129,724 aggregated taxi flows in Beijing. Explanatory variables are population and Euclidean distances among grids. The spatial weight matrix W is defined by Eq. (2), where $\alpha = 1.5$ and $\delta = 3$ km. The spatial lag model and the baseline model are estimated by Maximum Likelihood (ML), since Ordinary Least Square (OLS) estimation is inefficient and biased if spatial autocorrelation exists [17]. Estimated parameters and model's performance are shown in Table 1.

Table 1. The estimated parameters and performance of spatial lag model and log-additive gravity model(*** 0.001 significance level, ** 0.01 significance level).

Parameter estimates	Spatial lag model	Log-additive gravity model
Const	−0.919***	3.592***
P_i^O	0.270***	0.440***
P_i^D	0.232***	0.403***
distance	−0.277***	−1.04***
ρ	0.861***	−
Model performance		
Moran's I of residuals	0.028	0.186**
Likelihood-ratio test	−12786	−14982
Adjusted R^2	0.638	0.492

The result indicates that the spatial lag model performs better than the log-additive gravity model. First, the residuals of spatial lag model is closer to the independent distribution. The error terms of log-additive gravity model show significant positive spatial autocorrelation, which implies the existence of model misspecification. Second, the log likelihood increases from -14982 to -12786. The log-additive gravity model, which ignores spatial dependency among flow intensities and assumes independent residual flows, leads to a much lower likelihood function value. Third, the adjusted R^2 moves from 0.492 to 0.638. Therefore, capturing spatial dependency among flow intensities greatly reduces the residual variance and strengthens the inferential basis affiliated with the model. We can aslo find that the absolute values of coefficients of P_i^O, P_i^D and distance decay decrease from the log-additive model to the spatial lag model. Because the spatial dependency of flows is positive and highly significant, the flow intensities are largely explained by intensities of neighboring flows. The influence of nodal attractions and distance decay effect will diminish.

4 Conclusions

This article proposes an analytical framework for understanding spatial dependency among spatial interactions. Moran's I and LISA indices are extended to spatial interactions, integrating both spatial proximity represented by spatial weight matrix and intensity similarity of spatial interactions. Moreover, the potential factors lead to the spatial dependency of spatial interactions are explored. There is a transmission process from first-order spatial autocorrelation to second-order spatial autocorrelation, but the process will be affected by distance decay coefficient and consistency with the gravity model. Combining spatial dependency into the spatial interaction model mitigates the problem of model misspecification and improves the performance of model. This framework provides new insights into the spatial dependency among spatial interactions, and fills a gap in the literature exploring the potential mechanisms affecting second-order spatial autocorrelation. The case studies based on synthetic data and Beijing taxi flows validate this approach and also verify the importance of understanding spatial dependency among spatial interactions.

References

1. Anselin, L.: Spatial Econometrics: Methods and Models, vol. 4. Springer, Berlin (1988)
2. Anselin, L.: What is special about spatial data? alternative perspectives on spatial data analysis. National Center for Geographic Information and Analysis, Technical report, Santa Barbara, CA (1989)
3. Berglund, S., Karlström, A.: Identifying local spatial association in flow data. J. Geogr. Syst. **1**(3), 219–236 (1999). https://doi.org/10.1007/s101090050013
4. Cai, J., Kwan, M.P.: Detecting spatial flow outliers in the presence of spatial autocorrelation. Comput. Environ. Urban Syst. **96**, 101833 (2022). https://doi.org/10.1016/j.compenvurbsys.2022.101833

5. Chun, Y.: Modeling network autocorrelation within migration flows by eigenvector spatial filtering. J. Geogr. Syst. **10**(4), 317–344 (2008). https://doi.org/10.1007/s10109-008-0068-2

6. Chun, Y., Griffith, D.A.: Modeling network autocorrelation in space-time migration flow data: an eigenvector spatial filtering approach. Ann. Assoc. Am. Geogr. **101**(3), 523–536 (2011). https://doi.org/10.1080/00045608.2011.561070

7. Chun, Y., Kim, H., Kim, C.: Modeling interregional commodity flows with incorporating network autocorrelation in spatial interaction models: an application of the us interstate commodity flows. Comput. Environ. Urban Syst. **36**(6), 583–591 (2012). https://doi.org/10.1016/j.compenvurbsys.2012.04.002

8. Cliff, A., Ord, J.: Spatial Processes: Models & Applications. Pion (1981)

9. Fang, Z., et al.: Length-squared l-function for identifying clustering pattern of network-constrained flows. Int. J. Digit. Earth **16** (2023). https://doi.org/10.1080/17538947.2023.2265882

10. Fischer, M.M., Griffith, D.A.: Modeling spatial autocorrelation in spatial interaction data: an application to patent citation data in the European union. J. Reg. Sci. **48**(5), 969–989 (2008). https://doi.org/10.1111/j.1467-9787.2008.00572.x

11. Fotheringham, A.S., O'Kelly, M.E.: Spatial Interaction Models: Formulations and Applications. Kluwer Academic Publishers Dordrecht, Dordrecht (1989)

12. Gao, S., Wang, Y., Gao, Y., Liu, Y.: Understanding urban traffic-flow characteristics: a rethinking of betweenness centrality. Environ. Plann. B. Plann. Des. **40**(1), 135–153 (2013). https://doi.org/10.1068/b38141

13. Haining, R.P.: Spatial Autocorrelation, pp. 14763–14768. Pergamon, Oxford (2001)

14. Shu, H., et al.: L-function of geographical flows. Int. J. Geograph. Inf. Sci. **35**(4), 689–716 (2021). https://doi.org/10.1080/13658816.2020.1749277

15. Kan, Z., Kwan, M.P., Tang, L.: Ripley's k-function for network-constrained flow data. Geogr. Anal. **54**(4), 769–788 (2022). https://doi.org/10.1111/gean.12300

16. Kang, C., Ma, X., Tong, D., Liu, Y.: Intra-urban human mobility patterns: an urban morphology perspective. Phys. A **391**(4), 1702–1717 (2012). https://doi.org/10.1016/j.physa.2011.11.005

17. LeSage, J.P., Pace, R.K.: Spatial econometric modeling of origin-destination flows. J. Reg. Sci. **48**(5), 941–967 (2008). https://doi.org/10.1111/j.1467-9787.2008.00573.x

18. Liu, Y., Gong, L., Tong, Q.: Quantifying the distance effect in spatial interactions. Acta Scientiarum Naturalium Universitatis Pekinensis **50**(3), 526–534 (2014)

19. Liu, Y., Kang, C., Gao, S., Xiao, Y., Tian, Y.: Understanding intra-urban trip patterns from taxi trajectory data. J. Geogr. Syst. **14**(4), 1–21 (2012). https://doi.org/10.1007/s10109-012-0166-z

20. Liu, Y., Tong, D., Liu, X.: Measuring spatial autocorrelation of vectors. Geogr. Anal. **47**(3), 300–319 (2015). https://doi.org/10.1111/gean.12069

21. Liu, Y., et al.: Analytical methods and applications of spatial interactions in the era of big data. Acta Geogr. Sin. **75**(7), 1523–1538 (2020)

22. Lu, Y., Thill, J.C.: Assessing the cluster correspondence between paired point locations. Geogr. Anal. **35**(4), 290–309 (2003). https://doi.org/10.1111/j.1538-4632.2003.tb01116.x

23. Moran, P.A.: Some theorems on time series: Ii the significance of the serial correlation coefficient. Biometrika **35**(3/4), 255–260 (1948). https://doi.org/10.2307/2332344

24. Ord, J.: Tests of significance using nonnormal data. Geogr. Anal. **12**(4), 387–392 (1980). https://doi.org/10.1111/j.1538-4632.1980.tb00044.x

25. Roy, J.R., Thill, J.C.: Spatial interaction modelling. Pap. Reg. Sci. **83**(1), 339–361 (2003). https://doi.org/10.1007/s10110-003-0189-4
26. Sun, S., Zhang, H.: Flow-data-based global spatial autocorrelation measurements for evaluating spatial interactions. ISPRS Int. J. Geo-Inf. **12**(10) (2023). https://doi.org/10.3390/ijgi12100396
27. Tao, R., Chen, Y., Thill, J.C.: A space-time flow LISA approach for panel flow data. Comput. Environ. Urban Syst. **106**, 102042 (2023). https://doi.org/10.1016/j.compenvurbsys.2023.102042
28. Tao, R., Thill, J.C.: Spatial cluster detection in spatial flow data. Geogr. Anal. **48**(4), 355–372 (2016). https://doi.org/10.1111/gean.12100
29. Tao, R., Thill, J.C.: FlowAMOEBA: identifying regions of anomalous spatial interactions. Geogr. Anal. **51**(1), 111–130 (2019). https://doi.org/10.1111/gean.12161
30. Tao, R., Thill, J.C.: BiFlowLISA: measuring spatial association for bivariate flow data. Comput. Environ. Urban Syst. **83**, 101519 (2020). https://doi.org/10.1016/j.compenvurbsys.2020.101519
31. Thill, J.C.: Choice set formation for destination choice modelling. Prog. Hum. Geogr. **16**(3), 361–382 (1992). https://doi.org/10.1177/030913259201600303
32. Tiefelsdorf, M., Griffith, D.A.: Semiparametric filtering of spatial autocorrelation: the eigenvector approach. Environ. Plan. A **39**(5), 1193–1221 (2007). https://doi.org/10.1068/a37378
33. Tobler, W.R.: Spatial interaction patterns. J. Environ. Syst. **6**(4), 271–301 (1976). https://doi.org/10.2190/vakc-3grf-3xug-wy4w
34. Xiao, Y., Wang, F., Liu, Y., Wang, J.: Reconstructing gravitational attractions of major cities in china from air passenger flow data, 2001–2008: a particle swarm optimization approach. Prof. Geogr. **65**(2), 265–282 (2013). https://doi.org/10.1080/00330124.2012.679445
35. Yan, X., et al.: Spatiotemporal flow L-function: a new method for identifying spatiotemporal clusters in geographical flow data. Int. J. Geograph. Inf. Sci. **37**(7), 1615–1639 (2023). https://doi.org/10.1080/13658816.2023.2204345
36. Zhang, L., Cheng, J., Jin, C., Zhou, H.: A multiscale flow-focused geographically weighted regression modelling approach and its application for transport flows on expressways. Appl. Sci. **9**(21), 4673 (2019). https://doi.org/10.3390/app9214673
37. Zhang, W., Zhao, J., Liu, W., Tan, Z., Xing, H.: Geographically weighted flow cross k-function for network-constrained flow data. Appl. Sci. **12**(24) (2022). https://doi.org/10.3390/app122412796
38. Zhu, X., Guo, D.: Mapping large spatial flow data with hierarchical clustering. Trans. GIS **18**(3), 421–435 (2014). https://doi.org/10.1111/tgis.12100

An Improved DBSCAN Clustering Method for AIS Trajectories Incorporating DP Compression and Discrete Fréchet Distance

Xiliang Liu[1], Xiaoying Zhi[1(✉)], Peng Wang[2(✉)], Qiang Mei[3], Haoru Su[1], and Zhixiang He[1]

[1] Information Technology, Beijing University of Technology, Beijing 100124, China
{liuxl,suhaoru,zxhe}@bjut.edu.cn, s202375050@emails.bjut.edu.cn
[2] Key Laboratory of the Ministry of Education, Hainan Normal University, Haikou 570203, Hainan, China
pengwang621@163.com
[3] Navigation Institute, Jimei University, Xiamen 361000, China
meiqiang@jmu.edu.cn

Abstract. AIS provides a huge amount of maritime traffic data containing spatial and temporal information in a limited area. Trajectory clustering based on AIS data is a pre-task in intelligent maritime domain, providing typical movement patterns of vessels for follow-up studies in navigation safety and maritime supervision. This paper presents an AIS trajectory clustering method incorporating discrete Fréchet distance and Douglas-Peucker (DP) algorithm, based on improved density-based spatial clustering of applications with noise (DBSCAN). Experimental results on the dataset of vessels entering and leaving the Taiwan Strait in November 2017 demonstrate the effectiveness of our method.

Keywords: AIS · DP Compression · Discrete Fréchet Distance · Unsupervised KNN + Kneed · vessel trajectory clustering

1 Introduction

The Vessel Traffic System (VTS) collects traffic data through a maritime surveillance network. The maritime surveillance network consists of various infrastructure sources like Auto Identification System (AIS), shore-based radar, Long Range Identification and Tracking of ships (LRIT) and Synthetic-aperture radar (SAR) satellites [1]. AIS is one of the most important data sources of VTS, which can be used to verify the identification of radar targets and track ships in non-radar coverage areas. Raw AIS data includes dynamic information (position, speed, heading, etc.) and static information (size, length, width, draft, etc.) of the vessel with acceptance rate of information every 2–10 s [2]. The popularity of the system promotes the process of maritime informatization, massive track behavior data provides data support for exploring maritime intelligent management. With the continuously development of quality and availability of AIS data, there has been a growing interest in the research community in the use of data mining methods for maritime traffic analysis [1]. Vessel trajectory clustering has been often considered as a fundamental method for many AIS data mining tasks, like trajectory prediction, anomaly detection, collision avoidance, behavior recognition and knowledge extraction [3, 4].

Vessel trajectory clustering can be described as a modeling method that groups similar trajectories to obtain typical movement patterns of vessels in the water. One of the most commonly used methods is the density-based method DBSCAN. The main advantages of using DBSCAN for vessel trajectory clustering are the ability to find arbitrarily shaped vessel trajectory clusters, the robustness to abnormal ship trajectories, and the structure of trajectory aggregation independent of the traversal order of samples. However, it should be noted that DBSCAN is sensitive to the input parameters and vulnerable to the volume of ship trajectory data.

Owing to the difference of positioning error of different AIS data sources, environmental interference, human operation error or deliberate camouflage deception of the target, there are a lot of noises in the ship trajectory data that do not conform to the target movement pattern, resulting in the ship trajectory data is never completely accurate in the real environment. In addition, considering the high computational cost and memory load of clustering [4], this paper proposes a pre-processing framework for vessel trajectory data consisting of trajectory cleaning, trajectory segmentation and trajectory compression using the DP algorithm. After pre-processing of data, a method combining unsupervised KNN and kneed to obtain parameters is designed to solve the parameter-sensitivity problem of DBSCAN. For trajectory distance metric, this paper employs discrete Fréchet distance and compares its clustering performance with other two commonly used trajectory metrics to verify the effectiveness of our method.

2   Related Works

In this section, we introduce the current researches on trajectory similarity measurement and vessel trajectory clustering via DBSCAN.

The similarity measurements for trajectory clustering can be divided into warping-based methods and shape-based methods [5]. Warping-based methods find the distance between two trajectories by matching points. Widely used warping-based methods are Dynamic Time Warping (DTW) [6], Edit Distance on Real sequence (EDR) [7] and Longest Common SubSequence (LCSS) [8]. LCSS and EDR require manual parameter tuning and focus on either similarity or difference, which limits their effectiveness in cases of uneven sampling or minor trajectory changes [9].DTW aims to obtain the cumulative distance between all best-matched trajectory points by iteration without manual parameters. Li et al. combine DTW with Principal Components Analysis (PCA) for robust ship trajectory clustering [6, 10, 11]. DTW is sensitive to noise. If there are noise points in the trajectory, they will result in an excessive final distance.

Compared to point-based methods, shape-based methods like HD and Fréchet distances focus on trajectory shapes. HD measures the maximum distance between two trajectories, while Wang et al. enhance clustering by integrating a similarity function with

HDBSCAN [12]. Yang et al. use Hausdorff distance as a measure for DBTCAN cluster-ing [13], but it only considers spatial arrangement, not direction, so can't differentiate trajectories with similar shapes but different orientations.

Fréchet distance are divided into continuous Fréchet distance and discrete Fréchet distance (DFD) [14]. The metric is direction-sensitive, considering shape and temporal order. In practice, the discrete Fréchet distance is used due to trajectory points being discrete. Combined with PCA in AIS analysis, Nuocheng uses it with KDE and a prob-abilistic model to assess ship conflict likelihood [15]. Cao et al. take Fréchet distance as a similarity measure for hierarchical clustering and impute the number of clusters based on PCA [16].

DBSCAN is a commonly used density-based clustering algorithm for ship trajec-tories which can identify noise data and form arbitrarily shaped clusters. DBSCAN is designed to contain the clustering results by two parameters, minPts and ε.

The current researches on the improvement of DBSCAN algorithm for vessel tra-jectory clustering can be divided into three aspects: enhancement of computational data scale based on Hadoop platform [17–19], improvement of distance metric [10, 12, 13, 15, 16, 20, 21] and parameter optimization [22, 23]. In this section, we focus on parame-ter optimization for DBSCAN. Determining the optimal parameters is crucial. Lee et al. use OPTICS to set ε visually and find the best minPts through experiment results [22]. Zhao and Shi derive ε from a Gaussian distribution under fixed minPts, selecting the best parameters via experiments [23]. However, Lee's method can't ensure precise ε, and Zhao's requires manual filtering, limiting automation. Rahmah et al. automate the process by calculating the k-nearest neighbor distance curve slope; a 1% change indi-cates the optimal ε [24]. This approach is more automated and suitable for data without prior knowledge.

3 Methodology

3.1 Framework of the Research

Since the raw AIS trajectory data are low-quality, to ensure the accuracy and correct-ness of the clustering results, this paper first performs trajectory data pre-processing. Secondly, the discrete Fréchet distance matrix is calculated as the similarity measure between trajectories. In the last step, our unsupervised K-nearest neighbors (KNN) combined with Kneed's method is used to set the parameters of DBSCAN followed by clustering. Specific technical routes are shown in Fig. 1.

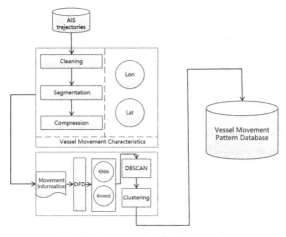

Fig. 1. Framework of this research.

3.2 Trajectory Data Pre-processing

Trajectory data pre-processing framework in this paper consists of trajectory data cleaning, trajectory data segmentation and trajectory data compression.

Trajectory data cleaning aims to filter out abnormal trajectory points in raw AIS data. Noises can be recognized as error data exceeding the threshold of normal range. Therefore, we set the normal speed range as (0, 25) in knots, the normal heading angle range as [0, 360] in degrees, the normal heading angle variation range as [0, 10] in degrees, and the minimum number of trajectory points of a trajectory as 10. Trajectory data cleaning process is shown in Fig. 2.

Afterwards, we identify two problems in single vessel trajectory extraction according to MMSI (Maritime Movement Service Identification) and time differences between two trajectory points varying from seconds to days and velocity differences which are not uniform. Thus, it is necessary to segment trajectories to ensure that only one movement mode exists in a trajectory. Trajectory data segmentation process is shown in Fig. 3, where spatial threshold (velocity) is set to 5 knots and temporal threshold (time) is set to 10 min.

The last step is trajectory compression. We first convert the latitude and longitude to UTM coordinates, and then employ the DP algorithm with an optimal distance threshold according to the experiment to improve the computational efficiency. When compressing trajectories, the distance threshold epsilon affects the compressed trajectory shape. If epsilon is too large, the local movement information of the ship will not be retained. On the other hand, if epsilon is too small, the number of trajectory points will not be sufficiently reduced. Choosing a suitable epsilon can retain sufficient local movement information while compressing redundant trajectory points in the trajectory. We take a vessel's trajectory as an example and compare the effect of DP algorithm under different epsilons in Fig. 4.

Figure 4(a) represents the original trajectory, Fig. 4(b) to (e) represent the compressed trajectories at epsilon of 0.01, 0.05, 0.1 and 1, respectively. Experimental results prove

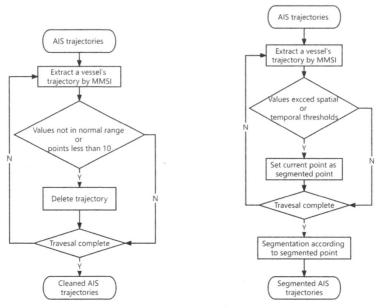

Fig. 2. (left) Trajectory data cleaning process. **Fig. 3.** (right) Trajectory data segmentation process.

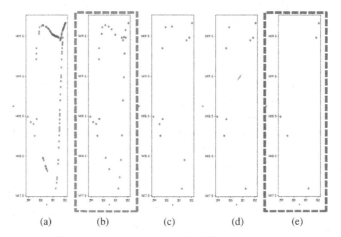

Fig. 4. DP compression under different epsilons.

that the best results can be obtained when epsilon equals to 0.01, where the shape of the trajectory is preserved and the redundant trajectory points are removed. From Fig. 4(c) to (e), the local movement information decreases as the epsilon becomes larger, when epsilon comes to 1, only a few critical rotation points remain.

In conclusion, our pre-processing framework removes noises, ensures spatial-temporal continuity and improves computing efficiency.

3.3 Computation of Distance Matrix

Definition of Vessel Trajectory
Trajectory dataset T can be presented by following Eq. (2).

$$T = \{t_i \mid i = 1, 2, \ldots, n\} \tag{1}$$

where n represents the number of trajectories, i.e., 1,218 trajectories in total after data pre-processing in this paper. A single trajectory in the dataset is expressed by the following Eq. (3).

$$t_i = \left\{ x_j, y_j, time_j, MMSI_j \mid j = 1, 2, \ldots, len(t_i) \right\} \tag{2}$$

Here x and y represent the UTM coordinates of the trajectory point at a specific time point.

Discrete Fréchet Distance Matrix
Continuous Fréchet distance can be interpreted intuitively as a human walking a dog: the human and the dog walk on two different curves. Both of them can control their walking speed independently but cannot go backwards. The minimum leash length that satisfies the requirement is the Fréchet distance between the curves. On the basis of continuous cases, discrete Fréchet distance assume that the human and dog jump between points of their trajectory. Vessel trajectories presented in Sect. 3.3.1 consist of discrete points, hence discrete Fréchet distance is applicable. Besides, discrete Fréchet distance considers both shape and temporal order of trajectory, which is inherently suitable for clustering.

Discrete Fréchet distance is also called coupling distance. Assuming a trajectory P of length n and a trajectory Q of length m, when the first and last trajectory points are matched, their coupling equation is as follow.

$$\|L\| = \max_{i=1,2,\ldots,m} dist\left(p_a^i, q_b^i \right) \tag{3}$$

$\|\ \|$ means Euclidean distance. By calculating couplings, we can obtain discrete Fréchet distance as follow.

$$\sigma_{dF}(P, Q) = min\{ \|L\| \} \tag{4}$$

After calculating the distances between all trajectories, we get a distance matrix of $1,218 \times 1,218$ saved in.npy format for future clustering.

3.4 Unsupervised KNN + Kneed

In this section, we propose an automated optimal parameter setting method for DBSCAN. Rahmah et al. employ the slope as a benchmark to determine the optimal ε value [24], but slope only considers the rate of change of the function, while curvature takes into account the concavity of the function based on the slope to reflect the degree of curvature, therefore, replacing the slope with the curvature as benchmark can lead to better results. Kneed is a method to find the point of maximum curvature in a curve, here we apply it to calculate the point of maximum curvature on the K-distance graph as the optimal ε value.

Based on sklearn [25], we first compute the average distance of each trajectory from its K (K = minPts) neighbor trajectories in discrete Fréchet distance matrix. All distance values computed in the previous step are stored in an array of length 1,218. After sorting the distance arrays in ascending order, we use the Kneed package [26] to compute the point with the largest curvature as the ε value. The K-distance graph and optimal ε value are shown in Fig. 5.

Considering the existence of noise trajectories in the dataset, we set the minPts range as 4–20. By traversing the range, we finally determine the final minPts as 8, and ε as 2.865 as shown in Fig. 5.

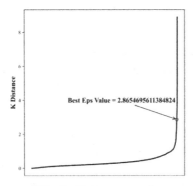

Fig. 5. K-distance graph.

4   Experiments

4.1   Dataset and Experimental Environment

The AIS trajectory dataset used in this paper includes 4,000 trajectories entering and leaving the Taiwan Strait in November 2017.

For the experimental environment, CPU is Intel(R) Core (TM) i9-10900X CPU @ 3.70 GHz, GPU is NVIDIA GeForce RTX 2080 Ti. Experiments are conducted using Python on Windows 10 OS.

4.2   Data Pre-processing

In this section, the clustering results before and after data pre-processing are compared as shown in Fig. 6, where Fig. 6(a) represents before pre-processing and Fig. 6(b) represents after pre-processing. The trajectory movement pattern clustered in (a) is messier, after data pre-processing the clustered movement pattern in (b) is more obvious than (a), which proves the effectiveness of the data pre-processing framework in this paper.

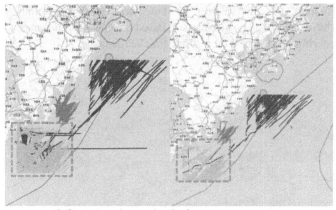

(left) AIS trajecrtories before pre-processing
(right) AIS trajecrtories after pre-processing

Fig. 6. Patterns before and after data pre-processing.

4.3 Comparison of Similarity Measures

In this section, we compared clustering results of other two commonly used similarity measures (point-based method DTW and shape-based method Hausdorff distance) with our measure discrete Fréchet distance by visualization.

Figure 7 shows the clustering result of employing DTW. It can be seen that DBSCAN divides most of the trajectories except noise into one cluster, which is less effective. All trajectories except anomalies are recognized as the same movement pattern resulting in the inability to perform subsequent route planning. Therefore, instead of using DTW, we further compare the shape-based similarity measurements to determine the final distance metric to be used.

Fig. 7. DTW clustering result.

Figure 8 compares the clustering results of the two shape-based similarity measures, of which Fig. 8(a) shows the clustering result based on Hausdorff distance and Fig. 8(b) shows the clustering result based on discrete Fréchet distance.

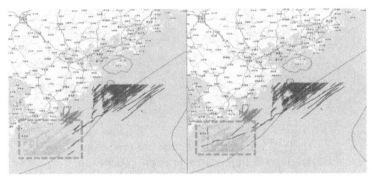

(left) Clustering result via Hausdorff distance
(right) Clustering result via discrete Fréchet distance

Fig. 8. Clustering results via Hausdorff distance and discrete Fréchet distance.

The clusters delineated by these two methods are approximately similar. However, in the lower right corner of the green frame, Hausdorff distance considers two trajectories that deviate from the region where most of the trajectories are located as red anomalous trajectories. By observing these two trajectories, we can find that the movement patterns of these two trajectories are similar to most trajectories in the frame. Since clustering aims to find trajectories with same movement patterns, we believe that these two trajectories should not be identified as anomalous, as the result of discrete Fréchet distance.

In addition, three apparently abnormal red trajectories in the green frame identified by discrete Fréchet distance are recognized as normal trajectories by Hausdorff distance. The figure of the three anomalous trajectories is shown in Fig. 9.

In the Fig. 9, trajectory 1 belongs to the unfiltered noise trajectory, which crosses an island and is clearly anomalous. Trajectories 2 and 3 have more steering, which are different from the common movement pattern in the region and can be considered as anomalous as well.

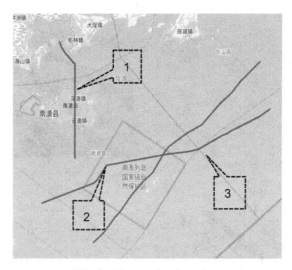

Fig. 9. Abnormal trajectories.

4.4 Description of Clusters

There are 29 noise trajectories among 1,218 trajectories which are pre-identified artificially according to maritime navigation regulations, these noise trajectories are denoted as −1; The remaining 1,189 normal trajectories are divided into three clusters according to actual geospatial locations. The normal movement patterns in the study area of this paper contain three parts: vessel movement trajectories near Nanpeng Islands National Nature Reserve, Dongshan County and Kinmen Island, which are represented by clusters 0, 1 and 2, respectively. Table 1 details the meaning of each cluster.

Table 1. Description of clusters.

Id	Trajectories	Description
−1	29	Noise trajectory that does not match the common movement pattern
0	704	Vessel movement near Nanpeng Islands National Nature Reserve
1	175	Vessel movement near Dongshan County
2	310	Vessel movement near Kinmen Island

All four clusters are shown in Fig. 10 in ID order, where Fig. 10(a), (b), (c) and (d) represent −1, 0, 1 and 2, respectively.

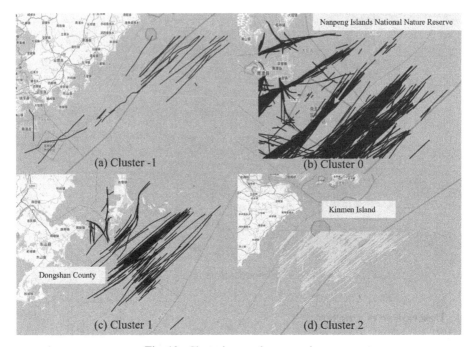

Fig. 10. Clustering results comparison.

5   Conclusions

In this paper, we propose an improved DBSCAN algorithm for vessel trajectory cluster-ing. First, the data quality is improved using the proposed data pre-processing framework including cleaning, segmentation, and DP compression. Then we combine unsupervised KNN and Kneed to automate the selection of parameters and use discrete Fréchet dis-tance as the similarity measure for clustering. Comparison experimental results prove that the discrete Fréchet distance in this paper performs better than other similarity mea-surements, and the data pre-processing framework effectively improves the clustering quality. In the end, the movement patterns of the clusters in visualization results clearly prove that our tuning method is effective.

Acknowledgments. This study was funded by the National Key R&D Program (2020YFB2104400), the Beijing Natural Science Foundation (Grant No. L222048), and the Young Scientists Fund of the National Natural Science Foundation of China (No. 62202018).

References

1. Xiao, Z., Fu, X., Zhang, L., Goh, R.S.M.: Traffic pattern mining and forecasting technologies in maritime traffic service networks: a comprehensive survey. IEEE Trans. Intell. Transp. Syst. **21**(5), 1796–1825 (2019)

2. Tetreault, B.J.: Use of the Automatic Identification System (AIS) for maritime domain awareness (MDA). In: Proceedings of OCEANS 2005 MTS/IEEE, 17–23 September 2005, Washington, DC, USA, pp. 1590–1594. IEEE (2005)

3. Yang, D., Wu, L., Wang, S., Jia, H., Li, K.X.: How big data enriches maritime research–a critical review of automatic identification system (AIS) data applications. Transp. Rev. **39**(6), 755–773 (2019)

4. Lu, N., Liang, M., Yang, L., Wang, Y., Xiong, N., Liu, R.W.: Shape-based vessel trajectory similarity computing and clustering: a brief review. In: 2020 5th IEEE International Conference on Big Data Analytics (ICBDA), 8–11 May 2020, Xiamen, China, pp. 186–192. IEEE (2020)

5. Besse, P.C., Guillouet, B., Loubes, J.-M., Royer, F.: Review and perspective for distance-based clustering of vehicle trajectories. IEEE Trans. Intell. Transp. Syst. **17**(11), 3306–3317 (2016)

6. Zhao, L., Shi, G.: A novel similarity measure for clustering vessel trajectories based on dynamic time warping. J. Navig. **72**(2), 290–306 (2019)

7. Zhai, W., Bai, X., Peng, Z.-R., Gu, C.: From edit distance to augmented space-time-weighted edit distance: detecting and clustering patterns of human activities in Puget Sound region. J. Transp. Geogr. **78**, 41–55 (2019)

8. Park, J., Jeong, J., Park, Y.: Ship trajectory prediction based on Bi-LSTM using spectral-clustered AIS data. J. Marine Sci. Eng. **9**(9), 1037 (2021)

9. Nie, P., Chen, Z., Xia, N., Huang, Q., Li, F.: Trajectory similarity analysis with the weight of direction and k-neighborhood for AIS data. ISPRS Int. J. Geo Inf. **10**(11), 757 (2021)

10. Li, H., Liu, J., Liu, R.W., Xiong, N., Wu, K., Kim, T.H.: A Dimensionality reduction-based multi-step clustering method for robust vessel trajectory analysis. Sensors **17**(8), 1792 (2017)

11. Yoo, W., Kim, T.W.: Statistical trajectory-distance metric for nautical route clustering analysis using cross-track distance. J. Comput. Design Eng. **9**(2), 731–754 (2022)

12. Wang, L., Chen, P., Chen, L., Mou, J.: Ship AIS trajectory clustering: an HDBSCAN-based approach. J. Marine Sci. Eng. **9**(6), 566 (2021)

13. Yang, J., Liu, Y., Ma, L., Ji, C.: Maritime traffic flow clustering analysis by density based trajectory clustering with noise. Ocean Eng. **249**, 111001 (2022)

14. Eiter, T., Mannila, H.: Computing discrete Fréchet distance (1994)

15. Nuocheng, X.: Study on the risk calculation model for traffic conflicts in intersecting waters. In: 2022 7th International Conference on Big Data Analytics (ICBDA), 4–6 March 2022, Guangzhou, China, pp. 115–122. IEEE (2022)

16. Cao, J., et al.: PCA-based hierarchical clustering of AIS trajectories with automatic extraction of clusters. In: 2018 IEEE 3rd International Conference on Big Data Analysis (ICBDA), March 9–12, 2018, Shanghai, China, pp. 448–452. IEEE (2018)

17. Chen, Z., Guo, J., Liu, Q.: DBSCAN algorithm clustering for massive AIS data based on the Hadoop platform. In: 2017 International Conference on Industrial Informatics-Computing Technology, Intelligent Technology, Industrial Information Integration (ICIICII), 2–3 December 2017, Wuhan, China, pp. 25–28. IEEE (2017)

18. Deng, D.: Application of DBSCAN algorithm in data sampling. J. Phys. Conf. Ser. **1617**(1), 012088 (2020)

19. Wang, X., Liu, X., Liu, B., de Souza, E.N., Matwin, S.: Vessel route anomaly detection with Hadoop MapReduce. In: 2014 IEEE International Conference on Big Data (Big Data), 27–30 October 2014, Washington, DC, USA, pp. 25–30. IEEE (2014)

20. Han, X., Armenakis, C., Jadidi, M.J.S.: Modeling vessel behaviours by clustering ais data using optimized DBSCAN. Sustainability **13**(15), 8162 (2021)

21. Wang, C., Li, G., Han, P., Osen, O., Zhang, H.: Impacts of COVID-19 on ship behaviours in port area: an AIS data-based pattern recognition approach. IEEE Trans. Intell. Transp. Syst. 1–12 (2022)

22. Lee, H.T., Lee, J.S., Yang, H., Cho, I.S.: An AIS data-driven approach to analyze the pattern of ship trajectories in ports using the DBSCAN algorithm. Appl. Sci. **11**(2), 799 (2021)

23. Zhao, L., Shi, G.: Maritime anomaly detection using density-based clustering and recurrent neural network. J. Navig. **72**(4), 894–916 (2019)

24. Rahmah, N., Sitanggang, I.S.: Determination of optimal epsilon (Eps) value on DBSCAN algorithm to clustering data on peatland hotspots in sumatra. In: IOP Conference Series: Earth and Environmental Science, vol. 31, p. 012012 (2016)

25. Pedregosa, F., et al.: Scikit-learn: machine learning in python. J. Mach. Learn. Res. **12**, 2825–2830 (2011)

26. Satopaa, V., Albrecht, J., Irwin, D., Raghavan, B.: Finding a "Kneedle" in a haystack: detecting knee points in system behavior. In: Proceedings of the 2011 31st International Conference on Distributed Computing Systems Workshops, pp. 166–171. IEEE Computer Society (2011)

Structure and Semantic Contrastive Learning for Nodes Clustering in Heterogeneous Information Networks

Yiwei Yu, Lihua Zhou[✉], Chao Liu, Lizhen Wang, and Hongmei Chen

Information Science and Engineering, Yunnan University, Kunming 650091, China
lhzhou@ynu.edu.cn

Abstract. Nodes clustering is an important approach to partition heterogeneous information networks based on the features and adjacent matrices from different metapaths. Some scholars have adopted contrastive learning methods on the basis of deep clustering, which has achieved promising clustering performance. Despite this, few of them pay attention to redundant information in features, while also not considering both the semantics and structure of the nodes. To fill these gaps, a Structure and Semantic Contrastive Learning for Nodes Clustering in HINs (SSCHC) method is proposed. Specifically, the proposed method explores the high-order neighbor relationship of the node by reconstructing the adjacency matrix containing path and processing the redundant information in the features. In addition, we design a structure and semantic contrastive learning module to obtain more comprehensive information about the nodes. Extensive experiments on several real-world benchmarks demonstrate the effectiveness of the proposed SSCHC method compared with the state-of-the-art baselines.

Keywords: Clustering · Contrastive Learning · Heterogeneous Information Networks

1 Introduction

Nodes clustering is a common data analysis technique, assigning similar nodes to the same group by analyzing the structure of the graph and the relationships between nodes. In many real-world applications, such as social networks, recommender systems, and biological networks [1, 2], data is made up of multiple types of data objects (nodes) and relationships (edges), known as heterogeneous information networks (HINs). Heterogeneous graph clustering helps us understand the structure and characteristics of the HINs network by dividing the nodes in HINs into disjoint groups [3].

For HINs, data has multiple types of data relationships, containing rich information. However, there are some correlations and differences between different nodes. How to capture and utilize the structural relationships between nodes and the semantic relationships between graphs brings challenges to heterogeneous graph clustering [4]. To solve this problem, many heterogeneous graph clustering methods have been proposed. Existing methods still have the following shortcomings: (1) Existing methods aggregate the feature and structure information between nodes, it may embed noise and redundant information into the low-dimensional represents of nodes, resulting in the mapping of nodes of different classes into similar representations. (2) The method based on contrastive learning only considers the correlation between nodes, but ignores the relationship between nodes and graph structure, and cannot capture the consistency information between metapaths, resulting in poor results.

We propose the Structure and Semantic Contrastive Learning for Nodes Clustering in HINs (SSCHC) to address these limitations. The model extracts specific topological information from each metapath of HINs and uses encoders to explore the nonlinear structure between nodes. By removing redundancy from node features, the duplicate information and noise between different features are reduced, so as to obtain a highly independent low-dimensional representation. According to the quality of each metapath, the topology of the metapath is fused and reconstructed to obtain the potential association of nodes. Meanwhile, contrastive learning between the fused metapath representations and independent representations, as well as the cross-graph summary and nodes, were carried out to enhance the consistency between the nodes of different metapaths. Our main contributions can be summarized as follows:

1. We capture the high-order neighbor relationships in heterogeneous data by fusing and reconstructing the topological information of multi-metapaths. Meanwhile, by eliminating redundant information of node features, SSCHC is encouraged to emphasize the independence of node features.
2. We conduct contrastive learning in two aspects, considering both semantic and structural aspects, to obtain consistent information between nodes.
3. Experiments on three benchmark datasets show that SSCHC achieves better performance than the baseline model in clustering tasks.

2 Related Work

In recent years, node clustering methods based on Graph Neural Network (GNN) have been proposed [5–8], such as SDCN [5] integrates Autoencoder and Graph Convolutional Network into one framework, One2Multi [6] integrates self-training strategy and heterogeneous graph reconstruction into a unified framework, and DIAGC [7] proposes a dual-information enhanced multi-view attribute graph clustering model. Since contrastive learning promote node representation and clustering tasks, many clustering methods based on contrastive learning have been proposed [9, 10], such as Heco [9] using a cross-view contrast mechanism to capture local and higher-order structures, and Graph Debiased Contrastive Learning[10] uses node class information to avoid the introduction of false positive samples. In addition, some excellent algorithms such as f-NSP [11], sc-NSP [12] and NegI-NSP [13] have been proposed to mine negative sequential pattern (NSP), which considers both positive (occurring) and negative (non-occurring) event/behavior and can provide more complement decision-making information. Although the above clustering methods have shown commendable performance to a certain extent, they cannot effectively utilize the node information of HINs. Therefore, we introduce a method based on contrastive learning, and compare them from two aspects: semantics and structure to obtain better heterogeneous graph clustering performance.

3 The Proposed Method

The overall framework of SSCHC is illustrated in Fig. 1. This model consists of three parts: adjacency matrix reconstruction, feature cleaning and contrastive learning. We first extract the metapaths-based adjacency matrices and nodes features from the HINs. Then, feed the data inputs into the encoders and decoder sequentially. Optimizing low-dimensional representations via two training strategies (i.e., adjacency matrices reconstruction, feature cleaning) and two contrastive learning (i.e., semantic contrastive learning and structure contrastive learning).

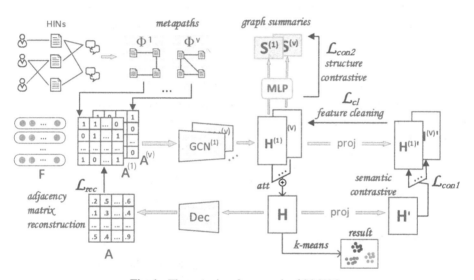

Fig. 1. The overview framework of SSCHC.

3.1 Adjacency Matrix Reconstruction

HINs is defined as graph $G = \{V, A, F, \Phi\}$ consisting of multiple types of nodes $V = \{v_i\}_{i=1}^{n}$ and adjacency matrixes $A^{(p)}$, where F represents attributes and Φ represents metapaths. We use $A^{(p)} = \left\{ a_{ij}^{(p)} | a_{ij}^{(p)} \in (0, 1) \right\}$ to store the structural relationship between the nodes with respect to each metapath. If there is a connecting relationship between the nodes v_i and v_j in the metapath Φ_p, $a_{ij}^{(p)} = 1$, otherwise $a_{ij}^{(p)} = 0$. We reconstruct the adjacency matrix $A^{(p)}$ containing metapath structure information to explore higher-order relationships and provide more accurate feature representations. First, the graph convolutional encoders $GCN^{(p)}$ is configured separately for each metapath to capture information between nodes:

$$H^{(p)} = GCN^{(p)}\left(A^{(p)}, F\right) \tag{1}$$

where $H^{(p)}$ is a low-dimensional representation learned from the p_{th} metapath. We use multi-channel attention mechanism $att(\cdot)$ fusion $\{H^{(p)}\}_{p=1}^{m}$ to obtain a multi-metapath fusion representation H, which enables the model to adaptively adjust the influence of different metapaths:

$$(\alpha_1, \alpha_2, \cdots, \alpha_m) = att\left(H^1, H^2, \cdots, H^m\right), \quad H = \sum_{p=1}^{m} \alpha_p \cdot H^{(p)} \tag{2}$$

α_p represents the attention coefficient of the metapath Φ_p. Subsequently, we send $\{H^{(p)}\}_{p=1}^{m}$ to the decoder $f_D(\cdot)$ to reconstruct the adjacency matrix $\tilde{A}$:

$$\tilde{A} = f_D(H).$$

In order to combine the loss functions $\mathcal{L}_{rec}$ of the metapaths $\{\Phi_p\}_{p=1}^{m}$, we fuse the loss of each metapath based on the attention mechanism, and use the mean square error(MSE) to compare the goals raw adjacency matrix $A^{(p)}$ and reconstructions adjacency matrix $\tilde{A}$ of each node v:

$$\mathcal{L}_{rec} = \sum_{p=1}^{m} \alpha_p \cdot \left(\sum_{v \in \mathcal{V}} (A_v^{(p)} - A_v)^2\right) \tag{3}$$

3.2 Cleaning Feature

By removing the correlation between features, it is possible to reduce interference among features, and enhance the discriminability and expressive power of features, making it easier for the model to capture important features in the data. Specifically, we use a linear transformation to project the low-dimensional representation $\{H^{(p)}\}_{p=1}^{m}$ into the space $\{H'^{(p)}\}_{p=1}^{m}$ to increase the nonlinear ability of the model. Define the feature similarity matrix $T^{(p)} \in \mathbb{R}^{d' \times d'}$ of $\{H^p\}_{p=1}^{m}$ and $\{H'^{(p)}\}_{p=1}^{m}$ as:

$$t_{ij}^{(p)} = \frac{\left(h_i^{(p)}\right)^{\mathrm{T}} \left(h'_j^{(p)}\right)}{\left\|h_i^{(p)}\right\| \left\|h'_j^{(p)}\right\|}, \forall i, j \in [1, d'], \tag{4}$$

where $t_{ij}^{(p)}$ represents similarity between $H_{i\cdot}^{(p)}$ and $H'_{j\cdot}^{(p)}$. d' represents the feature dimension of node projection. In order to make the features in $H^{(p)}$ and $H'^{(p)}$ as similar as possible in the same dimension and as different as possible in different dimensions, we enforce the feature similarity matrix $T^{(p)}$ to approximate the identity matrix $\tilde{I} \in \mathbb{R}^{d' \times d'}$ to obtain the feature cleaning loss function $\mathcal{L}_{fcl}$:

$$\mathcal{L}_{fcl} = \sum_{p=1}^{m} \frac{1}{d'^2} \sum \left(T^{(p)} - \tilde{I}\right)^2 = \sum_{p=1}^{m} \left[\frac{1}{d'^2} \sum_{i=1}^{d'} \left(t_{ii}^{(p)} - 1\right)^2 + \frac{1}{d'^2 - d} \sum_{i=1}^{d'} \sum_{j \neq i} \left(t_{ij}^{(p)}\right)^2\right] \tag{5}$$

3.3 Contrastive Learning

For raw data, if two nodes have edges connected in all metapaths, they are considered to be positive samples, otherwise they are negative samples. Sorting by the number of edges, the positive sample set of node v_i is denoted as $\mathbb{P}_i = \{v_{in} | v_{in} \in V\}$, and the negative sample set is denoted as $\mathbb{N}_i$. The contrast loss between $\{H^{(p)}\}_{p=1}^{m}$ and $\{H'^{(p)}\}_{p=1}^{m}$ can be expressed as:

$$\mathcal{L}_{con1} = -\frac{1}{|V|} \sum_{i \in V} \sum_{p=1}^{m} \log \frac{\sum_{j \in \mathbb{P}_i} \exp\left(sim\left(h'_i, h'^{(p)}_j\right)/\tau\right)}{\sum_{k \in (\mathbb{P}_i \cup \mathbb{N}_i)} \exp\left(sim\left(h'_i, h'^{(p)}_k\right)/\tau\right)}, sim\left(h'_i, h'^p_j\right) = \frac{h'^\mathsf{T}_i h'^{(p)}_j}{\|h'_i\| \|h'^{(p)}_j\|} \tag{6}$$

where $sim\left(h'_i, h'^{(p)}_j\right)$ represents the cosine distance between vector h'_i and vector $h'^{(p)}_j$, h'_i and $h'^{(p)}_j$ represents the projection of node v_i and v_j respectively. $\|\cdot\|$ represents the 2-norm, and τ represents the temperature parameter.

The graph summary $s^{(v)} = \mathcal{R}\left(\varepsilon(h^{(v)})\right)$ captures the global information content of the entire graph, compare the nodes with the graph summary, and the model understand the context and semantic meaning of the nodes in the graph better. $\varepsilon(\cdot)$ represents a multilayer perceptron MLP neural network, consisting of a bilinear layer and a parameterized rectifier linear unit. $\mathcal{R}(\cdot)$ consists of a mean pooling layer. Next, we use a discriminator $\mathcal{D}(\cdot)$ to measure the similarity between $h^{(v1)}$ and $s^{(v1)}$ to get the loss function:

$$\mathcal{L}_{con2} = \sum_{v1 \neq v2, v1, v2 \in V} -\log(\mathcal{D}(h^{(v1)}, s^{(v1)})) - \log(1 - \mathcal{D}(h^{(v2)}, s^{(v1)})) \tag{7}$$

$\mathcal{D}(\cdot)$ consists of a bilinear layer and sigmoid activation function. Therefore, we obtain the contrastive learning loss function:

$$\mathcal{L}_{con} = \mathcal{L}_{con1} + \mathcal{L}_{con2} \tag{8}$$

3.4 Objective Function

The overall objective function of SSCHC consists of three parts: feature cleaning loss $\mathcal{L}_{fcl}$, contrastive learning $\mathcal{L}_{con}$, and adjacency matrix reconstruction loss $\mathcal{L}_{rec}$.

$$\mathcal{L} = \mathcal{L}_{con} + \beta \mathcal{L}_{fcl} + \alpha \mathcal{L}_{rec} \tag{9}$$

α, β represents adjustable hyperparameters used to control the weights of the loss function. We stabilize the model by minimizing the $\mathcal{L}$. Once the model is stable, we apply the k-means algorithm in multi-metapath fusion representation H to obtain the cluster assignment results for nodes in HINs.

4 Experiments

4.1 Datasets and Baselines

To demonstrate the superiority of SSCHC, we conduct experiments on three public benchmark datasets, including ACM, DBLP and AMiner. Detailed descriptions of all datasets are summarized in Table 1.

Table 1. Data statistics

Datasets	Nodes	Metapath	Classes
ACM	Paper (P): 4019 Author (A): 7167 Subject (S): 60	Paper-Subject-Paper (PSP) Paper-Author-Paper (PAP)	3
DBLP	Paper (P): 14328 Author (A): 4057 Conference (C): 20 Term (T): 7723	Paper-Author-Paper (PAP) Paper-Paper-Paper (PPP) Paper-Author-Term-Author-Paper (PATAP)	4
AMiner	Paper (P): 6564 Author (A): 13329 Reference (R): 35890	Paper-Author-Paper (PAP) Paper- Reference -Paper (PRP)	4

4.2 Comparison Methods

We evaluate the performance of our model against various baselines, including DGI [14], MVGRL [15], GCC [16], SNMH [17], HDMI [18] and HeCo [9]. In the comparison experiments, we run each method 10 times and report their average values in terms of ACC, F1, NMI and ARI in Table 2. We have the following observations:

- The proposed method achieves the best clustering performance compared with the baselines. The results verify that SSCHC could leverage the complementary information between different views to generate a more comprehensive representation for clustering.
- Compared with the three models (DGI, MVGRL and GCC) that only clustered by a single element path, SSCHC can achieve better clustering results., the reason may be that GCN could incorporate both structural information embedded in the adjacent matrix and attribute information to mine the essential representation of attributed graph data.
- The rest of the baseline methods are both GCN-based graph heterogeneous clustering methods. They utilize the consensus representation generated by GCNs as the deep representation for clustering. From the results, it can be seen that the results of SSCHC on these three datasets are almost better than them, mainly because SSCHC considers the semantic information and structural information between nodes at the attribute level, and it can fully learn more discriminative representations.

Table 2. Comparison results. The best results are highlighted in bold.

Datasets	Indicators	DGI	MVGRL	GCC	SNMH	HDMI	HeCo	SSCHC
ACM	ACC	88.79 ± 0.30	86.71 ± 0.84	79.72 ± 0.81	70.47 ± 2.35	86.50 ± 2.04	85.73 ± 2.97	**89.57 ± 1.32**
	NMI	66.32 ± 0.49	60.48 ± 1.59	42.11 ± 1.74	43.10 ± 2.24	63.96 ± 2.09	59.73 ± 4.20	**67.56 ± 1.37**
	ARI	68.18 ± 0.74	63.02 ± 2.07	48.49 ± 1.57	38.38 ± 3.75	62.83 ± 4.67	61.69 ± 6.29	**70.18 ± 2.56**
	F1	89.25 ± 0.27	87.09 ± 0.76	79.20 ± 0.91	70.32 ± 0.93	87.34 ± 1.74	86.06 ± 2.79	**90.08 ± 1.66**
DBLP	ACC	89.56 ± 0.19	76.74 ± 4.01	79.05 ± 0.80	81.95 ± 8.15	88.91 ± 0.63	90.11 ± 0.31	**92.56 ± 0.16**
	NMI	70.57 ± 0.32	57.42 ± 4.09	47.45 ± 1.03	63.54 ± 8.44	69.48 ± 0.75	71.68 ± 0.59	**77.91 ± 0.66**
	ARI	76.11 ± 0.42	56.28 ± 4.66	53.09 ± 1.45	65.23 ± 9.57	74.89 ± 1.19	77.18 ± 0.64	**82.25 ± 0.45**
	F1	88.55 ± 0.27	74.75 ± 4.34	78.39 ± 0.76	79.97 ± 9.95	87.96 ± 0.66	89.22 ± 0.36	**92.05 ± 0.03**
AMiner	ACC	46.24 ± 0.53	30.89 ± 1.03	44.93 ± 0.35	43.74 ± 1.81	47.01 ± 3.56	**67.44 ± 5.43**	65.63 ± 4.34
	NMI	2.07 ± 0.14	3.35 ± 0.32	2.10 ± 0.13	3.45 ± 1.21	16.79 ± 2.36	40.86 ± 5.17	**51.28 ± 3.20**
	ARI	8.25 ± 0.65	0.34 ± 0.37	8.90 ± 0.26	6.03 ± 1.66	14.09 ± 2.43	42.73 ± 9.41	**44.28 ± 13.2**
	F1	29.17 ± 1.55	26.61 ± 0.89	31.39 ± 0.52	30.65 ± 1.85	42.67 ± 3.92	**59.03 ± 4.04**	54.01 ± 4.28

4.3 Ablation Experiments

We remove the three modules in the objective function separately to assess their importance. W/o-rec, w/o-fcl, and w/o-con represent the clustering results after the module is removed, respectively. Figure 2 illustrates the validity of these three modules on datasets, especially for the AMiner dataset. Missing any module will greatly reduce performance, because the dataset does not have the attribute information of the target node, only contains the topology of the graph, while the contrastive learning in the SSCHC model can learn the nodes information from the structural aspect. These results show that all the modules in the proposed SSCHC method are essential for improving the clustering performance.

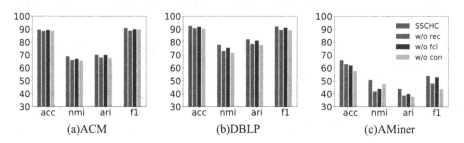

(a)ACM   (b)DBLP   (c)AMiner

Fig. 2. Clustering results of the module ablation experiments (**unit%**)

4.4 Parameter Analysis

We conduct the parameter analysis on all the benchmarks with the hyper-parameter α, β, which is tuned in the range of {0.001, 0.01, 0.1, 1, 10}. According to Fig. 3, we can observe that the clustering performance of SSCHC is relatively stable over all the benchmarks with different values of α, β, which indicates the robustness of SSCHC to obtain the promising clustering performance.

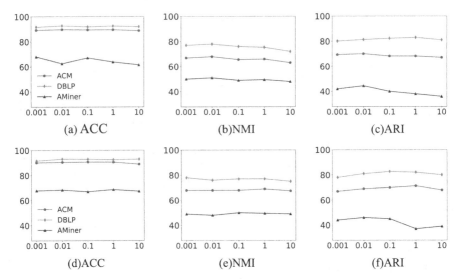

Fig. 3. (a) (b) (c), (d) (e) (f) are the parameter sensitivity analysis of α, β, the abscissa represents the value of the parameter, and the ordinate represents the index value (unit%)

5 Conclusion

In this paper, we propose SSCHC model. By reconstructing and fusing metapaths information, We obtain the higher-order nearest neighbor relationship of the node in HINs. We design a contrastive learning module, which combines the structural information and semantic information of the node. Meanwhile, we remove the redundant information through cleaning features. The experimental results on several real-world benchmarks demonstrate the effectiveness of the proposed method.

Acknowledgments. This research is supported by the National Natural Science Foundation of China (62062066, 62266050 and 62276227), Yunnan Fundamental Research Projects (202201AS070015); Yunnan Key Laboratory of Intelligent Systems and Computing (202205AG070003), the Block-chain and Data Security Governance Engineering Research Center of Yunnan Provincial Department of Education; the Postgraduate Research and Innovation Foundation of Yunnan University (KC-22222861).

References

1. Guo, X., Gao, L., Liu, X., Yin, J.: Improved deep embedded clustering with local structure preservation. In: Proceedings of the IJCAI, pp. 1753–1759 (2017)
2. Wang, C., Pan, S., Long, G., Zhu, X., Jiang, J.: MGAE: marginalized graph autoencoder for graph clustering. In: Proceedings of the CIKM, pp. 889–898 (2017)
3. Ester, M., Kriegel, H.P., Sander, J., Xu, X.: A density-based algorithm for discovering clusters in large spatial databases with noise. In: Proceedings of the KDD, vol. 96, no. 34, pp. 226–231 (1996)

4. Wang, T., et.al.: Neighborhood contrastive representation learning for attributed graph clustering. Neurocomputing, **562** (2023)
5. Bo, D., Wang, X., Shi, C., Zhu, M., Lu, E., Cui, P.: Structural deep clustering network. In: Proceedings of the WWW, pp. 1400–1410 (2020)
6. Lin, J.Q., Chen, M.S., Zhu, X.R., Wang, C.D., Zhang, H.: Dual information enhanced multi-view attributed graph clustering (2022). https://doi.org/10.48550/arXiv.2211.14987
7. Fan, S., Wang, X., Shi, C., Lu, E., Lin, K., Wang, B.: One2multi graph autoencoder for multi-view graph clustering. In: Proceedings of the WWW, pp. 3070–3076 (2020)
8. Fettal, C., Labiod, L., Nadif, M.: Simultaneous linear multi-view attributed graph representation learning and clustering. In: Proceedings of the WSDM, pp. 303–311 (2023)
9. Wang, X., Liu, N., Han, H., Shi, C.: Self-supervised heterogeneous graph neural network with co-contrastive learning. In: Proceedings of the SIGKDD, pp. 1726–1736 (2021)
10. Zhao, H., Yang, X., Wang, Z., Yang, E.. Graph debiased contrastive learning with joint representation clustering. In: Proceedings of the IJCAI, pp. 3434–3440 (2021)
11. Dong, X.J., Gong, Y.S., Cao, L.B.: F-NSP+: a fast negative sequential patterns mining method with self-adaptive data storage. Pattern Recogn. **84**, 13–27 (2018)
12. Gao, X.M., Gong, Y.S., Xu, T.T., Lu, J.H., Zhao, Y.H., Dong, X.J.: Towards to better structure and constraint to mine negative sequential patterns. TNNLS **34**(2), 571–585 (2023)
13. Qiu, P., Gong, Y.S., Zhao, Y.H., Cao, L.B., Zhang, C.Q., Dong, X.J.: An efficient method for modeling nonoccurring behaviors by negative sequential patterns with loose constraints. TNNLS. **34**(4), 1864–1878 (2023)
14. Veličković, P., Fedus, W., Hamilton, W.L., Liò, P., Bengio, Y., et al.: Deep graph infomax. In: ICLR (Poster), vol. 2, no. 3, p. 4 (2019)
15. Hassani, K., Khasahmadi A.H.: Contrastive multi-view representation learning on graphs. In: ICML, pp. 4116–4126 (2020)
16. Fettal, C., Labiod, L., Nadif, M.: Efficient graph convolution for joint node representation learning and clustering. In: Proceedings of the WSDM, pp. 289–297 (2022)
17. Park, C., Han, J., Yu, H.: Deep multiplex graph infomax: attentive multiplex network embedding using global information. Knowl.-Based Syst. **197**, 105861 (2020)
18. Jing, B., Park, C., Tong, H.: HDMI: high-order deep multiplex infomax. In: Proceedings of the WWW, pp. 2414–2424 (2021)

An Accuracy Evaluation Method
for Multi-source Data Based on Hexagonal
Global Discrete Grids

Yue Ma[1,2], Guoqing Li[1], Long Zhao[1], and Xiaochuang Yao[3(✉)]

[1] Aerospace Information Research Institute, Chinese Academy of Sciences, Beijing 100094, China

`{mayue,caoqq,liqg}@radi.ac.cn, zhaolong@aircas.ac.cn`

[2] School of Electronic, Electrical and Communication Engineering, University of Chinese Academy of Sciences, Beijing 100049, China

[3] College of Land Science and Technology, China Agricultural University, Beijing 100083, China

`yxc@cau.edu.cn`

Abstract. As a new form of data management, the global discrete grid can describe and exchange geographic information in a standardized way on a global scale, which can be used for efficient storage and application of large-scale global spatial data, and it is a digital multi-resolution geo-reference model, which helps to establish a new data model and is expected to make up for the deficiencies of the existing spatial data in the aspects of organization, processing and application. The representation of vector data based on hexagonal isoproduct projection of global discrete grids fundamentally solves the problems of data redundancy, geometric deformation, and data discontinuity that occur when multi-vector data are represented in grids. In this paper, different gridded methods are proposed for different types of vector data and remote sensing data to achieve efficient gridded processing of multi-source data. For the gridded vector data, a quantifiable accuracy evaluation index system is established to evaluate the accuracy of the gridded vector data in terms of geographic deviation, geometrical features and topological relationships, and for the gridded remote sensing data, a Kyoto evaluation index system is constructed based on the levels of information, image structure, and texture features, which further proves the usability of the hexagonal gridded vector-based and remotely sensed data. The evaluation method is generally applicable to all gridded vector and remote sensing data based on hexagonal grids and can be used to evaluate the usability of hexagonal grid data.

Keywords: multi-source data · global discrete grid · gridding · accuracy evaluation

1 Introductory

The Global Discrete Grid (GDG) supports data fusion, analysis and application of multi-resolution geospatial data by modeling the Earth's surface at multiple levels with appropriate spherical geometry [1, 2]. Global Discrete Grid The global discrete grid is an

X. Meng et al. (Eds.): SpatialDI 2024, LNCS 14619, pp. 66–79, 2024.

https://doi.org/10.1007/978-981-97-2966-1_6

infinite multi-level subdivision of the earth's surface according to certain rules, and the same level is covered by the same size and shape of the cells on the earth's surface, so that any data with geographic information can be expressed and fused according to the geographic information data on the grid [3]. Any data with geographic information can be expressed and integrated on the grid according to the geographic information data. The grid uses a unique code to index the grid cells, which not only extracts the geospatial coordinates of the grid, but also includes the level in which the grid cell is located as well as the attribute information of the grid cell (elevation, DN value, social data, etc.) [3, 4]. The Compared with traditional geospatial data organization and management frameworks, the global discrete grid can achieve multi-level nesting and data continuity management, and uses a unique code to index grid cells, thus avoiding projection distortion and enabling comprehensive management of data of different resolutions at different levels [5]. The grid can avoid projection distortion and provide comprehensive management of data of different resolutions at different levels.

Various types of global discrete grids have emerged, including equal latitude/longitude global discrete grids, variable latitude/longitude global discrete grids, adaptive global discrete grids, and orthopolyhedron-based global discrete grids. The orthopolyhedron-based discrete grid system is a multi-resolution hierarchical grid structure based on multi-level recursive dissections built on the basis of the Platonic stereo and projected on the sphere [6]. There are five types of Platonic cubes, ortho-tetrahedron, ortho-hexahedron, ortho-octahedron, ortho-dodecahedron and ortho icosahedron [7]. The polyhedron-based discrete grids cover the three-dimensional surface with grids of the same shape and size at the same level, and this unique pattern of grid composition is uniform and stable even after spherical projection. The ortho-polyhedral grids use a unique grid code to establish the index of grid cells, thus avoiding the defects of the latitude/longitude grids and adaptive grids to the greatest extent possible, and also enabling the interconnection of grid data between different levels [8]. The grid data can also be interconnected between different levels.

Whereas, the hexagonal grid based on ortho icosahedron has more consistent adjacency, better angular resolution and higher coverage. Besides, hexagonal cells share an edge with their six neighboring cells, and the hexagonal grid maintains the same distance between the center hexagonal cell and the neighboring cells, which makes it easier to perform spatial analysis and modeling. Besides, hexagonal grid is scalable, meaning that it can be used at different resolutions, from a global scale to a local scale. This makes it useful for analyzing and visualizing This makes it useful for analyzing and visualizing data at different levels of detail. Thus, hexagonal DGGS of ideal icosahedron is sometimes preferred as an organizational framework for GIS data.

In the existing technology, mainstream research teams have proposed accuracy evaluation indexes and characteristics for different global discrete grids.Goodchild proposed reference guidelines for grid evaluation in 1992, which were supplemented and summarized by Kimberling et al. and consolidated into 14 evaluation rules including complete coverage of grids without overlapping [9]. The evaluation rules are summarized by Kimberling et al. Based on the above 14 rules, many research teams at home and abroad have established various quantitative indicators to evaluate the geometric deformation of grids by combining the structural and geometric characteristics of different grids as well as the data requirements of different application scenarios. These indicators and features mainly evaluate the non-uniformity of grid cells, the irregularity of deformation distribution, and the complexity of deformation change with level, so as to be able to analyze the uncertainty of global discrete grid model in spatial data expression, analysis and decision-making [10]. However, there is still a gap in the research on the evaluation index system for the accuracy of multi-source data expression on hexagonal discrete grids.

This study analyzes the conversion model, error sources, and classification of vector and remotely sensed data on hexagonal global discrete grids to provide further support for hexagonal global discrete grids in the organization of multi-source data.

2 Multi-source Data Grids

2.1 Selection of Grid Levels

It is first necessary to select the appropriate grid level for modeling and sampling. Since the grid structure is fixed, the size of each level of grid cells is determined, and the spatial resolution of different data is also determined, so it is difficult to ensure a perfect match between the pixel cell of remote sensing image or the resolution of vector data and the size of the grid. In the actual operation process, the level of the grid cell that is closest to the remote sensing pixel size or vector data resolution is often selected for data conversion. The equal-area conversion can reduce data redundancy and information loss, if the equal-area data conversion cannot be realized, in order to reduce data loss, in the actual processing, the grid cell area is generally selected to be slightly smaller than the rectangular pixel area of the grid level. In Table 1, the area of the grid cells on the discrete grid with subdivision layer n is recorded, and the radius of the earth is 6,371,007.22347 m [11].

Table 1. Properties of hexagonal four-aperture global discrete grid cells

Res	Number of Cell*	Hex area (km)^2	Pen area (km)^2
1	32	17,002,187.39080	14168489.49230
2	122	4,250,546.84778	3542122.37308
3	482	1,062,636.71193	885553.59327
4	1,922	265,659.17798	221382.64832
5	7,682	66,414.79448	55345.66208
6	30,722	16,603.69862	13836.41552
7	122,882	4,150.92466	3459903883

(*continued*)

Table 1. (*continued*)

Res	Number of Cell*	Hex area (km)^2	Pen area (km)^2
8	491,522	1,037.73116	864.77597
9	1,966,082	259.43280	216.19400
10	7,864,322	64.85821	54.04850
11	33,457,282	16.21455	13.51212
12	125,829,122	4.05364	3.37803
13	503,316,482	1.01341	0.84451
14	2,013,265,922	0.25335	0.21113
15	8,053,063,682	0.06334	0.05278
16	32,212,254,722	0.01584	0.01320

2.2 Gridded Representation of Vector Data

Vector data is an abstract expression model of spatial entities, which abstracts spatial entities in the real world into targets with certain spatial relationships in the form of points, lines and surfaces mainly. It has been shown that in a generalized sense, the expression of raster data and vector data in the real world is the same, because vector data applies to an infinitely subdivided grid, and the size of its grid cells is the error range of vector data, but this error range does not affect the spatial relationship inference of vector data [12]. And the reorganization and management of vector data using hexagonal discrete grids is actually a process of vector data gridded reorganization [13]. The reorganization and management of vector data using hexagonal discrete grids is actually a process of vector data gridded reorganization.

The layout structure of hexagonal grid is different from that of raster data based on orthogonal coordinate system, so it is necessary to establish the grid coordinate system according to the layout structure of hexagonal grid. The establishment of the IJ coordinate system consists of three steps, selecting the geometric origin according to the geometric layout law of hexagonal grid; establishing the cell oblique 120° coordinate system (I,J coordinate system); and establishing the correspondence relationship between the geographic coordinates and the coordinates of hexagonal grid cells. The IJ coordinate system is shown in Fig. 1. The IJ coordinate system is shown in Fig. 1, starting from the coordinate origin, taking the two directions of the 120° angle as the coordinate direction, coding in integer mode, selecting the coordinate origin (0, 0), and for any case only need to carry out the coordinate translation.

Establish a transformation between IJ coordinates and orthogonal coordinate systems based on coordinate projections:

$$A(x, y) = A(i, j) \cdot \begin{pmatrix} 1 & 0 \\ -\frac{1}{2} & \frac{\sqrt{3}}{2} \end{pmatrix} \tag{1}$$

where A(x, y) are the coordinates of point A in the orthogonal coordinate system and A(i, j) are the coordinates of point A in the IJ coordinate system, and the side length of the hexagonal grid cell is 1.

Where for point data the drop marker method is used to obtain grid cells of a particular scale corresponding to the point vector data.

The Bresenham algorithm based on the transformation of hexagonal lattice structure is used for the line data to quickly generate straight line segments between the turning points. As shown in the figure, Bresenham algorithm is a method in computer graphics based on error discriminant to generate straight lines.

For faceted data, each edge of the polygon is traversed, gridded along the edges using Bresenham's algorithm, and marked on the grid. Based on the gridded boundary data, all edges of the polygon are traversed to find the points that intersect the scan lines. Perform scan line algorithm on the interior of the polygon to realize the activation and filling of the interior cells.

There are three types of information in such gridded vector data data records: geometric information, attribute information and topological information. Among them, geometric information is the basic and fundamental spatial information of all vector information, which consists of point coordinates. The basic steps in data recording are 1) replacement of coordinate points in the geometric information with coding sequences of grid cells, 2) attribute information retention, and 3) topological information retention. The vector data logging model on discrete grids differs from the traditional vector data logging model only in the coordinate logging, while all other aspects are equivalent. The difference is mainly in the data expression, because the grid subdivides the continuous space, so that the data expression must obey the spatial principle of subdivision.

2.3 Gridded Representation of Remotely Sensed Data

The data modeling of remote sensing images on the grid mainly includes the following steps, firstly, the pixel coordinates of the acquired remote sensing data (MODIS, Landsat 8 or Gaofen-1 remote sensing data) can be obtained by affine transformation to obtain the sinusoidal projection coordinates. The sinusoidal projection coordinates are obtained by inverse sinusoidal projection to obtain the WGS84 latitude and longitude coordinates. Based on the latitude and longitude coordinates, the grid cells corresponding to the pixel cells are determined, but because it is difficult to maintain the consistency between the size of the pixel cells and the size of the grid cells, the null-valued hexagonal cells will appear, and the pixel values of these cells can be obtained by interpolation. In order to determine the correspondence between the regional grid coordinates and the traditional orthogonal coordinates, the concept of "point to grid" is used to establish a planar hexagonal grid based on the orthogonal coordinate system. As shown in Fig. 1, the pixel coordinates of the rows and columns (i, j) where the grid is located are labeled.

According to the idea of "rasterization", in order to simplify the calculation, the geographic coordinates and attribute values of the entire grid cell are stored at the center of the grid, and the calculation and analysis of the grid cell are realized. The remote sensing data is also based on the correspondence between the coordinates of pixel units and the coordinates of the center point of the grid, which is the main basis for the conversion from rectangular pixel-based remote sensing data to hexagonal grid-based data.

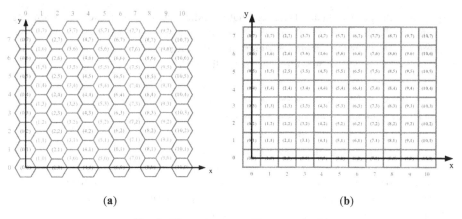

Fig. 1. Plane structure of hexagonal grid

According to the mismatch relationship between odd and even rows and the correspondence in orthogonal coordinate system shown inFig. 2-6, the correspondence between the coordinates of the planar hexagonal grid and the traditional orthogonal coordinate system can be defined as follows:

$$\begin{cases} Y(i,j) = \begin{cases} y_0 + \sqrt{3}l \times j, & i\%2 = 0 \\ y_0 + \sqrt{3}(j + \frac{1}{2})l, & i\%2 = 1 \end{cases} \\ X(i,j) = 1.5y_0 \times l \end{cases} \tag{2}$$

3 Accuracy Evaluation System for Gridded Data

3.1 Accuracy Evaluation Index System for Vector Data Gridding

Recognized GIS spatial data quality evaluation metrics include location accuracy, attribute accuracy, completeness, logical consistency, semantic accuracy, temporal accuracy and mileage information. The process of gridding different types of vector data changes the location, geometry and topological relationships of the data, etc. These changes vary with the data source, gridding algorithm and data structure. Discretizing vector features into grid cells is the core problem in the study of discrete global grid systems. Among vector features, point features are relatively simple to mesh and can be represented by grid cells corresponding to their scales, while for line and polygon features, all grid cells covered according to their scales must be determined. Therefore, in this paper, we will propose a generalized accuracy evaluation index system oriented to the three types of vector data for evaluating the similarity between the gridded vector data and the original vector data.

Point data have only data features such as geographic coordinates, attributes and topological relationships, but no geometric features, so the accuracy evaluation indexes for point data include geographic deviation and topological distortion. The geographic deviation is calculated as the straight-line distance between the geographic coordinates of the drop point of the point data and the coordinates of the center point of the corresponding hexagonal grid cell.

Figure 2-A shows the schematic diagram of the drop marker gridding of the point-like data, and Fig. 2-B shows the schematic diagram of the topological distortion of the point-like data. Where point I and point J are two vector point-like data, point O is the geographic coordinate of the center point of the corresponding grid cell, so the geographic coordinate deviation of point I is calculated as $D = \sqrt{(X_2 - X_1)^2 + (Y_I - Y_O)^2}$ Therefore, the geographic coordinate deviation of point I is calculated as $D =$. Where the topological distortion in the process of point data gridded is a spatial data scale problem, if the grid level is low, the process of gridded will appear in the process of gridded originally separated two vector points corresponding to the same grid cell, and the topological relationship of the separation becomes equal. This point topological distortion is evaluated by the criterion of If $x_i \neq x_j || y_i \neq y_j \cap code_i = code_j \rightarrow$ Intersects Distortions. If the spatial coordinates of the two original point features are exactly the same, the topologies of these two point features are equal; otherwise, they are disjoint from each other. After meshing the point features, two original disjoint point features can be converted into the same grid cell, and the topological relationship of the point feature objects changes from disjoint to equal.

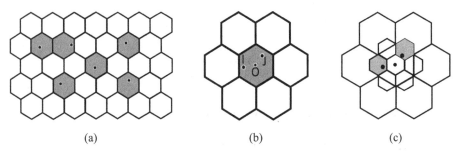

(a)   (b)   (c)

Fig. 2. Schematic diagram of gridding and topological distortion of point vector data (a) Schematic diagram of the drop marking method for point vector data; (b) Topological distortion of point data; (c) Solving the topological distortion of point data by increasing the grid level

And this topological distortion can be repaired by using the multilevel resolution feature of DGGS to improve the local resolution. This method can effectively maintain the topological relationship between the original vector data with a stable amount of data, which ensures the correct integration of vector features in DGGS.

The evaluation metrics of line vector data include three dimensions, which are geographic bias, shape bias and topological distortion. Linear vector data is a collection of point data of chained entities expressed by a series of ordered coordinate values or latitude and longitude, and the geographic deviation can be expressed as the median error of the geographic deviation of the multiple point data composing the linear vector data i.e. $D_l = \sqrt{\frac{\sum_1^n D_i}{n}}$.

Compared to point data without shape and geometric attributes, the accuracy evaluation of line data needs to consider the geometric structure change of the entity (Zhi-Ying

Xu et al. 2012). The geometric features of line data include two parameters, direction and length. Among them, the direction distortion (angular distortion) can be expressed as the average value of the angle between the direction of the gridded multi-segmented line data and the original data, where the angle towards clockwise direction is positive and the angle towards counterclockwise direction is negative. Thus the angular distortion of a line entity with n + 1 nodes and n segments of linear data is given by:

$$\theta_{dis} = \frac{\sum_{i=1}^{n} |\Delta\theta_i|}{n} \tag{3}$$

where $\Delta\theta_i$ is the angular error of the first i angular error of the line segment, the line entity has a total of n In order to better quantify the angular distortion, the cosine method is applied to normalize the angular distortion values $S_{dir} = cos\theta_{dis}$.

The Segment Length Difference refers to the ratio of the length of the gridded polyline data to the length of the vector data. If the side length of the grid cell is L, then the length distortion of the multisegmental line data covering a total of n grid cells is calculated as:

$$L_{distortion} = \frac{\sqrt{3}Ln}{L_{vector}} \tag{4}$$

where L_{vector} is the length of the vector line segment.

The accuracy evaluation for faceted data also includes three levels, namely, geographic bias, geometric features, and topological features.

Faceted vector data can be viewed as a different object type from closed line vector data, which also consists of multiple arc segments and nodes. The geographic deviation of faceted data is mainly used to assess whether the location of its data is accurate or not, which can be expressed as the median error of the geographic deviation of multiple arc segments, multiple nodes $\sqrt{\frac{\sum_{1}^{n} D_i}{n}}$.

Geometric features of faceted vector data are mainly shapes, specifically the geometric features of faceted vector data can be quantitatively evaluated in terms of distance similarity, orientation similarity and shape similarity:

Distance similarity. The Euclidean distance is used to calculate the distance between the center of mass position of the vector data before the transformation and the center of mass position of the gridded faceted data after the transformation. In the IJ coordinate system, the center of mass coordinates of polygons can be calculated using Eq:

$$\bar{x} = \frac{1}{6A} \sum_{i=1}^{n} (x_i + x_{i+1})(x_i y_{i+1} - x_{i+1} y_i) \tag{5}$$

$$\bar{y} = \frac{1}{6A} \sum_{i=1}^{n} (y_i + y_{i+1})(x_i y_{i+1} - x_{i+1} y_i) \tag{6}$$

Of these, the $\bar{x}$ and $\bar{y}$ are the coordinates of the center of mass of the polygon, respectively, and n are the number of sides of the polygon, and x_i and y_i are the coordinates of the starting point of the first i coordinates of the starting points of the sides of the polygon, and x_{i+1} and y_{i+1} are the coordinates of the endpoints of the i is the coordinate of the end point of the polygon's first edge, and A is the area of the polygon.

It is important to note that the formulas for calculating the area of a polygon in the IJ coordinate system are different from the formulas in the regular Cartesian coordinate system. Specifically, if the coordinates of the vertices of the polygon are $(x_1, y_1), (x_2, y_2), ..., (x_n, y_n)$, then the area of the polygon A can be calculated using the following formula:

$$A = \frac{1}{2} \sum_{i=1}^{n} (x_i y_{i+1} - (x_{i+1} y_i)) \tag{7}$$

where the $i = 1$ The values of the subscripts need to be calculated in cyclic order.

Orientation similarity. Calculate the diagonal of the smallest outer rectangle of the faceted data before and after conversion, and calculate the cosine of the angle between the two diagonals, i.e., the higher the geometrical similarity of the data before and after conversion, the closer the cosine of the angle of the diagonal is to 1. The formula is $S_{dir}(A, B) = \cos\theta_{AB}$ The cosine of the angle between the two diagonals is calculated as The formula is $S_{dir}(A, B)$ is the directional similarity between the vector data and the gridded data. θ_{AB} The diagonal angle of the smallest external rectangle of the vector data and the gridded surface data before and after conversion.

Shape similarity. Shape similarity metrics include area ratio, overlap area ratio, perimeter ratio, minimum externally connected circle (MEC) area ratio, minimum area external rectangle (MBR) area ratio, and so on. The error-based similarity of the metrics V (area, perimeter, etc.) of one of these features is calculated as:

$$S_V(A, B) = 1 - \frac{|V_A - V_B|}{\max(V_A, V_B)} \tag{8}$$

where $S_V(A, B)$ is the similarity of the area (perimeter) metric V; V_A is the value of V metric for vector data; V_B is the V indicator value of the gridded image B. This calculation of similarity indicators standardizes the results of all indicators to 1, i.e., the closer the results of the indicator calculation are to 1, the higher the accuracy of the parameter.

3.2 Accuracy Evaluation Index System of Remote Sensing Data Gridding

The basic evaluation index is an evaluation index based on the statistical information such as mean, variance and covariance between the original remote sensing image and the grid remote sensing image. This index is mainly used to evaluate the image composition information before and after the conversion, which has clear connotation, simple model and convenient evaluation, but the evaluation direction is only the amount of information and composition type of the image, which can not reflect the structure of the image and the image feature information. The basic evaluation indexes include five indexes: information entropy, interactive information quantity, joint entropy, spectral information deviation index, and structure similarity index (SSIM).

where the probability-based information entropy can be defined as:

$$H(N) = E\log\frac{1}{P_i} = \sum_{0}^{M} P_i \log P_i \tag{9}$$

Information entropy reflects the information richness of the image, and calculating the information entropy of the image before and after conversion can reflect the loss of information in the conversion process. The image before and after conversion A and B the amount of interactive information can be defined as:

$$M_{AB} = \sum_{b=0}^{L_1-1} \sum_{a=0}^{L_2-1} P_{AB}(a, b) \cdot \log_2[P_{AB}(a, b)/(P_A(a)P_B(b))] \tag{10}$$

Among them, the $P_{AB}(a, b)$ represents the joint probability density of the images before and after conversion, and the mutual information is an objective index reflecting the richness of information before and after data conversion. The larger its value is, the richer the information obtained from remote sensing data by hexagonal grid data, so as to assess the information loss or data redundancy in the conversion process.

The deviation index of the spectral information can reflect how well the spectral information matches between the data converted and resampled image and the original image. The main calculation method is to iteratively calculate the absolute value of all pixel values of the image and the ratio of the pixel values of the original image to the pixel values of the original image. The formula is:

$$D = \frac{1}{MN} \sum_{i=1}^{M} \sum_{j=1}^{N} \frac{|B(i,j) - A(i,j)|}{A(i,j)} \tag{11}$$

Based on the geometric features of hexagonal lattice grid, this paper proposes the HSobel gradient operator for hexagonal lattice grid images. As shown in Fig. 3, three operators are used to compute the gradient of the hexagonal lattice mesh in the three directions (x, y, z) is used to compute the integral gradient.

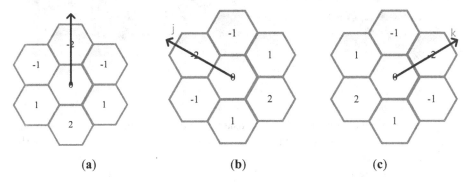

(a)   (b)   (c)

Fig. 3. 1. Sobel operator for hexagonal pixel image. 2. Sobel operator of hexagonal pixel image

In Fig. 3, (a) is the gradient operator in the vertical direction (x); (b) is the gradient operator in the direction (y) of 60° vertically to the left; (c) is the gradient operator in the direction (z) of 60° vertically to the right; the

$$g_B(i, j) = \frac{\sqrt{S_B^x(i,j)^2 + S_B^y(i,j)^2 + S_B^z(i,j)^2}}{3} \tag{12}$$

Among them $S_B^x(i, j)$ and $S_B^y(i, j)$ and $S_B^z(i, j)$ are the gradients of the hexagonal lattice mesh image in the i, j, and k directions. The relative edge intensity and orientation values of the hexagonal grid image B and the original image A are:

$$G^{AB}(i, j) = \begin{cases} \frac{g_B(i,j)}{g_A(i,j)}, \text{if } g_A(i, j) > g_B(i, j) \\ \frac{g_A(i,j)}{g_B(i,j)}, otherwise \end{cases} \tag{13}$$

Thus, we can obtain the edge retention of the converted image with respect to the source image:

$$Q^{AB}(i, j) = Q_g^{AB}(i, j)Q_a^{AB}(i, j) = \Gamma_g\Gamma_a\left[1 + e^{K_g(G^{AB}(i,j)-\sigma_g)}\right]^{-1}\left[1 + e^{K_a(G^{AB}(i,j)-\sigma_a)}\right] \tag{14}$$

of which $\Gamma_g, , , , , , ,$ and $\Gamma_a, , , , , , ,$ and $k_g, , , , , , , , , , , ,$ and $k_\alpha, , , , , , , , , , , ,$ and σ_g, σ_α are adjustable constants.

4 Experimental Results and Analysis

4.1 Conversion Results and Uncertainty Assessment of Remotely Sensed Data

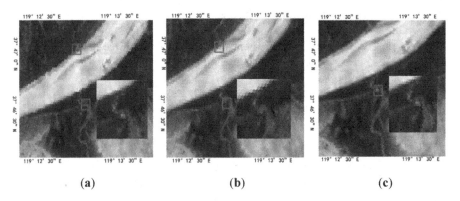

| (a) | (b) | (c) |

Hexagonal grid images converted from Landsat 8 images of the same region using different resampling methods. In Fig. 2-11 (a) generated by nearest neighbor interpolation, (b) generated by bilinear interpolation, and (c) generated by bicubic interpolation. Using different resampling methods to convert remote sensing images in the same area to hexagonal grid images has different effects (Table 2).

Table 2. Remote Sensing Data Accuracy Evaluation Results

imagery	interpolation method	information entropy	amount of interactive information	combinatorial entropy (physics)	similarity coefficient	structural similarity
Landsat 8	nearest neighbor interpolation	0.989	1.028	1.022	0.987	0.965
	bilinear interpolation	0.978	1.042	1.012	0.981	0.964
	Cubic Convolutional Interpolation	0.984	1.047	1.019	1.011	0.958

4.2 Transformation and Uncertainty Assessment of Vector Data

Linear data is adopted from Beijing Metro Line 13, and Bresenham algorithm is used to grid the linear vector data, and the converted grid levels are the 13th, 14th, and 15th layers, and the processing results are shown in Fig. 4.

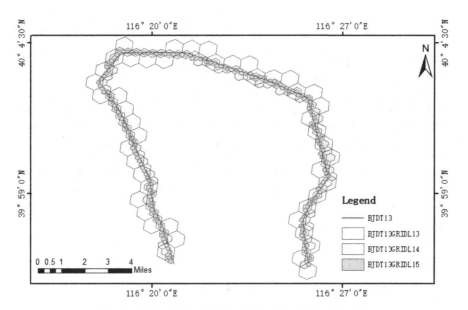

Fig. 4. Vector Data Gridding for Beijing Metro Line 13

For the line data, there are 18 stations and 17 segments in Beijing Metro Line 13. The geographic deviation is calculated for the 18 stations and the angular distortion and length distortion of the line data are calculated for each segment. The angular distortion is normalized by cosine, and the closer to 1, the higher the accuracy of the grid data relative to the original vector data, and the closer to 1, the higher the error in the length distortion, the higher the accuracy of the grid data relative to the original vector data (Table 3).

Table 3. Results of precision evaluation of line data

grid level	Geographic deviation (KM)	Angular Distortion Medium Error	Length Distortion Medium Error
13	8.67	6.4387	1.0927402
14	7.54	1.4903	0.9201187
15	2.18	2.2177	0.9723108

5 Summarize

Among many digital earth expression models, the global discrete grid has gradually shown superior performance in indexing, storing, fusing and analyzing massive multi-source data. In the foreseeable future, the theoretical research and practical application of global discrete grids have great research value, and in order to better utilize global discrete grids to play a greater role in the management and analysis of large amounts of data, the accuracy evaluation of the data is a very important research goal. This study aims to establish a suitable accuracy evaluation index system to evaluate the accuracy of vector data based on hexagonal grids through multiple levels, and provides a generalizable accuracy evaluation index system and evaluation method for hexagonal gridded multivariate data based on the features and image structure of remote sensing data, which provides support for the further use of hexagonal gridded data. These generalized accuracy evaluation indexes can achieve a better metric effect, but there are problems such as artificially specified index weights or threshold determination, so in specific practice, it is necessary to select appropriate feature indexes and similarity calculation methods for specific application scenarios to improve the accuracy of similarity metrics.

References

1. Sahr, K., White, D., Kimerling, A.J.: Discrete global grid system. Cartogr. Geogr. Inf. Sci. **30**(2), 121–134 (2003)
2. Yao, X., Li, G.: Big spatial vector data management: a review. Big Earth Data **2**(1), 108–129 (2018)
3. Zhao, X.S., Hou, M.L., Bai, J.J.: Spatial Numerical Modeling of Global Discrete Grids. Surveying and Mapping Press (2007)
4. Freeman, L.K.: WebGeochem: DGGS geochemical sample analysis search engine (2005)
5. Wang, S., Li, G., Yao, X., et al.: A distributed storage and access approach for massive remote sensing data in MongoDB. Int. J. Geo-Inf. **8**(12), 533 (2019)
6. Yao, X., et al.: Enabling the big earth observation data via cloud computing and DGGS: opportunities and challenges. Remote Sens. **12**(1), 62 (2019)

7. Li, M., Stefanakis, E.: Geospatial operations of discrete global grid systems - a comparison with traditional GIS. J. Geovis. Spat. Anal. **4**(2), 26 (2020)
8. Lee, D.R.: Prospecting geospatial informatics in the era of big data. J. Surv. Mapp. **45**(4), 379–384 (2016)
9. Goodchild, M.F.: The application of advanced information technology in assessing environmental impacts. Soil Science Society of America (1996)
10. Zhou, J., Ben, J., Wang, R., et al.: A novel method of determining the optimal polyhedral orientation for discrete global grid systems applicable to regional- scale areas of interest. Int. J. Digit. Earth **13**(12), 1553–1569 (2020)
11. Ma, Y., Li, G., Yao, X., et al.: A precision evaluation index system for remote sensing data sampling based on hexagonal discrete grids. Int. J. Geo-Inf. **10**(3), 194 (2021)
12. Jendryke, M., Mcclure, S.C.: Spatial prediction of sparse events using a discrete global grid system; a case study of hate crimes in the USA. Int. J. Digit. Earth (3), 1–17 (2021)
13. Zhao, L., Li, G., Yao, X., et al.: An optimized hexagonal quadtree encoding and operation scheme for icosahedral hexagonal discrete global grid systems. Int. J. Digit. Earth (English) (001), 015 (2022)

Applying Segment Anything Model to Ground-Based Video Surveillance for Identifying Aquatic Plant

Bao Zhu[1], Xianrui Xu[2], Huan Meng[1], Chen Meng[1], and Xiang Li[1,3,4(✉)]

[1] Key Laboratory of Geographic Information Science (Ministry of Education) and School of Geographic Sciences, East China Normal University, Shanghai 200241, China
{51213901091,hmeng}@stu.ecnu.edu.cn, xli@geo.ecnu.edu.cn
[2] School of Economics and Management, Shanghai University of Sport, Shanghai 200438, China
xuxianrui@sus.edu.cn
[3] Shanghai Key Lab for Urban Ecological Processes and Eco-Restoration, East China Normal University, Shanghai 200241, China
[4] Key Laboratory of Spatial-Temporal Big Data Analysis and Application of Natural Resources in Megacities (Ministry of Natural Resources), East China Normal University, Shanghai 200241, China

Abstract. Water hyacinth (*Eichhornia crassipes*), with its rapid growth and repro-ductive capacities, poses a formidable challenge to aquatic ecosystems worldwide. Traditional satellite remote sensing, while effective for large-scale monitoring, incurs high costs and limited applicability for localized surveillance. Unmanned aerial vehicle (UAV) offers higher spatial resolution but is hampered by oper-ational complexity, deployment costs, and weather-dependent limitations, pre-venting continuous monitoring. This study capitalizes on the cost-effectiveness and real-time capabilities of network surveillance cameras for persistent observa-tion, assembling a dataset from water hyacinth imagery captured in waterways in Shanghai. We developed a recognition and segmentation model tailored for water hyacinth by integrating the Segment Anything Model with the YOLOv8 algo-rithm. Complementary to ground-based data acquisition, UAV photogrammetry was utilized to establish a perspective transformation matrix, enabling accurate quantification of the water hyacinth's spread. Our approach demonstrates a scal-able and cost-effective solution with potential applicability in continuous aquatic plant management.

Keywords: Water hyacinth · YOLOv8 · Segment Anything Model · Video Surveillance

1 Introduction

Water hyacinth (*Eichhornia crassipes*), a perennial aquatic plant native to South Amer-ica, is among the fastest-growing aquatic weeds worldwide. It can rapidly blanket water surfaces, impeding light penetration into the waterbody and significantly degrading the

X. Meng et al. (Eds.): SpatialDI 2024, LNCS 14619, pp. 80–94, 2024.
https://doi.org/10.1007/978-981-97-2966-1_7

integrity and health of aquatic ecosystems. The invasive spread of water hyacinth has severely impacted numerous ecological environments globally.

Contemporary strategies for managing Water hyacinth, commonly known as water hyacinth, largely depend on physical removal methodologies, encompassing both manual extraction and mechanized harvesting. These conventional approaches necessitate the deployment of substantial resources, encompassing labor, equipment, and fiscal expenditure. Streamlining harvesting protocols can augment operational efficiencies, thereby attenuating associated costs, a proposition that is contingent upon refined monitoring frameworks for water hyacinth.

Remote sensing has emerged as a pivotal instrument for the detection of biological invasions and the surveillance of ecological milieus, boasting widespread applications within diverse ecological and environmental domains. Nevertheless, the acquisition of satellite imagery with high spatial resolution entails considerable expense and often fails to meet the requisites of real-time monitoring. The advent of deep learning, in conjunction with the ubiquity of unmanned aerial vehicle (UAV) and ground-based video surveillance, has engendered synergistic methodologies poised to economize and expedite invasion monitoring initiatives.

A growth monitoring system for water hyacinth, developed by Feng et al. [1], engages in the processing of imagery procured by cameras, delineating the vegetation in question and implementing binary segmentation to estimate the infestation footprint via the ratio of contrasting pixel intensities. After the processing, the accruing data are transmitted to a centralized server through wireless communication pathways, thereby enabling the contemporaneous tracking of water hyacinth proliferation. While this monitoring apparatus offers the merits of real-time observation at a deflated cost, it is not devoid of limitations in its extant form. The system predominantly leverages colorimetric differentiation for the identification of water hyacinth proliferations, which restricts its utility to simplistic environs with monotypic plant coverage.

Advancements by Qian et al. [2] have achieved the amalgamation of deep learning with unmanned surface vehicles (USVs) for water hyacinth surveillance, with specific improvements rendered to the YOLOv5 architecture to surmount the constraints of low receptive field accuracy and suboptimal detection outcomes frequently encountered within lightweight detection models. The refined detection paradigm has procured an increment of 7.1% in accuracy vis-a-vis its progenitor, delivering an average detection velocity of 62 frames per second (FPS), thus facilitating the real-time monitoring capability of USVs.

Complementarily, Qian and colleagues have leveraged the capabilities of UAV for the acquisition of color imagery within field environments [3]. They engineered an innovative classification model, IAPsNet, predicated on the foundational principles of deep convolutional neural networks, tailored for the identification of invasive botanical species within captured data sets. The trained model exhibits an accuracy of 93.39%, and provides, with expedience, robust metrics of average recall (93.3%), precision (93.74%), and F1-score (93.52%).

In summary, leveraging deep learning models facilitates more precise and rapid detection and identification of water hyacinth in imagery. UAV, employing oblique photography techniques, can capture high-resolution, geographically rich imagery of waterways. Concurrently, ground-based video surveillance can continuously record and transmit real-time data of riverine activities to a server, enabling sustained observation of water hyacinth proliferation. This paper presents an integrated approach that harnesses state-of-the-art deep learning models while amalgamating the advantages of ground-based video surveillance with UAV capabilities to achieve real-time monitoring and area estimation of water hyacinth proliferation.

The approach involves utilizing the YOLOv8 model for the detection of water hyacinth and the Segment Anything Model (SAM) for its segmentation. The captured imagery by UAV, in conjunction with camera parameters, allows for the computation of the water hyacinth coverage area. The proposed scheme promises to support the scientific harvesting and management of water hyacinth, bearing significant implications for its control and containment.

2   Methodology

2.1   Overview

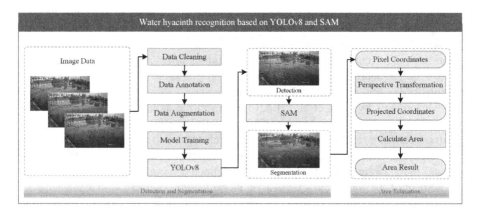

Fig. 1. Methodological Processes

As illustrated in Fig. 1, the methodological process can be generally divided into two stages, one is detection and segmentation, the other is area estimation. In the detection and segmentation phase, monitoring cameras are employed for timed image acquisition, and the resulting image data are preserved. Through data cleaning and processing, an image dataset is generated. To enhance the diversity of the training set samples, data augmentation techniques are applied to expand the image dataset, thereby improving the model training and enabling it to learn the characteristics of water hyacinth more effectively. Subsequently, the YOLOv8 model is used for training by feeding the image data into the model, which facilitates object detection and yields the positional results of the water hyacinth in the form of bounding boxes. SAM is then utilized to further process the object detection results, obtaining segmentation results that consist of a collection of pixel coordinates).

In the area estimation phase, an orthoimage of the river channel near the monitoring camera is initially obtained using oblique photogrammetry techniques with UAV. Subsequently, four sets of corresponding point coordinates are identified in both the orthoimage and the monitoring camera images to construct a perspective transformation matrix. The matrix enables the conversion of pixel coordinates from the camera images to orthoimage pixel coordinates, which can further provide projected coordinates. Based on these projected coordinates, the area of the water hyacinth is then estimated.

2.2 Detection and Segmentation

Detection Method. Object detection of water hyacinth was conducted using the YOLO (You Only Look Once) [4] algorithm, which has gained significant recognition in the field of object detection and image segmentation since its introduction in 2015. YOLOv8, the latest iteration of the YOLO series, has emerged as a state-of-the-art model, offering a remarkable balance between speed and accuracy. This version incorporates novel features and enhancements, further enhancing its performance, adaptability, and computational efficiency.

YOLOv8 not only exhibits outstanding capabilities in conventional tasks such as object detection and image segmentation but also demonstrates comprehensive proficiency in advanced computer vision tasks, including pose estimation, object tracking, and image classification. The YOLO architecture is designed with various configurations, typically denoted by n, s, m, l, and x, to accommodate different trade-offs between speed and accuracy.

As depicted in Fig. 2, YOLOv8 outperforms earlier versions in terms of both speed and accuracy. Comparative analysis reveals that within this spectrum, the 'n' variant of YOLOv8 offers the fastest inference speed and has a smaller parameter size, making it suitable for real-time monitoring requirements. However, as of now, the application of YOLOv8 in water hyacinth monitoring has not been realized. Therefore, in this study, we have chosen YOLOv8 'n' as the primary framework for water hyacinth identification. The objective is to achieve high-precision detection and efficient processing of water hyacinth imagery.

Segmentation Method. The segmentation method employed in this study is based on the SAM, which was developed by a team at Meta AI [7]. SAM is a versatile and foundational model designed for image segmentation, with the capability to accurately delineate a diverse array of objects within any given image. The development of SAM involved a robust annotation process spanning manual, semi-automated, and fully automated stages. This process utilized an extensive dataset consisting of 11 million images and over one billion annotated masks, resulting in the creation of the largest image segmentation dataset currently available. SAM has been trained on this extensive and meticulously annotated dataset to achieve its remarkable performance.

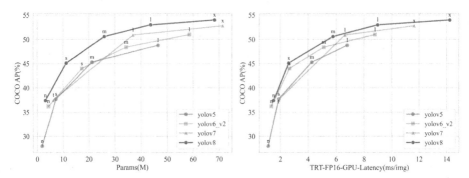

Fig. 2. Comparison of object detection accuracy and speed of each version of the YOLO model based on the COCO [5] dataset. Chart data from mmyolo [6]

Subsequent assessments through zero-shot transfer experiments have unveiled that SAM's accuracy on tasks such as edge detection, single-mask evaluation, and instance segmentation is comparable to, and in some cases surpasses, models trained with full supervision. Specifically, within the domain of instance segmentation, although SAM's predictive results are tantamount to those of ViTDet [8] on COCO and LVIS [9] benchmarks, a discernible gap in precision persists. However, SAM consistently outperforms in visual quality assessments determined by human evaluation, indicated by superior mask quality and higher scores. Therefore, SAM can effectively extract the water hyacinth mask for area estimation.

Moreover, SAM is equipped to accommodate various input modalities, such as point coordinates and bounding boxes, to generate segmentations. Interaction with the model through manual insertion of bounding boxes and point coordinates, or by leveraging the outputs from pre-existing object detection models, can swiftly yield annotated datasets, thereby enhancing the efficiency of the labeling process.

2.3 Area Estimation

The area estimation method consists mainly of camera calibration and perspective transformation.

Camera Calibration. Camera calibration methodologies can be broadly classified into three categories: traditional calibration, self-calibration, and active vision calibration. Traditional calibration methods necessitate the use of a known, high-precision calibration target, providing high accuracy at the cost of increased operational complexity. These methods are typically well-suited for scenarios demanding stringent precision. Self-calibration techniques forgo the use of a physical calibration artifact and instead rely on the intrinsic constraints of camera parameters for calculation. However, while offering simplicity, they exhibit lower robustness and are best suited for applications where lower precision is acceptable [10]. Active vision calibration involves manipulating the camera through specific motions and calculating camera parameters by correlating images with motion data. This approach is independent of calibration targets, offers algorithmic simplicity, and boasts higher robustness. However, it requires expensive equipment and is less suitable for unstructured environments. Among these methodologies, the calibration method developed by Zhang [11] strikes a balance between traditional and self-calibration techniques, providing both computational precision and cost-efficiency.

The computation of the camera's intrinsic matrix and radial distortion coefficient is the primary goal of the calibration process. Five variables (f_x, f_y, s, c_x, c_y) define the 3 × 3 camera intrinsic matrix. In this case, the pixel size of the focal length in the x and y directions is represented as $[f_x, f_y]$. The skew parameter s equals 0 when the x and y axes are exactly perpendicular to one another. Furthermore, the coordinates of the optical center in pixels are indicated by $[c_x, c_y]$. Crucial elements of the calibration procedure are also the radial distortion coefficients, k_1 and k_2. The following is an expression for the camera intrinsic matrix:

$$\begin{bmatrix} f_x & s & c_x \\ 0 & f_y & c_y \\ 0 & 0 & 1 \end{bmatrix} \tag{1}$$

The practical steps of our calibration process are as follows:

Print a checkerboard pattern image featuring 12 columns and 9 rows, affixing it to a flat surface.

Secure the camera in place, manipulate the position of the plane, and capture three or more images of the checkerboard pattern from varying angles.

Identify the characteristic points of the checkerboard pattern within each image.

Compute both the intrinsic and extrinsic parameters of the camera based on the detected characteristic points.

Employ the least squares method to determine the radial distortion coefficient.

Enhance the accuracy of our estimation by optimizing the results through the maximum likelihood method.

The distortion of the image is corrected by camera calibration. However, to calculate the area of the water hyacinth, the pixel coordinates have to be converted into physically meaningful coordinates, a process realized through perspective transformation.

Perspective Transformation. Perspective transformation stands as a fundamental technique in both computer vision and graphics, facilitating the projection of visual information from one plane to another while preserving the linearity of straight lines within the image. This process is integral to applications including image correction, simulation of depth of field, and 3D reconstruction.

The implementation of a perspective transform typically involves four crucial points. These points delineate a rectangular region within the source image and correspondingly map to designated points on the target plane. Depending on the application, these points may be the corners of the source image or other strategically chosen positions. The perspective transformation matrix, a 3 × 3 matrix, is computed based on these four points, providing the translation from pixel coordinates in the source image to their counterparts on the target plane. Each pixel from the source image undergoes this transformation to be remapped accurately onto the target plane.

Mathematically, the perspective transformation is represented as:

$$\begin{bmatrix} X \\ Y \\ Z \end{bmatrix} = M \begin{bmatrix} x \\ y \\ z \end{bmatrix} \tag{2}$$

where (M) is the perspective transformation matrix:

$$M = \begin{bmatrix} a_{11} & a_{12} & a_{13} \\ a_{21} & a_{22} & a_{23} \\ a_{31} & a_{32} & a_{33} \end{bmatrix} \tag{3}$$

Upon multiplication with the matrix (M), the original image coordinates $([x, y, z])$ undergo a transformation resulting in the new image coordinates $([X, Y, Z])$. Given that our study focuses on two-dimensional images, we convert the source coordinates from $([x, y, 1])$ to the target image coordinates $([X, Y, 1])$, which yields the following relationships:

$$X = \frac{a_{11}x + a_{12}y + a_{13}}{a_{31}x + a_{32}y + a_{33}} \tag{4}$$

$$Y = \frac{a_{21}x + a_{22}y + a_{23}}{a_{31}x + a_{32}y + a_{33}} \tag{5}$$

$$Z = 1 \tag{6}$$

Expanding these equations, we isolate the terms involving (X) and (Y):

$$a_{11}x + a_{12}y + a_{13} - Xa_{31}x - Xa_{32}y - X = 0 \tag{7}$$

$$a_{21}x + a_{22}y + a_{23} - Ya_{31}x - Ya_{32}y - Y = 0 \tag{8}$$

$$a_{33} = 1 \tag{9}$$

$$Z = 1 \tag{10}$$

The two equations have eight unknown coefficients to be solved. Therefore, to compute the perspective transform matrix successfully, four corresponding pairs of points must be selected between the source and target images.

3 Study Area and Data

The research area of this study is Shanghai. Since 2002, Shanghai has been carrying out specialized control measures targeting water hyacinth and has achieved certain success. In 2002 alone, approximately 1.68 million tons of water hyacinth were harvested from the Huangpu River and other water bodies in Shanghai, costing over 10 million USD in a single year. From 2002 to 2006, the Shanghai municipal government invested more than 1.2 million USD in comprehensive water hyacinth management projects [12]. However, due to environmental factors such as hydrology, climate, and geography, the influx of aquatic plants from upstream provinces and cities has remained high, posing ongoing challenges for water hyacinth control efforts in Shanghai. The distribution of surveillance camera stations, as shown in Fig. 3, is primarily concentrated along various rivers in Jinshan District, Songjiang District, Changning District, and Qingpu District. These stations effectively detect the invasion of water hyacinth from other provinces and cities based on the aforementioned locations.

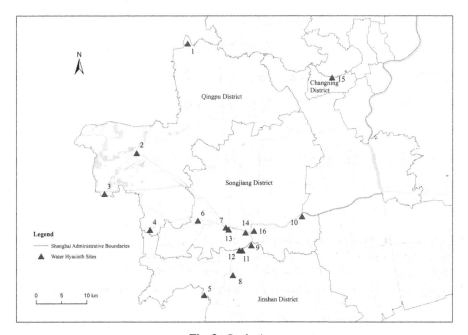

Fig. 3. Study Area

The dataset for our investigation was acquired through the deployment of network cameras in the vicinity of a riverbed. These cameras were programmed to systematically capture both videos and images at predetermined intervals. From this compendium of visual data, a subset of 511 representative images was meticulously selected by manual review to ensure the inclusion of water hyacinth specimens, thus constituting our dataset. To streamline the annotation process, we utilized the Segment Anything Labelling Tool (SALT, https://github.com/anuragxel/salt), which integrates the SAM to provide point-based annotation prompts. This innovative application of SAM within SALT exploited its segmentation capabilities to effectively delineate the water hyacinth within the images, facilitating the generation of a structured dataset adhering to the COCO format.

As delineated in Fig. 4, we harnessed the image encoding capabilities of the SAM to extract embeddings for each image in the dataset, subsequently conserving these as Numpy binary files for efficient storage and access. Consequent to the generation of embeddings, SAM was converted into the Open Neural Network Exchange (ONNX) format. This conversion facilitates the integration of SAM with the SALT, which enables the user to instantiate the annotation process through the simple act of mouse clicks on the image to provide point coordinates that guide the annotation file generation.

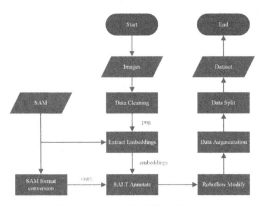

Fig. 4. Dataset Building Process

During the transfer of data to the Roboflow platform [13], it was noticed that the masks created by the SALT tool had deviations, which necessitated manual intervention to make minor adjustments and corrections. The purpose of this operation is to ensure that the accuracy and integrity of the resulting labeled data are not affected by the deviant masks. For the sake of uniformity in the data processing flow and to ensure efficient model training, the image data were uniformly adjusted to a resolution of 640x640 pixels, a measure designed to maintain the original aspect ratio of the image, while also minimizing the storage space and processing time required for the image data, taking into account the computational efficiency.

In deep learning applications, data augmentation is a pivotal technique for ameliorating data diversity and quantity through a set of transformations and manipulations applied to the original dataset. Acknowledging the limited sample size of the dataset in this study, we employed mosaic and flip augmentations to cultivate a more varied training set, tailored to ameliorate model robustness and generalizability to novel, unencountered data. This strategic approach to data augmentation plays a crucial role in mitigating the risk of overfitting and amplifying overall model performance.

As shown in Fig. 5, the 'images' folder contained the water hyacinth photographs, each saved in JPEG format. The 'embeddings' folder housed the embeddings data generated by the SAM, with each data stored as a Numpy binary (.npy) file. Annotations created using the SALT were cataloged in the 'annotation.json' file, formatted by the COCO dataset standard.

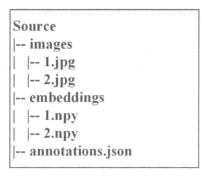

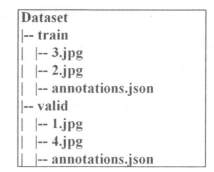

Fig. 5. Raw Data Catalog   **Fig. 6.** Dataset Catalog

During the preliminary annotation phase, discrepancies in the SALT-generated files necessitated subsequent revisions, which were accomplished through integration with the Roboflow platform. This facilitated the refinement of the annotation data to ensure higher accuracy and consistency. The final data set is split into the training set and the validation set by 80% and 20%, as shown in Fig. 6.

4   Experiment

4.1   Computational Environment

As shown in Table 1, the experimental environment for building the deep learning model in this paper mainly comprises hardware and software components. The hardware configuration includes an Intel(R) Xeon(R) CPU E5-2683 v4, an NVIDIA GeForce RTX 3090 graphics card, 64 GB RAM, and 24 GB GPU memory. The software components predominantly consist of Python, CUDA, PyTorch, and Ubuntu. Additionally, other equipment utilized includes a DJI PHANTOM 4 RTK drone, a Hikvision DS-2CD3T87WDA3-LS webcam, and a black-and-white checkerboard pattern.

4.2   Detection and Segmentation

In the software and hardware environment outlined in Table 2, the YOLOv8_Ultralytics [14] toolkit was utilized for model training on the water hyacinth dataset. The pre-trained model was YOLOv8, which underwent 100 epochs of training. Early Stopping was enabled to cease training when no significant improvements were observed after 50 epochs. The batch size was set to 16. Stochastic Gradient Descent (SGD) served as the optimizer, with momentum set at 0.937 and weight decay at 0.0005. Images were input at a resolution of (640,640) pixels, with specific parameters detailed in Table 2.

Table 1. Computational environment

Environments	Configuration	Details
hardware	CPU	Intel(R) Xeon(R) CPU E5–2683 v4
	GPU	NVIDIA GeForce RTX 3090
	Random-access memory (RAM)	64 GB
	GPU memory	24 GB
software	Python	3.8
	Cuda	11.1.1
	Pytorch	1.8.0
	Operating system	Ubuntu 20.04.3 LTS
other	Unmanned aerial vehicle	DJI PHANTOM 4 RTK
	Video surveillance	Hikvision DS-2CD3T87WDA3-LS
	Black-and-white checkerboard pattern	Length and width are 200 mm
		12×9 black and white array map
		Square edge length: 15 mm
		Precision: ± 0.005 mm

Table 2. Model Training Parameter

Training parameters	Detail
Epoch	100
Early Stopping Patience	50
Optimizer	SGD
Image Size	(640, 640)
Momentum	0.937
Weight decay	0.0005

Evaluation of the trained YOLO model was conducted on a validation set, yielding an average precision (AP) of 0.802. The model demonstrated high efficiency, processing images at an average rate of one image per 10.42 ms. When bounding boxes predicted by YOLOv8 were input into the SAM, segmentation results were obtained.

The segmentation performance of the SAM was evaluated using the validation set, following the COCO evaluation, and the results are shown in Table 3. The AP at a fixed IoU threshold of 0.5, denoted as AP50, was found to be 0.799. However, when considering the AP50-95 across the range of IoU values from 0.5 to 0.95 with a step size of 0.05, notable differences were observed between small and large objects.

Figure 7 shows the effect of SAM in segmenting water hyacinth in a complex scene. Using its powerful segmentation function, SAM can accurately recognize and isolate

Table 3. COCO evaluation metrics

AP50	AP50–95 all	AP50–95 large	AP50–95 medium	AP50–95 small
0.799	0.549	0.655	0.625	0.467

water hyacinth objects to generate fine mask images. These mask images can be further processed into polygonal boundaries, laying the foundation for the water hyacinth area estimation below.

Detection Results   Segmentation Results

Fig. 7. Model prediction results

4.3   Area Estimation

Imagery for calibration was captured using the Hikvision DS-2CD3T87WDA3-LS network camera. A standard black-and-white checkerboard pattern was maneuvered within the camera's operational range to amass a diverse set of calibration images, encompassing various positions and orientations. These images were then processed with the Camera Calibrator tool in MATLAB, which was tasked with the extraction of intrinsic parameters, extrinsic parameters, and lens distortion coefficients.

The computational results yielded intrinsic camera parameters f_x and f_y representing the focal lengths in pixel units, as 1481.84 and 1476.34, respectively. The skew parameter s equals 0, while the principal point coordinates c_x and c_y were calculated as 853.35 and 571.51. The radial distortion coefficients k_1 and k_2, were found to be -0.37 and 0.11. The average reprojection error across the calibration images was assessed to be a mere 0.24 pixels, a testament to the calibration accuracy.

Figure 8 and Fig. 9 clearly illustrate the significant enhancements in the images post-calibration. Notably, radial distortion was effectively rectified. Real-world riverbanks approximated a straight line but appeared as curves in pre-calibration images, and as the distortion intensifies away from the camera, these curves are corrected back to a straight line. The post-calibration portrayal of the riverine area could subsequently be construed as planar, laying the groundwork for ensuing perspective transformations.

Fig. 8. Pre-calibration   **Fig. 9.** Post-calibration

Aerial reconnaissance of a riverine area under surveillance by a network camera was conducted using a DJI PHANTOM 4 RTK UAV, following a meticulously arranged noughts-and-crosses pattern. The UAV was configured to achieve 80% side and front overlap, with a flight speed of 3.9 m/s and a forward-tilted camera gimbal angle of 5 degrees, optimizing the photogrammetry quality. This systematic flight yielded a dataset of 225 high-definition images. Leveraging OpenDroneMap (ODM), these images were subsequently stitched to generate an orthoimage.

As shown in Fig. 10, the perspective transformation of this orthoimage depends on the strategic placement of coordinate points, which have been carefully chosen to correspond to fixed, visually distinctive river markers and the base of the boulders. The fixed nature of these markers ensures that they are not subject to positional errors due to external environmental influences, making them ideal reference points. The area delineated by these four coordinates encompasses the main habitat of water hyacinth thus ensuring accurate area measurements after conversion.

Fig. 10. Perspective transformation mapping point selection

Figure 11 depicts the post-calibration image, while Fig. 12 showcases the outcome of the perspective transformation applied to Fig. 11. Figure 13 represents the orthoimage. In Fig. 14, an overlay image of Fig. 12 and Fig. 13 visually demonstrates the efficacy of the perspective transformation on the camera imagery. The processed camera image (Part A of Fig. 14) has been rectified to an orthographic projection, aligning nearly perfectly with the orthoimage (Part B of Fig. 14). This geometric correction enables the transformation of image pixel coordinates from the camera's perspective to orthoimage pixel coordinates, allowing for the retrieval of Universal Transverse Mercator (UTM) projection coordinates based on the pixel data. By applying this transformation to the polygonal outlines of water hyacinth clusters identified in the camera images, their coordinates were converted into the projection system. Utilizing these converted coordinates, the calculated area of the water hyacinth infestation (highlighted in red within Fig. 11) was determined to be 656.62 m^2.

Fig. 11. Post-calibration image

Fig. 12. Post-perspective transformation image

Fig. 13. Orthoimage

Fig. 14. Overlay image

5 Conclusion

The experimental results show that there is a significant difference in the performance of the trained YOLO model in recognizing large and small targets. The model performs well in identifying large areas of water hyacinth coverage, but performs poorly in identifying small areas of water hyacinth coverage. Therefore, future improvements can be made by balancing the data against the size of the target and exploring opportunities for further optimization.

The objective of this study is to achieve real-time monitoring of water hyacinth and calculate their coverage area by training a YOLOv8 object detection model and incorporating the SAM algorithm for water hyacinth instance extraction. Additionally, by utilizing oblique aerial photography from UAV and ground surveillance images, a perspective transformation matrix is constructed to estimate the area of water hyacinth in complex scenes. This approach combines the real-time data advantage of ground monitoring stations with the mapping capabilities of UAV. The perspective transformation matrix only needs to be established once after a flight, enabling future area estimation based on the matrix, which saves time and effort, and eliminates safety hazards associated with UAV flights. Statistical analysis of the estimated water hyacinth area can provide optimized strategies for the removal and control of water hyacinth.

Acknowledgments. This work was supported by the project funded by International Research Center of Big Data for Sustainable 740 Development Goals [Grant Number CBAS2022GSP07], Fundamental Research Funds for the Central Universities, Chongqing Natural Science Foundation [Grant Number CSTB2022NSCQMSX2069] and Ministry of Education of China [Grant Number 19JZD023].

References

1. Feng, Z., Pan, F., Li, Y.: Image recognition based on water hyacinth controlled breeding monitoring equipment. J. Phys. Conf. Ser. **1549**(3), 032116 (2020). https://doi.org/10.1088/1742-6596/1549/3/032116
2. Qian, Y., Miao, Y., Huang, S., et al.: Real-Time detection of eichhornia crassipes based on efficient YOLOV5. Machines **10**(9), 754 (2022). https://doi.org/10.3390/machines10090754
3. Qian, W., Huang, Y., Liu, Q., et al.: UAV and a deep convolutional neural network for monitoring invasive alien plants in the wild. Comput. Electron. Agric. **174**, 105519 (2020). https://doi.org/10.1109/CCDC.2010.5498574
4. Redmon, J., Divvala, S., Girshick, R., et al.: You only look once: unified, real-time object detection. In: CVPR, pp: 779–788, Seattle, WA (2016). https://doi.org/10.1109/CVPR.2016.91
5. Lin, T., Maire, M., Belongie, S., et al.: Microsoft COCO: common objects in context. In: Fleet, D., Pajdla, T., Schiele, B., Tuytelaars, T. (eds.) Computer Vision – ECCV 2014. ECCV 2014. LNCS, vol. 8693, pp. 740–755. Springer, Cham (2014). https://doi.org/10.1007/978-3-319-10602-1_48
6. MMYOLO: OpenMMLab YOLO series toolbox and benchmark. https://github.com/open-mmlab/mmyolo. Accessed 2022
7. Kirillov, A., Mintun, E., Ravi, N., et al.: Segment Anything. arXiv 2304, 02643 (2023)
8. Li, Y., Mao, H., Girshick, R., et al.: Exploring plain vision transformer backbones for object detection. In: Avidan, S., Brostow, G., Cissé, M., Farinella, G.M., Hassner, T. (eds.) Computer Vision – ECCV 2022. ECCV 2022. LNCS, vol. 13669, pp: 280–296. Springer, Cham (2022). https://doi.org/10.1007/978-3-031-20077-9_17
9. Gupta, A., Dollár, P., Girshick, R.: LVIS: a dataset for large vocabulary instance segmentation. In: CVPR, pp: 5351–5359, Long Beach, CA (2019). https://doi.org/ https://doi.org/10.1109/CVPR.2019.00550
10. Wang, Q., Fu, L., Liu, Z.: Review on camera calibration. In: 2010 Chinese Control and Decision Conference, pp. 3354–3358. IEEE, Xuzhou, China (2010). https://doi.org/10.1016/j.compag.2020.105519
11. Zhang, Z.: A flexible new technique for camera calibration. IEEE Trans. Pattern Anal. Mach. Intell. **22**(11), 1330–1334 (2000). https://doi.org/10.1109/34.888718
12. Chu, J., Ding, Y., Zhuang, Q.: Invasion and control of water hyacinth (Eichhornia crassipes) in China. J. Zhejiang Univ. Sci. B **7**(8), 623–626 (2006). https://doi.org/10.1631/jzus.2006.B0623
13. R. https://roboflow.com. Accessed 2022
14. Ultralytics YOLOv8. https://github.com/ultralytics/ultralytics. Accessed 2023

Spatiotemporal Data Mining

Mining Regional High Utility Co-location Pattern

Meiyu Xiong[1], Hongmei Chen[1,2(✉)], Lizhen Wang[1,2], and Qing Xiao[1]

[1] School of Information Science and Engineering, Yunnan University, Kunming, China
hmchen@ynu.edu.cn
[2] Yunnan Key Laboratory of Intelligent Systems and Computing, Yunnan University, Kunming, China

Abstract. A co-location pattern is a set of spatial features whose instances are frequently located together in geo-space. In real world, different instances have different distributions and different values. However, existing methods for mining pattern ignore these differences. In this paper, we propose a novel method for mining regional high utility co-location pattern by considering both instance distribution and value. First, local regions are obtained based on fuzzy density peak clustering. Then, the regional high utility co-location pattern is defined, and an efficient algorithm for mining the patterns in local regions is presented by pruning unpromising patterns. The experiment results show the patterns are meaningful and the mining algorithm is efficient.

Keywords: spatial data mining · co-location pattern · regional co-location pattern · high utility co-location pattern

1 Introduction

The rapid growth of spatial data advances spatial data mining. Co-location pattern mining, an important direction of spatial data mining, has attracted attentions due to the usefulness of patterns in applications such as environmental protection and urban computing. Different from prevalent co-location patterns based on clique instance model, sub-prevalent co-location patterns based on star instance model can capture richer spatial relationships by loosening the clique constraint of instances in a row instance [1, 2]. However, traditional methods mine pattern by the participation index of the pattern which measures the fraction of features' instances participating in the pattern, and ignore the values of instances. Thus, high utility co-location pattern is proposed [3].

Existing methods mine high utility co-location patterns in whole spatial dataset, and don't consider the distribution of instances, leading to missing some patterns which are not high utility patterns in the whole region but with high utility in a local region. Let us see an example of spatial dataset shown in Fig. 1. There are a spatial feature set {Chinese restaurant(A), Hotel(D), Parking lot(I), Airport(L)}and their instance set

---

M. Xiong—Student author.

X. Meng et al. (Eds.): SpatialDI 2024, LNCS 14619, pp. 97–107, 2024.
https://doi.org/10.1007/978-981-97-2966-1_8

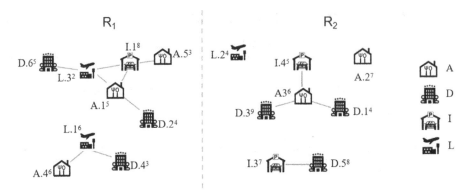

Fig. 1. An example of spatial data set

$\{A.1^5, \ldots, D.1^4, \ldots, I.1^8, \ldots, L.1^6 \ldots\}$, in which the utility attached to each instance denotes its value and a line between two instances denotes their neighbor relationship. We can see that instances are distributed in two local regions R_1 and R_2. For the pattern {ADI}, its utility in the local region R_2 is higher than that in the whole region. That is to say, {ADI} may be not a high utility pattern in the whole region but a high utility pattern in the local region R_2. In order to discover high utility patterns in local regions, it is necessary to partition the whole region into local regions and mine high utility patterns in each local region. A partition method based on fuzzy density peak clustering is proposed [4]. The method utilizes the fuzzy membership to get more reasonable local regions due to continuous geographic space.

In the paper, we first adopt the partition method mentioned above to get local regions. Further, we define regional high utility co-location pattern based on the star instance model which can capture more reasonable and richer spatial relationships, and design an efficient algorithm to mine patterns in each local region.

2   Related Work

Prevalent co-location pattern and participation index based on clique instance model are first introduced [5]. In order to capture richer spatial relationships, sub-prevalent co-location pattern based on the star instance model is proposed [1, 2].

Considering the values of features or instances, high utility co-location pattern is proposed [3, 6–8]. Ref. [3] mine high utility pattern based on the values of features. Further, Ref. [6] mines high utility pattern based on the values of instances. Ref. [7] defines the utility participation ratio of features in the pattern. Ref. [8] incorporates k-nearest neighbor relationships into mining high utility kernel patterns.

Considering the distribution of instances, regional co-location pattern is proposed [4, 9, 10]. The partition method of the region is key for regional pattern mining. Ref. [9] partitions the whole region into local regions based on k-nearest neighbors, and mines regional patterns in each local region. Ref. [10] uses a grid specified by user to divide the whole region into local regions, and the kernel function to measure the distribution of instances in each local region. The above partition methods obtain local regions with hard boundaries. However, the soft partition method is more reasonable due to continuous geographic space. Thus, based on the fuzzy theory, Ref. [4] extends density peak clustering to partition the whole region into local regions.

Different from the above methods for mining co-location pattern, this paper considers both the distribution of instances and the value of instances, and exploits the fuzzy density peak clustering [4] and the star instance model [1, 2] to mine regional high utility co-location patterns with more reasonable and richer spatial relationships.

3 Related Concepts and Problem Statement

Given a spatial feature set $F = \{f_1, f_2, ..., f_n\}$ and a spatial instance set $S = S_1 \cup S_2 \cup ... \cup S_n$, $S_i = \{f_i.1, ..., f_i.2, ..., f_i.m\}$ is the instance set of f_i, $f_i.j$ is attached a location $l(f_i.j)$ and utility $u(f_i.j)$. A co-location pattern C is a spatial feature subset, i.e., $C \subseteq F$, and $k = |C|$ is called the size of C.

According to the fuzzy density peak clustering [4], instances are clustered into fuzzy clusters $R = \{R_1, R_2, ..., R_L\}$, each of which represents a local region called maximal fuzzy region. Then, high utility co-location pattern is defined based on the star instance model [1], and is mined in each maximal fuzzy region. The related concepts are as follows.

Definition 1. Regional star neighbor instance set. Given a region R_l and a distance threshold d, the regional star neighbor instance set $RSNsI_l(f_i.j)$ of an instance $f_i.j \in R_l$ is defined as:

$$RSNsI_l(f_i.j) = \{f_s.t | distance(f_i.j, f_s.t) \leq d, f_s.t \in R_l\} \tag{1}$$

Definition 2. Regional star participation instance set. Given a region R_l and a k_size pattern $C_l = \{f_1, f_2, ..., f_k\}$, the regional star participation instance set $RSPIns_l(f_i, C_l)$ of a feature $f_i \in C_l$ is defined as:

$$RSPIns_l(f_i, C_l) = \{f_i.j | f_i.j \in$$
$$RSNsI_l(f_s.t), RSNsI_l(f_s.t) \text{ contains instances of all features in } C_l\} \tag{2}$$

Let us see the region R_2, $RSNsI_2(A.2^7) = \{A.2^7\}$, $RSNsI_2(A.3^6) = \{A.3^6, D.1^4, D.3^9, I.4^5\}$, $RSNsI_2(D.1^4) = \{D.1^4, A.3^6\}$, $RSNsI_2(D.3^9) = \{D.3^9, A.3^6\}$, $RSNsI_2(D.5^8) = \{D.5^8, I.3^7\}$, $RSNsI_2(I.3^7) = \{I.3^7, I.5^8\}$, $RSNsI_2(I.4^5) = \{I.4^5, A.3^6\}$. For the pattern AD_2, $RSPIns_2(A, (AD_2)) = \{A.3^6\} = \{A.3^6\}$, $RSPIns_2(D, (AD_2)) = \{D.1^4, D.3^9\}$, for the pattern ADI_2, $RSPIns_2(A, (ADI_2)) = \{A.3^6\}$, $RSPIns_2(D, (ADI_2)) = \{D.1^4, D.3^9\}$, $RSPIns_2(I, (ADI_2)) == \{I.4^5\}$.

Definition 3. Regional total utility. Given a region R_l, the regional total utility of a feature f_i in R_l is defined as:

$$u_l(f_i) = \sum_{f_i.j \in R_l} u(f_i.j) \tag{3}$$

Definition 4. Regional utility participation ratio RUPR. Given a region R_l and a k_size pattern $C_l = \{f_1, f_2, ..., f_k\}$, the regional utility participation ratio $RUPR(f_i, C_l)$ of each feature $f_i \in C_l$ is defined as:

$$RUPR(f_i, C_l) = \frac{\sum_{RSPIns_l(f_i, C_l)} u(f_i.j)}{u_l(f_i)}$$

$$\text{s.t. } RSPIns_l(f_i, C_l) \neq \phi \tag{4}$$

Definition 5. Regional utility participation index RUPI. Given a region R_l, the regional utility participation index $RUPI(C_l)$ of a k_size pattern $C_l = \{f_1, f_2, ..., f_k\}$ is defined as:

$$RUPI(C_l) = \min_{f_i \in C_l} RUPR(f_i, C_l) \tag{5}$$

Recall the region R_2, $u_2(A) = u(A.2^7) + u(A.3^6) = 7 + 6 = 13$, $u_2(D) = u(D.1^4)$ $+u(D.3^9) + u(D.5^8) = 21$, $u_2(I) = u(I.3^7) + u(I.4^5) = 12$. For the pattern ADI_2, $RUPR(A, ADI_2) = u(A.3^6)/u_2(A) = 6/13 = 0.46$, $RUPR(D, ADI_2) = (u(D.1^4) + u(D.3^9))/u_2(D) = 13/21 = 0.62$, $RUPR(I, ADI_2) = u(I.4^5)/u_2(I) = 5/12 = 0.42$. So, $RUPI(ADI_2) = min(0.46, 0.62, 0.42) = 0.42$.

Definition 6. Regional high utility co-location pattern. Given a region R_l, a utility threshold u, and a k-size pattern $C_l = \{f_1, f_2, ..., f_k\}$, if $RUPI(C_l) \geq u$, then the pattern C_l is a regional high utility co-location pattern.

Problem Statement. Given a maximal fuzzy region set $R = \{R_1, R_2, ..., R_l\}$ on a spatial feature set F and a spatial instance set S, a distance threshold d, and a utility threshold u, the goal is to mine all high utility co-location patterns in each region.

4   Algorithm

Firstly, the anti-monotonicity of RUPR and RUPI used to measure the pattern is proven, then an efficient algorithm for mining the patterns is designed based on the anti-monotonicity.

Lemma 1. The regional utility participation ratio (RUPR) and regional utility participation index (RUPI) are anti-monotonic. That is to say, given a region R_l, let C_l and C_l' be two patterns such that $|C_l| = k - 1$, $|C_l'| = k$, $C_l \subset C_l'$. For each feature $f_i \in C_l$, $RUPR(f_i, C_l) \geq RUPR(f_i, C_l')$ and $RUPI(C_l) \geq RUPI(C_l')$ hold.

Proof. For each feature $f_i \in C_l$, according to Definition 2, we have $RSPIns_l(f_i, C_l') \subseteq RSPIns_l(f_i, C_l)$. According to Definition 4, we have $RUPR(f_i, C_l) \geq RUPR(f_i, C_l')$.

According to Definition 5, we have:

$$RUPI(C_l) = \min_{f_i \in C_l} RUPR(f_i, C_l) \geq \min_{f_i \in C'_l - \{f_k\}} RUPR(f_i, C'_l)$$

$$\geq \min\left(\min_{f_i \in C'_l - \{f_k\}} RUPR(f_i, C'_l), RUPR(f_k, C'_l)\right) = RUPI(C'_l) \quad (6)$$

According to Lemma 1, we have the following Pruning 1 to prune candidate patterns.

Pruning 1. Given a region R_l, if $C_l \subset C'_l$ and $RUPI(C_l) < u$, then $RUPI(C'_l) < u$, i.e., C_l and it's all super patterns are not regional high utility patterns and can be pruned.

Algorithm 1: Regional high utility co-location pattern mining algorithm (RHUCP)

Input:
    $F = \{f_1, f_2, ..., f_n\}$: spatial feature set
    $S = S_1 \cup S_2 \cup ... \cup S_n$: spatial instance set
    d: distance threshold
    u: utility threshold
Output:
    $RSHUC$: regional high utility co-location pattern set
Variables:
    kn: number of neighbors of fuzzy density peak clustering
    R: maximal fuzzy region set
    $Candi_k$: k-size candidate pattern set
    $RSHUC_k$: k-size regional high utility co-location pattern set

1) $R = Fuzzy\_DPC(kn, S)$ //Generate maximal fuzzy region set
2) For each $R_l \in R$
3)   For each $f_i.j \in R_l$
4) $RSNsI_l(f_i.j) = gen\_RSNsI()$ //Calculate the regional star neighbor instance set
5)   For each $f_i \in R_l$
6) $u_l(f_i) = Caculate\_U()$ //Calculate the regional total utility of the feature
7) $Candi_k = gen\_candidate()$ //Generate 2-size candidate patterns
8) $k = 2$
9)   while $(Candi_k \neq \emptyset)$
10)   For each $C_l \in Candi_k$
11)   For each $f_i \in C_l$
12)   For each $RSNsI_l(f_i.j)$
13) $RSPIns_l(f_i, C_l) = gen\_SPInstance()$ //Generate star participation instance set
14) $RUPR(f_i, C_l) = Caculate\_RFUR(RSPIns_l(f_i, C_l), u_l(f_i))$ //Calculate the star participation ratio
15) $RUPI(C_l) = \min_{f_i \in C_l} RUPR(f_i, C_l)$
16)   if $(RUPI(C_l) \geq u)$ //Get regional high utility pattern
17) $RSHUC \Leftarrow RSHUC \cup C_l, RSHUC_k \Leftarrow RSHUC_k \cup C_l$
18) $Candi_{k+1} = gen\_candidate(RSHUC_k)$ //Generate $(k + 1)$-size candidate patterns
19) $k + +$

Based on Lemma 1 and Pruning 1, we design an efficient algorithm RHUCP for mining regional high utility co-location patterns in each region, as shown in Algorithm 1. First, RHUCP utilizes the fuzzy density peak clustering to partition the whole region into local regions. Then, in each region, RHUCP adopts the level-by-level and generation-test mechanism to obtain patterns. Specifically, starting from the 2-size pattern, RHUCP generates $(k + 1)$-size candidate patterns based on k-size patterns, and tests $(k + 1)$-size candidate patterns to get $(k + 1)$-size patterns.

5 Experiments

In order to evaluate the effect and efficiency of the proposed RHUCP algorithm, we conduct experiments on real datasets and synthetic datasets, and compare it with two baseline algorithms NRHUCP and KHUCP. The NRHUCP algorithm mines non-regional high utility patterns in the whole region, and the KHUCP algorithm mines regional high utility patterns in non-fuzzy local regions obtained by K-means clustering.

Data Set. The real dataset is from POI data in Beijing. The synthetic datasets are generated by using the method in Ref. [5]. The statistics of the datasets are shown in Table 1.

Parameter Settings. On three datasets, the default distance thresholds are all set to 100, and the default utility thresholds are set to 0.3, respectively. The default k-nearest neighbour kn of fuzzy density peak clustering are set to 250. The number of local regions of KHUCP is same with that of RHUCP.

Table 1. The description of dataset

Data set	Number of Features	Number of Instances	Utility	Range(meter)
Beijing-POI	16	23025	[1,10000]	22000 × 14000
Synthetic data 1	20	[20000,100000]	[1,1000]	10000 × 10000
Synthetic data 2	[10,25]	20000	[1,1000]	10000 × 10000

Environment Setup. The algorithms are coded in C++, and run on a computer with Intel Core i7 CPU, 32 GB RAM and Windows 10 OS.

5.1 Analysis of Mining Results

Results analysis of RHUCP and NRHUCP. First, we compare the results of RHUCP with that of NRHUCP.

Table 2. Mining results of RHUCP algorithm and NRHUCP algorithm

Algorithm	RHUCP	NRHUCP
2-size patterns	{Chinese restaurant, Cafe} {Chinese restaurant, Hotel} {Chinese restaurant, Guest house} **{Chinese restaurant, Park, bus station}** **{National attractions, Provincial attractions}**	{Chinese restaurant, Cafe} {Chinese restaurant, Hotel} {Chinese restaurant, Guest house}
3-size patterns	{Chinese restaurant, Cafe, Parking lot} {Chinese restaurant, Park, Parking lot} **{Chinese restaurant, Guest house, Train station} {Chinese restaurant, Hotel, Parking lot}**	{Chinese restaurant, Cafe, Parking lot} {Chinese restaurant, Park, Parking lot}

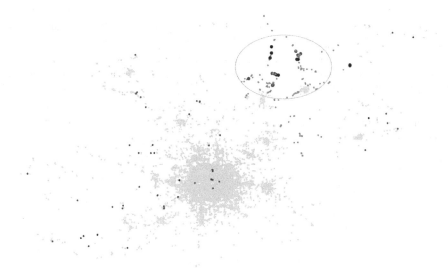

Fig. 2. A case of regional high utility pattern

Table 2 shows some patterns, and the patterns in bold are only mined by RHUCP. We can see that RHUCP discoveries some high utility patterns in local regions which are not high utility patterns in the whole region. Let us see a pattern {National attractions(G), Provincial attractions(H)}. We plot the distribution of instances in the whole region in Fig. 2, and the instances of the two features are colored, G is blue and H is black. We can see that these instances of the two features are neighbors in a local region in the circle, and the pattern is a regional high utility pattern which indicates the function of the local region may be a tourist center.

Table 3. Mining results of RHUCP algorithm and KHUCP algorithm

Algorithm	RHUCP	KHUCP
2-size patterns	{Chinese restaurant, Hotel} {Chinese restaurant, Hospitality} {Chinese restaurant, Park} **{Chinese restaurant, National attraction}** **{Chinese restaurant, Sporting goods supermarket}**	{Chinese restaurant, Hotel} {Chinese restaurant, Hospitality} {Chinese restaurant, Park}
3-size patterns	{Chinese restaurant, Cafe, Park}	{Chinese restaurant, Cafe, Park}

Results analysis of RHUCP and KHUCP. Second, we compare the results of RHUCP with that of KHUCP.

Table 3 shows some patterns, and the patterns in bold are only mined by RHUCP. We also see that RHUCP discoveries some high utility patterns in fuzzy local regions which are not high utility patterns in non-fuzzy local regions. In Fig. 3, we also plot the fuzzy/non-fuzzy local regions partitioned by fuzzy density peak clustering used in RHUCP and k-means clustering used in KHUCP, respectively. The fuzzy local regions are obviously different from non-fuzzy local regions. Due to the overlapping area of two fuzzy local regions, RHUCP discoveries meaningful high utility patterns, such as {Chinese restaurant, National attraction} and {Chinese restaurant, Sporting goods supermarket}.

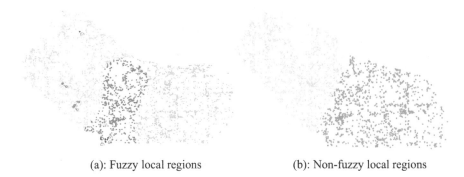

(a): Fuzzy local regions   (b): Non-fuzzy local regions

Fig. 3. Local regions obtained by RHUCP and KHUCP

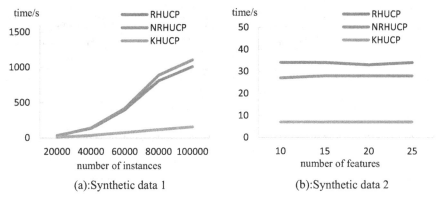

(a):Synthetic data 1   (b):Synthetic data 2

Fig. 4. Effect of the number of instances and the number of features

5.2 Efficiency Analysis

Effect of the Number of Instances and Features. We use Synthetic data 1, and Synthetic data 2 to evaluate the effect of the number of instances and features on the three algorithms. The results are shown in Fig. 4.

In Fig. 4(a), we can see that as the number of instances increases, the datasets become dense, which leads to the running time of three algorithms increasing. RHUCP is slower than KHUCP due to adopting fuzzy region partition method, while RHUCP is faster than NRHUCP. Figure 4 (b) shows that as the number of features increases, the running time of the three algorithms retains. The reason may be the number of features increasing leads the average number of instances decreases. We also see that RHUCP is slower than NRHUCP and KHUCP but mines more meaningful patterns.

Effect of different Parameters. We use synthetic data 1 and synthetic data 2 to evaluate the effect of parameters on the algorithm RHUCP respectively. The results are shown in Fig. 5. From Fig. 5(a), we can see that as the number of nearest neighbors kn increases, the number of fuzzy regions decreases and the running time also decreases. In Fig. 5(b), as the utility threshold u increases, the running time decreases due to less patterns mined. In Fig. 5(c), as the distance threshold d increases, the running time also increases because there are more regional star neighbor instances.

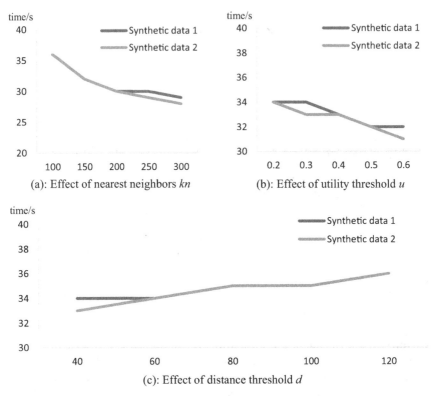

Fig. 5. Effect of the parameters

6 Conclusion

In this paper, we consider both the distribution of instances and the value of instances, and propose a novel method for mining regional high utility co-location pattern. We exploit the fuzzy density peak clustering to partition the whole into local regions. Then, we define regional high utility co-location pattern based on the star instance model. Further, we prove the anti-monotonicity of RUPR and RUPI used to measure the pattern, and design an efficient algorithm for mining the patterns in each local region based on the anti-monotonicity. The experiments show that the proposed pattern is meaningful and the proposed algorithm is efficient.

Acknowledgments. This work is supported by the National Natural Science Foundation of China (62266050, 62276227), the Program for Young and Middle-aged Academic and Technical Reserve Leaders of Yunnan Province (202205AC160033), Yunnan Provincial Major Science and Technology Special Plan Projects (202202AD080003), Yunnan Fundamental Research Projects (202201AS070015).

References

1. Wang, L., Bao, X., Zhou, L., et al.: Maximal sub-prevalent co-location patterns and efficient mining algorithms. In: Bouguettaya, A., et al. (eds.) Web Information Systems Engineering – WISE 2017. WISE 2017. LNCS, vol. 10569, pp. 199–214. Springer, Cham (2017). https://doi.org/10.1007/978-3-319-68783-4_14
2. Wang, L., Bao, X., Zhou, L., et al.: Mining maximal co-location patterns. World Wide Web **22**(5), 1971–1997 (2019)
3. Yang, S., Wang, L., Bao, X., Lu, J.: A framework for mining spatial high utility co-location patterns. In: FSKD 2015, Proceedings of the 12th International Conference on Fuzzy Systems and Knowledge Discovery, pp. 595–601. IEEE, Zhangjiajie, China (2015)
4. Jiang, X., Wang, L., Tran, V.: A parallel algorithm for regional co-location mining based on fuzzy density peak clustering. Sin Sci. Inform. **53**(7), 1281–1298 (2023)
5. Huang, Y., Shekhar, S., Xiong, H.: Discovering colocation patterns from spatial data sets: a general approach. IEEE Trans. Knowl. Data Eng. **16**(12), 1472–1485 (2004)
6. Wang, L., Jiang, W., Chen, H., Fang, Y.: Efficiently mining high utility co-location patterns from spatial data sets with instance-specific utilities. In: Candan, S., Chen, L., Pedersen, T., Chang, L., Hua, W. (eds.) Database Systems for Advanced Applications. DASFAA 2017. LNCS, vol. 10178, pp. 458–474. Springer, Cham (2017). https://doi.org/10.1007/978-3-319-55699-4_28
7. Xiao-Xuan, W., Li-Zhen, W., Hong-Mei, C., et al.: Mining spatial high utility co-location patterns based on feature utility ratio. Chin. J. Comput. **42**(8), 1721–1738 (2019)
8. Luo, J., Wang, L.-Z., Wang, X.-X., Xiao, Q.: Mining spatial high utility core patterns under k-nearest neighbors. Chin. J. Comput. **45**(2), 354–368 (2022)
9. Qian, F., Chiew, K., He, Q.M., et al.: Mining regional co-location patterns with kNNG. J. Intell. Inf. Syst. **42**, 485–505 (2014)
10. Yu, W.H.: Identifying and analyzing the prevalent regions of a co-Location pattern using polygons clustering approach. ISPRS Int. J. Geo-Inf. **6**(9), 259 (2017)

Local Co-location Pattern Mining Based on Regional Embedding

Yumming Zeng[1], Lizhen Wang[2]($\boxtimes$), Lihua Zhou[1], and Hongmei Chen[1]

[1] School of Information Science and Engineering, Yunnan University, Kunming 650091, China
[2] Dianchi College, Kunming 650228, China
lzhwang@ynu.edu.cn

Abstract. Local co-location pattern (LCP) presents the spatial correlation between various categories in local regions. Regional partitioning is a pivotal step in LCP mining. Existing regional partitioning methods may ignore potential LCPs due to subjective elements. Additionally, with the diversity of geographic data increases, previous mining techniques disregarded the semantic information within the data, and limited the interpretability of local regions and LCPs. In response to these issues, this paper introduces an approach for LCP mining based on regional embedding. Initially, the entire study region is finely divided into local regions through natural data like road networks. Next, leveraging regional embedding techniques, local regions are embedded using human trajectory events, resulting in the creation of regional embedding vectors. Subsequently, the k-means method is employed to find functional clusters of local regions, and self-attention mechanisms is used for functional annotation. Then, the semantic LCPs are mined in these annotated local regions. Experiments on real-world datasets comprising urban population trajectories and Points of Interest (POI) confirm the efficiency and interpretability of the proposed framework for LCP mining based on regional embedding.

Keywords: Spatial Data Mining · Regional Embedding · Local Co-location Pattern

1 Introduction

With the rapid evolution of technology and the continuous advancement of the internet, spatial technologies like Geographic Information Systems, Global Positioning Systems, and high-resolution remote sensing techniques have garnered extensive global application. Constantly, we generate copious amounts of spatiotemporal data laden with location information. Through the scrutiny of these data, we uncover and address myriad crucial issues that permeate everyday human life, such as earth resource assessment [1], geographic information recommendation [2], and traffic planning problems [3].

Spatial co-location pattern mining, as an essential component of spatial data mining [4], assumes a critical role. By mining spatial co-location patterns such as {hospital,

---

The first author is a student.

X. Meng et al. (Eds.): SpatialDI 2024, LNCS 14619, pp. 108–119, 2024.
https://doi.org/10.1007/978-981-97-2966-1_9

flower shop}, we acquire pivotal insights into geographical co-occurrence of regional functional locations. These insights find multifaceted applications across urban planning, crime prevention, and various other domains, providing robust support for urban development and societal amelioration.

The existing spatial partitioning strategies primarily include methods like geographical partitioning and grid-based partitioning. These approaches, focusing on localized regions, mine certain LCPs that might elude detection within a global scope. However, these methods tend to subjectively partition regions, disregarding the spatial distribution of data, potentially compromising the discovery of latent LCPs. Furthermore, the lack of semantic information diminishes the interpretability of both LCPs and their prevalently occurring local regions, thereby impeding the practical application of LCP mining.

To obtain regional partitions with semantic information, this paper introduces a regional embedding method. By employing a regional embedding framework akin to natural language processing model "word2vec" on spatiotemporal trajectory data of human mobility, embeddings for finely delineated regions structured by road networks are obtained. Subsequently, through clustering of regional embedding vectors, a delineation of local regions imbued with semantic information is obtained, allowing for the exploration of LCPs within annotated local regions. At last, this paper proposed a semantic LCP mining algorithm based on embedded functional local region. The algorithm improves the joinless algorithm by semantic importance index, which improves the mining efficiency while obtaining the semantic information of patterns and regions. A case study is used to prove the validity of the proposed algorithm and the interpretability of the mining results.

2 Related Works

In order to embed the semantic information in the words into the vector, Mikolov T et al. first proposed two word2vec model structures, CBOW and Skip-gram in 2013, and used the recurrent neural network language model to train word vectors with semantic representation ability on large-scale corpus [5]. Furthermore, the details of Skip-gram model and the training methods of hierarchical softmax and negative sampling are elaborated [6]. Rong X et al. elaborated on the technical details of word2vec, such as word vector extraction and training process [7]. Barkan O et al. expanded the application scope of word2vec from the field of natural language processing directly to any field where sequence can be generated, such as recommendation, advertising, and search [8]. In 2018, Yao et al. applied the word embedding approach to regional embedding of urban functional representations [9]. In the same year, Fu et al. proposed a collective learning model with heterogeneous human mobility data, using human trajectory data for representation learning of urban functions [10].

On the other hand, in the research of co-location pattern mining, researchers have proposed many different partitioning schemes for the division of regions. In 2014, Qian et al. developed a k-nearest neighbor based partitioning method in order to reduce the subjectivity of determining partitioning schemes [11], which divides the study area into several homogeneous local regions. In each local region, the edge weights in the k-nearest neighbor graph are slightly different. Then in 2023, Jiang X et al. proposed a parallel algorithm based on fuzzy density peak clustering [12], and Wang D et al. applied regional co-location pattern mining on online decision support system at the same year [13]. In order to alleviate the computational burden on identifying candidate co-location patterns, multiple methodologies for filtering and pruning instances are devised. For example, joinless method [14], the maximal clique and hash table-based method [15], and fuzzy grid clique approach [16]. In addition, negative sequential pattern (NSP) mining, which considers both positive (occurring) and negative (non-occurring) event/behavior and can provide more complement decision-making information, is also an interesting topic. Some excellent algorithms such as f-NSP [17], sc-NSP [18] and NegI-NSP [19] have been proposed to mine NSP.

3 Basic Concepts

The process of mapping the representation of each word to a numerical vector space based on the relationships between words is termed as word embedding. Similar to the contextual associations inherent in word embedding, in the regional embedding model, we extract trajectory events from human trajectories likened to context. We scrutinize the functional aspects of the occurrence points of mobility events in the trajectory movement, learning the functional embedding of associated regions from these trajectory events, and local regions are divided based on this. The definitions of mobility event and trajectory event are as follows:

Definition 1 (Trajectory Event). During a personnel travel activity, trajectory events are derived from the utilization of origin-destination (O-D) region pairs, departure and arrival times, as well as travel distance data, represented as $TE = \{te_1, , te_2, ..., te_n\}$, where each trajectory event $te = (r_O, r_D, t_O, t_D)$ comprises the origin region r_O, destination region r_D, departure time t_O, and arrival time t_D.

Definition 2 (Mobility Event). Within the trajectory events, two types of personnel mobility events can be extracted: departures and arrivals. These mobility events encapsulate region and temporal data, denoted as $ME = (me.r, me.t, me.flag)$. Here, $me.r$ represents the region, $me.t$ signifies time categorized by period and date type, and $me.flag \in \{Arrive, leave\}$ indicates the directional flag, elucidating the directionality of mobility event.

After the partitioning of the region is completed, to mine prevalent LCP with semantic information, the basic concept is given below. The spatial feature set represents the set of different kinds of things in space, denoted $F = \{f_1, f_2, ..., f_k\}$, where the spatial feature $f_i (1 \leq i \leq k)$ refers to the conceptual abstraction of a set of spatial objects with the same feature type.

Objects corresponding to spatial characteristics at specific locations in space are called spatial instances, and their sets are called spatial instance sets, denoted as $S = S_1 \cup S_2 \cup \cdots \cup S_k$, where $S_i (1 \leq i \leq k)$ represents the set of space instances of the space feature f_i. In order to mine the semantic information contained in regions and features, the spatial instance contains the basic information of the instance number, spatial feature and location. If the Euclidean distance between two spatial instances is less than or equal to a distance threshold d given by the user, then the two spatial instances are said to be neighbors in space. For a subset c of the spatial feature set, called spatial pattern c, denoted as $c = \{f_1, f_2, \ldots, f_s\}$, where the length of c is called the size of the pattern. The prevalence measure for a pattern is defined as follows:

Definition 3 (Participation Rate and Participation Index). The participation rate is expressed as $PR(c, f_i)$, which is the ratio of the number of instances of f_i that appear in instances of spatial co-location pattern c to the total number of instances of f_i. The participation index is expressed as $PI(c)$, which is the minimum of the PR values of all spatial features in spatial co-location pattern c.

Definition 4 (Semantic Importance Index of Pattern). Given the semantic importance index of instances, the importance index of the pattern c can be measured by the weighted average of the importance index of the instance, denoted as $IM(c)$.

Definition 5 (Semantic LCP). Given a minimum participation threshold p_{min} and a minimum importance threshold IM_{min}, for a spatial pattern c that meets $IM(c) \geq IM_{min}$, if it's also meets $PI(c) \geq p_{min}$, that is, if c not only satisfies the importance of regional semantic representation, but also occurs prevalently in the functional local region, then it is called a semantic LCP.

4 Mining Framework

4.1 Regional Embedding

To find semantic information in trajectory events, POI data in regions is integrated. The distribution of these POI unveils the distinct functionalities of various regions, indirectly reflecting population densities across different regions. Integrating POI data with trajectory event data not only enables a coherent interpretation of spatial correlations within local regions but also furnishes a foundational understanding for subsequent work.

Fig. 1. Distribution of different POI data.

An illustration of the distribution of POI, as depicted in Fig. 1, reveals the diverse array of POI within the whole region. In different local regions, directed trajectories unfold over time, capturing both temporal and directional facets that reflect distinctions and correlations among regions. Figure 2 is an example of trajectory events. In trajectory event 1, movement follows the directional arrows, passing through three different POI over a time span. In trajectory event 2, an individual departs from the triangular marked POI at the first time point, arrives at the square marked POI at the second time point, and returns to the triangular marked POI at the third time point. This visualization emphasizes how the time and direction of trajectory events can portray the functional landscape of regions, while the function of the origin and destination also influences the function of local regions.

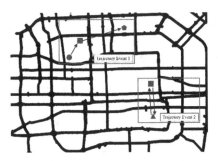

Fig. 2. An example of trajectory events.

To facilitate the learning of regional embeddings, employing the current region as the focal point and trajectory events as context, we minimize the following objective function involving all concurrently appearing regions and trajectory events:

$$\min_{V,V'} \frac{1}{2} \sum_{r \in RE} \sum_{e \in TE} \left(M(r, t) - v_r^T v_t' \right)^2 \tag{1}$$

where $M = |TE| \times |RE|$ represents the Positive Pointwise Mutual Information (PPMI) matrix, elucidating the co-occurrences between regions and trajectory events. TE represents the trajectory event set, and RE represents the region set. v_r and v_t' correspondingly denote the embeddings of trajectory events t and their associated regions r. The computation of the matrix M is as follows:

$$M(r, t) = \max\left(0, \log\left(\frac{\#(t, r) \cdot |T|}{\#(r) \cdot \#(t)} \right) \right) \tag{2}$$

where T represents the migration frequency of trajectory events. $\#(t, r)$ stands for the global frequency of concurrent occurrences of regions and trajectory events, while $\#(t)$ and $\#(r)$ denotes the local frequencies of individual occurrences for trajectory events and regions, respectively. By taking derivatives of v_r and v_t', and employing gradient descent, the embeddings are optimized. Ultimately, this process yields the embedding vector matrices for both trajectory events and regions.

4.2 Region Functional Annotation

The annotation of regional functions stands as a pivotal foundation rooted in discovering semantic LCPs and local regions where they occur prevalently. Thus, the K-means algorithm is employed to cluster the region embedding vectors. This process effectively delineates various types of local regions into local regions characterized by diverse functionalities. Leveraging the region embeddings as feature vectors, we proceed with the annotation of regional functionalities.

The spatial distribution of instances often correlates significantly with regional population density. Regions with higher population density tend to harbor a richer set of instances, making it more challenging to assess regional functionalities comprehensively. Conversely, regions with lower population density may contain fewer instances, yet their regional functionalities are more discernible.

In order to mitigate the impact of population density on regional functional classification and better capture the instance properties within each region, this paper employs a self-attention model for dynamic adjustments within classified regions. The model is represented as follows:

$$Attention(Q, K, V) = softmax(\frac{QK^T}{\sqrt{d_k}} + P)V \qquad (3)$$

Herein, Q, K, and V denote the query, key, and value matrices, respectively, corresponding to three distinct attributes of the feature vector matrix, $\sqrt{d_k}$ represents the square root of the vector dimension and P represents the position vector. The self-attention model conducts unsupervised secondary learning based on the statistical properties of instances within each categorized functional local region. This approach dynamically adjusts the functionalities associated with each region. Through this adaptive refinement, it not only mitigates the impact of population density on regional functional annotations but also assimilates a richer array of regional insights, thereby elevating the precision of functional local region annotation.

4.3 Mining Semantic LCPs

The partitioning of local regions derives from learned trajectory event embeddings passing through instances. Post-processing by the self-attention model, these embeddings serve in learning the weighted ranking of features corresponding to functional trajectory events, based on their functionality and visit frequencies. For instance, features such as residential buildings or restaurants, ubiquitously distributed across all regions and exerting minimal impact on classification outcomes, receive lower feature weights. Conversely, features like governmental institutions, indicative of regional functionalities, are given higher feature weights.

In the LCP mining conducted within local regions, an improved join-less algorithm was proposed, called Semantic Local Co-location Pattern Mining Algorithm (SLCPM). During the generation of candidate patterns, consideration was given to the semantic importance index of patterns, facilitating the pruning of lower-importance patterns to enhance mining efficiency. The mined LCPs recurring within local regions not only significantly contribute to interpreting regional functionalities but also exhibit high interpretability. For instance, within leisure and entertainment regions, the {cinema, fastfood restaurant} pattern prevalently emerges, enhancing our understanding of urban functionalities and supporting applications in commercial decision-making.

Algorithm 1. SLCPM

Input: Functional local region set FR, Spatial instance set S, Semantic importance index matrix SII

Output: Semantic LCP set $SLCP$

Variables: p_{min}: Minimum participation threshold; IM_{min}: Minimum importance index threshold; F: Spatial feature set; c: Current candidate pattern; sn: The neighbors of current feature; $IM(c)$: Semantic importance index of pattern; p: The participation index of pattern

Steps:

```
 1:  init: FR, S, p_min, IM_min, F, c
 2:  for each functional_region in FR do
 3:      F.clear()
 4:      for each S_i in S do
 5:          F.add({S_i})
 6:      end for
 7:      while F is not empty do
 8:          for each f_j in F do
 9:              sn = find_neighbors(f_j, I)
10:              c = merge(f_j, sn)
11:              IM(c) = calculate_importance(c, SII)
12:              if IM(c) >= IM_min then
13:                  p = calculate_participation(c)
14:                  if p >= p_min then
15:                      SLCP.add(c)
16:                  end if
17:              end if
18:              F = expand_feature_set(F)
19:          end for
20:      end while
21:  end for
22:  return SLCP
```

Algorithm 1 shows the steps to mine the semantic LCPs in local regions: first initializing input data and variables (Step 1), adding spatial instances within each functional local region into the feature set (Steps 2–6). Subsequently, an evaluation of the neighbor relations of each spatial feature within the feature set leads to the generation of candidate patterns (Steps 7–10). Then the candidate patterns that meet the thresholds for semantic importance index and participation index is included in the semantic LCP set, while those failing to meet the criteria are pruned (Steps 11–15). At last, upon completing iterations across all local regions, the algorithm returns the Semantic LCP set including information about regions where semantic LCPs frequently occur (Step 16–22).

4.4 Algorithm Analysis

Time Complexity Analysis: The initialization process operates in constant time. Denoted the number of local regions as $|FR|$, and the average number of instances of regions as $|I_{avg}|$, the initialization of the feature set might require traversing all instances in the region in the worst case, resulting in a time complexity of $O(|I_{avg}|)$. The main loop iterates continuously until the feature set is empty. During each iteration, operations such as finding neighbors, merging features, computing importance, and involvement of each pattern are performed. The time required for handling each pattern depends on the complexity of specific operations including neighbor search, feature merging, and importance and participation calculations. Let's assume these operations take $O(f)$ time on average for each pattern. In each iteration, the worst-case scenario might involve processing the entire feature set. Hence, the time complexity of the algorithm might reach $O(|FR| * |I_{avg}| * F_{size} * f)$, where F_{size} denotes the size of the feature set.

Space Complexity Analysis: The space consumption mainly comes from two aspects: (1) In the generation of the spatial feature set, the size of the spatial feature set is influenced by the number of instances within the local regions and their neighboring relations. Assuming a maximum feature set size of F_{max}, the total space complexity of feature set generation can be approximated as $O(|I_{avg}| * F_{max} * |FR|)$, where $|I_{avg}|$ represents the average number of instances and $|FR|$ denotes the number of local regions. (2) As for the storage of spatial features, within the iterative process for each functional local region, operations are performed on spatial features, such as merging and neighbor relations. As the size of features per instance is constant and additional storage is required for these features during merging and neighbor relation computations, the space complexity of this portion becomes $O(|I_{avg}| * F_{max})$.

5 Experimental Evaluation

5.1 Description of Datasets

In this paper, 3 datasets are used to evaluate the efficiency of the proposed SLCPM algorithm, and illustrate the semantic and application of the mining results.

The first dataset comprises the trajectories of taxi journeys, epitomizing the bustling pulse of human life. Taxis, emblematic of city transit, serve as a lens through which we capture the intricate tapestry of human trajectory events within Beijing. This dataset meticulously captures the GPS trajectories of 10,357 taxis traversing the cityscape in February 2008. It encompasses an impressive 15 million data points, painting a narrative spanning an expansive 9 million kilometers. Structured around vehicle IDs, temporal markers, and GPS coordinates, this dataset provides a comprehensive portrayal of the city's human movement dynamics.

The second dataset delineates Beijing's comprehensive road network, segmented into ten tiers encompassing urban expressways, subway lines, rapid highways, steadfast railways, national routes, provincial passages, county lanes, rural pathways, pedestrian thoroughfares, and miscellaneous routes.

The third dataset, procured from the Amap API, embraces 597,704 entries enriched with precise positional coordinates and specific geographic nomenclature within Beijing. These entries are grouped into 125 distinct classes.

5.2 Region Partitioning and Function Annotation Based on Regional Embedding

Given the intricate complexity of Beijing's road network, particularly within the ten-tier classification, which includes redundant data and disjointed pedestrian paths, delineating regions becomes challenging. Hence, we focused on the five primary levels of roads to derive a representative segmentation of the road network.

Subsequently, leveraging the cartographic editing tool, Arcmap, we undertook a process of deduplication and refinement, elongating the principal roadways in Beijing. This meticulous effort resulted in the creation of finely partitioned, disconnected local regions, derived from the segmentation of the road network. As illustrated in the Fig. 3, the road network was delineated into 760 fine-grained local regions, each exhibiting distinct characteristics.

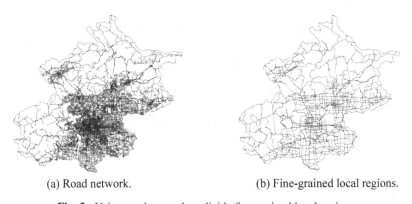

(a) Road network.   (b) Fine-grained local regions.

Fig. 3. Using road network to divide fine-grained local regions.

Following the fine-grained division of local regions, this paper proceeded to curate the 15 million discrete GPS points from taxi trip data, filtering out duplicate and erroneous entries. These refined points were then transformed into trajectory events, serving as representative indicators of inter-regional correlations. By scrutinizing the categories of POI within each region and leveraging the correlation between trajectory events, we conducted functional embeddings for the 760 regions, culminating in the identification of 12 distinct local regions by clustering the regional embedding vectors. The visual representation of this analysis is depicted in Fig. 4(a).

Subsequently, harnessing the statistical attributes of POI within each functional local region, an unsupervised secondary learning phase was executed using a self-attention model. This dynamic process facilitated the adjustment of each region's associated functionality, resulting in annotated functional labels for the regions, as illustrated in Fig. 4(b). This approach allowed for a dynamic reconfiguration of regional functionalities based on the aggregated attributes of POI, enhancing the accuracy of functional delineations within each region.

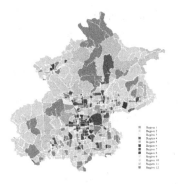
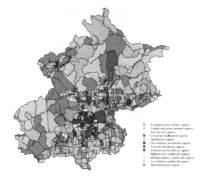

(a) The division of local regions obtained through regional embeddings.

(b) The local regions after dynamic adjustments via the self-attention model

Fig. 4. The delineation and optimization of regions enriched with functional information.

5.3 Case Study of Semantic LCP Mining

Through the previously mentioned regional embedding and functional annotation, we have attained regions imbued with functionality and gauged the significance of each instance's functionality. Employing the SLCPM algorithm proposed in this paper for LCP mining on the Beijing POI dataset, compared against the join-less algorithm, as illustrated in Fig. 5.

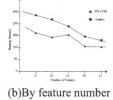
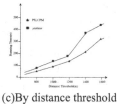

(a)By instance number

(b)By feature number

(c)By distance threshold

Fig. 5. Comparison by different parameters.

Figure 5 shows the influence of changes in the number of instances, number of features and distance thresholds on the algorithm running time. Due to the existence of semantic importance pruning, it can be seen that the algorithm is more efficient than the joinless algorithm. In addition, to validate the explicability of the SLCPM algorithm results, analysis through patterns mined from real-world data is imperative.

Table 1 enumerates some 2-size and 3-size LCPs discovered by the SLCPM algorithm along with their prevalent local regions. From Table 1, we observe the 2-size pattern {Government offices, Chinese restaurants}, showcasing a prevalent local region within the government sector. This pattern signifies a recurring geographical co-occurrence of government offices and Chinese restaurants within the governmental sphere, which is substantiated in real-world scenarios. Furthermore, the joinless algorithm, reliant solely on participation index, overlooks these niche yet semantically influential patterns crucial

Table 1. Examples of semantic LCPs on real dataset

Size	Region	Semantic LCP
2	Government institution region	{Government offices, Chinese restaurants} {Public security organs, Parking lot} {Cinema, Fast food restaurant}
3	Leisure and entertainment region	{Coach station, Hotel, Chinese restaurant} {Karaoke room, Bath center, Hair salon}

for understanding regional functionality due to the scarcity of instances like government office.

As an additional example, within the 3-size pattern of the Leisure and Entertainment region, the {Coach station, Hotel, Chinese restaurant} pattern unravels the practical life logic wherein individuals arriving at the coach station seek accommodation and dining solutions. This real-world scenario further substantiates the interpretability of semantic LCPs discovered by the SLCPM algorithm.

6 Conclusion

This paper delves into the lack of regional interpretability within existing LCP mining algorithms, proposing an LCP mining algorithm based on regional embedding as a solution to these issues. By modeling embeddings associated with region-related events extracted from extensive human mobility traces, it characterizes regional functionalities as distributed low-dimensional vectors. Incorporating movement direction and departure/arrival times, a direction and time-aware regional co-occurrence is constructed to annotate regional functionalities. Building upon this, the LCP mining within function-annotated regions yields LCPs and their corresponding semantically enriched prevalent local regions. This amplifies interpretability for both regions and LCPs. Experiment on real-world datasets confirm the effectiveness of the proposed method.

In future work, we plan to further explore the dynamic function of the region by analyze the data differences at different times, explore the various attributes of the region at different times, and grasp the dynamic changes of spatiotemporal data in more detail.

Acknowledgments. This work is supported by the National Natural Science Foundation of China (62276227, 62306266), the Yunnan Fundamental Research Projects (202201AS070015) and the Scientific Research Fund Project of Yunnan Provincial Department of Education (2023Y0248).

References

1. Lin, L., et al.: Application of spatiotemporal data mining in Marine gas hydrate resource evaluation. Mar. Geol. Front. **34**(11), 41–45 (2018)
2. Yin, P., et al.: Geographic big data mining and recommendation technology based on topic characteristics. Geogr. Spatiotemporal Inf. **18**(04), 41–44+6 (2020)

3. Wang, X., et al.: Spatio-temporal co-location congestion pattern mining and application in traffic data. Yunnan University (2019)
4. Mennis, J., Guo, D.: Spatial data mining and geographic knowledge discovery—an introduction. Comput. Environ. Urban Syst. **33**(6), 403–408 (2009)
5. Mikolov, T., Chen, K., et al.: Efficient estimation of word representations in vector space. Comput. Sci. (2013)
6. Mikolov, T., Yih, W.-T., Zweig, G.: Linguistic regularities in continuous space word representations. In: Proceedings of the 2013 Conference of the North American Chapter of the Association for Computational Linguistics: Human Language Technologies, pp. 746–751 (2013)
7. Rong, X.: Word2vec parameter learning explained. Comput. Sci. (2014)
8. Barkan, O., Koenigstein, N.: Item2Vec: neural item embedding for collaborative filtering. In: 2016 IEEE 26th International Workshop on Machine Learning for Signal Processing (2016)
9. Yao, Z., Fu, Y., Liu, B., et al.: Representing urban functions through zone embedding with human mobility patterns. In: Twenty-Seventh International Joint Conference on Artificial Intelligence, vol. 545 (2018)
10. Fu, Y., Liu, G., Ge, Y., et al.: Representing urban forms: a collective learning model with heterogeneous human mobility data. IEEE Trans. Knowl. Data Eng. **31**, 535–548 (2018)
11. Qian, F., Chiew, K., He, Q., et al.: Mining regional co-location patterns with kNNG. J. Intell. Inf. Syst. **42**(3), 485–505 (2014)
12. Jiang, X., Wang, L., Tran, V.: A parallel algorithm for regional co-location mining based on fuzzy density peak clustering. Sci. Sin. Inform. **53**, 1281–1298 (2023)
13. Wang, D., Wang, L., Yang, P.: ODSS-RCPM: an online decision support system based on regional co-location pattern mining. In: Processing of the 28th International Conference on Database Systems for Advanced Applications, pp. 663–668 (2023)
14. Yoo, J.S., Shekhar, S.: A joinless approach for mining spatial colocation patterns. IEEE Trans. Knowl. Data Eng. **18**(10), 1323–1327 (2006)
15. Zhang, S., Wang, L., Tran, V.: CPM-MCHM: a spatial co-location pattern mining algorithm based on maximal clique and hash table. Chin. J. Comput. **45**(3), 526–541 (2022)
16. Hu, Z., Wang, L., Tran, V., et al.: Efficiently mining spatial co-location patterns utilizing fuzzy grid cliques. Inf. Sci. **592**, 361–388 (2022)
17. Dong, X., Gong, Y., Cao, L.: F-NSP+: a fast negative sequential patterns mining method with self-adaptive data storage. Pattern Recogn. **84**, 13–27 (2018)
18. Gao, X., Gong, Y., Xu, T., et al.: Towards to better structure and constraint to mine negative sequential patterns. IEEE Trans. Neural Netw. Learn. Syst. **34**(2), 571–585 (2023)
19. Qiu, P., Gong, Y., Zhao, Y., et al.: An efficient method for modeling non-occurring behaviors by negative sequential patterns with loose constraints. IEEE Trans. Neural Netw. Learn. Syst. **34**(4), 1864–1878 (2023)

RCPM_RLM: A Regional Co-location Pattern Mining Method Based on Representation Learning Model

Yi Cai[1], Lizhen Wang[2(⊠)], Lihua Zhou[1], and Hui Chen[2]

[1] School of Information Science and Engineering, Yunnan University, Kunming 650091, China
caiyi@mail.ynu.edu.cn
[2] Dianchi College, Kunming 650228, China
lzhwang@ynu.edu.cn

Abstract. Due to the heterogeneity of spatial data, spatial co-location patterns are not all global prevalent patterns. There are regional prevalent patterns that can only appear in specific local areas. Regional co-location pattern mining (RCPM) is designed to discover co-location patterns like these. The regional co-location patterns can reveal the association relationships among spatial features in the local regions. However, most studies only divide the functional regions through density of instances, ignoring the spatial correlation within, which makes the identification results biased towards a higher number of instances (such as restaurants, convenience stores, etc.), and may not present the functional characteristics of regional differences effectively. In the stage of RCPM, we propose a new algorithm for mining regional co-location patterns. By using the method of representation learning to extract the feature vectors of POI types with the help of the word embedding model, and then the functional areas of the city are divided. This method uses word vector to represent the semantic information of words, so that semantically similar words are close to each other in the representation space, and the division of regions is more reasonable. Compared to the existing algorithms, our method demonstrates a greater potential, as evidenced by experimental results.

Keywords: Spatial data mining · Regional pattern · Representation Learning · Urban functional regions

1 Introduction

Rapid population growth, traffic congestion and environmental degradation bring opportunities and challenges to urban spatial planning and management. At the same time, the rapid development of spatial information technology such as remote sensing technology, global positioning system and geographic information system is widely used in People's Daily production and life. For example, vehicle trajectory data, bus card data, social media data, mobile phone signaling data and Point of Interest (POI) data are widely used in land use classification and urban functional area identification. The application of these technologies produces a large amount of spatial data every day, which contains

© The Author(s), under exclusive license to Springer Nature Singapore Pte Ltd. 2024
X. Meng et al. (Eds.): SpatialDI 2024, LNCS 14619, pp. 120–131, 2024.
https://doi.org/10.1007/978-981-97-2966-1_10

location information. A spatial co-location pattern is a subset of a set of spatial features whose instances occur prevalently in the neighborhood of each other and are neighbors. Spatial association rules mining is one of the main tasks of spatial data mining, and the spatial co-location pattern mining studied in this paper is a special case of spatial association rules mining. Its research has been widely used in environmental protection [1], public safety [2], urban planning [3], transportation [4] and location-based services [5, 19].

Due to the heterogeneity of spatial data, spatial co-location patterns are not all global prevalent patterns that can appear globally in the whole research area, but also regional prevalent patterns that can only appear in local areas [6, 18]. For example, the crime rate in a city is not high overall, but it may be high near bars. Through regional co-location pattern mining studies, new insights will be provided into the interactions between different spatial phenomena.

Previous regional partition methods can be broadly categorized into two categories, that is, clustering-based methods, partition-based methods. The main challenge of the existing partition-based methods lies in how to identify the spatial partitioning scheme of the local region. Cluster-based methods may miss some regional co-location patterns [7, 8]. However, these methods have given a determined boundary for the region of division. To crack this nut, Jiang [9] introduced a density peak based clustering combining with fuzzy set theory and k-nearest neighbor distance to an applicable regional co-location pattern mining algorithm.

In negative sequential pattern (NSP) mining area, some excellent algorithms, such as e-NSP [15], f-NSP [10], sc-NSP [11] and NegI-NSP [12] have been proposed. In addition, two other algorithms e-RNSP [13] and Topk-NSP [14] are used to mine repetition negative sequential patterns and top-k useful NSPs respectively.

However, most studies only divide the functional regions through density of instances, ignoring the spatial correlation within [9, 17], which makes the identification results biased towards a higher number of instances (such as restaurants, convenience stores, etc.), and may not present the functional characteristics of regional differences effectively [16].

Based on the above background and theory, this paper proposes a new algorithm for mining regional co-location patterns. Firstly, the method of representation learning is used to extract the feature vectors of POI types with the help of the word embedding model, and then the functional areas of the city are divided. This method uses word vector to represent the semantic information of words, so that semantically similar words are close to each other in the representation space, and the division of regions is more reasonable.

2 Related Concepts

2.1 Regional Co-location Patterns Mining

The various types of objects in space are spatial features, and the concrete things with spatial attributes are spatial instances. Generally, spatial instances with location attributes can be regarded as points with characteristic attributes in space. A spatial co-location pattern c is a subset of the set of spatial features F, that is, $c = \{f_1, f_2, \cdots, f_k\} \subseteq F$.

With the length of the bit pattern c is called the order with a pattern, as the $size(c) = |c|$. For example, $\{A, B\}$ is a second-order pattern.

To measure the prevalence (i.e., the degree of interest) of co-location patterns, engagement [17] is used to measure the prevalence of patterns in spatial data mining.

Given a spatial co-location pattern $c = \{f_1, f_2, \cdots, f_k\} \subseteq F$, the participation rate of a spatial feature $f_i (1 \leqslant i \leqslant k)$ is denoted by $PR(c, f_i)$, which is the ratio of the number of non-recurring instances of feature f_i in the spatial co-location pattern c to the total number of instances, i.e.

$$PR(c, f_i) = \frac{|\pi_{f_i}(T(c))|}{|T\{f_i\}|} \tag{1}$$

where π is the projection operation of the relation. The participation of a co-location pattern c is the minimum of the PR values of all spatial features in c, denoted by $PI(c)$, i.e.

$$PI(c) = min_{i=1}^{k}\{PR(c, f_i)\} \tag{2}$$

The minimum participation threshold is specified as θ. If $PI(c) \geq \theta$, the co-location pattern c is said to be prevalent.

The regional spatial co-location pattern consists of two parts: the spatial co-location pattern and the prevalent region of the pattern, that is, $P = (pattern, c)$, where pattern belongs to F and c is the prevalent region.

2.2 Word Embeddings Representation Model

Word embedding is a language feature learning technique that has been used to boost the performance in NLP tasks such as sentiment analysis [5, 18]. Word2Vec, proposed by Mikolov et al. (Mikolov, Chen, Corrado, & Dean, 2015) [19], is an open-source, state-of-the-art model that produces word embedding. Taking a large corpus as input, by training two-layer neural networks (NNs), linguistic contexts of words are re constructed, and each word is represented as a unique vector. Word2Vec model provides two mathematical models, skip-gram and continuous BoW [20, 23], for training NNs. The Skip-Gram model is more suitable, due to the data size of this study is relatively small. By embedding each word as a unique word vector, the vectors of the target word are used as features to predict the context words. The maximum likelihood function of the skip-gram can be estimated as:

$$I(\theta) = \frac{1}{n} \sum_{i=1}^{n} \log p\left(w_i \mid w_{i-s}^{i+s}\right) \tag{3}$$

where s denotes the window size, n denotes the number of words vocabulary, and w_{i-s}^{i+s} denotes context words of target word w_i. The softmax function is used in skip-gram for computing the probability $p\left(w_i \mid w_{i-s}^{i+s}\right)$ as:

$$p\left(w_i \mid w_{i-s}^{i+s}\right) = \frac{\exp\left(w_i, w_{i-s}^{i+s}\right)}{\frac{1}{n} \sum_{i=1}^{n} \exp\left(w_i, w_{i-s}^{i+s}\right)} \tag{4}$$

2.3 Similarity Measurement

In our study, a cosine distance-based similarity measurement [19] was introduced to implement the correlation analysis of POIs categories and the preprocessing of the clustering method. In high-dimensional vector space, given two high-dimensional vectors w_i and w_j, the measurement of word similarity is usually calculated by the cosine distance, denoted as:

$$S(w_i, w_j) = 1 - \cos(\theta) = 1 - \frac{w_i \cdot w_j}{|w_i||w_j|} \tag{5}$$

The change interval of $S(w_i, w_j)$ is $[-1, 1]$.

2.4 Clustering Method

A single word vector does not explicitly express the semantics of a word due to the word vectors have features such as high dimensionality, denseness, and unclear semantics in the embedding space. Therefore, it is particularly important to find an efficient clustering method, which can divide the high-dimensional embedding space based on the cosine based distance and accurately cluster the vectors of words, thus effectively mining the internal features of the word vectors and clustering attributes.

HDBSCAN is a hierarchical density-based clustering algorithm which allows varying density clusters by condensing the dendrogram into a smaller tree that is used to select the most stable clusters [5, 21]. It extends DBSCAN by converting it into a hierarchical clustering algorithm, and then using a technique to extract a flat clustering based in the stability of clusters.

The DBSCAN algorithm defines the following concepts:

1. Directly density-reachable: We call sample point p is by the sample points q for parameters $\{Eps, MinPts\}$ density direct, if they meet the $p \in NEps(q)$ and $|NEps(q)| \geq MinPts$ (that is, sample points q is the core).
2. Density-reachable: We say that a sample point p is reachable by a sample point q with respect to the parameter $\{Eps, MinPts\}$ density if there exists a sequence of sample points $p_1, ..., p_n$ (where $p_1 = q, p_n = p$) such that for $i = 1, ..., n - 1$, the sample point $p_i + 1$ is reachable by the sample point p_i density-reachable.
3. Density-connected: We say that a sample point p is density-connected to a sample point q with respect to the parameter $\{Eps, MinPts\}$ if there exists a sample point o such that both p and q are o-density-reachable.

The HDBSCAN proposes that five steps are required to implement the algorithm as:

1. Transform the space according to the density or sparsity.
2. Build the minimum spanning tree of the distance weighted graph.
3. Construct a cluster hierarchy of connected components.
4. Condense the cluster hierarchy based on minimum cluster size.
5. Extract the stable clusters from the condensed tree.

Two more variables are defined:

1. The core distance defined for parameter k for a point x and denote as:

$$\text{core}_k(x) = d\left(x, N^k(x)\right) \tag{6}$$

2. Mutual reachability distance:

$$d_{\text{mreach}-k}(a, b) = max\{\text{core}_k(a), \text{core}_k(b), d(a, b)\} \tag{7}$$

where $d(a, b)$ is the original metric distance between a and b. Under this metric dense points (with low core distance) remain the same distance from each other but sparser points are pushed away to be at least their core distance away from any other point.

3 Study Area and Data

In this study, we choose is Baiyun District as the study area, Guangzhou City. It is the largest area and the largest permanent population in the central urban area of Guangzhou. It ranks in the forefront of Guangzhou in terms of economy, transportation and industry, and has perfect infrastructure service facilities. The POIs dataset is obtained by an open-source data platform, Peking University Research Data (State Information Center). This dataset is derived from the Gaode Map Services (https://ditu.amap.com/), which is a famous map service provider in China, with a time span to September 30, 2019. We extracted a total of 156603 POIs in the study area. In geographic information systems (GISs), a POIs can be a house, a shop, a bus stop, even a mailbox, and so on.

Among them, multilevel categories are mainly divided into three categories: top-level, second-level and third-level, where the descriptions of the POIs are provided in greater detail along with the category-level upgrades. In this POIs dataset, there are 12 labels in the top-level category, 200 labels in the second-level category and 537 labels in the third level category. In this study, we use two level categories, the top and second-level category, are employed and ignore the third-level category because the third-level category is relatively complex and superfluous. For example, Chinese food restaurants in the second-level category can be divided into more than 112 third-level labels, such as Sichuan food restaurants and Cantonese food restaurants, which seem to be unnecessary and could be ignored.

4 Regional Co-location Pattern Mining Method Based on Representation Learning Model (RCPM_RLM)

With the help of the word embedding model, the algorithm proposed in this paper use the method of representation learning to extract the feature vectors of POI types. Then find the cluster core instance and divided the functional regions of the city by means of the HDBSCAN clustering algorithm. Finally, perform co-location pattern mining on the functional regions by using the joinless co-location pattern mining algorithm [22].

Algorithm 1 RCPM_RLM

Input: $c, s, \lambda, minPI, I$
Output: P
1. $D \Leftarrow$ Representation learning (I, m)
2. Mark all objects in dataset D as unprocessed
3. for （each object v in the dataset D） do
4.   if （p Has been assigned to a certain cluster or marked as noise） then
5.   continue;
6.   else
7.   Check the Eps neighborhood of object v NEps(v) ;
8.   if (NEps(v) Contains less than objects MinPts) then
9.   Mark the object v as boundary point ornoise point;
10.   else
11.   Mark the object v as a core point, and build a new
               cluster C, and add all points in the neighborhood of v to C
12.   for (All objects q in NEps(v) that have not yet
                   been processed) do
13.   Check its Eps neighborhood NEps(q),
               If NEps(q) contains at least MinPts objects, the objects in NEps(q)
               that are not classified in any of the clusters are added to C;
14.   end for
15.   end if
16.   end if
17. end for
18. $P \Leftarrow \varnothing$
19. for $Fj \in F$ do
20. $P \Leftarrow P \cup$ (Joinless($Fj, minPI, dj$), Fj)
21. end for

Firstly, Algorithm 1 extract the feature vectors of POI types, by using the word embedding model. Word2Vec model has two network structures: CBOW and Skip-Gram. When the amount of data is small, Skip-Gram model is more suitable to choose [23, 24]. In this study, the data scale is relatively small, so the Skip-Gram model is used to train the neural network. The neighboring POI types are predicted based on the central POI types, and the goal is to simulate the probability distribution of the real POI types from the training data. In this paper, referring to the study of Yan et al. [25], Cross-Entropy is used to measure the difference between the predicted probability and the true probability.

Secondly, the HDBSCAN clustering algorithm should have at least 1 min-cluster-size, the larger this parameter is, the smaller the number of clusters will be. So, the parameter c must be set greater than one. A point must have at least min-samples samples in its neighborhood to be considered a core point. The larger the value of min-samples provided, the more conservative the clustering, the more points will be declared as noise, and the clustering will be restricted to gradually dense regions.

5 Algorithm Complexity Analysis

Suppose the dataset comprises n instances, m clusters, and k nearest neighbors are taken into account. The algorithm needs $O(n^2)$ time complexity to calculate the neighborhood of the instance, and $O(n^2)$ time complexity to calculate the relative distance. Because we can use prim minimum spanning tree and other methods to optimize the algorithm, the time complexity of the algorithm is lower than $O(n^2)$. Assuming that the average complexity of Join-less algorithm on each cluster is T_l, the total time complexity of the algorithm is $O(n^2 + m * T_l)$. The algorithm requires $O(k * n)$ space to store the nearest neighbor distance, and the space complexity to store the minimum spanning tree is $O(k * n)$. Assuming that the average space complexity of Join-less algorithm on each cluster is S_l, the total time complexity of the algorithm is $O(k * n + m * S_l)$.

6 Results

6.1 Clustering Results

Several trials were conducted to determine the optimal values for the key parameters of the HDBSCAN cluster method, namely min cluster size (represented by c) and min samples (represented by s), in our case study. This was achieved by executing the cosine-distance measurement-based HDBSCAN cluster method with varying values of c (ranging from 2 to 126) and s (ranging from 1 to 126). The evaluation of results was based on both the silhouette metric and the number of clusters. To interpret the clustering outcomes, we utilized a POIs database, and subsequently calculated enrichment factors for POIs.

When $c = 90$ and $s = 50$, cluster 1 primarily represents corporate business areas or factories, while cluster 2 can be categorized as shopping malls. Cluster 3 predominantly comprises hospitals, daily life service establishments, and food and beverage locations. Cluster 4 largely encompasses tourism attractions, science and education areas, as well as transportation facilities (Tables 1). When $c = 50$ and $s = 50$, the clusters exhibit greater specificity. Specifically, Cluster 1 represents corporate business areas or factories; Cluster 2 predominantly comprises shopping malls; Cluster 3 primarily encompasses tourism attractions and public facilities; Cluster 4 largely denotes transportation facilities; Cluster 5 signifies science and education locations; Cluster 6 mainly consists of hospitals, food and beverage establishments, as well as daily life service places; while Cluster 7 predominantly represents governmental and public organizations (Table 2).

Therefore, our findings indicate that cluster 1 and cluster 2 from scheme A, as well as cluster 1 and cluster 2 from scheme B, exhibit identical characteristics in terms of both geography (Fig. 1) and category attributes (Table 3). Consequently, it can be inferred that scheme B represents a further decomposition of the clusters identified in scheme A. Furthermore, through an analysis of regional clustering, we are able to gain a comprehensive visual understanding of the distribution patterns pertaining to urban land use.

Table 1. Enrichment factors of POIs categories (EP) grouped by clusters for c = 90 and s = 50

Types	Cluster1	Cluster2	Cluster3	Cluster4
1. Transportation	0.757	0,750	0.565	1.086
2. Residence	0.683	0.765	0.750	1.035
3. Sports	0.593	0.646	0.113	1.117
4. Food	1.113	0.453	0.675	0.968
5. Tourism attraction	3.534	0.142	0.523	0.765
6. Medical service	0.650	0.356	0.452	0.690
7. Business building	0.943	0.147	0.464	0.563
8. Public organizations	0.834	0.573	0.879	0.673
9. Daily life service	1.032	0.768	1.201	0.897
10. Science/Education	0.123	0.131	0.678	0.789
11. Shopping mall	0.976	0.567	0.797	0.903
12. Bank/Financial	0.111	0.563	0.569	0.324

Table 2. Enrichment factors of POIs categories (EP) grouped by clusters for c = 50 and s = 50

Types	Cluster1	Cluster2	Cluster3	Cluster4	Cluster5	Cluster6	Cluster7
1.	0.764	0.735	1.279	2.413	1.135	0.694	0.812
2.	0.657	0.715	0.665	0.711	1.105	0.817	0.586
3.	0.483	0.633	1.154	1.055	1.087	1.206	0.679
4.	1.076	0.635	3.926	1.055	0.704	0.565	0.865
5.	2.875	1.015	0.569	0.541	0.964	0.479	0.828
6.	0.617	0.679	0.247	0.756	1.107	1.679	1.240
7.	1.004	0.795	0.531	1.035	1.631	0.863	1.147
8.	0.947	0.912	0.875	0.679	0.791	1.126	2.785
9.	0.868	0.763	0.532	1.001	0.625	1.612	1.117
10.	0.712	0.465	0.500	0.975	3,579	0.570	0.824
11.	0,769	2.450	0.317	0.648	0.504	1.137	0.902
12.	1.048	0.719	0.206	0.675	0.302	0.655	0.836

6.2 RCPM_RLM Mining Results

In this study, we applied the RCPM_RLM algorithm to analyze the Baiyun District Guangzhou City dataset (Table 4) and compared its performance with both global spatial co-location pattern methods and other regional spatial co-location pattern mining algorithms. It is important to note that, in order to facilitate a fair comparison between

Table 3. The correspondence between the functional areas of the city and clusters

Functional area types	$c = 90$ and $s = 50$	$c = 50$ and $s = 50$
Business	Cluster1	Cluster1
Shopping mall	Cluster2	Cluster2
Tourism attraction	Cluster4	Cluster3
Public organizations	Cluster4	Cluster3
Transportation	Cluster4	Cluster4
Science/Education	Cluster4	Cluster5
Medical service, food and daily life service	Cluster3	Cluster6
Bank/Financial	Cluster3	Cluster7

the results obtained from the global spatial co-location pattern mining algorithm and our proposed algorithm, we set the neighbor distance threshold of the former to 100, which exceeds the actual core distance of 90 determined by the HDBSCAN clustering algorithms. The min cluster size c is set to 90, min cluster size s is set to 50, and the prevalent threshold is set to 0.6. The proposed RCPM_RLM algorithm mines 63 patterns, including 12 regional patterns that cannot present in the global spatial co-location patterns (Table 5).

Multi-level algorithm is a method to mine global and regional co-location patterns based on uniform coefficient of instance distribution. But this method uses grid division to divide the area, and gives a clear boundary to the mining area artificially. FDPC-PRCPM algorithm introduced a density peak based clustering combining with fuzzy set theory and k-nearest neighbor distance to an applicable regional co-location pattern mining. However, it only divides the functional regions through density of instances, ignoring the spatial correlation within, which makes the identification results biased towards a higher number of instances. RCPM_RLM algorithm uses word vector to represent the semantic information of words, so that semantically similar words are close to each other in the representation space, and the division of regions is more reasonable. This could potentially explain why the RCPM_RLM algorithm is capable of mining a greater number of regional co-location patterns.

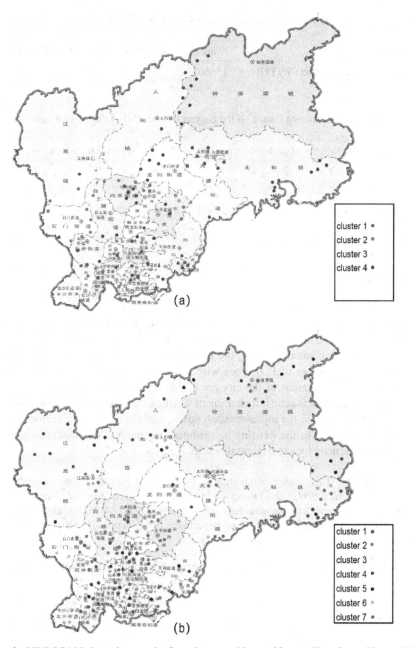

Fig. 1. HDBSCAN clustering results for schemes with $c = 90$, $s = 50$ and $c = 50$, $s = 50$.

Table 4. The Baiyun District Guangzhou City dataset

Dataset	Number of incidences	Number of features
Baiyun District Guangzhou City POI	156603	12

Table 5. The mining results on the Baiyun District Guangzhou City dataset

Algorithm	Number of co-location patterns	Number of regional co-location patterns
RCPM_RLM	63	12
FDPC-PRCPM	61	10
Multi-level	58	8
Reference [22]	51	0

7 Summary

We propose a new algorithm for mining regional co-location patterns, which aims to investigate an NLP-driven approach for inferring urban functional regions, with a primary focus on addressing the prevalent challenges of ubiquitous homonymy and polysemy within urban contexts. Firstly, the method of representation learning is used to extract the feature vectors of POI types with the help of the word embedding model, and then the functional areas of the city are divided. Secondly, the method uses word vector to represent the semantic information of words, so that semantically similar words are close to each other in the representation space, and the division of regions is more reasonable. Compared to the existing algorithms, our method demonstrates a greater potential, as evidenced by experimental results.

Acknowledgments. This work is supported by the National Natural Science Foundation of China (62276227, 62306266), the Project of Innovative Research Team of Yunnan Province (2018HC019), the Yunnan Fundamental Research Projects (202201AS070015) and the Scientific Research Fund Project of Yunnan Provincial Department of Education (2023Y0248).

Disclosure of Interests.   The authors have no competing interests to declare that are relevant to the content of this article.

References

1. Zhang, H., Zhou, X., et al.: Detecting colocation flow patterns in the geographical interaction data. Geogr. Anal. **54**, 84–103 (2022)
2. Baride, S., Saxena, A.S., Goyal, V.: Efficiently mining colocation patterns for range query. Big Data Res. **31**, 1–13 (2022)
3. Roya, H., Ali, A., Sayeh, B.: An event-based model and a map visualization approach for spatiotemporal association relations discovery of diseases diffusion. Sustain. Cities Soc. (2022)

4. Wang, Y., Zhu, D.: A hypergraph-based hybrid graph convolutional network for intracity human activity intensity prediction and geographic relationship interpretation. Inf. Fusion **104**, 102149 (2024)
5. McInnes, L., et al.: HDBSCAN: hierarchical density based clustering. J. Open Source Softw. **2**(11), 205 (2017)
6. Yao, X., Chen, L., Peng, L., Chi, T.: A co-location pattern-mining algorithm with a density-weighted distance thresholding consideration. Inf. Sci. **396**, 144–161 (2017)
7. Cai, J., Deng, M., et al.: Nonparametric significance test for discovery of network-constrained spatial co-location patterns. Geogr. Anal. **51**(1), 3–22 (2019)
8. Zhou, M., Ai, T., et al.: A visualization approach for discovering colocation patterns. Int. J. Geogr. Inf. Sci. **33**(3), 567–592 (2019)
9. 蒋希文, 王丽珍, 周丽华. 基于模糊密度峰值聚类的区域同位模式并行挖掘算法. 中国科学: 信息科学 **53**(7), 1281–1298 (2023)
10. Dong, X., Gong, Y., Cao, L.: F-NSP+: a fast negative sequential patterns mining method with self-adaptive data storage. Pattern Recogn. **84**, 13–27 (2018)
11. Gao, X., Gong, Y., Xu, T., Lu, J., Zhao, Y., Dong, X.: Towards to better structure and constraint to mine negative sequential patterns. IEEE Trans. Neural Netw. Learn. Syst. **34**(2), 571–585 (2023)
12. Qiu, P., Gong, Y., Zhao, Y., Cao, L., Zhang, C., Dong, X.: An efficient method for modeling non-occurring behaviors by negative sequential patterns with loose constraints. IEEE Trans. Neural Netw. Learn. Syst. **34**(4), 1864–1878 (2023)
13. Dong, X., Gong, Y., Cao, L.: E-RNSP: an efficient method for mining repetition negative sequential patterns. IEEE Trans. Cybern. **50**(5), 2084–2096 (2020)
14. Dong, X., Qiu, P., Lv, J., Cao, L., Xu, T.: Mining top-k useful negative sequential patterns via learning. IEEE Trans. Neural Netw. Learn. Syst. **30**(9), 2764–2778 (2019)
15. Dong, X., Zheng, Z., Cao, L., et al.: e-NSP: efficient negative sequential pattern mining based on identified positive patterns without database rescanning. In: CIKM, pp. 825–830 (2011)
16. Wang, D., Wang, L., Jiang, X., Yang, P.: RCPM_CFI: a regional core pattern mining method based on core feature influence. Inf. Sci. 119895 (2023)
17. 刘新斌, 王丽珍, 周丽华. MLCPM-UC: 一种基于模式实例分布均匀系数的多级co-location模式挖掘算法. 计算机科学 **48**(11), 208–218 (2021)
18. Celik, M., Kang, J., Shekhar, S.: Zonal co-location pattern discovery with dynamic parameters. In: Proceedings of the 7th IEEE International Conference on Data Mining, pp. 28–31 (2007)
19. Mikolov, T., Chen, K., Corrado, G.S., Dean, J.A.: Computing numeric representations of words in a high-dimensional space. Google Patents (2015)
20. Rong, X.: word2vec parameter learning explained. arXiv preprint arXiv:1411.2783 (2014)
21. Sheng, H., Zhan, J., Liang, W., et al.: A framework for extracting urban functional regions based on multiprototype word embeddings using points-of-interest data. Comput. Environ. Urban Syst. **80**, 101442 (2020)
22. Yoo, J., Shekhar, S.: A joinless approach for mining spatial colocation patterns. IEEE Trans. Knowl. Data Eng. **18**(10), 1323–1337 (2006)
23. Yang, J., Cao, J., He, R., et al.: A unified clustering approach for identifying functional zones in suburban and urban areas. In: IEEE INFCOM 2018-IEEE Conference on Computer Communications Workshops (INFOCOM WKSHPS), pp. 94–99 (2018)
24. Yao, Y., Li, X., Liu, X., et al.: Sensing spatial distribution of urban land use by integrating points-of-interest and Google Word2Vec mode. Int. J. Geogr. Inf. Sci. **31**(4), 825–848 (2017)
25. Yan, B., Janowicz, K., Mai, G., et al.: From ITDL to Place2vec: reasoning about place type similarity and relatedness by learning embeddings from augmented spatial contexts. In: Proceedings of the 25th ACM SIGSPATIAL International Conference on Advances in Geographic Information Systems, vol. 35, pp. 1–10. ACM (2017)

Construction of a Large-Scale Maritime Elements Semantic Schema Based on Heterogeneous Graph Models

Xiaotong Liu[1], Yong Li[1], Peng Wang[2], and Qiang Mei[3(✉)]

[1] School of Software Engineering, Beijing University of Technology, Beijing, China
[2] Institute of Computing Technology, Chinese Academy of Sciences, Beijing, China
[3] Navigation College, Jimei University, Xiamen, China
meiqiang@jmu.edu.cn

Abstract. From the perspective of optimizing maritime logistics, a key focus in the field of maritime information research has been how to extract behavioral patterns and deep behavioral characteristics of vessels from vast amounts of shipping statistics. Additionally, aligning these characteristics with infrastructure such as berths for effective association and recommendation to vessels is a critical requirement for the evolution of intelligent maritime systems. Traditional methods primarily focus on the behavioral trajectories of vessel navigation, failing to explore the geographical interconnections between vessels and port infrastructure. In light of this, this paper proposes a framework for deep mining of shipping information based on knowledge graph technology. Utilizing AIS data and spatial data of port facilities, it constructs a semantic relationship in the form of triplets between vessels, berths, and waterways, and semantically models vessel behaviors. Effective identification of vessels is achieved based on various semantic information. Simultaneously, based on the berthing semantic relationship between vessels and berths, a reverse semantic knowledge graph of berths is constructed with respect to vessel type, size, and class. This study compares different graph embedding methods, dimensionality reduction techniques, and classification approaches to achieve optimal experimental results. The findings indicate that the vessel type recognition accuracy in the proposed framework reached 83.1%, and the number of Identical Relationships between the recommended and original berths in similar berth recommendations was 3.755. The experiments demonstrate that the framework can provide a technical foundation for deep mining of vessel behavior, vessel type identification, and berth recommendation, as well as a semantic basis for large-scale maritime models.

Keywords: Knowledge Graph · Graph Embedding · Intelligent Maritime · Ship Classification · Similar Berth Recommendation

---

X. Liu—Student Author.

X. Meng et al. (Eds.): SpatialDI 2024, LNCS 14619, pp. 132–151, 2024.
https://doi.org/10.1007/978-981-97-2966-1_11

1 Introduction

With the increasing global maritime business and the growing number of ships, maritime traffic systems are facing challenges such as congested waterways and inflexible ship scheduling. Therefore, focusing on the complexities of shipping route connectivity, imbalances in cargo flow, and dynamic changes in sea conditions, research on intelligent transportation management systems for the maritime sector has become a key research direction in the field of maritime traffic. The advantage of intelligent maritime systems lies in providing more intelligent and efficient decision support for shipping. Through deep learning and analysis of historical shipping data, these systems are capable of predicting future shipping trends, offering scientific bases for vessel scheduling, port planning, and route optimization. The application of intelligent maritime systems not only helps to improve the efficiency of the entire shipping network but also provides sustainable path planning and management tools for the realization of green and low-carbon shipping.

Early intelligent maritime systems were primarily implemented through distributed devices integrated with artificial intelligence and machine learning systems. For example, equipping vessels with various sensors, such as GPS, radar, and meteorological sensors, enabled real-time monitoring of the vessel's position and other state information. However, the maritime domain involves complex spatiotemporal relationships, including vessel motion trajectories, weather changes, and port activities. Traditional artificial intelligence and machine learning methods have relatively limited capability in representing knowledge, making it challenging to capture and model the spatiotemporal relationships among these complex interactions. Furthermore, data from multiple sources may be in different formats and standards, generated by different devices and systems, leading to heterogeneity among the data. Integrating these heterogeneous data is a challenge, especially in early intelligent maritime systems where issues of standardization and interoperability had not been fully addressed. The introduction of knowledge graphs enables better modeling of the complex spatiotemporal relationships among entities. This provides a more comprehensive means of modeling and analysis in the maritime field, particularly for information fusion considering spatiotemporal factors. Knowledge graph modeling offers strong semantic consistency by defining entities and relationships, making information easier to understand and interpret. This helps eliminate semantic discrepancies in information fusion, ensuring standardization and consistency across data. Moreover, compared to early distributed device and machine learning approaches, knowledge graphs store knowledge in the form of graph data, supporting more complex intelligent queries and reasoning, while being highly scalable to flexibly integrate new entities and relationships. This characteristic, applied in the maritime field, allows systems to conduct more in-depth analysis through the rules and relationships in the knowledge graph and to flexibly adapt to changing information needs for a wider range of downstream tasks. The architecture of the intelligent maritime system proposed based on the knowledge graph is illustrated in Fig. 1.

A knowledge graph is a network composed of entities and the relationships between them. Each entity and its associated attribute values are used to describe knowledge points, while the relationships connecting entities describe the associations between knowledge points. A knowledge graph G can be represented as G $\in$ (E, R, S), where

$E = \{e_1, e_2, \ldots, e_n\}$ represents the set of entities in the knowledge base, containing $|E|$ different entities; $R = \{r_1, r_2, \ldots, r_n\}$ represents the set of relationships in the knowledge base, containing $|R|$ different relationships; and $S \subseteq E \times R \times E$ represents the set of triples in the knowledge base. The basic form of a triple can be represented as $s = (h, r, t)$, where $h, t \in E$ represent the head and tail entities in the triple, and $r \in R$ represents the relationship connecting the head and tail entities. For example, in the triple (Cat, Belongs to, Mammals), the head and tail entities are "Cat" and "Mammals," respectively, which are two concrete things in the real world, while "Belongs to" is the relational attribute connecting the head and tail entities.

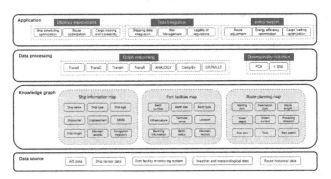

Fig. 1. Intelligent Maritime Application Framework Architecture

The graph data in knowledge graphs contain a large number of nodes and edges, constituting a high-dimensional data form. While processing high-dimensional data is feasible in some cases, it often leads to several issues such as computational complexity, the curse of dimensionality, and challenges in interpretability and visualization. Therefore, to transform high-dimensional graph data into lower-dimensional vector data, graph embedding methods are introduced. Graph embedding techniques involve converting the nodes and edges in knowledge graphs into vector representations in vector space. Vectors derived from graph embedding technology can capture relationships, similarities, and structural features between nodes in the graph, facilitating the application of knowledge graphs in various data analysis and machine learning tasks. Common graph embedding techniques include TransE [1], TransD [2], and RESCAL [19], among others. These methods achieve dimensionality reduction and vector representation of graphs through different principles. There are already some studies that have applied knowledge graphs and graph embedding techniques in intelligent transportation and maritime-related industries [11, 20–23], such as in areas related to traffic anomaly detection, marine environmental monitoring, and maritime geographical analysis.

This paper combines knowledge graphs with the maritime domain to propose an intelligent maritime application framework based on knowledge graphs. The main contributions of this paper are as follows:

1. This paper presents practical solutions to real-world problems in the maritime industry. Utilizing knowledge graph embedding technology, we addressed the uncertainties in ship type prediction and the complexities in similar berth recommendation for these

two business scenarios. These solutions are beneficial in enhancing the operational efficiency of shipping companies, optimizing berth allocation, and reducing waiting times.

2. We propose an intelligent maritime application framework based on knowledge graphs and graph embedding technology. This framework not only integrates complex data of ships and infrastructure but also captures deep semantic relationships between entities through graph embedding algorithms. The design of this framework takes into account the specific needs of the maritime industry, and its modular design ensures scalability and adaptability for future applications.

3. The paper explores how to use this framework to support specific downstream tasks, namely ship type prediction and similar berth recommendation. We optimized combinations of embedding models, classification models, etc., significantly improving task accuracy. Furthermore, we experimentally validated the impact of different weight distributions in the combined model on the performance of the berth recommendation system, providing new insights for the design of intelligent recommendation systems.

The organization of this paper is as follows: Sect. 1 primarily introduces the challenges in the intelligent maritime domain and the proposition of methods integrating knowledge graphs. Section 2 discusses related work on knowledge graphs and ship behavior mining. Section 3 proposes an intelligent maritime application framework based on knowledge graphs and graph embedding technology. Section 4 validates the effectiveness and optimal performance of this framework for different downstream tasks through comparative experiments. Section 5 concludes the paper and presents future prospects.

2   Related Work

2.1   Overview of Related Work on Knowledge Graphs

Knowledge graphs, as a powerful tool for knowledge storage and representation, have had a widespread impact across multiple domains. With the rapid development of big data and artificial intelligence technologies, the research and application of knowledge graphs have increasingly become a topic of great interest in fields such as computer science, natural language processing, information retrieval, machine learning, and human-computer interaction.

In the research of knowledge graph-related algorithms, the main directions currently include enhancing downstream task performance and improving the accuracy of knowledge graph embeddings. Traditional knowledge graph embedding models have achieved impressive results in tasks like knowledge graph completion. However, most of these methods do not incorporate temporal dimensions and background knowledge. Li et al. [8] proposed a new rule-based embedding method that separates attributes from entities and uses logical rules to expand datasets, thereby improving the accuracy of knowledge graph completion tasks. Jiang et al. [9] introduced a novel link prediction framework based on a knowledge graph embedding multi-source hierarchical neural network to overcome challenges in effectively extracting complex graph information from knowledge graphs and building multiple feature knowledge semantic fusions.

Thanks to the strong knowledge representation capability of knowledge graphs, they have been widely applied in fields such as recommendation systems, intelligent search, and industrial production. Chen et al. [10] used official migration information of infected individuals from provincial and city websites to construct a knowledge graph containing COVID-19 patients' activity information, which was utilized for tracking, visualizing, and reporting in applications related to COVID-19. In the maritime domain, Liu et al. [11] developed a model based on Transformer-multi convolution bidirectional encoders to extract information needed for frontline management from maritime pollution prevention-related laws, regulations, and rules, addressing port state control inspections to prevent ship pollution. Gan et al. [12] collected and analyzed ship collision accident investigation reports published by the China Maritime Safety Administration in recent years, proposing a new method for constructing knowledge graphs to explore ship collision accidents, aiming to demonstrate the correlations between critical factors of accidents and thereby enhance maritime traffic safety.

Despite the widespread application of knowledge graphs in many domains, there are still some issues to be addressed in the realm of geographical information, particularly in maritime transportation. The first is real-time updating; maritime information, such as ship positions and weather conditions, can change at any moment. Therefore, knowledge graphs need to be capable of real-time updates to reflect the latest situations. Furthermore, integrating information from different data sources to ensure data consistency and interconnectivity for constructing a complete knowledge graph is challenging. Different data sources use various standards and formats, necessitating the development of effective data integration and cleansing methods.

2.2 Overview of Related Work on Ship Behavior Mining

Due to the powerful feature extraction capabilities demonstrated in recent years in the fields of deep neural networks, computer vision, and natural language processing, ship behavior mining has emerged as a significant application direction in the domain of intelligent maritime. Current research on ship behavior mining mainly focuses on ship trajectory detection, ship intention prediction, and ship classification.

A significant portion of work in ship behavior mining is based on convolutional neural networks (CNNs) and recurrent neural networks (RNNs). In the aspect of ship trajectory prediction, Wang et al. [13] proposed a novel ship trajectory prediction model based on a sparse multi-graph convolutional hybrid network. This model simulates effective interactions and motion trends between ships in both spatial and temporal dimensions and embeds temporally-aware ship trajectory features into the prediction framework. Ma et al. [14], through statistical analysis of observed ship movement trajectories, found that ship movements are often highly correlated with long-term past trajectories. Thus, they introduced an augmented long short-term memory network (ALSTM), which adds skip connections and adaptive memory modules to LSTM, allowing current memory units to interact with historical data for advanced representation of the uncertainty and diversified movement of individual ships. In terms of ship classification, Escorcia-Gutierrez et al. [15] utilized masked convolutional neural networks for small ship detection and employed a collision body optimization algorithm and weighted regularized extreme learning machine technique for effective classification of detected ships. Liang et al.

[16] proposed MVFFNet to achieve ship classification with imbalanced data. It first extracts multiple multi-view features from AIS-based ship trajectories and then introduces a bidirectional gated recurrent unit network to combine these multi-view features to generate ship classification results.

Another mainstream method for ship behavior mining is through multimodal approaches that extract features from different sensing modes and integrate these features together to achieve a more comprehensive understanding and data mining capability. Guo et al. [17] proposed a multimodal ship trajectory prediction method through pattern distribution modeling. This method introduces a vector randomly sampled from a multivariate Gaussian distribution as the encoding of trajectory patterns to generate multiple predicted trajectories, using adversarial learning to enable this Gaussian distribution to capture ship trajectory patterns. Ye et al. [18] proposed an adaptive data fusion model based on multi-source AIS data for predicting ship trajectories. This model integrates maritime mobile service identifiers and timestamps with multi-source AIS data, applying deep learning methods for feature learning and improving adaptability.

3   Technical Framework and Dataset

3.1   Technical Framework

Leveraging the flexible application of knowledge graphs in the maritime domain, this paper proposes an application framework based on two application scenarios: ship classification and similar berth recommendation. The framework involves embedding knowledge graphs using extensive port and ship AIS data, and utilizing the embedded vectors to accomplish corresponding downstream tasks. Additionally, our framework also offers a visualization feature, enabling the visualization of maritime knowledge graphs constructed based on the dataset.

Process Flowchart. The workflow of this framework is depicted in Fig. 2. Initially, ship and berth knowledge graphs are constructed based on triplet data. The knowledge graph embedding model is then employed for training to learn the representation vectors of ships and berths. To enhance computational efficiency, the learned representation vectors are subjected to dimensionality reduction. Finally, the reduced vectors are used for data analysis corresponding to downstream tasks. The types of tasks applied in this paper are ship classification models and similar berth recommendation.

Graph Embedding Model. The graph data in knowledge graphs contain a large number of nodes and edges, representing a high-dimensional data form. While processing high-dimensional data is feasible in some cases, it often leads to several challenges such as computational complexity, the curse of dimensionality, and difficulties in interpretability and visualization. Therefore, graph embedding methods are introduced to transform high-dimensional graph data into lower-dimensional vector data. Graph embedding involves converting the nodes and edges in knowledge graphs into vector representations in vector space. Vectors derived from graph embedding technology can capture relationships, similarities, and structural features between nodes in the graph, making the knowledge graph more conveniently applicable to various data analysis and machine

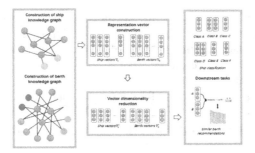

Fig. 2. Framework Flowchart

learning tasks. Our framework employs graph embedding models such as TransE [1], TransD [2], TransH [3], TransR [4], ANALOGY [5], ComplEx [6], and Distmult [7]. By extracting and learning the latent features of each relationship and entity related to berths, each berth is encoded into vectors of the same dimension, thus obtaining a quantifiable analysis feature representation of the berth.

Dimensionality Reduction Model. Although the aforementioned graph embedding models have already transformed graph data into vector representations in vector space, to enhance computational efficiency and more accurately focus on the important features of each berth representation vector, filtering out noise or redundant information in the data to make subsequent analyses more accurate, our framework incorporates traditional dimensionality reduction methods PCA and t-SNE for further processing of the representation vectors.

Classification Model. Based on the ship representation vectors obtained from dimensionality reduction, our framework integrates various classification models to categorize ships. These include K-Nearest Neighbors (KNN), Decision Trees, Random Forests, Support Vector Machines (SVM), and Gaussian Naive Bayes methods, among others. Utilizing a variety of machine learning classification models allows for exploration from multiple perspectives and different classification paradigms to identify the most suitable model for downstream tasks.

Similarity Calculation. The framework utilizes the cosine similarity metric for similarity analysis, thereby achieving the objective of discerning berth similarity. The formula for calculating cosine similarity is as follows:

$$Similarity = \cos\theta = \frac{A \cdot B}{||A||||B||}$$

where A and B represent two vectors, the denominator is the product of the magnitudes of the two vectors, and the numerator is the dot product of the two vectors. Cosine similarity is independent of vector dimensionality and is unaffected by the scale of the vectors, making the results easy to understand.

3.2 Dataset

The port-related dataset used in this paper is derived from AIS data, comprising two parts: the annual berth utilization rate statistics of Shanghai Port from 2021 to 2022 and the statistics of ships entering and leaving a certain port from January to May 2022. The dataset includes the number of ships in each category as shown in Table 1. In our experiments, we adopted the basic structure of knowledge graphs, triplets, to construct semantic relationships between ships and infrastructure. Through the format of triplets, we can build a rich semantic network that not only contains detailed information about ships and infrastructure but also various relationships between them, such as docking and affiliation. Figure 3 shows the visualization results of the berth knowledge graph constructed by this framework based on the port-related dataset, where Fig. 3a is an example of the ship knowledge graph, and Fig. 3b is an example of the berth knowledge graph.

This triplet-based construction method allows the knowledge graph to flexibly represent complex relationships between ships and infrastructure and provides a basis for using machine learning algorithms, especially embedding models. Through this semantic construction, we can more deeply illustrate and understand the dynamic relationships between ships and infrastructure, and further develop downstream tasks based on this.

In the classification task, we established 21,374 triplets of three types: (MMSI, Waterway, Waterway ID), (MMSI, Berth, Berth ID), and (MMSI, Anchorage, Anchorage ID) based on the statistics of ships entering and leaving the port. For the similar berth recommendation, we established 12,885 triplets of six types based on the annual berth utilization rate statistics of Shanghai, including (Berth ID, Affiliated, Port), (Berth ID, Belonging, Harbor District), (Berth ID, Berthed Ship Type, Ship Type), (Berth ID, Affiliated, Berth Office), (Berth ID, Berth Usage, Usage), and (Berth ID, Berthed Ship's Tonnage, Tonnage Type). The ship's tonnage types are divided into four categories: small-medium (0 t–5000 t), medium (5000 t–20000 t), large (20000 t–50000 t), and extra-large (over 50000 t).

Table 1. Number of Ships in Each Category in the Port-Related Dataset

Ship Category	Quantity
Dry bulk carrier	2610
Product oil tanker	600
Container vessel	365
Fishing boat	510
Roll-on-roll-off ship	115
LNG/LPG carrier	105
Total	4305

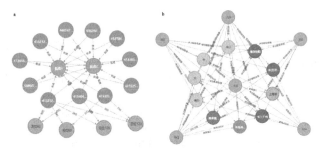

Fig. 3. Example of Graph Visualization Results

3.3 Introduction to Application Scenarios of the Framework

Scenario 1 - Ship Type Prediction. Ship type prediction, a key foundational technology in the intelligent maritime domain, plays a crucial role in ship traffic monitoring, port management, cargo tracking, as well as coastal patrol and border security. This paper utilizes knowledge graph embedding models to extract features across multiple dimensions and generate feature vectors. Subsequently, through dimensionality reduction and classification operations, test ships are categorized into predefined types.

Scenario 2 - Similar Berth Recommendation. Similar berth recommendation is one of the practical application scenarios in the intelligent maritime domain, employing modern information technology to provide optimal docking location suggestions for ships. This can assist ports in resource optimization, route optimization for shipping companies, and enhancing the efficiency of cargo loading and unloading. This paper establishes a berth knowledge graph and uses similarity calculation and recommendation to provide each berth with other similar berths that match it.

4 Experimental Results and Analysis

In this section, we conducted tests on the proposed model in typical downstream tasks to evaluate its performance in different datasets and application scenarios. We used our custom-built port-related dataset and conducted experiments for two downstream tasks: similar berth recommendation and ship type prediction. First, we introduce the semantic construction method of ships and infrastructure through the graph. Next, we discuss the evaluation metrics for each dataset, then test the performance capability of individual graph embedding models on the datasets. Finally, we evaluate the performance of combined models on the datasets and introduce ablation experiments and internal analysis to verify the effectiveness of each module in our framework.

4.1 Ship Type Prediction

Evaluation Metrics. For ship type prediction, we employed a supervised approach for classifying and validating ships. Therefore, traditional evaluation metrics for assessing the efficacy of classification models were adopted, namely Accuracy, Precision, Recall, F1 Score, Macro Average, and Weighted Average.

Accuracy: The proportion of correctly classified ship samples in the test set.

Precision: The proportion of correctly classified ship samples among all ship samples classified by the model.

Recall: The proportion of correctly classified samples in each category of the test set.

F1-Score: The harmonic mean of Precision and Recall.

Macro Average: The arithmetic mean of each metric for each classification. This metric treats each category equally but can be influenced by categories with fewer samples.

Weighted Average: The weighted average of each classification's metrics, based on the distribution of sample counts in each category in the total sample set. This metric considers the imbalance in the number of samples in each category.

Experimental Setup. In this experiment, within the port-related dataset, a series of relational triplets were constructed based on the ships' entry and exit data. The experiment implemented graph embedding models and supervised machine learning classification models using the PyTorch and Sci-kit Learn frameworks, respectively. The embedding vectors for each entity in the graph embedding model were set to 50, 100, and 200 dimensions. For classification models, comparative experiments were conducted using K-Nearest Neighbors (KNN), Decision Trees, Random Forests, Support Vector Machines (SVM), and Gaussian Naive Bayes methods to categorize ships into six classes: Dry Bulk Carriers, Product Oil Tankers, Container Vessels, Fishing Boats, Roll-on/Roll-off Ships, and LNG/LPG Carriers. The dataset was randomly split into 80% for the training set and 20% for the test set, with this random partitioning repeated five times to obtain the average results for each metric.

Experimental Results and Analysis. Applying the framework proposed in this paper to the port-related dataset for classifying ships, Figs. 4a, 4b, and 4c respectively show the precision, recall, and F1 scores for different graph embedding models and embedding dimensions in the port-related dataset, using all dimensionality reduction methods and classification approaches for classification experiments. The TransR model exhibited the best average classification performance across all metrics at an embedding dimension of 50, while the ComplEx and Distmult models also demonstrated notable performance in various metrics at different dimensions.

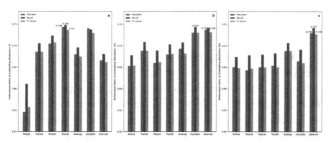

Fig. 4. Average Classification Results for Port-Related Dataset Classification Task Using Different Embedding Models

To determine the optimal dimensionality reduction method and dimensions, we selected the TransR, ComplEx, and Distmult models, which showed superior average performance, for the dimensionality reduction experiments. Figures 5, 6, and 7 display the average precision (Figs. 5a, 6a, 7a), recall (Figs. 5b, 6b, 7b), and F1 scores (Figs. 5c, 6c, 7c) obtained for ship classification tasks in the port-related dataset at different embedding dimensions using various dimensionality reduction methods and dimensions, employing all classification methods within our framework. The TransR model achieved the best classification performance at an embedding dimension of 50 using t-SNE for dimensionality reduction.

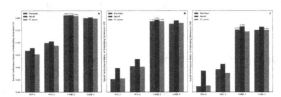

Fig. 5. Classification Results of TransR Using Different Dimensionality Reduction Methods and Dimensions

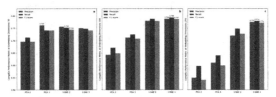

Fig. 6. Classification Results of ComplEx Using Different Dimensionality Reduction Methods and Dimensions

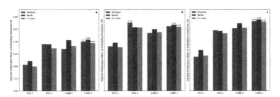

Fig. 7. Classification Results of Distmult Using Different Dimensionality Reduction Methods and Dimensions

Based on the optimal embedding model and dimensionality reduction combination, namely using the TransR model with an embedding dimension of 50 and t-SNE for dimensionality reduction, this paper further investigated the impact of different machine learning classification methods on ship classification results. Figures 8 and 9 display the visualization results of classifying each ship in the test set once, using the TransR model with an embedding dimension of 50 and t-SNE reduced to 2 or 3 dimensions, applying different classification methods under the same dataset partition and the same dimensionality distribution. Figures 8a, 8b, 8c, 8d, and 8e show the classification results when choosing KNN, Decision Trees, Random Forests, SVM, and Gaussian Naive Bayes methods as the classification model with a dimensionality reduction to 2 dimensions. Figures 9a, 9b, 9c, 9d, and 9e show the results for the same classification models with a dimensionality reduction to 3 dimensions. Based on the visualization results of different classification models, when all ship vectors are projected onto the same coordinate system, most models can effectively distinguish the accurate categories of ships in areas with unique and significant features.

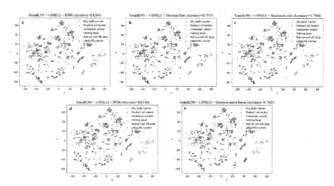

Fig. 8. Classification Results Using Different Methods with 50-Dimensional TransR Model Embedded and t-SNE Reduced to 2 Dimensions

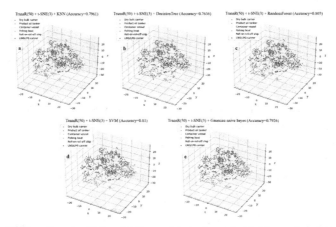

Fig. 9. Classification Results Using Different Methods with 50-Dimensional TransR Model Embedded and t-SNE Reduced to 3 Dimensions

To achieve more accurate experimental results, this paper randomly split the dataset into the same proportion five times and then used the t-SNE method to reduce the dimensions to 2D and 3D, conducting five classification experiments for each model and taking the average results. Figures 10a, 10b, and 10c show the average precision, recall, and F1 scores for different ship categories when the dimensionality reduction is 2D. Figures 10d, 10e, and 10f show these metrics for 3D dimensionality reduction.

Figures 11a and 11b present a comparison of macro-average results for overall test data precision, recall, and F1 scores at different dimensionality reductions. Figures 11c and 11d compare the weighted average results of these metrics. Figure 12 compares classification accuracy at different dimensionality reductions. The results indicate that using the TransR model with an embedding dimension of 50 and t-SNE reduction to 2D combined with the KNN model displays more precise classification performance in the majority of categories in the ship classification task on the port-related dataset. The optimal performance of this experimental model combination may be due to the dataset used being particularly suited to the relationships and hierarchies captured by the TransR model, and the 50-dimensional embedding vectors manage to preserve sufficient semantic information of the graph while avoiding overfitting. Combining t-SNE reduced to 2D with the KNN classification model effectively utilizes the ability of t-SNE to maintain local features of data, and the 2D space allows KNN to more effectively use its distance-based classification logic.

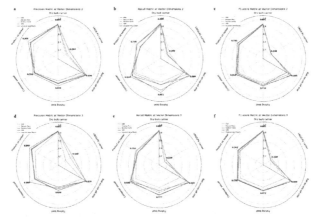

Fig. 10. Classification Results for Each Ship Category Using Different Dimensionality Reduction Dimensions and Classification Methods with 50-Dimensional TransR Model Combined with t-SNE Reduction

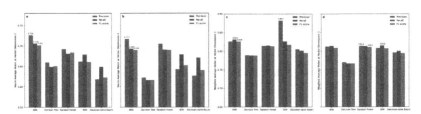

Fig. 11. Macro Average and Weighted Average Results Using Different Dimensionality Reduction Dimensions and Classification Methods with 50-Dimensional TransR Model Combined with t-SNE Reduction

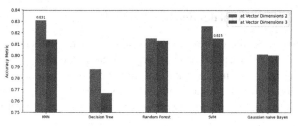

Fig. 12. Accuracy Using Different Dimensionality Reduction Dimensions and Classification Methods with 50-Dimensional TransR Model Combined with t-SNE Reduction

Ablation Study. To further evaluate the effectiveness of the components in our framework, we conducted an ablation study on the port-related dataset and analyzed the experimental results. Below are the designed model variants:

w/o DRM: Removed the embedding vector dimensionality reduction module to explore the impact of the dimensionality reduction module on ship classification.

Figures 13a, 13b, and 13c display the classification accuracy, recall, and F1 scores obtained by classifying ships in the port-related dataset using the 50-dimensional TransR model combined with the KNN classification method, as mentioned earlier as the most effective. The results are shown both with t-SNE reduction to 2D and without any dimensionality reduction. Compared to the classification results before dimensionality reduction, the performance in categories with a larger number of samples was better after applying t-SNE reduction. Overall, the classification precision, recall, and F1 scores were also better after using t-SNE reduction, demonstrating the effectiveness of the dimensionality reduction module in ship classification tasks. The use of dimensionality reduction techniques serves to filter out noise and typically retains the most important semantic features, aiding the classification model in focusing on distinctive features, thereby improving classification accuracy. Additionally, dimensionality reduction can result in a more uniform distribution of vectors in space, while similar vectors are relatively clustered together, aiding distance-based classifiers like KNN in classification.

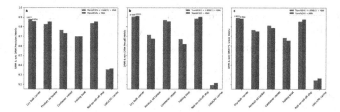

Fig. 13. Classification Results Before and After Using t-SNE Reduction with 50-Dimensional TransR Model Combined with KNN Classification Method

4.2 Similar Berth Recommendation

Evaluation Metrics. In the context of the similar berth recommendation system, we adopted six initial dimensions for construction: affiliated port, belonging harbor district, affiliated berth office, berth usage, type of ships berthed at the berth, and tonnage of ships berthed at the berth, to evaluate and determine the similarity between two berths. For each model, the evaluation accuracy p_a for a single berth a can be defined as follows:

$$p_a = r_a t (0 \leq r \leq 6)$$

In the formula, t represents the total number of similar berths output for a single compared berth, and r_a is the count of identical relationships between each similar berth and the compared berth a. If the calculation of similar berths is performed across the entire dataset, then the evaluation accuracy of the model, i.e., the Total Count of Identical Relationships P_{Full}, can be defined as:

$$P_{Full} = \sum_{i=1}^{n} p_i = \sum_{i=1}^{n} r_i t (0 \leq r_i \leq 6)$$

where n is the number of all berths in the dataset. The greater the number of identical relationships between the similar berths output for the entire dataset and the corresponding compared berths, the better the performance of the model is reflected. Additionally, we have defined the Average Count of Identical Relationships for Top t Recommended Berths P_{Topt} and the Average Count of Identical Relationships per Recommended Berth P_{Single}. These metrics respectively reflect the model's general recommendation capability for a single compared berth and the accuracy of the model's recommendation for a single similar berth:

$$P_{Topt} = \frac{P_{Full}}{n} = \frac{\sum_{i=1}^{n} p_i}{n} = \frac{\sum_{i=1}^{n} r_i t}{n} (0 \leq r_i \leq 6)$$

$$P_{Single} = \frac{P_{Topt}}{t} = \frac{P_{Full}}{nt} = \frac{\sum_{i=1}^{n} p_i}{nt} = \frac{\sum_{i=1}^{n} r_i}{n} ((0 \leq r_i \leq 6))$$

Experimental Setup. In this experiment within the port-related dataset, relevant triplets were pre-constructed, and for each berth to be compared, the top 20 berths with the highest similarity were recommended. The experiment implemented graph embedding models and berth similarity analysis models using the PyTorch framework. The dimensions of the embedding vectors generated by the graph embedding models were set to 50, 100, and 200 respectively.

Experimental Results and Analysis. The framework proposed in this paper was tested in the port-related dataset, first verifying the impact of dimensionality reduction methods on the results of recommending similar berths. Figures 14a, 14b, and 14c display the comparative results of the Total Count of Identical Relationships, the Average Count of Identical Relationships for the Top 20 Recommended Berths, and the Average Count of Identical Relationships per Recommended Berth for the TransE model's different dimensions after dimensionality reduction using various methods and dimensions for the task of recommending similar berths. It is observed that the best results for recommending similar berths are achieved when no dimensionality reduction method is used. The potential reason for this could be that in constructing the similar berth knowledge graph, this paper used more relationship dimensions compared to the ship classification mentioned earlier, leading to a richer feature set in the embedding vectors. Dimensionality reduction might result in the loss of these features, thereby causing a decline in the accuracy of the recommendations.

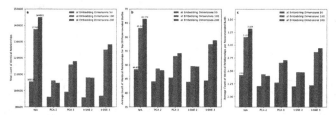

Fig. 14. Recommendation Accuracy of Different Dimensionality Reduction Methods in the Port-Related Dataset

Figures 15a, 15b, and 15c display the Total Count of Identical Relationships, the Average Count of Identical Relationships for the Top 20 Recommended Berths, and the Average Count of Identical Relationships per Recommended Berth for similar berth recommendation tasks in the port-related dataset using different embedding methods in our framework. The results show that Analogy performs best in terms of recommendation accuracy at an embedding dimension of 50. Considering that the port-related dataset includes six types of triplets, this may suggest that the berth knowledge graph has diverse relationship types, and Analogy may be more adept at capturing this diversity, especially at lower dimensions, effectively expressing these relationships without causing overfitting. Additionally, the Analogy model is particularly suited for processing analogical relationships, which in the context of the port-related dataset, may manifest as similar characteristics or functionalities between different berths.

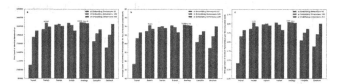

Fig. 15. Recommendation Accuracy of Different Embedding Models in the Port-Related Dataset

Based on the single base embedding model, this paper also designed a combined model for recommending similar berths. Figures 16a, 16b, and 16c show the comparative results of the Total Count of Identical Relationships, the Average Count of Identical Relationships for the Top 20 Recommended Berths, and the Average Count of Identical Relationships per Recommended Berth in the port-related dataset for the task of recommending similar berths when the similarity score weights of the two sub-models in the combined model are set at a 1:1 ratio. On the basis of the combined model, the combination of any two models shows higher recommendation accuracy than either of the single models involved in the combination, demonstrating that the combined model has better adaptability and performance in the task of recommending similar berths.

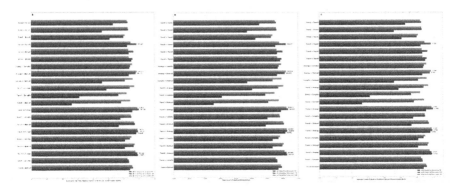

Fig. 16. Recommendation Accuracy of Various Combined Models in the Port-Related Dataset

As seen in Fig. 16, the combined models involving TransD, Analogy, and DistMult perform better in recommending similar berths compared to other combined models. The combination of TransD and Analogy models shows the best recommendation effect at an embedding dimension of 100, with an Average Count of Identical Relationships per Recommended Berth reaching 3.748. The TransD model captures complex semantic relationship features by defining a mapping matrix for each entity-relation, while the Analogy model emphasizes the symmetry and anti-symmetry of relationships between entities, which can help the model to capture finer similarities between berths. When these two models are combined, TransD's dynamic mapping capability and Analogy's symmetry capturing ability may complement each other, enabling the combined model to more comprehensively understand and represent the similarities between berths. To further investigate the impact of weight distribution on similarity results, this paper introduces a weight value n to the combined model of TransD, Analogy, and Distmult, exploring the influence of the two models on the results in the combined model based on these three embedding models. The computational impact of combining models A and B with a weight value n is assumed as follows:

$$Similarity_{union} = nSimilarity_A + (1 - n)Similarity_B$$

By fusing the similarity calculation values of two models, the combined model can inherit the recommendation tendencies and strengths of both sub-models. Figures 17, 18, and 19 show the trends of the Average Count of Identical Relationships per Recommended Berth for the TransD, Analogy, and Distmult models at different dimensions, using the port-related dataset for recommending similar berths. Figures 17a, 17b, and 17c show the trends for the TransD model at embedding dimensions of 50, 100, and 200, respectively. Figures 18a, 18b, and 18c show the trends for the Analogy model at the same dimensions, and Figs. 19a, 19b, and 19c show the trends for the Distmult model. The figures reveal that introducing the combined model significantly enhances the performance of similar berth recommendations, with the optimal recommendation effects at different dimensions showing variations in the weight value n. The combination of TransD and Analogy models performs best at n = 0.4, achieving an Average Count of Identical Relationships per Recommended Berth of 3.755. This indicates that the Analogy model may more effectively capture similarities between berths in the task of similar berth recommendation and the dataset used in this experiment. Although TransD's weight is slightly lower, it still makes a significant contribution to the final similarity calculation. The dynamic mapping mechanism provided by the TransD model may assist in capturing certain structured relationships, which might be less emphasized by the Analogy model.

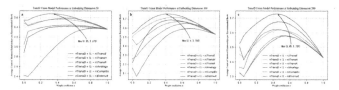

Fig. 17. Trend of Similar Berth Recommendation Results by TransD Model at Different Dimensions with Changes in Weight Value *n*

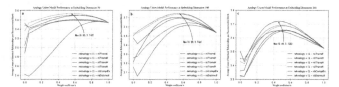

Fig. 18. Trend of Similar Berth Recommendation Results by Analogy Model at Different Dimensions with Changes in Weight Value *n*

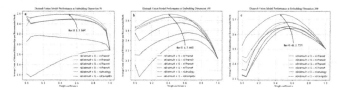

Fig. 19. Trend of Similar Berth Recommendation Results by Distmult Model at Different Dimensions with Changes in Weight Value *n*

5 Conclusion and Future Work

This study proposes an innovative intelligent maritime application framework based on knowledge graphs and graph embedding technologies, aimed at addressing key issues in the maritime industry, such as ship type prediction and berth recommendation. We first constructed a comprehensive knowledge graph, which not only contains rich information about ships and infrastructure but also accurately describes various relationships between them through triplets. Subsequently, we employed various graph embedding models to transform these complex relationships into operable vector forms, a crucial step for efficient prediction and recommendation. Through a series of comparative experiments, this paper not only validates the effectiveness of different embedding models in maritime applications but also explores the patterns of model performance variations with embedding dimensions and weight distribution. These experimental results provide empirical support for intelligent maritime applications and valuable data and insights for future research. This study showcases the immense potential of knowledge graphs and graph embedding technologies in practical industry applications, offering a feasible research template for researchers in other fields. Despite the achievements of this study, there remains room for further research. Future work could focus on enhancing model fusion and optimization, real-time data integration and dynamic updating, construction and application of cross-domain knowledge graphs, as well as scalability and improved generalization capabilities.

References

1. Bordes, A., Usunier, N., Garcia-Duran, A., Weston, J., Yakhnenko, O.: Translating embeddings for modeling multi-relational data. In: Advances in Neural Information Processing Systems, vol. 26 (2013)
2. Wang, Z., Zhang, J., Feng, J., Chen, Z.: Knowledge graph embedding by translating on hyperplanes. In: Proceedings of the AAAI Conference on Artificial Intelligence, vol. 28, no. 1 (2014)
3. Lin, Y., Liu, Z., Sun, M., Liu, Y., Zhu, X.: Learning entity and relation embeddings for knowledge graph completion. In: Proceedings of the AAAI Conference on Artificial Intelligence, vol. 29, no. 1 (2015)
4. Ji, G., He, S., Xu, L., Liu, K., Zhao, J.: Knowledge graph embedding via dynamic mapping matrix. In: Proceedings of the 53rd Annual Meeting of the Association for Computational Linguistics and the 7th International Joint Conference on Natural Language Processing (Volume 1: Long Papers), pp. 687–696 (2015)
5. Liu, H., Wu, Y., Yang, Y.: Analogical inference for multi-relational embeddings. In: International Conference on Machine Learning, pp. 2168–2178. PMLR (2017)
6. Trouillon, T., Welbl, J., Riedel, S., Gaussier, É., Bouchard, G.: Complex embeddings for simple link prediction. In: International Conference on Machine Learning, pp. 2071–2080. PMLR (2016)
7. Yang, B., Yih, W.T., He, X., Gao, J., Deng, L.: Embedding entities and relations for learning and inference in knowledge bases. arXiv preprint arXiv:1412.6575 (2014)
8. Li, J., Xiang, J., Cheng, J.: EARR: using rules to enhance the embedding of knowledge graph. Expert Syst. Appl. 120831 (2023)
9. Jiang, D., Wang, R., Xue, L., Yang, J.: Multisource hierarchical neural network for knowledge graph embedding. Expert Syst. Appl. **237**, 121446 (2024)
10. Chen, L., Liu, D., Yang, J., Jiang, M., Liu, S., Wang, Y.: Construction and application of COVID-19 infectors activity information knowledge graph. Comput. Biol. Med. **148**, 105908 (2022)
11. Liu, C., Zhang, X., Xu, Y., Xiang, B., Gan, L., Shu, Y.: Knowledge graph for maritime pollution regulations based on deep learning methods. Ocean Coast. Manag. **242**, 106679 (2023)

12. Gan, L., Ye, B., Huang, Z., Xu, Y., Chen, Q., Shu, Y.: Knowledge graph construction based on ship collision accident reports to improve maritime traffic safety. Ocean Coast. Manag. **240**, 106660 (2023)

13. Wang, S., Li, Y., Zhang, Z., Xing, H.: Big data driven vessel trajectory prediction based on sparse multi-graph convolutional hybrid network with spatio-temporal awareness. Ocean Eng. **287**, 115695 (2023)

14. Ma, J., Jia, C., Shu, Y., Liu, K., Zhang, Y., Hu, Y.: Intent prediction of vessels in intersection waterway based on learning vessel motion patterns with early observations. Ocean Eng. **232**, 109154 (2021)

15. Escorcia-Gutierrez, J., Gamarra, M., Beleño, K., Soto, C., Mansour, R.F.: Intelligent deep learning-enabled autonomous small ship detection and classification model. Comput. Electr. Eng. **100**, 107871 (2022)

16. Liang, M., Zhan, Y., Liu, R.W.: MVFFNet: multi-view feature fusion network for imbalanced ship classification. Pattern Recogn. Lett. **151**, 26–32 (2021)

17. Guo, S., Zhang, H., Guo, Y.: Toward multimodal vessel trajectory prediction by modeling the distribution of modes. Ocean Eng. **282**, 115020 (2023)

18. Xiao, Y., Li, X., Yin, J., Liang, W., Hu, Y.: Adaptive multi-source data fusion vessel trajectory prediction model for intelligent maritime traffic. Knowl.-Based Syst. **277**, 110799 (2023)

19. Nickel, M., Tresp, V., Kriegel, H.P.: A three-way model for collective learning on multi-relational data. In: Proceedings of ICML (International Conference on Machine Learning), vol. 11, no. 10.5555, pp. 3104482–3104584 (2011)

20. Liu, X., et al.: Multi-source knowledge graph reasoning for ocean oil spill detection from satellite SAR images. Int. J. Appl. Earth Obs. Geoinf. **116**, 103153 (2023)

21. Wang, H., et al.: A knowledge graph for standard carbonate microfacies and its application in the automatical reconstruction of the relative sea-level curve. Geosci. Front. **14**(5), 101535 (2023)

22. Ahmed, U., Srivastava, G., Djenouri, Y., Lin, J.C.W.: Knowledge graph-based trajectory outlier detection in sustainable smart cities. Sustain. Cities Soc. **78**, 103580 (2022)

23. Li, W., et al.: Location and time embedded feature representation for spatiotemporal traffic prediction. Expert Syst. Appl. **239**, 122449 (2024)

OCGATL: One-Class Graph Attention Networks with Transformation Learning for Anomaly Detection for Argo Data

Yongguo Jiang, Hua Liu$^{(\boxtimes)}$, Jiaxing Wang, and Guangda Zhai

Faculty of Information Science and Engineering, Ocean University of China,
Qingdao 266000, Shandong, China
jiangyg@ouc.edu.cn, liuhuaouc@stu.ouc.edu.cn

Abstract. As the typical representative of marine big data, the Argo plan conducts high-quality and scientific anomaly detection on Argo data, which is an important step in ocean science big data. However, in classical anomaly algorithms, Argo anomaly detection mostly has low accuracy, poor efficiency, and neglects the spatial continuity of Argo data. In the research on anomaly detection of spatial and regional data, graph anomaly detection has achieved excellent results. In the research of graph anomaly detection, depth based classification as a downstream anomaly detection method performs well, but at the same time, there are also problems of hyper sphere collapse and performance flipping. This article focuses on the research work related to the above issues: (1) Based on the study of Argo data and graph data, combined with the three-dimensional spatial characteristics of Argo buoy data, a novel graph data construction method is proposed. (2) Propose to incorporate neural transformation learning into the architecture, improve data learning expression ability, and further improve the shortcomings of graph neural classification, enabling it to adapt to the spatiotemporal and multi-dimensional characteristics of Argo buoy data for outlier detection. This article conducts experiments on five simulation datasets to demonstrate that the improved idea outperforms five state-of-the-art graph anomaly detection algorithms in various indicators, successfully improving the problems of hyper sphere collapse and performance flipping, and enhancing the accuracy and robustness of graph anomaly detection; The effectiveness of graph construction was demonstrated by comparing it with classical anomaly algorithms on real Argo sample data.

Keywords: Marine Data · Graph Anomaly Detection · Hypersphere Learning · Transformation learning

1 Introduction

Over the past 20 years, the Argo program has formed a global observation network consisting of more than 3,000 Argo profiling buoys with implementation

X. Meng et al. (Eds.): SpatialDI 2024, LNCS 14619, pp. 152–173, 2024.
https://doi.org/10.1007/978-981-97-2966-1_12

and maintenance. Not only can these buoys continue to operate, but they can also continuously return data to the data center, helping researchers understand large-scale changes in the ocean. In this context, high-quality scientific data management and anomaly detection of Argo data are necessary. Common Argo anomaly types are shown in the Fig. 1. The anomaly type in the left picture is the Argo profile point anomaly, and the anomaly type in the right picture is the overall Argo profile anomaly. Among the anomaly detection algorithms related to Argo data, the statistical anomaly detection method based on ARMA [1] only considers a single attribute; the improved K-means algorithm [2] has high time complexity and is not suitable for high-dimensional data; Zhang et al. [3] Combined with the Gaussian mixture model for detection, this method can identify profiles containing outliers, but the accuracy is not high enough and the error is large. In addition, these methods generally ignore the spatial continuity of Argo data and the impact of ocean changes on Argo data. At present, graph data is widely used in data representation in various fields to construct representations of spatiotemporal connections between data, and its anomaly detection algorithms have also achieved good results.

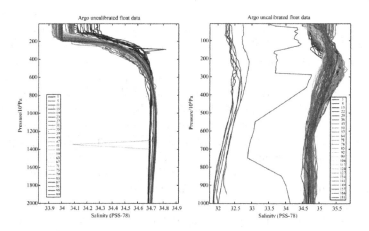

Fig. 1. Common Argo exception types

Graph data representation possesses unique advantages in expressing complex relationships, providing rich contextual information, handling unstructured data, overcoming local constraints, and adapting to dynamic changes. As a result, it has been widely applied in various fields. Concurrently, graph anomaly detection, which aims to identify anomalous nodes within a graph, has become an urgent and significant research problem that demands social attention [4]. It finds crucial applications in multiple security-related domains, such as detecting spam senders in social networks [5], diagnosing sensor faults [6], identifying financial fraudsters [7], and defending against graph adversarial attacks [8].

The development of deep learning has led to the development of Graph Neural Networks (GNN) [9]. In essence, GNN is a message-passing (or neighbor node aggregation) system where each node computes a new feature vector by averaging the feature data from its neighbors. The node's feature vector gathers the structural information of its nearby nodes through numerous iterations of information aggregation, which enables GNN to perform very well across a range of graph mining applications [10–12].

In graph anomaly detection, relationship learning-based methods show good performance.Among them, Wang et al. [13] proposed an end-to-end relation learning model called OCGNN (One-Class Graph Neural Network). This model leverages GNNs to automatically extract information from the graph and combines it with a deep one-class anomaly detection method, namely hypersphere learning [14]. By training on labeled normal data, OCGNN establishes a compact hypersphere boundary to separate normal and anomalous data. This strategy successfully blends the traditional hypersphere learning aim with the potent representation capabilities of GNNs. Moreover, the end-to-end manner ensures that the learned node representations are highly relevant to the GAD task. The utilization of Graph Attention Network (GAT) [15] in this method achieves the highest accuracy in anomaly detection.

However, Zhao and Akoglu et al. [16] discovered that in the task of graph anomaly detection using classification datasets, even when using such datasets where one class of samples is designated as "inlier" samples and the other class is significantly undersampled to create (real) "outlier" samples, the performance of deep anomaly detection methods is comparable to random methods. Through analysis, it has been found that this issue primarily stems from propagation-based graph neural networks amplifying the similarity among different inlier samples, thereby affecting the key features of the outlier distribution and indirectly impacting the difficulty of the outlier detection task, leading to performance reversal. This issue is commonly referred to as "performance flip".

A recent trend in anomaly detection tasks is to apply transformations to images [17] or tabular and sequential data [18] in order to enhance data representation and improve anomaly detection accuracy. These methods have shown excellent performance when applied to Euclidean data. However, the research on transformation learning in deep anomaly detection for graphs is very limited. So far, attempts to combine contrastive self-supervised deep learning methods with deep one-class anomaly detection and apply them to graph anomaly detection have not been successful.

In this paper, an Argo graph construction method and a graph anomaly detection model are proposed. Among them, the Argo graph construction method is based on studying Argo data and graph data, combined with the three-dimensional spatial regional characteristics of Argo buoy data, defining node data and edge data, and improving ocean data mining capabilities. A new graph anomaly detection method One-Class Graph Attention Networks with Transformation Learning (OCGATL), which leverages the expressive power of Graph Attention Networks (GAT) and combines deep one-class classification (Deep OCC) methods with self-supervised learning. The $T + 1$ Graph Attention Networks (GAT) that make up the OCGATL architecture are concurrently trained on two complementing deep anomaly detection losses. We show that this new combined loss alleviates the hypersphere collapse problem in previous deep-class anomaly detection methods, as well as experimentally confirm that we overcome the "performance flip" problem.To summarize, the following are our significant contributions:

- We proposed a method for constructing Argo spatial graphs, combining the three-dimensional spatial regional characteristics of Argo buoy data: defining dimensional data including pressure, temperature, salinity and other dimensional data in Argo data as node data, and at the same time using seawater flow speed, distance, direction, etc. Data related data is defined as edge data.
- We propose a novel end-to-end method for graph anomaly detection called OCGATL. This method combines the powerful representation capability of Graph Attention Networks with the advantages of the classical one-class hypersphere learning objective, while incorporating the idea of transformation learning.
- We study seven methods (four newly developed methods) on five real-world graph datasets, improving the architecture of existing depth map anomaly detection methods. Compared with previous work, OCGATL significantly improves the accuracy of anomaly detection and improves performance rollover and hypersphere collapse issues. Comparative experiments with classic anomaly detection methods on real Argo data confirmed the effectiveness of the Argo graph structure for Argo anomaly detection.

2   Related Work

This study's main objective is to discover nodes in a network that significantly diverge from the rest, which is a challenge known as "graph node anomaly detection." We looked into recent papers on deep anomaly detection techniques using one-class classifiers, transformation learning techniques, and graph anomaly detection to make sure our research was thorough.

2.1   Graph Anomaly Detection

Various studies have been conducted in graph anomaly detection to identify potential anomalies in real-world networks, such as fraudsters and network intruders [4,19]. The majority of conventional graph anomaly detection techniques use a two-stage approach. First, they use graph kernel techniques like the Weisfiler-Leman kernel [20] and propagation kernel [21] to develop graph vector representations. Second, they use shallow anomaly detectors like isolation forests (IF) [22], local outlier factors (LOF) [23], and one-class support vector machines (OCSVM) [24] to discover abnormal graphs based on these graph representations. However, the anomaly detection scores obtained by these methods rely on upstream task representation learning and depend on human expertise and prior knowledge for data analysis.

However, these methods are often limited by the architecture of autoencoders and suffer from overfitting issues between normal and abnormal data. To address such challenges, many researchers have employed approaches based on relational learning or contrastive self-supervised learning, which have demonstrated promising performance.

2.2   One-Class Classification

In Support Vector Data Description (SVDD) [25], the idea of hypersphere learning was first proposed. SVDD aimed to develop an efficient hypersphere boundary that covers all training data and determines which data points are similar to the training set. With the development of deep learning, Ruff et al. [14] created Deep SVDD, which trains a neural network model in accordance with the search for a minimal enclosing hypersphere to encapsulate the network representation of the data. The network can extract common features from a variety of data by minimizing the hypersphere that surrounds the representation of the training data.

One-class classification have been widely applied in graph anomaly detection. Wang et al. [13] proposed the OCGNN model, which utilizes graph neural networks (GNNs) to automatically extract information from the graph. By training on labeled normal data, the model obtains a compact hypersphere boundary to separate normal and anomalous data. Zhang et al. [26], on the other hand, measure anomalies from both the structural and attribute perspectives using structural hypersphere learning and attribute hypersphere learning. They demonstrate stronger performance than OCGNN, but their network size is significantly larger and time complexity is higher. Both approaches combine the powerful representation capabilities of GNNs with classical hypersphere learning, with GAT consistently achieving the best performance. These methods construct feature representations directly for the anomaly detection task, employing an end-to-end learning approach that allows joint training of deep neural networks and optimization of the data containing hyperspheres in the output space, resulting in better integration. However, there is a possibility of hypersphere collapse during the construction of the hypersphere model. Additionally, when Zhao and Akoglu [16] extended deep one-class classification for graph-level anomaly detection and developed OCGIN, they reported a "performance flip" issue, where the model performs worse than random on at least one experimental variant. This study aims to address these limitations and improve upon them.

2.3   Contrastive Learning

Self-supervised anomaly detection methods have made significant progress in the field of image analysis [27]. This task typically requires data augmentation, with two commonly used methods being transformation prediction [17] and contrastive learning [28].

Contrastive learning has also been extensively studied in the field of graph analysis. In these studies [29,30], leverage the maximization of mutual information to obtain rich feature representations by utilizing instances with similar semantic information. This approach has found wide application in recent research on graph representation learning. DGI [31] used local mutual information maximization to learn efficient representations of graph data and was the first to incorporate contrastive learning into methods for learning graph representations. To learn node representations, GMI [32] creates contrastive examples from both the edges' and nodes' perspectives. By utilizing adaptive graph data augmentation, GCA [33] creates a variety of contrastive perspectives in order to produce successful contrastive learning instances. For the purpose of creating pairs of graphs for contrastive learning, GraphCL [34] develops four different augmentation methods.

In the field of graph anomaly detection, many researchers have made attempts. Liu et al. [35] leverage instance pair sampling to capture the relationships between nodes and neighboring substructures by utilizing local information in attribute graphs, and employ a contrastive learning method based on GCN to learn node representations. Zheng et al. [36] combine generative and contrastive self-supervised learning strategies to fully utilize attribute information and contextual information by means of generative attribute reconstruction and multi-view level contrastive learning mechanisms, capturing anomalous patterns in multi-view settings. Subsequently, Zheng et al. [37] employ contrastive learning at both the patch level and the context level for multi-view anomaly detection, and further extend it by utilizing labeled small-sample anomaly data for training to enhance the accuracy of detection results.

In order to combine the benefits of connection learning with contrastive self-supervised learning for anomaly detection, it is proposed in this research to implement the concept of contrastive self-supervised learning by incorporating a data-driven transformation learning module into the model.

3 Preliminaries

In this section, we present an overview of graph node anomaly detection and introduce other relevant symbols and definitions.

Definition 1 (Attributed graph). *An attributed graph is $\mathcal{G} = (\mathcal{V}, \mathcal{E}, \mathcal{X})$, where $\mathcal{V}$ and $\mathcal{E}$ denote the node set $\{v_i\}_{i=1}^{n}$ and the edge set $\{e_{ij}\}$ of $\mathcal{G}$, respectively. $e_{ij} = (v_i, v_j)$ denotes an edge connecting nodes v_i and v_j. The node attributes are represented by $\mathcal{X} = [x_1, x_2, ..., x_n] \in \mathbb{R}^{n \times d}, x_i \in \mathbb{R}^d$, the attribute vector associated with node v_i and d is the attribute dimension.*

Definition 2 (Argo anomaly detection). *The model is trained to characterize the boundary of normal data given the anomaly-free training argo dataset $\{x_i\}_{i=1}^{n}$, and it then generates the anomaly score $S(x_u)$ for a hidden data point x_u. An outlier is a data point having a high anomaly score.*

Definition 3 (Performance Flip). *In benchmarks for anomaly detection built from binary classification datasets, Zhao and Akoglu [16] found a phenomenon they called "performance flip". We expand their definition to include several classes: if a model performs worse than random on at least one experimental variant, the model displays performance reversal on the anomaly detection benchmark derived from the classification dataset.*

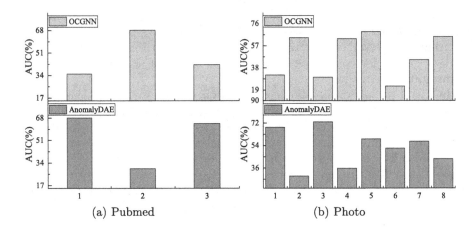

(a) Pubmed   (b) Photo

Fig. 2. Details of Performance Flip in Pubmed and Photo

For example, in Fig. 2, on the Pubmed dataset, OCGNN shows optimal performance on class 3 data, but inferior to random performance on both classes 1 and 2; AnomalyDAE performs exactly the opposite of OCGNN. A similar problem occurs in the industry on the Photo dataset.

4   Methodology

In this section, we first propose the Argo graph construction method and describe the data used in our work. Based on this graph, we finally propose a method called OCGATL to perform anomaly detection on Argo's spatial dependence.

4.1   Graph Construction

As mentioned before, Argo data is affected by many factors. In order to improve the prediction accuracy, we build a graph by taking domain knowledge as attributes on nodes and edges, and then learn the transfer and diffusion process based on the graph.

Node Attributes. We select the data collected by the Argo buoy itself as the node data, as shown Table 1:

Table 1. Argo node data dimension information

Variable Name	Unit
Date	(yymmdd-hh:mm:ss)
Latitude	(°)
Longitude	(°)
Pressure	dbar
Temperature	(°)
Salinity	PSU
Dissolved Oxygen	micromole/kg
Chlorophyll-a	mg/m^3
Backscattering700	m^{-1}
Nitrate	micromole/kg
Depth	m

Table 2. Argo edge data dimension information

Variable Name	Unit
Upward Sea Water Velocity	m/s
Eastward Sea Water Velocity	m/s
Northward Sea Water Velocity	m/s
Velocity	m/s
Distance	m
Advection coefficient	%

Edge Attributes. Changes in ocean currents in ocean areas will affect Argo buoy data collection. Among them, the data collected by the Argo buoy is related to various flow rates. Research [38, 39] shows that, the chlorophyll a mass concentration, dissolved oxygen, and ocean velocity are related. In the Colombia Maritime Network, sea velocity can be decomposed into upward sea velocity, eastward sea velocity, and northward sea velocity. The distance between nodes also determines the impact of changes. To incorporate these domain knowledge, an advection coefficient is defined capturing the transport from one place to another. As shown in Fig. 3, the starting location is denoted as source node i, and the target location is denoted as point j. We incorporate several variables related to these two nodes into the model and take inspiration from the literature [32] to estimate the amount of impact migration.

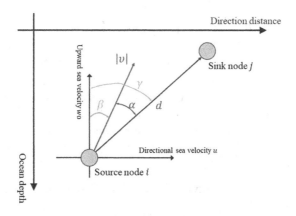

Fig. 3. A simplified model of influencing factors

Among them, $|v|$ is the combined speed from source node i to sink node j, d is the distance between nodes j and i, α is the angle between two directions: one is the direction flow velocity of the source node itself and the direction of the upward flow velocity β, the other is the direction γ from the source node to the sink node, and the direction flow velocity is the direction from the source node to the sink node in the plane The sum of the eastward ocean current velocity and the northward ocean current velocity in the direction of the node can be obtained by $\alpha = |\gamma - \beta|$. It is worth noting that the ReLU function only captures one-way transmission from the source point to the destination point, because each node has the opportunity to be a source node. For source node i to sink node j, if and only if the direction coefficient is not 0, the topological structure can be constructed. Among them, the specific calculation of the advection coefficient S is:

$$S = ReLU\left(\frac{|v|}{d}\cos(\alpha)\right) \tag{1}$$

In summary, we summarize the edgedata information of Argo data as shown in Table 2

4.2 OCGATL Model

Graph Attention Network. The attention mechanism enables a neural network to focus only on the information required for task learning, allowing it to selectively attend to specific inputs [40]. Introducing attention mechanisms into graph neural networks enables the network to prioritize nodes and edges that are more relevant to the task, thereby enhancing the effectiveness of training and the accuracy of testing, giving rise to graph attention networks. Depending on the specific attention mechanism, it can be categorized into self-attention, multi-head attention, hierarchical attention, etc. In this study, we employ a combination of multi-layer and multi-head attention. Among them, each GAT layer is configured with 8 attention heads, and the output obtained from each layer is defined as:

$$\boldsymbol{h}_i^{(l+1)} = \|_{k=1}^K \sigma\left(\sum_{j\in\mathcal{N}_i} \alpha_{ij}^{(k)} \boldsymbol{W}^{(k)} \boldsymbol{h}_j^{(l)}\right) \tag{2}$$

where K represents the number of attention heads, $\|$ denotes the concatenation operation, $\mathcal{N}_i$ for the collection of v_i's one-hop neighboring nodes, $\alpha_{ij}^{(k)}$ represents the weight between the node v_i and node v_j, coefficients computed by the kth attention mechanism, and $\boldsymbol{W}^{(k)}$ corresponds to the learnable parameters. In the final layer, to reduce the dimensionality, we replace the concatenation operation with the average operation. Where the complete formula for the initial GAT weight coefficients is:

$$e_{ij} = \text{LeakyReLU}(\boldsymbol{a}^{\mathrm{T}} \cdot [\boldsymbol{W}\boldsymbol{h}_i\|\boldsymbol{W}\boldsymbol{h}_j]) \tag{3}$$

$$\alpha_{ij} = \frac{\exp(e_{ij})}{\sum_{k\in\mathcal{N}_i}\exp(e_{ik})} \tag{4}$$

In GATv2 [41], improvements were made to GAT by transforming the original static attention into dynamic attention and making slight modifications to Eq. (3), which is now represented as:

$$e_{ij} = \boldsymbol{a}^{\mathrm{T}} \mathrm{LeakyReLU}(\boldsymbol{W} \cdot [\boldsymbol{h}_i \| \boldsymbol{h}_j]) \tag{5}$$

In our experiments, we will conduct experiments with GAT and GATv2 to compare the impact of these two representation models on OCGATL.

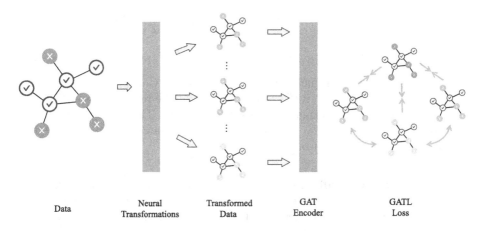

Data   Neural   Transformed   GAT   GATL
          Transformations   Data   Encoder   Loss

Fig. 4. Detail of Graph Transformation Learning

Graph Transformation Learning. Deep anomaly detection uses neural transformation learning as a self-supervised training goal and has seen success in fields including time series and tabular data. Here, we provide an overview of Qiu et al.'s [18] training objective and adapt it to graph data. When using GAT for feature extraction, for feature extractors f and $f1, \cdots, f_T$, according to Eq. (2), the learned node embeddings from each GAT feature extractor can be represented as:

$$h_i^{(l)} = \mathrm{GAT}^{(l)} \left(h_j^{(l-1)}; \boldsymbol{W}^{(l-1)} \mid j \in \mathcal{N}_i \right) \tag{6}$$

Then, by applying an readout function to combine $\boldsymbol{h}_i^{(l)}$ into layer-specific graph embeddings $\boldsymbol{f}_t(G)^{(l)}$, the graph embedding $\boldsymbol{f}_t(G)^{(l)}$ can be represented as:

$$\boldsymbol{f}_t(G)^{(l)} = \mathrm{READOUT}^{(l)} \left(h_i^{(l)} \mid i \in \mathcal{G} \right) \tag{7}$$

which are concatenated into a holistic graph representations,

$$\boldsymbol{f}_t(G) = \mathrm{CONCAT} \left(f_t(G)^{(l)} \mid l \in 1, ..., L \right) \tag{8}$$

This connection introduces information from different hierarchical levels into the graph representation [42], which is particularly important for reliable anomaly detection.

The loss function of GAT transformation learning promotes the diversity of combined embeddings $f_t(G)$ learned by each GAT feature extractor as shown in Fig. 4. Therefore, each GAT feature extractor f_t is capable of generating different views of G, thereby learning different node and attribute features. The contribution of each graph pair to the loss function can be expressed as:

$$\mathcal{L}_{GATL}(G) = -\sum_{t=1}^{T} \log \frac{\mathcal{Z}(g_t, g)}{\mathcal{Z}(g_t, g) + \sum_{l \neq t} \mathcal{Z}(g_t, g_l)} \tag{9}$$

$$\mathcal{Z}(g_t, g_l) = \exp\left(\text{sim}\left(f_t(G), f_l(G)\right)/\tau\right) \tag{10}$$

Here, the temperature parameter is denoted here by τ. Cosine similarity is used to define the similarity, $\text{sim}(z, z') := z^T z'/\|z\|\|z'\|$. The restrictions on parameter sharing between transformations have been left out. This decision was motivated by the finding made by You et al. that various categories of graphs favor various kinds of transformations.

Deep One-Class Classification. Our OCGATL approach integrates with the hyperbolic space learning objective to learn informative node representations. To achieve this goal, we introduce joint training of GAT and graph neural transformations. By considering the attributes and relationships of graph nodes and incorporating diverse data views, we learn node embeddings. These embeddings are then constrained within a minimum hypersphere to facilitate anomaly detection. Our goal in the deep one-class module is to decrease the hypersphere data volume defined by the radius r and center c while simultaneously learning the network parameters W. The loss function for deep one-classification may be written as: Given a graph G and n training nodes with the values v_i and v_j, the loss function can be written as:

$$\mathcal{L}_{OCC}(G) = \sum_{t=1}^{T} \mathcal{L}_t(G) \tag{11}$$

$$\mathcal{L}_t(G) = \frac{1}{\beta n} \sum_{v_i \in \mathcal{V}} \left[\|f_t(G)_{v_i} - c\|^2 - r^2\right]^+ + r^2 + \frac{\lambda}{2} \sum_{l=1}^{L} \left\|W^{(l)}\right\|^2 \tag{12}$$

Equation (11) represents the sum of all deep one-class losses of the feature extractors. In Eq. (12), the graph attention network receives information about all the nodes and edges in the graph. When the embedding vector's distance from the center c exceeds the radius r of the hypersphere, a penalty for embeddings of nodes outside the hypersphere is applied. Controlling the trade-off between the hypersphere's volume and the penalty is the hyperparameter $\beta \in (0, 1]$. The hypersphere's volume is minimized by the second term, which also minimizes r^2. The final term is a weight decay regularizer on the hyperparameter $\lambda > 0$ of the network parameters W. The goal of OCGATL is to train the network to map node embeddings contained within the c hypersphere. The training nodes are all normal, hence OCGATL extracts their shared characteristics. As a result, it is possible to identify problematic nodes and establish descriptive limits for normal nodes.

Loss Function. In this section, we will introduce our loss function and demonstrate the contribution of our method in addressing the limitation of ordinary solutions being optimal in deep one-class classification anomaly detection models.

OCGATL integrates the excellent expressive power of GAT, as well as the advantages of deep one-class classification and neural transformation learning. OCGATL jointly trains the extraction results of multiple feature extractors, including one feature extractor f on the original data and multiple feature extractors f_t $(t = 1, ..., T)$ after transforming the data. During the training process, each graph contributes to the loss in two ways:

$$\mathcal{L}_{OCGATL}(G) = \mathcal{L}_{OCC}(G) + \mathcal{L}_{GATL}(G) \tag{13}$$

The first term, $\mathcal{L}_{OCC}(G)$, is a deep one-class classification term that encourages all normal data to be as near together as possible and creates an enclosed hypersphere space for all data. The second term, $\mathcal{L}_{GATL}(G)$, requires that the GAT features produced by each feature extractors be identical to the original data, but that additional extractors must be distinct from one another.

Hypersphere collapse [14] is a known difficulty in training OCC-based deep anomaly detectors, like deep SVDD. A hypersphere collapse occurs when the ideal solution degenerates into a simple one. This phenomena can also happen in the OCGATL model. When all inputs are precisely mapped to the center by the feature extractor f, it occurs. Anomaly detection is impossible under such circumstances because the hypersphere's radius r becomes zero. Fixing c and staying away from bias terms in f was recommended by Ruff et al. and has produced positive outcomes in real-world applications. Not all f architectures, however, can be guaranteed to be free of simple solutions. We show how OCGATL fixes this issue.

Proposition 1. *The constant feature extractors, $f_t(G) = c$ for all t and all inputs G, minimize $\mathcal{L}_{OCC}(G)$ (Eq. 11)*

Proof. $0 \le \mathcal{L}_{OCC}(G)$ is the squared ℓ^2 norm of the distance between the embedding of $\mathcal{V}$ and the center r. Plugging in $f_t(G) = c$ attains the minimum 0.

Assuming that under a constant encoder, all potential views $f_t(G)$ are the same and equal to c, they are at least close to the reference embedding, resulting in $\mathcal{L}_{OCC}(G) \ge T \log T$. However, the goal of transformation learning is to make the reference embeddings similar to the original data while they are not identical to each other. In this case, it is required that $\mathcal{L}_{OCC}(G) < T \log T$. As a result, we can conclude that the two components in our loss function are complimentary, preventing hypersphere collapse and giving two directions of measurement for anomaly identification.

$\mathcal{L}_{OCGATL}(G)$ (Eq. 13) is used directly as the scoring function for anomaly detection during training. When the training sample loss is minimal, the graph is probably normal, and when the loss is significant, an anomaly is present.

5   Experiments

We carried out comprehensive experiments and compared our proposed framework with four cutting-edge graph anomaly detectors on five real-world attribute graph datasets to assess its performance. To evaluate the efficiency of specially created functional modules, we also conducted ablation analysis.

5.1   Simulation

Datasets. For fairness, we selected five real-world attribute graph datasets previously used in [13,43], to verify the effectiveness of our model. Tables 3 lists the statistical data of these five datasets.

Table 3. Datesets Statistics

Dataset	#Nodes	#Edges	#Feat.	Degree	Class
Cora	2708	10556	1433	3.9	7
Citeseer	3327	9104	3703	2.74	6
Pubmed	19717	88648	500	4.5	3
Photo	7650	238162	745	31.13	8
Computers	13752	491722	767	35.76	10

Publicly accessible citation network datasets like Cora, Citeseer, and Pubmed [44] have been extensively used in prior studies [15,45,46]. As nodes and edges in a graph, they represent scientific publications and the connections between citations made to them. Each publication's node features are specified by sparse bag-of-words feature vectors that were generated from dictionaries. The Amazon co-purchase graph [43], whose nodes represent products and edges signify frequent co-purchase relationships, is where the Photo and Computers datasets are drawn from. The category labels are provided by the product categories, while the node attributes are bag-of-words encoded product reviews.

Baselines. By contrasting our suggested framework with four representative, cutting-edge deep graph-based anomaly detectors, we were able to assess its effectiveness. The following four detectors are listed:

- **DONE** [47] is an anomaly detection model based on autoencoders, designed to identify abnormal nodes with high structural and attribute reconstruction errors. During the learning phase, the model automatically learns the scores for each node's anomalies and classifies the top K nodes with the highest scores as anomalies.
- **DOMINANT** [48] employs two separate decoders to reconstruct the node characteristics and graph topology after encoding the graph using GCN. The model uses the reconstruction error to give each node an anomaly score.
- **AnomalyDAE** [49] encodes the graph using a fully connected neural network and the node characteristics using an encoder with graph attention layers. Similar to DOMINANT, this model computes anomaly ratings based on reconstruction loss.
- **OCGNN** [13] uses hypersphere learning to define the line between abnormal and regular nodes. The class of graph neural networks that this work proposes is trained on typical data and recognizes anomalous nodes as those that are outside the taught hypersphere boundary.

Experimental Setup. In our trials, we constructed anomaly detection tasks from classification datasets [14] using the same settings as earlier research. The N experimental variations were produced by the N classifier datasets. One class was regarded as "normal" and the other classes as anomalies in each experimental version. The test set included both normal and anomaly samples, with the anomalies needing to be found during testing because the training and validation sets only included normal samples. To create the test set for each experimental variant, 10% of the data from the normal classes were set aside, and 10% from each of the other classes were added as anomalies. Training and validation were conducted using the remaining 90% of the normal class samples. To assess the models' performance, we used 10-fold cross-validation, with 10% of the training set being kept for validation after each fold. To achieve the final test results for each fold, we ran three training runs for each model, averaging the outcomes of the three runs. It facilitated the evaluation of methods with robustness to random initialization and ensured a fair comparison by allowing for several training runs.

Overall Performance Comparison. We evaluated our suggested framework, baselines, and their variations' capacity to detect anomalies using generally accepted assessment measures. Specifically, we reported the average metric values of our model and baselines over ten runs. The detection outcomes are reported as average AUC (%) and standard deviation in the Table 4.

The last column in Table 4 presents the average performance rankings across all 5 datasets. The asterisk (*) denotes instances where the method's performance was reversed from random in at least one experimental variant. It is evident that our method works better than previous methods and does not show Performance Flip.

Table 4. Average AUCs (%) with standard deviations of 7 methods of 5 datasets.

Methods	Cora	Citeseer	PubMed	Computers	Photo
DONE	48.43 ± 0.51*	50.66 ± 0.31*	49.15 ± 0.11*	51.47 ± 0.50	52.43 ± 0.21*
Dominant	48.66 ± 0.66*	49.90 ± 0.32*	49.77 ± 0.11*	49.08 ± 0.63*	50.00 ± 0.32*
AnomalyDAE	49.28 ± 0.45*	50.27 ± 0.26*	48.48 ± 0.03*	46.09 ± 0.60*	52.34 ± 0.43*
OCGAT	80.14 ± 0.57*	61.19 ± 1.00*	53.75 ± 0.03*	47.07 ± 0.25*	48.76 ± 0.28*
OCGCNL	64.31 ± 1.03*	60.35 ± 0.93	70.83 ± 0.21	71.93 ± 0.62*	68.22 ± 0.37
OCGATL(Ours)	**85.06 ± 1.07**	**76.43 ± 0.52**	**91.28 ± 0.54**	85.78 ± 0.54	**85.29 ± 0.45**
OCGATLv2(Ours)	84.10 ± 0.88	75.71 ± 0.66	90.90 ± 0.60	**85.99 ± 0.56**	84.58 ± 0.38

In the average results of three-fold ten-fold cross-validation on the five datasets, OCGATL significantly outperforms the baseline methods in terms of performance, showing an improvement of over 20% compared to any baseline method. As a result, we can say that OCGATL greatly improves the precision of graph-level anomaly identification. At the same time, most existing baseline methods suffer from performance reversal issues, whereas our approach is the only model that does not exhibit performance reversal on any dataset, successfully overcoming the limitations associated with performance reversal. Next, we will conduct an ablation analysis to further investigate the effectiveness of the GAT encoder and the transformer learning module in our framework.

Ablation Study. By reviewing the GAT neural network module and the transformation neural module, two functional modules specifically designed to address the challenges of anomaly detection accuracy and performance reversal, we conducted extensive ablation tests on five datasets, including four additional variants, as follows:

– OCGAT: The transformation neural module is excluded in OCGAT. It deploys a three-layer GAT architecture with 8 attention heads, consisting of dimensions 64, 64, and 32, respectively. The model is trained using the deep OCC loss.
– OCGCNL: The GAT module is excluded in OCGCNL. It utilizes the GCN encoder as the method for graph representation learning and incorporates six transformers to enhance the learning representation of graph data. The GCN layers employ a hidden layer of 128 dimensions and are trained using the balanced GCNL loss and deep OCC loss.
– OCGATL and OCGATLv2: Equipped with both the GAT neural network module and the GATv2 neural network module for learning graph data representation, along with six transformers for self-supervised contrastive learning. In each transformer, a three-layer GAT with 8 attention heads is deployed, with hidden layer dimensions of 64, 64, and 32, respectively. The models are trained using the balanced GATL loss and deep OCC loss.

We seek to comprehend the benefits of the GAT network and transformation neural module in the context of graph node-level anomaly detection within

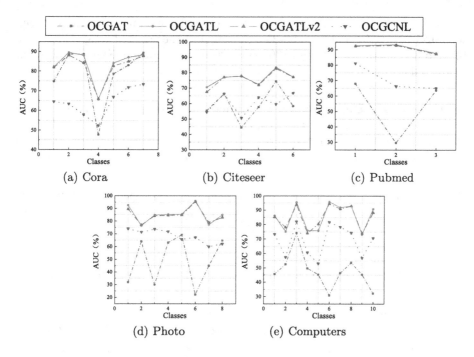

Fig. 5. Ablation experiment results

the deep OCC model from the standpoint of ablation study. Firstly, the analysis from Fig. 5 reveals that OCGATL achieves significantly higher AUC scores than OCGAT on four out of five datasets, and it is evident that the model with the addition of the transformation neural module exhibits more balanced performance across various classes in each dataset. This provides sufficient evidence that the inclusion of the transformation learning module overcomes the performance reversal issue in graph anomaly detection within the deep OCC model, particularly in scenarios involving classification data, and to some extent, enhances the accuracy of anomaly detection. On the Cora dataset, the transformation learning module demonstrates an advantage in terms of performance reversal, but the superiority in AUC scores for detecting anomaly accuracy is not significant. A reasonable inference is that GAT's learned feature representations on the Cora dataset are more distinct and accurate compared to those learned by GCN, and the impact of the GAT module on anomaly detection results is more pronounced.

5.2   Argo Real Data Experiment

In addition to the graph anomaly detection model in the simulation experiment, this article will use the classic anomaly detection algorithms DBSCAN algorithm, LOF algorithm, and iForest algorithm for the data before graph processing, and use the baseline model compared in the simulation experiment for the data after graph processing. In this experiment, the selected observation time is between 2023-02-14 15:13:24 and 2023-02-23 04:18:56, and the selected range is between 10° and 35° north latitude and 130° and 180° east longitude. Experiments were conducted on 658 real core Argo buoy measurement data.

Argo Anomaly Detection Performance. The average evaluation index of the comparison results of the three experiments is shown in Table 5. It can be seen that the improved graph neural network OCC algorithm has improved compared with the baseline task in four aspects: TPR, FRP, F1 score and AUC value.

Table 5. Experimental results of different anomaly types of models and comparison algorithms on the Argo data set

Method	Exception type 1				Exception type 2			
	TPR	FPR	F1	AUC	TPR	FPR	F1	AUC
OCGATL	**90.36**	1.14	**92.67**	**90.85**	**89.26**	1.10	**93.28**	**91.18**
DONE	81.37	2.46	87.38	82.05	84.78	2.64	88.29	85.63
Dominant	82.37	1.38	85.31	84.42	83.06	1.69	86.25	85.52
AnomalyDAE	80.19	2.25	85.47	82.36	79.98	2.56	86.77	84.96
LOF	70.29	3.18	73.82	74.9	66.32	3.13	66.73	68.4
iForest	70.21	2.85	70.16	73.28	62.23	2.16	63.03	64.32
DBSCAN	56.1	**0.96**	63.29	67.43	58.67	**1.02**	59.88	62.75

It can be seen from the data that the TPR of the OCC model of the improved graph neural network is 90.36 and 89.26 respectively, which performs best among all algorithms. Regarding the FPR value, although the FPR values of DBSCAN are 0.96 and 1.02 respectively, which is the best performance, the TPR value is only 56.1 and 58.57. Although the algorithm does not misdetect normal data as abnormal data, only about 60% of the abnormal data is detected. Correctly detected as abnormal data, the overall effect is not good. In addition, the graph anomaly detection algorithm after graph structure conversion is better than the Euclidean anomaly detection algorithm in four aspects. It can be seen that for Argo data, the construction and learning of graph structure has an improvement effect.

For different anomaly types, the F1 and AUC of the improved graph neural network OCC model perform better in anomaly type 1 than in anomaly type 2. The methods of DONE, Dominant, and AnomalyDAE after graph structure conversion perform better in the two anomaly types. There is not much difference in performance. In the classic Euclidean anomaly detection algorithm, F1 and AUC perform better in anomaly type 1 than in anomaly type 2. As shown in the introduction, anomaly type 1 is a sudden abnormal point, and anomaly type 2 is an overall offset. On the basis of stably improving the detection effect of sudden anomalies, the graph anomaly detection algorithm enhances the detection of overall offset anomalies. It is more sensitive and has better overall performance in anomaly detection.

Argo Graph Construction Parameter Experiment. In the construction of Argo graph, the correlation between all nodes will inevitably lead to an exponential increase in edge data. In this experiment, we control the connections between nodes through the coverage radius and TopK value. The coverage radius refers to any edge constructed by other Argo data sample nodes within the influence radius cd of the current Argo data sample node. The TopK value means that any Argo data sample node only constructs edge connections with the k nodes with the closest Euclidean distance in its space, and does not form edge connections with other Argo data sample node nodes. In the coverage path, this article distinguishes the situation where excessive data volume within the radius may still occur after the coverage distance interval. In this regard, the interval is scaled and selected, and the k nodes with the closest Euclidean distance are selected to construct edge connections.

In this experiment, we conducted the experiment in an arithmetic manner, and the experimental results are as shown in the Fig. 6.

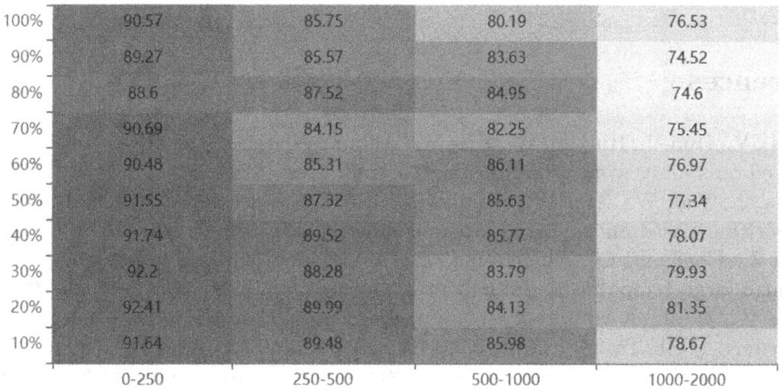

	0-250	250-500	500-1000	1000-2000
100%	90.57	85.75	80.19	76.53
90%	89.27	85.57	83.63	74.52
80%	88.6	87.52	84.95	74.6
70%	90.69	84.15	82.25	75.45
60%	90.48	85.31	86.11	76.97
50%	91.55	87.32	85.63	77.34
40%	91.74	89.52	85.77	78.07
30%	92.2	88.28	83.79	79.93
20%	92.41	89.99	84.13	81.35
10%	91.64	89.48	85.98	78.67

Fig. 6. AUC heat map of different parameter settings in the improved graph neural network OCC model

Among them, the horizontal axis of the heat map represents the interval of the coverage path, and the vertical axis represents the value of TopK. The value in the heat block is the AUC value obtained from the operation. The darker the color, the higher the AUC value and the higher the model anomaly detection performance. It can be seen from the figure that when the TopK value is the same, as the coverage path increases, its anomaly detection performance decreases. For Argo graph data, the optimal coverage path can be set as 0–250 m. When covering the same path, the AUC value reaches the maximum when the TopK value is 20%–30%, but in fact the difference in AUC values between different TopK values is small, indicating that the TopK value has a small impact on the model. From the heat map, the optimal TopK of Argo graph data can be 20%.

The AUC value in the heat map is relatively stable in the experiment, which also shows that the OCC model of the improved graph neural network has strong stability.

6   Conclusion

We propose a novel Argo graph construction method and develop a new end-to-end graph anomaly detection method. The Argo diagram construction method takes into account the spatiality of the ocean and improves the information extraction of Argo data. The anomaly detection model named OCGATL combines the advantages of deep OCC and neural transformation learning based on the excellent representation of GAT, and uses graph transformation learning as regularization to make up for the shortcomings of deep OCC. Our comprehensive empirical research supports our claims and theoretical results. It shows that OCGATL performs best in various challenging domains and is the only method without performance flip that achieves state-of-the-art results on the Argo real-world dataset.

References

1. Yidi, Y., Hua, J., Huijiao, W., Xin, W.: Anomaly detection algorithm of argo profile based on sliding window and arma. Comput. Eng. Appl. **54**(19), 254 (2018)
2. Hua, J., Yao, W., Xin, W., Huijiao, W.: Study on ocean data anomaly detection algorithm based on improved k-means clustering. Comput. Sci. **46**(7), 6 (2019)
3. Qi, Z., Chenyan, Q., Changming, D.: A machine learning approach to quality-control argo temperature data. Atmos. Oceanic Sci. Lett. **16**(4), 100292 (2023)
4. Ma, X., et al.: A comprehensive survey on graph anomaly detection with deep learning. IEEE Trans. Knowl. Data Eng. **35**, 12012–12038 (2021)
5. Ye, J., Akoglu, L.: Discovering opinion spammer groups by network footprints. In: Appice, A., Rodrigues, P., Santos Costa, V., Soares, C., Gama, J., Jorge, A. (eds.) ECML PKDD 2015 Part I. LNCS, vol. 9284, pp. 267–282. Springer, Cham (2015). https://doi.org/10.1007/978-3-319-23528-8_17
6. Gaddam, A., Wilkin, T., Angelova, M., Gaddam, J.: Detecting sensor faults, anomalies and outliers in the internet of things: a survey on the challenges and solutions. Electronics **9**(3), 511 (2020)
7. Dou, Y., Liu, Z., Sun, L., Deng, Y., Peng, H., Yu, P.S.: Enhancing graph neural network-based fraud detectors against camouflaged fraudsters. In: Proceedings of the 29th ACM International Conference on Information & Knowledge Management, pp. 315–324 (2020)
8. Ioannidis, V.N., Berberidis, D., Giannakis, G.B.: Unveiling anomalous nodes via random sampling and consensus on graphs. In: ICASSP 2021-2021 IEEE International Conference on Acoustics, Speech and Signal Processing (ICASSP), pp. 5499–5503. IEEE (2021)

9. Xu, K., Hu, W., Leskovec, J., Jegelka, S.: How powerful are graph neural networks? In: International Conference on Learning Representations (2019). https://openreview.net/forum?id=ryGs6iA5Km

10. Yu, B., Yin, H., Zhu, Z.: Spatio-temporal graph convolutional networks: a deep learning framework for traffic forecasting. In: Lang, J. (ed.) Proceedings of the Twenty-Seventh International Joint Conference on Artificial Intelligence, IJCAI 2018, July 13-19, 2018, Stockholm, Sweden, pp. 3634–3640 (2018)

11. Peng, H., et al.: Fine-grained event categorization with heterogeneous graph convolutional networks. CoRR **abs/1906.04580** (2019)

12. Wang, D., et al.: A semi-supervised graph attentive network for financial fraud detection. In: 2019 IEEE International Conference on Data Mining (ICDM), pp. 598–607. IEEE (2019)

13. Wang, X., Jin, B., Du, Y., Cui, P., Tan, Y., Yang, Y.: One-class graph neural networks for anomaly detection in attributed networks. Neural Comput. Appl. **33**, 12073–12085 (2021)

14. Ruff, L., et al.: Deep one-class classification. In: International Conference on Machine Learning, pp. 4393–4402. PMLR (2018)

15. Veličković, P., Cucurull, G., Casanova, A., Romero, A., Liò, P., Bengio, Y.: Graph attention networks. In: International Conference on Learning Representations (2018)

16. Zhao, L., Akoglu, L.: On using classification datasets to evaluate graph outlier detection: p[eculiar observations and new insights. Big Data **11**, 151–180 (2021)

17. Golan, I., El-Yaniv, R.: Deep anomaly detection using geometric transformations. In: Advances in Neural Information Processing Systems, vol. 31 (2018)

18. Qiu, C., Pfrommer, T., Kloft, M., Mandt, S., Rudolph, M.: Neural transformation learning for deep anomaly detection beyond images. In: International Conference on Machine Learning, pp. 8703–8714. PMLR (2021)

19. Akoglu, L., Tong, H., Koutra, D.: Graph based anomaly detection and description: a survey. Data Min. Knowl. Disc. **29**, 626–688 (2015)

20. Shervashidze, N., Schweitzer, P., Van Leeuwen, E.J., Mehlhorn, K., Borgwardt, K.M.: Weisfeiler-lehman graph kernels. J. Mach. Learn. Res. **12**(9) (2011)

21. Neumann, M., Garnett, R., Bauckhage, C., Kersting, K.: Propagation kernels: efficient graph kernels from propagated information. Mach. Learn. **102**, 209–245 (2016)

22. Liu, F.T., Ting, K.M., Zhou, Z.H.: Isolation forest. In: 2008 Eighth IEEE International Conference on Data Mining, pp. 413–422. IEEE (2008)

23. Breunig, M.M., Kriegel, H.P., Ng, R.T., Sander, J.: LOF: identifying density-based local outliers. In: Proceedings of the 2000 ACM SIGMOD International Conference on Management of Data, pp. 93–104 (2000)

24. Schölkopf, B., Williamson, R.C., Smola, A., Shawe-Taylor, J., Platt, J.: Support vector method for novelty detection. In: Advances in Neural Information Processing Systems, vol. 12 (1999)

25. Tax, D.M., Duin, R.P.: Support vector data description. Mach. Learn. **54**, 45–66 (2004)

26. Zhang, F., Fan, H., Wang, R., Li, Z., Liang, T.: Deep dual support vector data description for anomaly detection on attributed networks. Int. J. Intell. Syst. **37**(2), 1509–1528 (2022)

27. Ruff, L., et al.: A unifying review of deep and shallow anomaly detection. Proc. IEEE **109**(5), 756–795 (2021)

28. Chen, T., Kornblith, S., Norouzi, M., Hinton, G.: A simple framework for contrastive learning of visual representations. In: International Conference on Machine Learning, pp. 1597–1607. PMLR (2020)
29. He, K., Fan, H., Wu, Y., Xie, S., Girshick, R.: Momentum contrast for unsupervised visual representation learning. In: Proceedings of the IEEE/CVF Conference on Computer Vision and Pattern Recognition, pp. 9729–9738 (2020)
30. Wang, Y., Wang, J., Cao, Z., Barati Farimani, A.: Molecular contrastive learning of representations via graph neural networks. Nat. Mach. Intell. **4**(3), 279–287 (2022)
31. Velickovic, P., Fedus, W., Hamilton, W.L., Liò, P., Bengio, Y., Hjelm, R.D.: Deep graph infomax. ICLR (Poster) **2**(3), 4 (2019)
32. Peng, Z., et al.: Graph representation learning via graphical mutual information maximization. In: Proceedings of The Web Conference 2020, pp. 259–270 (2020)
33. You, Y., Chen, T., Sui, Y., Chen, T., Wang, Z., Shen, Y.: Graph contrastive learning with augmentations. Adv. Neural. Inf. Process. Syst. **33**, 5812–5823 (2020)
34. Zhu, Y., Xu, Y., Yu, F., Liu, Q., Wu, S., Wang, L.: Graph contrastive learning with adaptive augmentation. In: Proceedings of the Web Conference 2021, pp. 2069–2080 (2021)
35. Liu, Y., Li, Z., Pan, S., Gong, C., Zhou, C., Karypis, G.: Anomaly detection on attributed networks via contrastive self-supervised learning. IEEE Trans. Neural Netw. Learn. Syst. **33**(6), 2378–2392 (2021)
36. Zheng, Y., Jin, M., Liu, Y., Chi, L., Phan, K.T., Chen, Y.P.P.: Generative and contrastive self-supervised learning for graph anomaly detection. IEEE Trans. Knowl. Data Eng. (2021)
37. Zheng, Y., et al.: From unsupervised to few-shot graph anomaly detection: a multiscale contrastive learning approach. arXiv preprint arXiv:2202.05525 (2022)
38. Ying, C., Hui, Z.: Spatio-temporal distribution of chlorophyll in the mid-western south china sea. J. Mar. Sci. **39**, 84–94 (2021)
39. Peng, H., Qing, Y., Zefan, Y., Kun, H., Jiangguang, P.: Experimental study on dissolved oxygen content in water and its physical influence factors. J. Hydraul. Eng. **50**(6), 8 (2019)
40. Vaswani, A., et al.: Attention is all you need. In: Advances in Neural Information Processing Systems, vol. 30 (2017)
41. Brody, S., Alon, U., Yahav, E.: How attentive are graph attention networks? In: International Conference on Learning Representations (2022)
42. Xu, K., Li, C., Tian, Y., Sonobe, T., Kawarabayashi, K.i., Jegelka, S.: Representation learning on graphs with jumping knowledge networks. In: International Conference on Machine Learning, pp. 5453–5462. PMLR (2018)
43. Shchur, O., Mumme, M., Bojchevski, A., Günnemann, S.: Pitfalls of graph neural network evaluation. CoRR **abs/1811.05868** (2018)
44. Sen, P., Namata, G., Bilgic, M., Getoor, L., Galligher, B., Eliassi-Rad, T.: Collective classification in network data. AI Mag. **29**(3), 93–93 (2008)
45. Kipf, T.N., Welling, M.: Semi-supervised classification with graph convolutional networks. In: International Conference on Learning Representations, ICLR 2017 (2017)
46. Hamilton, W., Ying, Z., Leskovec, J.: Inductive representation learning on large graphs. In: Advances in Neural Information Processing Systems, vol. 30 (2017)
47. Bandyopadhyay, S., Vivek, S.V., Murty, M.: Outlier resistant unsupervised deep architectures for attributed network embedding. In: Proceedings of the 13th International Conference on Web Search and Data Mining, pp. 25–33 (2020)

48. Ding, K., Li, J., Bhanushali, R., Liu, H.: Deep anomaly detection on attributed networks. In: Proceedings of the 2019 SIAM International Conference on Data Mining, pp. 594–602. SIAM (2019)
49. Fan, H., Zhang, F., Li, Z.: Anomalydae: dual autoencoder for anomaly detection on attributed networks. In: ICASSP 2020-2020 IEEE International Conference on Acoustics, Speech and Signal Processing (ICASSP), pp. 5685–5689. IEEE (2020)

RGCNdist2vec: Using Graph Convolutional Networks and Distance2Vector to Estimate Shortest Path Distance Along Road Networks

Xiangfu Meng$^{(\boxtimes)}$ ⓘ, Weipeng Xie ⓘ, and Jiangyan Cui ⓘ

Liaoning Technical University, Huludao 43017-6221, Liaoning, China
marxi@126.com

Abstract. Computing shortest distance estimation for road networks is an important component of map service systems. Existing embedded-based shortest path distance estimation methods either have a long training time or the model training time is reduced by sacrificing the estimation accuracy. To address the above problems, this paper proposes a Road Graph Convolutional Networks and Distance2Vector (RGCNdist2vec), which is suitable for road network scenarios, as an embedding method of road network vertices. Used to capture network structure information. In the aspect of sampling model training samples, a three-stage sampling method based on graph logical partition is designed, which can select a small number of high-quality samples for model training. In order to verify the validity of the model and sampling scheme, experiments were carried out on four real road network datasets and compared with existing relevant models. The results show that the proposed model has high estimation accuracy, and the training time of the model is nearly 4 times lower than that of the existing baseline model.

Keywords: Graph neural network · Shortest path distance · Data Sampling · Representation learning

1 Introduction

The calculation of the shortest distance between two points in a road network is a core problem in the field of road network applications, which has wide applications in map services and navigation systems. The shortest path distance calculation falls into two categories: accurate calculation [1–4]and estimation calculation [5–14].The estimation method offers quick calculation speed, efficiency, and prompt feedback when millions of simultaneous calculations occur, compared to accurate calculations.Besides, the estimation method's use does not compromise accuracy for multiple calculation tasks.

Recently, researchers have proposed a road network shortest path distance estimation method that employs graph embedding techniques [11–14]. These methods utilize deep learning technology to construct an index for calculating

X. Meng et al. (Eds.): SpatialDI 2024, LNCS 14619, pp. 174–187, 2024.
https://doi.org/10.1007/978-981-97-2966-1_13

the shortest path distance. The main idea is to utilize the graph embedding method to embed each vertex in the road network. Each vertex is transformed to a vector representation by embedding it into either Euclidean [15] or hyperbolic [16] space. Calculating the shortest distance between two points of the road network can be achieved by assessing the similarity score of the corresponding embedding vectors of the two vertices. Nevertheless, current estimation methods overlook the structural information of the road network during the embedding process, and use all vertex pairs within the graph for training purposes. This approach remains inadequate in terms of estimation accuracy and training time. Graph Convolutional Networks (GCN) [17] are among the most representative approaches for graph neural networks in recent years. The fundamental idea is to update the vertex embedding vectors through convolutional operations. This approach leverages both structural and feature information of vertices within the graph to extract high-level features and is particularly adept at capturing spatially critical information. As such, this paper aims to enhance the GCN approach and apply it towards estimating shortest path distances within road networks.

The contributions of this paper are summarized as follows:

- Decoupling the core component based on embedding method, RSDE framework (Road Shortest Distance Estimation, RSDE) is proposed, which takes advantages of the core process of estimating the shortest path distance in road networks.
- For model training sample selecting, a three stage sampling method is proposed that utilizes graph logical partitioning. This method enables selection of a small yet high-quality sample set, which significantly reduces the time required for constructing training samples and training the models.
- Extensive experiments are conducted on four real road networks for evaluating the effectiveness and efficiency of the proposed models.

2   Related Work

2.1   Shortest Path Distance Calculation

Classical algorithms for calculating shortest path distances include Dijkstra and Floyd algorithms, among others. Since these algorithms require accessing all points within the distance range between the end and beginning points, their computational complexity is high. To enhance computational efficiency, Robert et al. [3] devised a shortened hierarchical network method called CH algorithm, which accelerates queries by computing shortest paths between select vertices within the graph and storing them in an optimal fashion. Similarly, Ouyang et al. [4] proposed the H2H method, which assigns distance labels to each vertex for improved computational speed.Nevertheless, these methods necessitate extensive preprocessing to construct indexes and are unsuitable for large-scale road networks.

The landmark-based methods [8–10] are a typical class of methods for estimating the shortest path distances of road networks.The basic idea of this class of methods is to select some of the vertices in the graph as landmark vertices, and then assign distance labels to each vertex. Although landmark-based methods can reduce memory overhead, the computational accuracy of such methods cannot be guaranteed because selecting landmark vertices is an NP-hard problem. Embedding-based methods are a breakthrough from the landmark methods, which incorporate graph embedding techniques to estimate the shortest path distance of a road network.Rizi et al. [11] were the first to propose using deep learning to embed graph vertices in order to approximate the shortest path distance in large-scale graphs. Their method employed node2vec [18] and Poincare [19] as embedding techniques, which yielded promising results on social networks. However, experiments revealed that node2vec is unsuitable for road networks. Qi et al. [12] presented a learning-based method for estimating the shortest path distance in large-scale road networks. The method attains a high level of estimation accuracy. However, since it uses all vertex pairs in the graph as training data, it leads to a prolonged training time for the model. Chen et al. [14] proposed an estimation method using landmark-based sampling and learning. This method reduces the training time. However, the randomness associated with landmark-based sampling means that the training results' estimation accuracy cannot be guaranteed.

2.2   Graph Neural Network

In recent years, numerous graph neural networks models have emerged, including the graph convolutional neural network [17] and graph attention network [20]. Most of these approaches follow Gilmer et al.'s [21] neural message passing framework. Existing literature [22,23] describes significant research breakthroughs in the GNN field in recent years. The GCN model [17] proposed by Kipf et al. is a type of transductive learning that generates vector representations of vertices by aggregating information of neighbor vertices. Meanwhile, Hamilton et al.'s GraphSAGE model [24] is an inductive learning framework that generates embedding vectors of unknown vertices efficiently using vertex attribute information. GraphSAGE treats all neighbors equally while fusing neighbor information, which may not be suitable for some practical problems. Veličković et al.'s GAT model [20] addresses this issue by incorporating a self-attention mechanism to allow adaptive allocation of weights to different neighbors. There have been numerous real-world application tasks using graph neural network related methods, and we propose a new perspective by applying the graph neural network method to the shortest path distance estimation task of a road network as an embedding method for extracting the structure of the road network.

3   Definitions and Solutions

3.1   Definition

Road Networkx. The road network is represented as a weighted undirected graph $G = (V, E, W)$, where V is a set of vertices and $v_i \in V$ is a vertex in the graph, E is the set of edges, $e_{v_i,v_j} \in E$ is an edges from v_i to v_j, $w_{v_i,v_j} \in W$ is the weight of e_{v_i,v_j}.

Road Network Shortest Path Distance Calculation. Given any two points from v_i to v_j, calculation method of accurate distance between them is $d_{ij}^* = w_{v_i,v_u} + \ldots + w_{v_n,v_j}$, where v_u and v_n are the vertices on the path.

Network Shortest Path Distance Estimation. Given a road network $G=(V, E, W)$, embedding each vertex into d-dimensional space to obtain embedding vector $v^{(i)}$, $H = \{v^{(1)}, v^{(2)}, \cdots, v^{(i)}\}$ is embedded in the matrix. Given any vertices v_i and v_j, the formula to calculate the estimated distance is:

$$\hat{d}_{ij}^* = |H[i] - H[j]|_1 \tag{1}$$

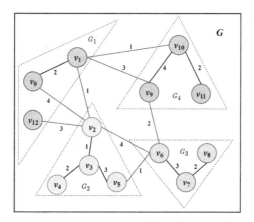

Fig. 1. The Partition Results for G

Graphic Partitioning. Given a graph G, use the $\Delta(G) = G_1, G_2, ..., G_n$ represents the partition result of graph G. Graph G is divided into n sub-graphs, the $\Delta(G)$ of the element for $G_i = (V_i, E_i, W_i)$, $(i \in [1, n])$. Each subgraph satisfies the following three conditions: (1)$V = \bigcup_{i \in [1,n]} V_i$; (2) if $i \neq j, V_i \cap V_j = \phi$; (3) Each subgraph G_i is the induction subgraph of G, that is, the attribute of subgraph G_i is consistent with that of G.

Given a graph G and an area threshold of k_f, the graph is divided into approximately k_f subgraphs each having a similar number of vertices $(|V_1| \approx \cdots \approx |V_{k_f}|)$. This paper adopts the METIS multi-layer graph partitioning framework [25] to achieve this and minimize the number of graph cuts found in the resulting subgraphs. The Fig. 1 shows Graph G being divided into four subgraphs using the set $\Delta(G) = G_1, G_2, G_3, G_4$, with an area threshold of $k_f = 4$.

Degree of Vertex. The degree of a vertex in a graph represents the number of edges attached to it and is represented as $D(v_i)$. As shown in the Fig. 1, v_3 has a degree of 3, with $D(v_3) = 3$.

Border. Given the graph $G_x = (V_x, E_x, W_x)$, a subgraph $G_x = (V_x, E_x, W_x)$ is formed. If an edge $e_{v_i,v_j} \in E$ but $e_{v_i,v_j} \notin E_x$, it is considered a boundary edge of the subgraph. The endpoint of the boundary edge is referred to as a boundary vertex of the subgraph. As shown in the Fig. 1, the boundary set of G_x is defined as $B(G_x)$. Hence, $B(G_2) = v_2, v_5, B(G_3) = v_6$.

3.2 Solution

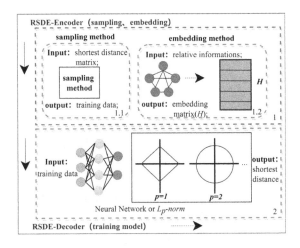

Fig. 2. Overall Frame Structure of RSDE

This paper proposes the Road Shortest Distance Estimation (RSDE) framework, which refines and organizes the core ideas and steps of the embedded-based method while also reducing the dependencies between critical components. The RSDE framework, illustrated in Fig. 2, consists of an RSDE-encoder and an RSDE-decoder. The decoder has two components, namely the sample selection process (1.1 in Fig. 2) and the graph embedding process (1.2 in Fig. 2).

4   Road Network Shortest Path Estimation Method

4.1   RGCNdist2vec

The RGCNdist2vec model workflow is depicted in Fig. 3, consisting of two parts: (1) RGCNdist2vec-encoder layer, which uses an improved GCN to build the Road Graph Convolutional Network (RGCN). By combining the weight and structure data of the road network, embedding vectors are derived for each vertex. (2)

RGCNdist2vec-decoder layer that receives the output and training data from the encoder layer. It selects an appropriate measurement method and loss function to optimize the learnable weight matrix in the encoder layer for calculating the shortest path distance between two points.

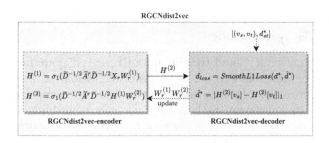

Fig. 3. Base Architecture of RGCNdist2vec

4.2   RGCNdist2vec-Encoder

The core component of the RGCNdist2vec model is the graph embedding function, which integrates road network information and outputs low dimensional embedding vectors for each vertex. GCN can effectively extract spatial features from graphs, so this paper uses GCN as an embedding method for shortest path distance estimation. The message passing mechanism of the GCN is depicted in Eq. (2),

$$H^{(l+1)} = \sigma \left(\tilde{D}^{-\frac{1}{2}} \tilde{A} \tilde{D}^{-\frac{1}{2}} H^{(l)} W^{(l)} \right) \tag{2}$$

Among them, $\tilde{A} = A_v + I_{|V|}$ is an adjacency matrix attached to a self-join, A_v is a adjacency matrix, $I_{|V|}$ is the identity matrix of size $|V|$, $\tilde{D}_{ii} = \sum_j \tilde{A}_{ij}$ is a degree matrix, $W^{(l)}$ is the learnable weight matrix of layer l, $H^{(l)} \in \mathbb{R}^{|V| \times |d|}$ is the vertex matrix of layer l, $\sigma(\cdot)$ takes the ReLU function.

The connections between the neighbor vertices of a road network usually have different degrees of connection weights. As GCN integrates neighbor and vertex information in an unbiased manner, relying solely on it to exploit the road network's neighborhood structure is not justifiable. We propose the Road Graph Convolutional Networks (RGCN) model that mainly comprises of two parts: First, replacing the unweighted adjacency matrix with the road network's weighted adjacency matrix and incorporating the road network weight information as the integrated neighborhood information to account for varying degrees of preference. Second, selecting the neighborhood mean as the self-connectivity measure for vertices. The neighborhood mean is suitable because it is both in the same range as the neighbor weight and can reflect the concentration level of data sets. To sum up, RGCN's message passing rules are shown in Formula (3),

$$H^{(l+1)} = \sigma_1 \left(\tilde{D}^{-\frac{1}{2}} \tilde{A}_{ij}^r \tilde{D}^{-\frac{1}{2}} H^{(l)} W_r^{(l)} \right) \tag{3}$$

Among them, $\widetilde{A}_{ij}^r = A_v^w + eye\left(mean\left(w_{v_i,v_j}\right)\right)$ is the adjacency matrix after self-connection by weight mean, $eye\left(mean\left(w_{v_i,v_j}\right)\right)$,$w_{v_i,v_j} \in W$ said neighbor weighted average diagonal matrix, $\widetilde{D}_{ii} = \sum_j \widetilde{A}_{ij}^r$ for degree matrix, $W_r^{(l)}$ represents the l-level learnable weight matrix, $\sigma_1(\cdot)$ is the activation function $LeakyReLU(\cdot)$.

4.3   RGCNdist2vec-Decoder

The embedded matrix $H^{(2)}$ and training data $[(v_s, v_e), d_{se}^*]$ are first received by the decoder layer from the encoder layer. The weight matrix is updated iteratively by calculating Eq. (1) to optimize the model's representation ability. The selection of the measurement method for the vertex embedding vector greatly impacts the training results. This paper uses L_1-norm as a measurement method as outlined in prior research [13], which provides reasons and relevant proofs for its selection. The SmoothL1Loss is used as a loss function to evaluate the accuracy of the regression model during the training process. It is a combination of L1loss and L2Loss, as shown in Eq. (4), which has advantages of both. This experimental setup used the Adam optimizer to train the model parameters, which automatically updated the learning rate during training and resulted in quick model convergence.

$$d_{\text{loss}} = \text{SmoothL1Loss}\left(d^*, \hat{d}^*\right) =$$

$$\begin{cases} \frac{0.5}{N} \sum_{i=1}^N \left(d^* - \hat{d}^*\right)^2 & \text{if } \left|d^* - \hat{d}^*\right| < 1 \\ \frac{1}{N} \sum_{i=1}^N \left(\left|d^* - \hat{d}^*\right| - 0.5\right) & otherwise \end{cases} \quad (4)$$

5   Sampling Method

The selection of training data plays a critical role in learning the embedding vector representations for each vertex in the road network. To balance the model's estimation accuracy against the cost of training it, we designed a three-level sampling method based on logical partitioning of the graph. Three-Stage sampling includes: (1) subgraph sampling, (2) inter-subgraph sampling, (3) Whole graph sampling.

5.1   Subgraph Sampling Method

Dividing the vertices of the road network creates a subgraph with a relatively equal number of vertices. The boundary point of a subgraph is the necessary point for calculating the distance between two points belonging to different subgraphs.

The centrality of a graph can be measured by the degree of its vertices. Thus, the entry point for sampling is determined by selecting the point with a larger moderate degree values within the subgraph and the corresponding boundary point. Adopting a specific graph partition method results in a fixed and known set of boundary points for the subgraph, denoted as $Set(B_n)$, representing the boundary point set of G_n. Uncertainty exists in the selection of vertices with larger degree values. The degree set, represented by $Set(D_n)$, is defined as the set of vertices with larger degree values within the subgraph G_n. In order to determine the appropriate degree set, the normality of vertex degree values is tested on multiple real road network datasets. Additionally, a peak distribution phenomenon is observed in the vertex degree values. Sampling is performed on the degree set using the degree value corresponding to the peak value as the threshold to ensure an adequate number of data points.

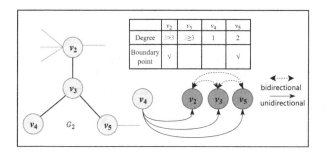

Fig. 4. The Intra-subgraph Sampling Process

The vertices $Set(G_n)$ of the subgraph is divided into 3 parts, namely $Set(E_n) = Set(G_n) - Set(B_n) - Set(D_n)$, $Set(B_n)$ and $Set(D_n)$. First, $v_i \in Set(E_n)$ and $v_j \in Set(D_n) \cup Set(B_n)$ are selected. Secondly, $v_i \in Set(D_n)$ and $v_j \in Set(B_n)$ are selected respectively. Finally, the selected data is spliced to form the sampling result of subgraph G_n. Assuming a degree set threshold of 3 for subgraph G_2, the sampling process for G_2 is depicted in Fig. 4.

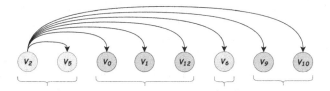

Fig. 5. The Inter-subgraph Sampling Process

5.2   Sampling Method Between Subgraphs

Learning the structural associations between subgraphs is also an essential task for embedded vectors. This paper proposes the following sampling method to achieve this goal. A sampling process is carried out by selecting each subgraph boundary point to the boundary point of other subgraphs except itself. This local sampling method aims to achieve fine-grained learning of subgraph structural information. Figure 5 illustrates the process of sampling the boundary point v_2 of subgraph G_2.

5.3 Whole Graph Sampling Method

Whole-graph sampling learns global information about the graph by sampling across the graph hierarchy, commonly referred to as coarse-grained learning. The first two stages involve sampling subgraphs of vertices within the graph. In other subgraphs, each vertex randomly selects $10\% \sim 15\%$ of the vertices from other subgraphs, excluding its own subgraph vertices.

6 Experiment

6.1 Experimental Introduction

Datasets and Experimental Environment. To validate the RGCNdist2vec model, its performance was evaluated on four road network datasets of varying sizes. To preprocess the data, the model input consists of the maximum connected component of the road network. Table 1 displays specific information about the selected road network, including its number of vertices, number of edges, vertex degree value, and average weight.

Table 1. Details of Datasets

Datasets	#Region	#Vertices	#Edges	#Degree	#Mean
SU	Surat, India	2508	3591	7182	244.78
DG	Dongguan, China	7658	10,542	21,084	446.32
HA	Harbin, China	10,132	14,185	28,370	621.55
AH	Ahmedabad, India	12,747	18,117	36,243	191.73

The RGCNdist2vec model was developed using Python language and implemented in the PyTorch deep learning framework. Training and testing experiments were conducted on two RTX2080Ti 12GB graphics cards with 32GB of RAM running Ubuntu 16.04 operating system.

Evaluation Index. Two sets of evaluation indices are utilized in this paper to assess the model's performance. MAE and MRE quantify the error between the estimated and actual distances, with a smaller error indicating better model performance. Equations (5) and (6) present the definitions for MAE and MRE, respectively, where N represents the number of validation data. Training time (PT, precomputation/training time) and query time (QT, query time) are utilized to assess the model's training and query efficiency.

$$MRE = \frac{1}{N} \sum \left| \hat{d}_{ij}^* - d_{ij}^* \right| \tag{5}$$

$$MRE = \frac{1}{N} \sum \frac{\left| \hat{d}_{ij}^* - d_{ij}^* \right|}{d_{ij}^*} \tag{6}$$

Parameter Setting. The experimental process for the RGCNdist2vec model proposed in this paper uses 2-order message passing. The model uses four hyper-parameters: the hidden layer dimension (hid) in 1-order message passing, the embedded dimension (d) of the model, the learning rate (lr), and the number of training rounds ($epoch$). Different values for hyperparameters were used to obtain better training results in the various road network datasets. Optimal hyperpa-rameter values were selected as follows: for SU and DG datasets, $hid = 512$, $k = 32$, $lr = 0.05$, while for the HA and AH datasets, $hid = 1024$, $k = 64$, $lr = 0.05$. In all experiments, the training data, obtained through the three-stage sampling method, was randomized and fed into the network. Verification data comprised of $1M$ vertex pairs randomly sampled from the road network.

6.2   Ablation Experiment

To evaluate the impact of each module in the RGCNdist2vec model on overall estimation accuracy, we perform a self-comparison of sampling and embedding method combinations, while selecting the optimal embedding dimension and parameter settings.

The Effect of Setting Strategy and Sampling Method on Partition Threshold k_f. The experimental results for different values of k_f in the SU and DG datasets are presented in Fig. 6, respectively. Varying the partition threshold k_f in the three-stage sampling method provides insight into its impact on training data quality and overall estimation accuracy of the model. Figures 6 present the comparison results between landmark and three-stage sampling techniques applied to SU and DG datasets. According to the experimental evidence, the accuracy of the three-stage sampling approach surpasses that of the landmark method when dealing with various partition thresholds k_f. A more systematic selection of vertex pairs in the road network, focused on the structural and weight learning dynamics, supports the better accuracy of the three-stage sampling compared to the landmark-based method.

The Effect of the Order of Message Passing on the Accuracy of Model Estimation. As previously discussed, excessive order message passing can lead to over-smoothing in GCN. We examined RGCN to determine if it suffers from the same issue. To evaluate the influence of message passing order on model accuracy, we performed 2, 3 and 4 order message passing within RGCN, the results of which are presented in Fig. 7. The experimental evidence indicates a considerable increase in the average relative error of the model when transition-ing from 2-order to 3 and 4-order message passing. These results suggest that RGCN is also not suitable for excessively deep message passing orders.

6.3   Effect Experiment

In order to evaluate the estimation effect of RGCNdist2vec model, the following mainstream models were used for experimental comparison:

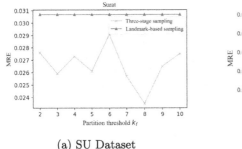

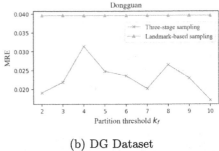

(a) SU Dataset   (b) DG Dataset

Fig. 6. Performance Comparison Under The Change of k_f of SU and DG Dataset

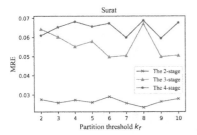

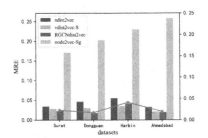

Fig. 7. Performance Comparison of Different Messaging Stages

Fig. 8. Comparison on Effects of Different Models

(1) ndist2vec [14] : The model applies a depth-first algorithm to select a specific proportion of vertices and thus create landmark vertices. The training data is then sampled from both landmark vertices and other vertices to train the neural network model;

(2) vdist2vec [12] : This model embeds the graph vertex using the weight matrix, then trains a multilayer perceptron to approximate the shortest distance of the road network;

(3) Node2vec-sg [11] : To predict the shortest distance of a social network, the neural network is trained using either the node2vec [18] or Poincare [19] embedding method;

The estimation accuracy of the four models is presented in Table 2, while a visualization analysis of experimental results is shown in Fig. 8. In terms of estimation accuracy in three different-sized real road networks (excluding HA), the results indicate that the proposed RGCNdist2vec model outperforms the other three models in both MAE and MRE. This could be attributed to the fact that other models' graph embedding methods use random walks (node2vec) or simple weight matrix multiplication. Compared to the graph embedding methods proposed in this paper, these methods struggle to effectively learn the road network's structure and weight information.

Table 2. Comparison on Effects of Different Models

		S U		D G		H A		A H	
		MAE	MRE	MAE	MRE	MAE	MRE	MAE	MRE
Baseline	ndist2vec	99.74	0.034	278.41	0.046	256.47	0.0548	146.32	0.033
	vdist2vec-S	87.22	0.028	144.32	0.030	**158.60**	**0.0351**	100.98	0.021
	node2vec-Sg	642.09	0.171	2421.34	0.203	3646.78	0.230	3711.44	0.258
proposed	RGCNdist2vec	**60.92**	**0.0227**	**127.65**	**0.0174**	179.85	0.0409	**98.36**	**0.0196**

6.4   Efficiency Experiment

The results of efficiency comparison between RGCNdist2vec model and baseline model are presented in Table 3. Analysis of the experimental results indicates that the RGCNdist2vec model has a significant advantage in the performance metric PT, outperforming the compared model on all four datasets. While the embedded-based method has significantly reduced training times compared to the traditional method, graph neural network approaches have even faster training speeds than previous methods used for this task.

Table 3. Comparison on Effects of Different Models

		S U		D G		H A		A H	
		PT	QT(us)	PT	QT(us)	PT	QT(us)	PT	QT(us)
Baseline	ndist2vec	0.10h	7.79	0.48h	16.95	1.20h	**23.45**	2.50h	**25.56**
	vdist2vec-S	0.41h	8.11	2.40h	17.12	3.7h	37.48	12.00h	40.37
	node2vec-Sg	0.35h	8.02	1.37h	18.06	37.45h	36.64	9.74h	35.69
proposed	RGCNdist2vec	**93.3997 s**	**7.52**	**0.14h**	**15.47**	**0.43h**	28.34	**1.22h**	30.48

To calculate the query time QT, we took the query mean of the vertex pair of the road network, which is $n(n-1)$. Our experiments indicate that the query time directly relates to the embedding dimension of the road network. In datasets SU and DG, we used $d = 32$ for the RGCNdist2vec model, $d = 50$ for ndist2vec, $d = 0.02n$ for vdist2vec-S, and 128 for node2vec-Sg. The RGCNdist2vec model has smaller dimensions than the other three models, resulting in the shortest query time. In datasets HA and AH, the RGCNdist2vec model has a slightly higher query time than ndist2vec but lower than vdist2vec-S and node2vec-Sg. This is because we fixed $k = 64$ for the RGCNdist2vec model while keeping all settings of other models unchanged.

7   Conclusion

In order to balance the estimation accuracy and training time of the road network shortest path distance estimation task, this paper proposes a road network shortest path distance estimation framework. By improving the graph convolutional neural network, it is used as an embedding method for road network shortest path distance estimation. Meanwhile, in order to further improve the training efficiency, this paper partitions the road network processing and designs a three-stage sampling method based on graph logic partitioning. Finally, experiments are carried out on four real datasets, which show that the proposed method has significant effects in both estimation accuracy and training efficiency. The network structure of the model will be further optimized in the future to improve the performance of the model.

References

1. Dijkstra, E.W.: A note on two problems in connexion with graphs. Numer. Math. **1**, 269–271 (1959)
2. Floyd, W.: Algorithm 97: shortest path. Commun. ACM **5**(6), 345 (1962)
3. Geisberger, R., Sanders, P., Schultes, D., Delling, D.: Contraction hierarchies: faster and simpler hierarchical routing in road networks. In: McGeoch, C.C. (ed.) WEA 2008. LNCS, vol. 5038, pp. 319–333. Springer, Heidelberg (2008). https://doi.org/10.1007/978-3-540-68552-4_24
4. Ouyang, D., et al.: When hierarchy meets 2-hop-labeling: efficient shortest distance queries on road networks. In: Proceedings of the 2018 International Conference on Management of Data, pp. 709–724. Houston, 10–15 June 2018. ACM, New York (2018)
5. Geisberger, R., Schieferdecker, D.: Heuristic contraction hierarchies with approximation guarantee. In: Proceedings of the Third Annual Symposium on Combinatorial Search, pp. 31–38. Stone Mountain, 8–10 July 2010. AAAI, Menlo Park (2010)
6. Chechik, S.: Approximate distance oracles with improved bounds. In: Proceedings of the Forty-seventh Annual ACM Symposium on Theory of Computing, pp. 1–10. Portland, 14–17 June 2015. ACM, New York (2015)
7. Tang, L., Crovella, M.: Virtual landmarks for the internet. In: Proceedings of the 3rd ACM SIGCOMM Conference on Internet Measurement, pp. 143–152. Miami Beach, 27–29 October 2003. ACM, New York (2003)
8. Zhao, X.H., et al.: Orion: shortest path estimation for large social graphs. Networks **1**, 5 (2010)
9. Zhao, X., et al.: Efficient shortest paths on massive social graphs. In: Proceedings of the 7th International Conference on Collaborative Computing, pp. 77–86. Orlando, 15–18 October 2011. IEEE, Piscataway (2011)
10. Gubichev, A., et al.: Fast and accurate estimation of shortest paths in large graphs. In: Proceedings of the 19th ACM International Conference on Information and Knowledge Management, pp. 499–508. Toronto, 26–30 October 2010. ACM, New York (2010)
11. Rizi, F.S., Schloetterer, J., Granitzer, M.: Shortest path distance approximation using deep learning techniques. In: Proceedings of the 2018 International Conference on Advances in Social Networks, pp. 1007–1014. Barcelona, 28–31 August 2018. IEEE, Piscataway (2018)
12. Qi, J., et al.: A learning based approach to predict shortest-path distances. In: Proceedings of the 23rd International Conference on Extending Database Technology, 367–370. Copenhagen, 30 March – 02 April 2020. OpenProceedings, Greece (2020)

13. Huang, S., et al.: A learning-based method for computing shortest path distances on road networks. In: 2021 IEEE 37th International Conference on Data Engineering, pp. 360–371. IEEE, Chania, 19–22 April 2021. IEEE, Piscataway (2021)

14. Chen, X., Wang, S., Li, H., et al.: Ndist2vec: node with landmark and new distance to vector method for predicting shortest path distance along road networks. ISPRS Int. J. Geo Inf. **11**(10), 514 (2022)

15. Darmochwal, A.: The Euclidean space. Formalized Math. **2**(4), 599–603 (1991)

16. Kleinberg, R.: Geographic routing using hyperbolic space. In: Proceedings of the 26th IEEE International Conference on Computer Communications, pp. 1902–1909. Anchorage, 6–12 May 2007. IEEE, Piscataway (2007)

17. Kipf, T.N., Welling, M.: Semi-supervised classification with graph convolutional networks. arXiv:1609.02907 (2016)

18. Grover, A., Leskovec, J.: node2vec: Scalable feature learning for networks. In: Proceedings of the 22nd ACM SIGKDD International Conference on Knowledge Discovery and Data Mining, pp. 855–864. San Francisco, 13–17 August 2016. ACM, New York (2016)

19. Nickel, M., Kiela, D.: Poincaré embeddings for learning hierarchical representations. In: Advances in Neural Information Processing Systems, arXiv:1705.08039 (2017)

20. Veličković, P., et al.: Graph attention networks. arXiv:1710.10903 (2017)

21. Gilmer, J., et al.: Neural message passing for quantum chemistry. In: Proceedings of the 34th International Conference on Machine Learning, pp. 1263-1272. Sydney, 6–11 August 2017. PMLR, New York (2017)

22. Zhou, J., et al.: Graph neural networks: a review of methods and applications. AI Open **1**, 57–81 (2020)

23. Wu, Z., et al.: A comprehensive survey on graph neural networks. IEEE Trans. Neural Netw. Learn. Syst. **32**(1), 4–24 (2021)

24. Hamilton, W.L., Ying, R., Leskovec, J.: Inductive representation learning on large graphs. In: Advances in Neural Information Processing Systems, arXiv:1760.2216 (2017)

25. Hoang, N.T., Maehata, T.: Revisiting graph neural networks: all we have is low-pass filters. arXiv:1905.09550 (2019)

Self-supervised Graph Neural Network Based Community Search over Heterogeneous Information Networks

Jinyang Wei, Lihua Zhou[✉], Lizhen Wang, Hongmei Chen, and Qing Xiao

Information Science and Engineering, Yunnan University, Kunming 650091, China
lhzhou@ynu.edu.cn, keyoungwell@mail.ynu.edu.cn

Abstract. Community search in heterogeneous information network (CSH) based on deep learning methods has received increasing attention. However, almost all the existing methods are semi-supervised learning paradigms, and the learning models based on meta path only consider the end-to-end relationship of meta path, ignoring the intermediate information of meta path. To address these issues, a CSH method based on Self-supervised Graph Neural Network (SGNN) is proposed. The model training is self-supervised by contrastive learning between the network schema view and the meta path view, and the two views capture the local and global information of the meta path from different angles. We then introduce a greedy algorithm called k-$core$ and $\mathcal{K}$-$sized$ attribute-scores maximization community search ($k\mathcal{K}$ - ASMcs) to explore target communities. A large number of experiments on real datasets have verified the effectiveness and efficiency of the proposed method.

Keywords: community search · heterogeneous information network · self-supervised · contrastive learning

1 Introduction

Heterogeneous information network (HIN) [1] is a type of network that includes multiple types of objects and connections. Different types of objects and connections depict the semantics of the network from different dimensions, allowing for a more complete and natural modeling of real-world network data. The research on community search in heterogeneous networks (CSH) [2, 3] is to find specific types of nodes containing query nodes in a cohesive subgraph from HIN. Due to its excellent application value, the CSH problem has received widespread attention.

Recently, more and more scholars are starting to use deep learning methods to solve the CSH problem. The idea of this method is to infer node scores through GNN classification [4], and then introduce a Maximum-GNN-scores and the largest connected subgraph as the target community. Therefore, the calculation of node scores is crucial. However, existing research has several main problems in node scores calculation. Firstly, Most methods are semi-supervised learning paradigms [5], which require a portion of node labels to supervise learning. However, in some practical environments, obtaining labels can be challenging or very costly. Therefore, constructing a self-supervised learning CSH model is of great significance. Secondly, capturing semantic relationships through meta paths is an effective approach [2], but most methods only consider the end-to-end relationship of meta paths, ignoring the intermediate information of meta paths, resulting in information loss and ultimately affecting the judgment of node and query node relevance. Furthermore, ensuring only the connectivity of the target community does not meet the requirements of community cohesion. It is necessary to capture the community cohesion structure while maximizing the search node rating.

To address the aforementioned issues, this paper proposes a CSH method based on SGNN. Specifically, unlike previous methods that rely on meta path view learning, we add a network schema view to achieve contrastive learning between two views. Through the Masked mechanism [5], partial information of the two views is hidden, and this information is constructed as a complementary relationship, so that the two views can supervise each other to complete the learning. The information lost in the middle of the meta path can be captured in the embedding of the newly added network mode view. We then introduce a greedy algorithm called $k-core$ and $\mathcal{K}-sized$ attribute-scores maximization community search ($k\mathcal{K}$ - ASMcs) to explore target communities.

2 Related Work

In order to solve the CSH problem, many scholars have proposed works from the perspective of community structure, such as $(k, \mathcal{P})-core$ [2, 3, 6] and so on. These methods are based on predefined rules and can find communities with strong interpretability, but adjusting the parameters in the rules is not easy, which affects the flexibility of community search. To address this issue, some scholars have started using deep learning methods to query communities. According to the learning model, it can mainly be divided into those based on random walks. For example, in [7] and [8], GNNs are used, such as ICS-GNN [4], QD-GNN [9], but these methods are all modeled on homogeneous networks. For heterogeneous networks, there are also ICSMIM [10]. These methods are almost all semi-supervised paradigms, which pose a challenge for constructing unsupervised CS learning models. Secondly, they may not distinguish the impact of different semantic relationships, or only consider one meta path, or fail to distinguish the importance of each meta path. Moreover, meta path based embeddings often only consider end-to-end information, which can easily overlook intermediate information and cause information loss. Therefore, this paper to solve these problems.

3 Community Search Model and Algorithm over HIN

HIN is a graph containing multiple types of nodes and edge relationships, as shown in Fig. 1(HIN). The network schema describes different types of nodes and relationships of HIN. The meta path $\mathcal{P}$ describes a specific path between entities in the HIN, such as author-paper-author. This paper presents a community search algorithm based on SGNN, which is introduced from two aspects: node attribute score calculation and community search, as shown in Fig. 1.

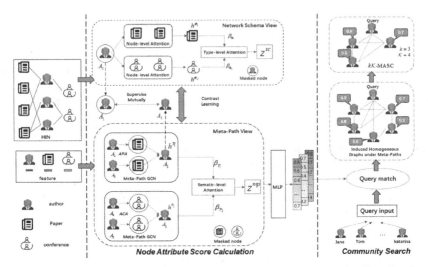

Fig. 1. The network schema view and meta path view achieve mutual supervised learning through a view mask mechanism, embedding the learned meta path view into MLP transformed node attribute score. The community search objective is to find Maximum-attribute-scores community.

3.1 Node Attribute Score Calculation

We constructed two views (network schema view and meta path view) guided encoder for embedding of HIN, and introduced how the two views supervise each other to complete learning.

3.1.1 Meta-path View Guided Encoder

This view encoder is designed to learn the embedding of target nodes affected by different semantic relationships. Firstly, for the meta-path neighbors [11] under the same meta path of node i, they are fused through the meta path GCN [12]. Therefore, an embedding $h_i^{\mathcal{P}_n}$ can be learned through $\mathcal{P}_n$. Aggregating the embeddings learned from e-ach meta path through semantic-attention mechanism to obtain the final embeddings z_i^{mp} under the meta path view:

$$h_i^{\mathcal{P}_n} = \frac{1}{d_i + 1} h_i + \sum_{j \in N_i^{\mathcal{P}_n}} \frac{1}{\sqrt{(d_i + 1)(d_j + 1)}} h_i$$

$$z_i^{mp} = \sum_{n=1}^{M} \beta_{\mathcal{P}_n} \cdot h_i^{\mathcal{P}_n} \tag{1}$$

where $\beta_{\mathcal{P}_n}$ weighs the importance of meta-path $\mathcal{P}_n$, which is calculated as follows:

$$w_{\mathcal{P}_n} = \frac{1}{|V|} \sum_{i \in V} \mathbf{a}_{mp}^{\mathrm{T}} \cdot \tanh\left(\mathbf{W}_{mp} h_i^{\mathcal{P}_n} + \mathbf{b}_{mp}\right)$$

$$\beta_{\mathcal{P}_n} = \frac{\exp(w_{\mathcal{P}_n})}{\sum_{i=1}^{M} \exp(w_{\mathcal{P}_i})} \tag{2}$$

where V is the target node set, $\boldsymbol{W}_{mp}$ and $\boldsymbol{b}_{mp}$ are learnable parameters. $\mathbf{a}_{mp}^{\mathrm{T}}$ is a semantic-level attention [11] vector.

3.1.2 Network Schema View Guided Encoder

This view encoder is designed to learn the embedding of the influence of different types of neighbors on the target node, first the node-level attention [11] is used to fuse neighbors with type Φ_m of node i to get embeddings $\boldsymbol{h}_i^{\Phi_m}$. Therefore, the neighb-or of type m has $\{\boldsymbol{h}_i^{\Phi_1}, ..., \boldsymbol{h}_i^{\Phi_m}\}$. We utilize Type-level attention [5] to fuse them together to get the final embedding z_i^{sc} for node i under network schema view:

$$z_i^{sc} = \sum_{m=1}^{S} \beta_{\Phi_m} \cdot \boldsymbol{h}_i^{\Phi_m} \tag{3}$$

where β_{Φ_m} is interpreted as the importance of type Φ_m to target node i, which is calculated as follows:

$$
\begin{aligned}
w_{\Phi_m} &= \frac{1}{|V|} \sum_{i \in V} \mathbf{a}_{sc}^{\mathrm{T}} \cdot \tanh\left(\boldsymbol{W}_{sc} \boldsymbol{h}_i^{\Phi_m} + \boldsymbol{b}_{sc}\right) \\
\beta_{\Phi_m} &= \frac{\exp(w_{\Phi_m})}{\sum_{i=1}^{S} \exp(w_{\Phi_i})}
\end{aligned}
\tag{4}
$$

where V is the set of target nodes $\boldsymbol{W}_{mp}$ and $\boldsymbol{b}_{mp}$ are learnable parameters, and $\mathbf{a}_{sc}^{\mathrm{T}}$ denotes Type-level attention vector. $\beta_{\phi m}$ is interpreted as the importance of type Φ_m to target node i

3.1.3 View Mask Mechanism

During the generation of z_i^{sc} and z_i^{mp}, we introduce a view mask mechanism that hi-des different parts of network schema and meta path views, respectively. As shown in Fig. 1, in network schema view, only the neighboring nodes of A_i, papers, and conferences are aggregated to form embeddings z_i^{sc}. The A_i own information is hidden, and the hidden nodes are represented by red circles. In the meta path view, infomation flo-ws through meta paths (APA, ACA) to form embeddings z_i^{mp}, and the information of intermediate nodes, such as P in APA and A in ACA, is hidden. The embedding information of A_i learned by these two views is relevant and complementary, and they can supervise mutually and train each other.

3.1.4 Contrastive Optimization

After getting the z_i^{sc} and z_i^{mp} for node i from the above two views, we feed them into a MLP with one hidden layer to get embeddings $\mathcal{H}_i^{sc}$ and $\mathcal{H}_i^{mp}$, in order to map them into the space where contrastive loss is calculated.

We define positive samples as nodes connected by multiple meta paths. Specifcall-y, mp_i^j represents the number of meta paths connected between node i and node j. We arrange mp_i^j in descending order, with the first γ nodes being positive samples, denoted as pos_i, and the remaining nodes as negative samples, denoted as neg_i. With the positive sample set pos_i and negative sample set neg_i, we have the following contrastive loss under network schema view:

$$\mathcal{L}_i^{sc} = -\log \frac{\sum_{j \in pos_i} \exp(sim(\mathcal{H}_i^{sc}, \mathcal{H}_j^{mp})/\tau)}{\sum_{u \in \{pos_i \cup neg_i\}} \exp(sim(\mathcal{H}_i^{sc}, \mathcal{H}_u^{mp})/\tau)} \tag{5}$$

where $sim(u, v)$ denotes the cosine similarity between the vectors u and v, and τ denotes the temperature parameter.

In the contrastive loss $\mathcal{L}_i^{sc}$, the target embedding from the network schema vie an-d the embeddings of positive and negative samples are from the meta-path view, By doing the opposite, we can obtain loss $\mathcal{L}_i^{mp}$. In this way, we realize the cross-view self-supervision.

The overall objective is given as follows:

$$\mathcal{L} = \frac{1}{|V|} \sum_{i \in V} [\lambda \cdot \mathcal{L}_i^{sc} + (1 - \lambda) \cdot \mathcal{L}_i^{mp}] \tag{6}$$

where λ is a coefficient to balance the effect of two views. We can optimize the proposed model via back propagation and learn the attribute score of target nodes.

Definition: Attribute Score. We use an MLP to transform the embeddings learned from the meta path view into probabilities of nodes belonging to different categories, which is defined attribute score $S \in \mathcal{R}^{V \times T}$, V is the number of target nodes, and T is the number of classification categories, it can also be described as $S = \{S_1, S_2, ..., S_T\}$, where $\{S_i \in \mathcal{R}^{V \times 1} | i \in (1, T)\}$, when query input, it is necessary to match the S_i corresponding to query for searching.

3.2 Community Search

3.2.1 Target Community Definition

After obtaining attribute score of target nodes, we can introduce the target community. We use node attribute ratings to describe the attribute similarity between nodes. If a community within a certain scale has the highest total score, it indicates that the community has the highest attribute similarity. We use *k-core* to further improve the cohesion of community structure. Therefore, the target community is defined as *k-core* and $\mathcal{K}-sized$ maximum-attribute-scores community ($k\mathcal{K}$ - MASC) as follows:

Definition: $k\mathcal{K}-$MASC. Given a HIN $G = (V, E)$, a querying node v_q, an integer $k(k > 0)$, community size $\mathcal{K}$ and attribute score S_q corresponding to node v_q. The target community is a connected subgraph $C = (V_c, E_c, S_c)$ that satisfies the following conditions: (1) $v_q \in V_c$, $\phi(v_i) = \phi(v_q)$ and C is connected; (2) $|V_c| \leq \mathcal{K}$ and $\{v_i \in V_c | deg(v_i) \geq k\}$; (3) The total score $\sum_{v \in V_c} S_c[v]$ of C is the largest.

3.2.2 Search for $k\mathcal{K}-$MASC

Based on the category of query node q, find the S_q of all nodes belonging to the same category as the query from S, and then construct an induced homogeneity gr-aph $G' = (V', E', S_q)$ to CS. The implementation process is shown in Algorithm 1.

Algorithm 1: $k\mathcal{K}$-ASMcs

Input: $G' = (V', E', S_q)$, q , k , $\mathcal{K}$;

Output: $C = (V_c, E_c, S_c)$;

1   Initialize $V_c = \{q\}$; $E_c = \{\}$

2   **while** $|V_c| < 2\mathcal{K}$ **do**

3       $v = \arg_{u,x} \max S_q[u], u \notin V_c, u \in N_x, x \in V_c$

4       $V_c = V_c \cup \{v\}$, $E_c = E_c \cup \{(x, u)\}$;

5   **while** $\exists v \in V_c, |N_v| < k$ **do**

6   **foreach** vertex $v \in V_c$ **do**

7   **if** $|N_v| < k$ **then** $V_c = V_c \setminus \{v\}$, $E_c = E_c \setminus \{(v, u) | u \in V_c, u = N_v\}$;

8   **if** $|V_c| > \mathcal{K}$ **then** $x = \arg_u \min S_q[u], u \in V_c$, $V_c = V_c \setminus \{x\}$;

9   Jump to the 5 line of the algorithm 1 ;

10   return C ;

The idea of Algorithm 1($k\mathcal{K}$ - ASMcs) is to first find a maximum-attribute-score co-mmunity that satisfies twice the preset size $\mathcal{K}$, in order to facilitate the adjustment of community members to meet the community structure of *k-core*. Next, we will check the community members one by one until the degree of satisfying all the node is not less than k, here we use the number of neighbors to calculate the node degree, where N_x represents the number of neighbors of node x on the induced homogeneity graph. It is worth noting that when all conditions are met, if the number of community members is still greater than the preset size $\mathcal{K}$, select a node with the lowest attribute sco-re value from the community and delete it, and then check the community members again until $|V_c| > \mathcal{K}$ is met to complete the community search.

4 Experiments

4.1 Experiment Settings

Datasets. We employ the following three real HIN datasets: ACM [11], DBLP [5], IMDB[10], where the basic information are summarized in Table 1.

Baselines. We chose 3 community search methods for comparative experiments to demonstrate the effectiveness of the proposed method, including the deep learning method ICS-GNN [4] for homogeneous networks, the non deep learning method Fas-tBCore [2] for heterogeneous networks, and the deep learning method ICSMIM [10] for heterogeneous networks.

Table 1. The statistics of the datasets

Datasets	Node	Edges	Meta-path
ACM	paper (P):4019 author (A):7167 subject (S):60	P-A:13407 P-S:4019	PAP PSP
DBLP	author (A):4057 paper (P):14328 conference (C):20 term (T):7723	P-A:19645 P-C:14328 P-T:85810	APA APCPA APTPA
IMDB	movie (M):3492 actor (A):33401 direct (D):2502 writer (W):4459	M-A:65341 M-D:3762 M-W:6414	APA APCPA APTPA

Evaluating Indicator. This paper uses Community Precision [4], F1-score [13], and Density [14] to measure community quality, and uses query time to measure community query efficiency.

Implementation Details. In all methods, we set the community size $\mathcal{K} = 30$ uniformly, and randomly select 50 query nodes for query, and take the average value for comparison. For the method that cannot set the $\mathcal{K}$, such as FastBCore, we flexibly adjust its parameters, so that it can meet the conditions as much as possible and ensure the f-airness of the experiment. The running environment of the model is: CPU is AMD R-yzen 7 5800H with Radeon Graphics 3.20 GHz, memory is 16g, and GPU is GeFor-ce RTX 3070.

4.2 Effectiveness Evaluation

Community Evaluation. Table 2 shows the results of the different community search methods. It can be clearly seen that the communities found by $k\mathcal{K}$ - ASMcs method ach-ieve the highest precision, F1-score and community density on the three data sets, indicating that the quality of the communities mined by $k\mathcal{K}$ - ASMcs is better than that of the baseline method. Because FastBcore enhances structural cohesion like $k\mathcal{K}$ - ASMcs, community density achieves good results, but because it does not capture attribute similarity, precision and F1-score are much lower than other methods using deep learning. ICS-GNN is inferior to ICSMIM and $k\mathcal{K}$ - ASMcs, indicating that capt-uring semantic information is conducive to more accurate judgment of node similarity. Compared with ICSMIM, $k\mathcal{K}$ - ASMcs achieves better results, indicating that capturing missing information in meta paths is conducive to more accurate calculation of node similarity.

Search Efficiency Evaluation. Figure 2 shows the efficiency comparison of community search. ICS-GNN's community positioning process requires the construction of candidate subgraphs first, so it takes the most time. Second, ICSMIM only uses BFS to find the nodes with the most mutual information, and does not strengthen the structure

Table 2. Community quality comparison of different methods.

Datasets	Indicator	FastBCore	ICS-GNN	ICSMIM	$k\mathcal{K}$-ASMcs
ACM	Precision	0.430	0.905	0.952	**0.978**
	F1-score	0.420	0.885	0.920	**0.942**
	Density	0.747	0.664	0.668	**0.764**
DBLP	Precision	0.310	0.848	0.852	**0.974**
	F1-score	0.300	0.815	0.820	**0.945**
	Density	0.960	0.930	0.930	**0.963**
IMDB	Precision	0.425	0.564	0.570	**0.728**
	F1-score	0.400	0.550	0.562	**0.676**
	Density	0.670	0.612	0.633	**0.673**

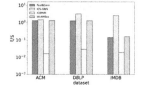 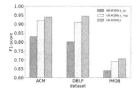

Fig. 2. Comparison of efficiency.   **Fig. 3.** Precision of Ablation.   **Fig. 4.** F1-score of Ablation.

of the community, so it takes the least time. However, it is necessary to improve the cohesion of the community, so while $k\mathcal{K}$ - ASMcs's query time is higher than ICSMIM, CSDS-SGNN leads in community precision, F1-scores, and community density, so the time spent is more valuable.

4.3 Ablation Study

We conducted ablation experiments from two aspects, node attribute score calculation and community search, to verify the effectiveness of each module of the proposed method.

Node Attribute Score Calculation. We design two variants of $k\mathcal{K}$-ASMcs: $k\mathcal{K}$-ASMcs_ *sc* and $k\mathcal{K}$-ASMcs_*mp* to verify the effect of network schema view and meta path view on community attribute similarity, respectively. $k\mathcal{K}$-ASMcs_ *sc* means that the node attribute score is calculated only through the network schema view, and the corresponding positive and negative sample embeddings are also from the network schema embeddings. $k\mathcal{K}$-ASMcs_*mp* means that the node attribute score is calculated only through the meta path view, and the corresponding positive and negative sample embeddings are also from the meta path view embeddings. Figure 3 and Fig. 4 shows the comparison before and after ablation. The precision and F1-scores found by

Table 3. Ablation study of CS.

Datasets	algorithm	Precision	F1-score	Density	Time
ACM	$\mathcal{K}$-ASMcs	**0.980**	**0.951**	0.656	**0.081**
	$k\mathcal{K}$-ASMcs	0.978	0.942	**0.764**	0.291
DBLP	$\mathcal{K}$-ASMcs	**0.978**	**0.952**	0.871	**0.154**
	$k\mathcal{K}$-ASMcs	0.974	0.945	**0.963**	0.312
IMDB	$\mathcal{K}$-ASMcs	**0.734**	**0.680**	0.592	**0.006**
	$k\mathcal{K}$-ASMcs	0.728	0.676	**0.673**	0.012

$k\mathcal{K}$-ASMcs_ sc and $k\mathcal{K}$-ASMcs_mp are lower than those found by $k\mathcal{K}$-ASMcs. Cross-perspective comparative learning can calculate node attribute scores more accurately and find communities with more similar attributes.

Community Search Algorithm. We removed the restriction on community structure in the algorithm, we only found a community of size $\mathcal{K}$ with the maximum attribute score sum, which we defined as $\mathcal{K}$-ASMcs. Table 3 shows the comparison results of different indicators before and after ablation.

It can be seen that community precision and F1-score are improved to a certain extent after the restriction of structure is removed. Moreover, community density has a significant decline, which further indicates that enhancing community structure cohesion will affect community attribute similarity, but community structure is an important indicator of community, and it is meaningful to sacrifice a certain degree of accuracy in exchange for higher community density.

4.4 Community Sensitivity Analysis

This section tests the effects of k and $\mathcal{K}$ on community precision, F1-score and community density, and community search efficiency on three datasets.

Figure 5 shows the effect of $\mathcal{K}$, where the experiment controls for $k = 5$. It can be seen that when the $\mathcal{K}$ is small, such as $\mathcal{K} = 10$, the community precision and F1-score are relatively low, because when the $\mathcal{K}$ is low, some query nodes cannot find the community that meets the conditions, which will reduce the average level. With the increase of $\mathcal{K}$, the accuracy and F1-score tend to be stable, but the community density will show a downward trend, because the current k value cannot meet the increasing edge density caused by the increase of nodes. Finally, as the scale increases, so does the query time.

Figure 6 shows the effect of k, and the default $\mathcal{K} = 30$. It can be seen that increasing the value of k will improve the community density, but will reduce the community precision and F1-score, indicating that strengthening the community structure will affect the community attribute similarity. In addition, increasing the value of k will increase the community search query time.

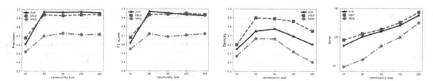

(a) Pre of variable $\mathcal{K}$ (b) F1-score of variable $\mathcal{K}$ (c) Density of variable$\mathcal{K}$ (d) time of variable$\mathcal{K}$

Fig. 5. Sensitivity analysis of $\mathcal{K}$.

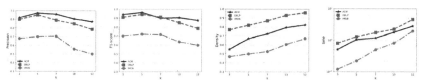

(a) Pre of variable k (b) F1-score of variable k (c) Density of variable$k$ (d) time of variable$k$

Fig. 6. Sensitivity analysis of k.

5 Conclusion

This paper studies the CSH problem based on deep learning and proposes the CSH method $k\mathcal{K}$ - ASMcs based on the SGNN model. SGNN uses network schema view and meta path view as two views to capture the local and global structures in HIN. They achieve mutual supervision through view mask mechanism, and contrastive learning to calculate the attribute scores of nodes for query nodes. After obtaining the attribute socre of target nodes, we first capture the maximum-attribute-scores community, and then mine the k-core subgraph to discover the target community. A large number of experimental results demonstrate the effectiveness of the method proposed in this paper.

Acknowledgments. This research is supported by the National Natural Science Foundation of China (62062066, 62266050 and 62276227), Yunnan Fundamental Research Projects (202201AS070015); Yunnan Key Laboratory of Intelligent Systems and Computing (202205AG070003), the Block-chain and Data Security Governance Engineering Research Center of Yunnan Provincial Department of Education.

References

1. Shi, C., Wang, R.J., Wang, X.: Survey on heterogeneous information networks analysis and application. J. Softw. **33**(2), 598–621 (2022)
2. Fang, Y., Yang, Y., Zhang, W., et al.: Effective and efficient community search over large heterogeneous information networks. Proc. VLDB Endowment **13**(6), 854–867 (2020)
3. Yang, Y., Fang, Y., Lin, X., et al.: Effective and efficient truss computation over large heterogeneous information networks. In: 2020 IEEE 36th (ICDE), 901–912 (2020)
4. Gao, J., Chen, J., Li, Z., Zhang, J.: ICS-GNN: lightweight interactive community search via graph neural network. Proc. VLDB Endowment **14**, 1006–1018 (2021)

5. Wang, X., Liu, N., Han, H., Shi, C.: Self-supervised Heterogeneous Graph Neural Network with Co-contrastive Learning, 1726–1736 (2021)
6. Qiao, L., Zhang, Z., Yuan, Ye., Chen, C., Wang, G.: Keyword-centric community search over large heterogeneous information networks. In: Jensen, C.S., et al. (eds.) DASFAA 2021. LNCS, vol. 12681, pp. 158–173. Springer, Cham (2021). https://doi.org/10.1007/978-3-030-73194-6_12
7. Guo, Y., Gu, X., Wang, Z., Fan, H., Li, B., Wang, W.: RCS: an attributed community search approach based on representation learning. In: 2021 (IJCNN), pp. 1–8 (2021)
8. Zhao, W.J., Zhang, F.B., Liu, J.L.: Community search algorithm based on node embedding representation learning. Control Decis. **36**(8), 7 (2021)
9. Jiang, Y., Rong, Y., Cheng, H., et al.: Query driven-graph neural networks for community search: from non-attributed, attributed, to interactive attributed. arXiv:2104.03583 (2021)
10. Wang, Y.F., Zhou, L.H., Chen, W., Wang, L.Z., Chen, H.M.: Community search with mutual information maximization over heterogeneous information networks. J. Zhejiang Univ. (Eng. Sci.) **57**(02), 287–298 (2023)
11. Wang, X., Ji, H., Shi, C., et al.: Heterogeneous graph attention network. In: The World Wide Web Conference, 2022–2032 (2019)
12. Kipf, T.N., Welling, M.: Semi-Supervised Classification with Graph Convolutional Networks (2016)
13. Zhu, J.C., Wang, C.K.: Approaches to community search under complex conditions. J. Softw. **30**(3), 21 (2019)
14. Wang, J., Zhou, L., Wang, X., Wang, L., Li, S.: Attribute-sensitive community search over attributed heterogeneous information networks. Expert Syst. Appl. **235**, 121153 (2024)

Measurement and Research on the Conflict Between Residential Space and Tourism Space in Pianyan Ancient Township

Hong Hui, Lan Feng, and Renjun Zhang[✉]

Chongqing University of Technology, Chongqing, China
zrj@cqut.edu.cn

Abstract. Studying spatial behavioral conflicts is the main method to understand the conflicts between tourists and residents. However, academic research on spatial conflict mostly involves urban macro-level discussions, and is not deeply involved in micro-scale spatial conflict. And most of them analyze spatial conflict from a qualitative perspective, lacking quantitative research on tourism spatial conflict. In this paper, we identify the spatial conflict areas in the township and quantitatively analyze the structural characteristics of the conflict areas through the method of multi-intelligence body simulation.

Keyword: Multi-Agent · Spatial conflict · Tourism space · Living space

1 Introduction

Traditional ancient towns are legacies left behind by Chinese traditional culture and have great cultural, historical, aesthetic and economic values. As one of the hot tourist towns in Chongqing, in 2007, it became one of the third batch of famous historical and cultural towns in China. Carrying multiple functions such as residence, tourism, etc., different groups of people are gathered in this specific space of the ancient town of Pianyan, and there are differences in the demands of different groups, which will inevitably lead to contradictions and conflicts, and at the spatial level, it will be manifested in the competition for the established spatial resources, which will lead to a conflict between the residents' living space and the tourists' traveling space in the off-peak seasons, and it needs to be urgently dealt with.

Ancient towns cannot be developed without tourism, and it is difficult to get rid of the impact of spatial conflicts caused by tourism development, which is also the main dilemma faced by the tourism development and protection of ancient towns. The objective existence of spatial conflict, the demand for fair distribution of tourism space and residential space is also becoming more and more urgent, but it is difficult to achieve fair distribution, but it is difficult to completely subvert overnight. Therefore, it is particularly important to strengthen the research on tourism space and residential space to identify spatial conflicts. Research methods for spatial conflict at home and abroad have also experienced a shift from qualitative analysis to quantitative calculation, but the existing research is mainly based on qualitative research, including mathematical and statistical analysis [1, 2], GIS modeling analysis [3, 4], etc., and lacks the research on quantitative spatial conflict. The research perspectives are mainly from sociology or psychology on human spatial behavioral conflicts [5], or their spatial patterns [6], spatial changes [7], etc. are studied individually. In terms of spatial optimization strategies, crowd guidance [8], control of crowd behavior [9] and other measures are mainly adopted to optimize it.

Based on the study of spatial conflict, it is found that the existing spatial conflict research methods are mainly based on qualitative research and lack quantitative research on spatial conflict. This study provides a microsimulation method to analyze tourism spatial conflicts with the object of space-using subjects, and the microsimulation method provides a virtual experimental tool for analyzing and optimizing spatial relationships. The same spatial structure of the ancient town of Pianyan is stripped into tourist space and resident space, and through field observation and other means, we collect data related to the behavior of tourists and residents, understand their general behavioral trajectory, analyze the behavioral decision-making patterns of tourists and residents, and use multi-intelligent body analog simulation technology to simulate the behavior of tourists and residents in a single day. The conflict areas between visitors' open space and residents' living space in the ancient town of Pianyan are identified. And optimization strategies are proposed based on the performance of conflict areas at different moments in a day.

2 Overview of the Study Area and Data Sources

2.1 Overview of the Study Area

The ancient town is located in Beibei District, Chongqing City, between the two branches of the Huaying Mountains in the southwest of the mountain range, because of the north of the town there is a rock wall tilted high, overhanging steeply named. 2007, the ancient town of the Pianyan approved to become the third batch of the country's famous historical and cultural towns. Over the past 300 years, the town has basically maintained the architectural characteristics of the ancient town. The main streets of Yiyan Ancient Town are laid out in parallel along the river, which roughly divides it into three parts, the main neighborhood, the old neighborhood and the new village area. The total length of the old streets and alleys of the old town is about 500 m, and the buildings are staggered and continuously arranged along both sides of the streets and alleys, and the width of the streets and alleys is about 2–4 m. The main block of dense buildings, the main road intersected horizontally and vertically, forming a crossroads, the main road road width of about 7 m, the northernmost is for recreation of the writing square, infrastructure, interlocking alleys. The new village is mainly residential, with streets and alleys distributed vertically and neatly arranged.

Ancient buildings, rustic environment, long historical and cultural relics, and pro-found humanistic connotations together constitute the unique scenery of the ancient town. There are old buildings such as old neighborhoods, ancient theaters, Yuwang Temple, ancient stone bridges, Yuping Academy and other old buildings, folk arts such as playing Lianrong, mountain songs, rice-planting dances and other folk crafts such as wood carvings, stone carvings, ironware, costumes and other folk crafts. Of course, the ancient trees are also important landscape elements of the ancient town. The ancient tree clusters that have been preserved along the river as well as the husband and wife trees by the Yuanyang Bridge at the southeastern end of the ancient town attract a lot of tourists to go sightseeing because of their simplicity and naturalness. The tourism of the ancient town of Pianyan is mainly characterized by the Heishuitan River, which is surrounded by trees on both sides of the river, and the water in the river is clear and cool, making it a good place to play in the water and cool off in the summer in Chongqing.

In this study, the data of road network, attraction distribution and street distribution in the ancient town of Pianyan are selected to construct the basic database. The area of the ancient town of Pianyan is drawn as an axial map, and the unique ID of each road section is formed to get the basic database of the ancient town of Pianyan.

2.2   Data Sources

(1) Spatial distribution data. Obtain the spatial base map of the old town by downloading the satellite map of the old town, Baidu map, etc., and utilize the field research to obtain the spatial data including the length of the road, the road time consumed, the path condition, and the distribution of attractions. Utilize CAD software to draw the axial map to form the base data.

(2) Spatial distribution data of tourists and residents. 2023 was carried out in three times to target the behavioral trajectory data of tourists and residents, the investigators consisted of a total of 14 postgraduate students from the team, the investigation location was the ancient town of Pianyan, including the old street, the new street as well as the new village of the three regions, to obtain the flow data of the important nodes such as the school, the bus station, the writing square and other important nodes, and record them in real time by the counter, and through the professional software to obtain the More than 600 behavioral trajectory data of tourists and residents.

3   Multi-intelligence Body Simulation

The spatial behavior simulation based on GIS and Multi-Agent system technology can microsimulate the spatial mobile behavior of groups in scenic spots, and realize the tracking analysis of the spatial for location and behavioral state changes of each tourist and resident in scenic spots [10]. The application of intelligent body technology in the field of tourism is the earliest foreign research, only need to consider a very small number of assumptions, can be highly restored to the complex system simulation simulation [11]. STUDENT et al. [12] used NetLogo to simulate the growth of the number of tourists, diversification of business measures, etc., on the impact of Antarctica. Compared with traditional models, multi-intelligence body-based modeling can fully consider the heterogeneity between individuals and the adaptability of behavior, and show the interaction between intelligences [13]. At present, for multi-intelligent body simulation is mainly applied to the study of optimized protection of tourist areas [14], pedestrian walking characteristics [15], and so on, and there are fewer researches on tourists' behaviors. Using computer technology to simulate the spatial movement behavior of human beings, it is convenient to grasp the basic data such as the flow of people in a certain area at a certain moment or a certain period of time, the walking position and distance of an individual at a certain moment, and so on, which is of great significance to understand the characteristics of the spatial movement behavior of tourists and residents [10]. The basic structure of Agent consists of an environment information module, an execution module, an information storage module, and a simulation result analysis module. The basic structure of Agent consists of environment information module, execution module, information storage module and simulation result analysis module.

3.1 Environmental Information Module

The environment information module is mainly for the perception of the environment information that Agent needs to walk, including several primitive tables, team initial table: team ID, number of teams, team type, team age composition, team gender composition, team travel time, etc.; probable paths table: path ID, location ID, path order, path length, path segment area, etc.; path length table: path ID, starting point, time length and number of attractions; destination probability table: destination ID, location ID, location name, longest and shortest duration of stay at destination, etc. These four basic tables are related to Agent definition, Map definition and Rule definition, Agent definition includes the definition of the number of Agents entering the simulation, time, Agent attributes, the team they belong to and so on. Map definition includes the description of the spatial structure, road sections, nodes, etc. of the simulation case place. Rule definition refers to the definition of the relationship between each Agent acting on the spatial walking, including the process of Agent attribute change rules into the database.

3.2 Implementation Module

The algorithm implemented in the Agent Execution Module is shown in Fig. 1, where the whole system is controlled by a virtual clock, and for every step increase of the clock, the system calculates a brand new position and time for all agents, and stores the structure of each calculation into the agent team state database. Several key techniques in the algorithm are described below.

(1) Agent spatial movement destination determination. Tourist spatial behavior destinations include visiting attractions, playing and entertaining, etc., and resident spatial behavior purposes include playing and entertaining, living and shopping, etc. The proposed destination table is generated by querying through SQLserver calls based on the existing destination probability table as well as the initial table of the team, and each team has a corresponding table of the proposed destinations of the team.

(2) Virtual Clock. The virtual clock is the center that controls the operation of the whole system, the clock increases every step, the system calculates all Agents once, the total time of the clock is the simulation of the time period, the clock's step is selected 1min.

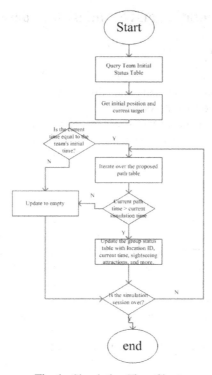

Fig. 1. Simulation Flow Chart

3.3 Information Storage Module

The spatial base database contains several table data, including team initial table, possible path table, spatial destination table, final path table and so on. The team status table updates the relevant data in the team status table according to the step of the virtual clock and saves it, which is mainly realized by PyCharm software connecting to SQLserver, and every time a step is run, the dynamic, spatial location of the Agent in the team status table is recorded once. Therefore, the team state table is equivalent to a spatio-temporal database, including the spatial location and other data of different Agents at different times.

3.4 Module for Analyzing Simulation Results

The main data for the experimental results analysis module comes from the team state table. The team state database obtained through Agent simulation of residents and tourists, which includes the position change data of each Agent at each moment. It can be visualized and analyzed by GIS software, and the virtual experimental process can be displayed graphically, which can show the required results more intuitively.

4 System Implementation and Simulation Experiments

4.1 Spatial Form of the Ancient Town of Pianyan

The space of the ancient town of Pianyan is mainly building blocks. Ancient town is to experience the development process of point - line - surface and form the current complete space structure of the ancient town. As the basic spatial model of the ancient town, faceted space contrasts sharply with the form of street space; the spatial configuration is different in terms of aspect ratio, and does not have the directionality of linear space; linear space is also more open and flexible. Faceted space also involves public space and private space, the privacy of faceted space corresponds to its function, the residential area is relatively private, while the public area is relatively open, which is also an important spatial structure for spatial conflict measurement. The ancient town of Pianyan is divided into three main parts by the natural linear barrier of the Heishuitan River, the new neighborhood, the old neighborhood, and the new village area, as shown in Fig. 3.

Transportation roads crisscross each space, forming a unique spatial form, and numerous alleys are interspersed, forming multiple intersections, which is very convenient. The old neighborhood mainly consists of the old street, the river street and various attractions. The buildings in the old street are on the old side, dating from a long time ago, with the foot-hanging towers as the main feature, and the distribution of the husband and wife tree, the ancient theater and other attractions, which is the place where tourists are concentrated. The new neighborhood is mainly a commercial area with many stores and residential buildings, with modern brick buildings, a kindergarten in the westernmost part, and a writing plaza in the northern part of the new neighborhood for residents' daily activities and recreation, and also for temporary parking during the peak season. The new village, on the other hand, is more recent, with mainly residential buildings and a few farmhouses and restaurants arranged in a coherent manner. The new village is mainly a place for residents to live, the houses are arranged neatly, the government square has become the main activity and entertainment place for residents, and it is also a place for tourists to drop off their guests and vehicles to park temporarily. The new neighborhood is mainly a commercial area, all kinds of stores are distributed, banks, mahjong parlors, restaurants, food markets and other facilities are available, it is a place where residents and tourists converge. As shown in Fig. 4 (Fig. 2 and Table 1).

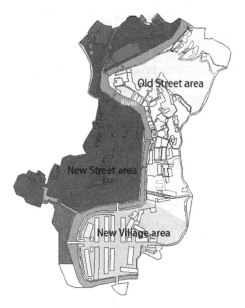

Fig. 2. Pianyan Ancient Town Area Map

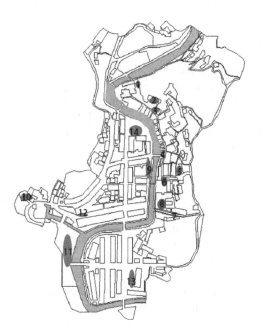

Fig. 3. Distribution map of nodes in the old town of Pianyan

Table 1. Main nodes of the old town of Pianyan

serial number	Location ID	nodal	shore
1	256	The Female Blacksmith's Shop	old neighborhood
2	336	Yu Wang Temple	old neighborhood
3	335	old theater	old neighborhood
4	221	River Street Entrance	old neighborhood
5	186	Duanmeng Academy	old neighborhood
6	189	Old Street Entrance	old neighborhood
7	114	Couples' tree	old neighborhood
8	160	secondary schools	old neighborhood
9	200	food market	new neighborhood
10	133	nursery school	new neighborhood
11	118	West parking lot	new neighborhood
12	111	station	new neighborhood
13	78	Government Plaza	New Village area
14	269	sketching gallery	new neighborhood

4.2 Spatial Conflict Identification

Through Multi-Agent system technology, the behavior of tourists and residents in a day is simulated with SQLserver database and PyCharm software, and the simulation data are obtained. The data of tourists and residents in the morning, midday and evening were obtained respectively, and visualized and analyzed by ArcGis software. Figures 3, 4, 5 and 6 show the simulated conflict areas of tourists and residents in the morning, midday and evening, respectively.

The behavior of residents and tourists in the morning, midday and evening of a day can reflect the conflict size of a place to a certain extent. From the simulation results, the conflict areas in the three different moments in the morning, midday and evening of the ancient town of Pianyan are different, and the size of the conflict is also different. Through ArcGis and SQLserver software to get the number of residents and tourists in three moments of the day and visualize them, we get: 1) The conflict area in the morning at nine o'clock in the ancient town of Pianyan is less, and it is mainly at the entrance, and the conflict of people flow is not obvious in the old street and the main street. According to the information obtained from the survey, the source of the ancient town of Pianyan is mainly the main city of Chongqing, and the ancient town of Pianyan to the main city of almost 2 h by car, this moment is almost the tourists just arrived at the time, the tourists are mainly concentrated in the entrance area, not yet entered the old street. 2) twelve o'clock with the increase in the number of tourists, the conflict area of the ancient town of Pianyan increased significantly, mainly in the old streets of old streets, the entrance to the old street, bus stops, as well as near the vegetable market in the new neighborhood. Obviously, this simulation result is in line with the actual behavior,

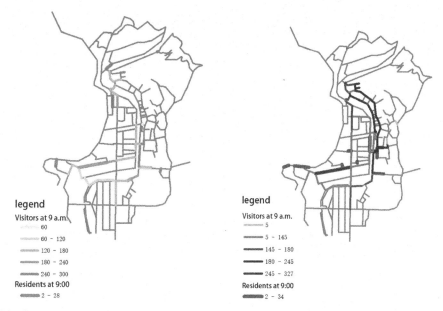

Fig. 4. Map of space conflict zones at 9 o'clock

Fig. 5. Map of areas of conflict in space at 12 o'clock

most of the residents are at home, and the tourists are almost exploring the attractions in the old neighborhood. Some tourists arrived in the ancient town of Pianyan at noon, showing a conflict at the bus station. 3) At 6:00 p.m., the number of tourists decreased compared to noon, the number of residents increased, some residents concentrated on walking in the main street of the new neighborhood, and the conflict area shifted from the old street to the new street area, and the conflict was more obvious, with a larger number of people.

As far as the experimental results are concerned, the establishment of the pedestrian intelligent body model based on the vector data structure using the multi-intelligent body method better reflects the dynamics of the crowd flow process in the outdoor space. The group flow of the group in the ancient town of Pianyan in a day simulated based on the behavioral trajectories of different groups better reflects the actual situation in the ancient town of Pianyan.

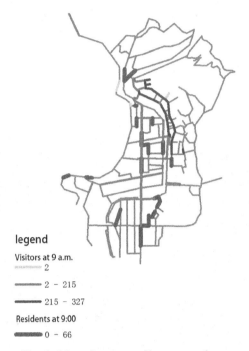

Fig. 6. Map of space conflict areas at 6 p.m.

4.3 Optimization Strategies

According to the above situation of conflict areas in different moments, corresponding strategies can reduce the spatial overlap between tourists and residents in the peak season of the ancient town, reduce the management cost and conflict management cost of the ancient town, and achieve the reasonable distribution of spatial resources to maintain good spatial order. 1) For the performance of conflict in different moments, it is noted that tourists in the ancient town of migrants mainly visit the main attractions after midday, and that the old neighborhood has a large flow of people and the new neighborhood has a small flow of people, which can be optimized according to different spatial properties. And the new neighborhoods have less flow of people, the living places and recreational facilities of the residents can be set in the new village and new street area to reduce the overlap between the two groups spatially. 2) Optimize according to different spatial natures. Appropriately increase the diversity of activities in the old neighborhood to extend the tourists' visiting time and avoid spreading to the residents' space. At the same time, increase the accessibility of the old neighborhoods and set up guiding facilities such as attraction tour maps and signposts in the areas where tourists are concentrated, so as to avoid tourists entering the residential space due to getting lost on their way to visit, which will result in conflicts. 3) Reasonable planning of infrastructures. The current vegetable market in the ancient town of Pianyan is set on the side of the street, and there is a cross overlap with the tourists' excursion activities, coupled with the fact that the site has more residents and a large time span, it is the place where the conflict area manifests itself more obviously, and it is possible to reasonably plan the construction of a closed-type vegetable market, with its site mainly in the new street or new village area, avoiding the tourists. Formulate appropriate development intentions to meet the needs of activities from tourists and residents.

5 Conclusion

The simulation of group behavior through multi-intelligent body simulation simulation technology, using the method of virtual experiment, is an effective research way to measure spatial conflict. Moreover, the simulation based on behavioral data can more realistically reflect the state of crowd flow. In this study, the multi-intelligent body system formed by simple behavioral rules from a single intelligent subject can simulate the state of a specific crowd under a specific space, obtain the positional movement status at different time points, identify the spatial conflict between groups, which is of certain practical significance for spatial planning and design. Based on the simulation results, the conflict in the ancient town of Pianyan is optimized to realize the planning concept with the goal of reducing group conflicts, and the optimization strategy of rationally planning space and infrastructure for different moments is proposed, which provides a reference for the optimization of spatial conflicts in the ancient town in the future, and deepens the application of multi-intelligent body simulation in spatial optimization.

This study measured the spatial conflict in the ancient town of Pianyan using a multi-intelligence simulation experiment, which is exploratory both in terms of the theoretical study of spatial conflict and spatial optimization. However, the population behavior research data in the study is only a part of the data, and the simulated data is better suited to the reality, and the accuracy can be further improved. The focus of this study is to explore the measurement method of spatial conflict between different groups in the region of town, which has theoretical and practical significance. Spatial conflicts are constantly changing and developing, and more in-depth research is needed.

References

1. Murtagh, B., Ellis, G.: Skills, conflict and spatial planning in Northern Ireland. Plann. Theory Pract. (3) (2011)
2. Tanulku, B.: Gated communities: ideal packages or processual spaces of conflict? Housing Stud. **28**(7), 937–959 (2013)
3. Tuda, A.O., Stevens, T.F., Rodwell, L.D.: Resolving coastal conflicts using marine spatial planning. J. Environ. Manage. 13359–13368 (2014)
4. Chen, J., Liu, W., Li, Z., Zhao, R., Cheng, T.: Detection of spatial conflicts between rivers and contours in digital map updating. Int. J. Geograph. Inf. Sci. (10) (2007)
5. Zhao, S.: Research on the relationship between conflict perception and participation willingness of residents in tourist communities. Jinan University (2015)
6. Zhang, X., Che, Z.: Research on spatial morphology change of tourist villages based on spatial syntax–taking Shuhe Ancient town of Lijiang as an example. Cent. China Archit. **30**(09), 105–109 (2012). https://doi.org/10.13942/j.cnki.hzjz.2012.09.021
7. Tian, J., Zhou, X., Li, Z., Yu, C.: Syntactic study on the development of urban spatial structure in Kunming. Urban Plann. **40**(04), 41–49 (2016)

8. Li, Y., Xie, J., Wang, Q.: Research on the evaluation of tourism spatial behavioral conflict and spatial optimization strategy - taking Gulangyu Island as an example. Geogr. Geogr. Inf. Sci. **34**(01), 92–97 (2018)

9. Muying, O., Lin, Z.: A study of residents' tourism impact perception and conflict adjustment behavior–taking Shanghai Innovation Village as an example. Resident. Sci. Technol. **42**(05), 34–39 (2022). https://doi.org/10.13626/j.cnki.hs.2022.05.002

10. Zhang, R., Yang, Y.: Walking simulation system based on GIS and multi-agent. J. Chongqing Technol. Bus. Univ. (Nat. Sci. Edn.) (02), 160–163 (2005)

11. Gilbert, N., Terna, P.: How to build and use agent-based models in social science. Mind Soc. **1**, 57–72 (2000)

12. Student, J., Amelung, B., Lamers, M.: Towards a tipping point? Exploring the capacity to self-regulate Antarctic tourism using agent-based modelling. J. Sustain. Tour. **24**(3), 412–429 (2016)

13. Gross, D., Strand, R.: Can agent-based models assist decisions on large-scale practical problems: a philosophical analysis. Complexity **5**(5), 26–33 (2000)

14. Fu, L.-H., Xie, B.-G., Li, X.-Q., et al.: Decision-making for tourism land protection behavior based on multi-intelligence simulation. Geogr. Res. **31**(03), 555–564 (2012)

15. Li, M.: Agent-based simulation modeling and application of tourists' behavior in scenic spots–taking the summer palace as an example. J. Tour. **29**(11), 62–72 (2014)

Spatiotemporal Data Prediction

Spatio-Temporal Sequence Prediction of Diversion Tunnel Based on Machine Learning Multivariate Data Fusion

Zenghui Bi, Huan Zhao[✉], Changping Li, and Yan Xia

Yunnan Institute of Water and Hydropower Engineering Investigation Design and Research, Kunming 650000, China
zhaohuan111531@126.com

Abstract. The safety monitoring of hydraulic structures is an important measure to ensure the safe construction and operation of water diversion projects. The traditional data analysis and prediction of water conservancy monitoring mostly uses geometric models, and the accuracy of short-term prediction is reasonable, while the accuracy of long-term prediction is greatly reduced. Moreover, the traditional time series analysis method only considers the temporal correlation of the monitoring time series, but does not consider the spatial correlation between the multivariate monitoring time series, and can not make full use of the spatio-temporal correlation information between the multivariate monitoring data. To solve the above problems, this paper proposes a spatio-temporal prediction method, ARIMA-b-DLSSVM, which integrates multiple time series. The model is based on least square support vector machine (LSSVM) for multivariate data fusion, auto-regressive integral moving average (ARIMA) model for trend extraction, bisquare spatial basis to establish spatial correlation of monitoring data, and discounted least square method (DLS) for model optimization. The results show that the accuracy of ARIMA-b-DLSSVM long-term prediction is higher than that of traditional model and single machine learning model. The spatio-temporal fusion of multivariate data can better predict the spatio-temporal sequence changes of diversion tunnels with large fluctuations.

Keywords: multivariate data fusion · auto-regressive integral moving average · least square support vector machine

1 Introduction

The core of water conservancy safety monitoring lies in the analysis and prediction of various monitoring data. Currently, the commonly used time series analysis methods can be divided into traditional analysis methods and machine learning methods, and the traditional analysis includes geometric analysis, physical analysis and spatio-temporal analysis methods [1–4]. Among them, geometric analysis is to build a time series to analyze and predict the change process of the deformable by analyzing the change amount of the deformable and the relationship between its spatial distribution and time dimension [5, 6]. Physical analysis is to approach the physical process by certain mathematical methods, analyze the physical process and cause of deformation, simulate the analysis by establishing mechanical and dynamic models, and analyze and predict the deformation of deformable body by using the evolution of physical process. Spatio-temporal analysis method breaks through the limitation of single time series analysis, and integrates multiple time series into the model for overall modeling, taking into account the spatial correlation, and then obtains good robustness and prediction accuracy.

Although the traditional deformation analysis method has obtained a good effect in short-term prediction, the error increases rapidly in long-term prediction, and the prediction effect is not ideal, and the safety problems often start to breed in the long rainy season. Machine learning [7, 8] is more suitable for long-term prediction. Machine learning methods include neural network [9], support vector machine (SVM), etc. [10]. Computer is used for thinking simulation, models are built under certain rules, and multi-layer perception and multi-dimensional information features are learned and optimized to obtain optimal solutions, which can better solve nonlinear problems. However, these algorithms only consider the temporal dimension of the data, ignoring the temporal and spatial correlation between the multivariate data. In this case, it is difficult to draw accurate and reliable conclusions for various monitoring data of long-distance diversion tunnels due to the loss of correlation information.

Organic fusion of information from different sources, different modes, different times, and different spatial locations can not only eliminate contradictions and redundancy between sensors, but also integrate multiple data features to obtain a more complete and systematic model and improve decision accuracy. Among mainstream machine learning algorithms, neural networks are Mired in local optimality and the topology is difficult to determine [11]. The SVM has better generalization ability, which can reduce data overfitting. At the same time, kernel function is introduced to map low-dimensional space samples to high-dimensional space for solving, which can better solve the time-consuming high-dimensional inner product operation of neural network and effectively avoid the "dimensional disaster" problem [12].

Support vector machine regression algorithm has always played an important role in the field of data analysis and prediction. With the proposed DLSSVM algorithm, the related problems of SVM are transformed into solving linear equations, which not only reduces the calculation consumption, but also achieves better prediction effect in small sample problems [13, 14]. However, the LSSVM model does not consider the time correlation of time series, which affects the generalization ability. In order to improve the time prediction performance of LSSVM, Taiwan scholar Yuxiang Huang proposed the DSVM model based on DLS method [15].

In order to make effective use of the advantages of various models, considering the linear, non-linear, temporal and spatial correlation characteristics of time series of various monitoring data such as safety monitoring of diversion tunnels [16], ARIMA [17], which has excellent linear prediction performance in traditional models, is combined with LSSVM model based on DLS method for multivariate data fusion prediction. At the same time, in order to improve the lack of spatial correlation of support vector machines, this paper introduces the spatial basis construction method of spatio-temporal random effect model(STRE) in spatio-temporal Kalman model [18, 19], adopts bisquare spatial basis to construct kernel function in the optimal classification hyperplane, and introduces spatial distance of monitoring instrument to describe spatial correlation. The ARIMA-b-DLSSVM model was formed. Compared with a single machine learning model, this model overcomes the defects of a single model, while taking into account the correlation between time and space, and obtains the optimal model prediction accuracy with faster computing speed.

2 Methodology

2.1 ARIMA Model

The autoregressive integral moving average model makes the difference on the basis of the autoregressive moving average model. If the difference series is still non-stationary, the difference is continued until the difference series is stationary, thus transforming the non-stationary time series into a stationary series. The basic principle is as follows:

The D-order difference calculation for the original non-stationary time series $\{X_t, t = 0, \pm 1, \pm 2, \cdots\}$ can make the sequence stationary, then

$$\nabla^d X_t = (1 - B)X_t \tag{1}$$

$$\nabla^d = 1 - \begin{bmatrix} d \\ 1 \end{bmatrix} B + \begin{bmatrix} d \\ 2 \end{bmatrix} B^2 + \cdots + (-1)^{d-1} \begin{bmatrix} d \\ d-1 \end{bmatrix} B^{d-1} + (-1)^d B^d \tag{2}$$

According to the difference operator and the displacement operator, the general form of ARIMA model can be obtained as follows:

$$X_t - \varphi_1 X_{t-1} - \varphi_2 X_{t-2} - \cdots - \varphi_p X_{t-p} = \varepsilon_t - \theta_1 \varepsilon_{t-1} - \theta_2 \varepsilon_{t-2} - \cdots - \theta_q \varepsilon_{t-q} \tag{3}$$

where B is the linear shift operator vector, ∇^d is the difference operator of order d, ε_t is the Gaussian white noise of zero mean, p is the autoregressive coefficient, q is the moving average coefficient, $\varphi_1 \ldots \varphi_p$ is the partial correlation coefficient of X_t, $\theta_1 \ldots \theta_q$ is the moving average paramete $\begin{bmatrix} d \\ 1 \end{bmatrix}, \begin{bmatrix} d \\ 2 \end{bmatrix} \cdots \begin{bmatrix} d \\ d-1 \end{bmatrix}$ for 2-d column vector, X_t remember as ARIMA (p, d, q) sequence.

2.2 Order of ARIMA Model

The ARIMA model of multivariate data needs to model each time series separately. In order to improve the modeling efficiency, the difference order d is determined by calculating the variance function.

Let $Z(x)$ be the regionalized variable, when $Z(x)$ satisfies the second-order stationary hypothesis, the expectation of the regionalized variable $Z(x)$ is constant, and the covariance function is only related to h. Let $Cov(Z(x), Z(x + h))$ be $C(x, x + h)$, that is: $E(Z(x)) = c$, therefore:

$$Cov(Z(x), Z(x + h)) = E(Z(x)Z(x + h)) - c^2 \tag{4}$$

$$C(x, x + h) = f(h) \tag{5}$$

In geostatistics, the variance function $2\gamma(h)$, which describes the spatial correlation between random fields and random processes, is represented by the second order central moment of the increment of the regionalized variables separated by h,

$$2\gamma(h) = E(Z(x) - Z(x + h))^2 \tag{6}$$

$$\gamma(h) = f(0) - f(h) \tag{7}$$

where $f(0)$ is the prior variance, and $\gamma(h)$ is called the semi-variance function. For the convenience of use, the semi-variance function is often used to replace the variance function to describe the spatial correlation. Because the observational data are discrete and finite. Let $(x_i, i = 1, 2, \ldots, n)$ is the regionalized variable, and $Z(x_i)$ and $Z(x_i + h)$ are the observed values of the x_i and $x_i + h$ positions, respectively, then the experimental semi-variation function of $Z(x_i)$ is:

$$\gamma(h)^* = \frac{1}{2N(h)} \sum_{i=1}^{N(h)} [Z(x_i) - Z(x_i + h)]^2 \tag{8}$$

where $\gamma(h)^*$ is the experimental semi-variation function, $N(h)$ is the number of observed data pairs, and h is the spatial lag distance. The semi-variation function corresponding to each lag distance is fitted to obtain the semi-variation function. As shown in Fig. 1.

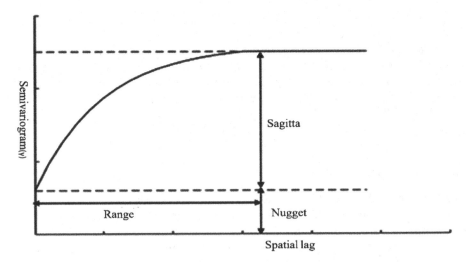

Fig. 1. Semi-variogram

When the space lag distance h is the time lag distance, that is, the time interval of the time series, the time series correlation described by the semi-variation function can be used to determine the order of the model, and the difference order d can be quickly obtained.

The determination of p and q directly affects the complexity and prediction accuracy of the model. Traditional order determination methods include Akaike information criterion (AIC), Bayesian information criterion and cross confirmation method, etc. However, traditional order determination methods often have poor prediction accuracy. Therefore, a better ordering method, genetic algorithm, is adopted here. The ordering steps of the ARIMA model by genetic algorithm are as follows:

1. Set the basic parameters of genetic algorithm. The basic parameters of genetic algorithm include population size, crossover probability, mutation probability, iteration number, individual form and individual length. The group size affects the final result and execution efficiency, and the general group size ranges from 10 to 200. The cross probability controls the frequency of use of the cross operation, generally 0.25–1.00, and the mutation probability maintains the diversity of the population, usually 0.01–0.1.
2. Select the fitness function. The ratio of the sum of the squares of the difference between the predicted value and the actual value of the monitoring data and the sum of the squares of the difference between all the real data and its average value is used to measure the distance ratio error, as shown in Eq. 9:

$$E = \frac{\sum_{i=1}^{N}(x_i - \hat{x}_i)^2}{\sum_{i=1}^{N}(x_i - \overline{x}_i)^2} \tag{9}$$

where N is the number of data, x_i is the actual value of the monitoring data, $\overline{x}_i$ is the average of the actual value of the monitoring data, and $\hat{x}_i$ is the predicted value of the monitoring data. A smaller E means a better prediction. AIC is also used to measure the advantages and disadvantages of the model, as shown in Formula 10:

$$Q = NIn\hat{\sigma}^2 + 2(p + q + 1) \tag{10}$$

where, $\hat{\sigma}^2$ is the estimate of σ^2, and this criterion is related to p and q, where Q is the best fit of the model, and the smaller Q is, the better the prediction effect is. The two model criteria are combined as a fitness function:

$$f(x) = \frac{1}{E + A} \tag{11}$$

In the formula, the larger the fitness function $f(x)$ value, the better the prediction effect.

2.3 The LSSVM Model

SVM is a process of solving the optimal solution through convex quadratic programming, while LSSVM is a variant formed on the basis of SVM, which converts the problem into solving linear equations and improves the accuracy while reducing the calculation amount. The calculation principle is shown in Fig. 2.

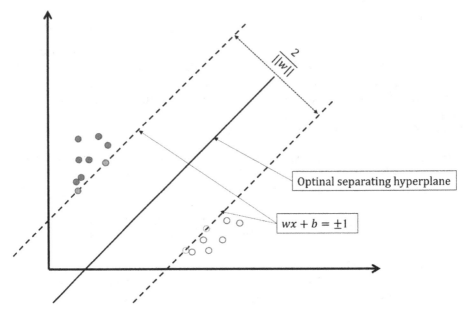

Fig. 2. Schematic diagram of LSSVM principle

Let the sample data be (x_i, y_i), $x_i \in R^k$ represents the input variable, $y_i \in R^k$ represents the output variable, $f(x)$ is the unknown function to be estimated, the nonlinear mapping of $f(x)$, then the estimated function $f(x)$ can be expressed as:

$$f(x) = w^T \cdot \varphi(x) + b \tag{12}$$

where b is the bias quantity, w is the weight vector, and $\varphi(x)$ is the nonlinear mapping function, then the LSSVM regression problem can be expressed as:

$$min\, J(w, e) = \frac{1}{2}w^T w + \frac{1}{2}r \sum_{i=1}^{m} e_i^2 \tag{13}$$

$$y_i = w^T \varphi(x_i) + b + e_i \tag{14}$$

where $e_i \in R^k$ is the error variable, $i = 1, 2, \cdots, m$. Since the w dimension is unknown, direct solution is quite difficult, so Lagrange multipliers are introduced to transform the quadratic programming problem into a dual problem for solution, namely:

$$L(w, b, e, \alpha) = J(w, e) - \sum_{i=1}^{m} \alpha_i \left[w^T \varphi(x_i) + b + e_i - y_i \right] \tag{15}$$

If the partial derivative of L with respect to w, b, e_i, α_i is equal to zero, then the constraint of the optimal solution is:

$$
\begin{cases}
\frac{\partial L}{\partial w} = 0 \Rightarrow w = \sum_{i=1}^{m} \alpha_i \varphi(x_i) \\
\frac{\partial L}{\partial b} = 0 \Rightarrow \sum_{i=1}^{m} \alpha_i = 0 \\
\frac{\partial L}{\partial e_i} = 0 \Rightarrow \alpha_i = re_i, i = 1, \cdots, m \\
\frac{\partial L}{\partial \alpha_i} = 0 \Rightarrow y_i = w^T \varphi(x_i) + b + e_i, i = 1, \cdots, m
\end{cases}
\tag{16}
$$

In the formula, $\alpha_i = re_i$ makes LSSVM no longer have the sparsity of SVM. If the above formula is converted into a linear system of equations and b, α_i is solved, then the estimated function $f(x)$ can be expressed as:

$$
f(x) = \sum_{i=1}^{m} \alpha_i k(x, x_i) + b
\tag{17}
$$

2.4   The DLSSVM Model

In standard SVM, the model fitting accuracy is controlled by the parameter ε of the sensitivity of the response model to the noise contained in the input sequence, but the ε corresponding to all training samples is constant. The DLSSVM model improves the standard LSSVM by introducing the DLS method. The improvement of DLSSVM model lies in the processing of recent data to obtain better accuracy by reducing ε, and to obtain better sparsity by increasing ε for long-term data, so as to construct the time correlation of time series. That is:

$$
\varepsilon(i) = w(i)\varepsilon
\tag{18}
$$

$$
w(i + 1) < w(i), i = 1, 2, \cdots, n
\tag{19}
$$

where $w(i)$ is the weighting function of ε, and n is the number of training sample cycles. When the data is from far to near, the weight tends to decline, and the weight function is usually defined as an exponential form:

$$
w(i) = \frac{1}{1 + exp(a - 2a_i/n)}
\tag{20}
$$

where a_i is the Lagrange multiplier and a is the decrement rate parameter, a is adjusted so that $w(i)$ is the decreasing function between 0 and 1 and converges to both ends, then the empirical error term in DLSSVM can be expressed as:

$$
E_{\text{DLSSVM}} = c\frac{1}{n} \sum_{i=1}^{n} (|f(x_i) - y_i| - \frac{e}{1 + exp(a - 2a_i/n)})
\tag{21}
$$

Then the corresponding DLSSVM risk function becomes:

$$
R_{\text{DLSSVM}} = c\frac{1}{n} \sum_{i=1}^{n} (|f(x_i) - y_i| - \frac{e}{1 + exp(a - 2a_i/n)}) + \frac{1}{2}||w||^2
\tag{22}
$$

2.5 DLSSVM Kernel Function

In the optimal classification hyperplane construction, the proper kernel function is used to realize the linear classification after a linear transformation without increasing the computational complexity, which provides a solution to the dimension disaster problem. In the process of LSSVM modeling, the choice of kernel function directly affects the performance of the established model. Each time series has its own applicable function type. When the prior knowledge is lacking, the performance of the radial basis kernel function model is usually better than that of the model with other kernel functions. Considering the spatial correlation construction of monitoring data, this paper selects bisquare spatial base function whose reliability is equivalent to covariance function in geoscience field. The form of bisquare spatial base kernel function is as follows:

$$S_{i,j} = \begin{cases} \{1 - (\|s_{i,t} - v_{j,t}\|/r)^2\}^2 & \|s_{i,t} - v_{j,t}\| < r, i \neq j \\ 0 & other \end{cases} \tag{23}$$

where s and v are the observed values at different positions at time t, $\|s_{i,t} - v_{j,t}\|$ is the Euclidean distance between two points i and j, and r is the variable determined by the variance function.

Select the right amount of spatial basis, so that most of the spatial details of the time series can be captured. Spatio basis distribution of two scale are shown in Fig. 3, including 25 space bases, 9 in the first scale and 16 in the second scale.

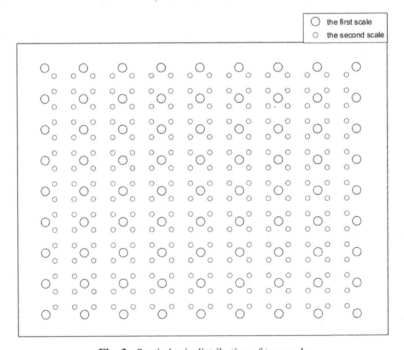

Fig. 3. Spatio basis distribution of two scale

2.6 ARIMA-Bi-DLSSVM Modeling

1. Normalize the time series. Due to the different dimensions of various monitoring data, the performance and operation speed of the model will be affected. Therefore, before modeling, each time series is normalized. The normalization formula is as follows:

$$x_i' = \frac{x_i'{}_{max} - x_i'{}_{min}}{x_{max} - x_{min}}(x_i - x_{min}) + x_i'{}_{min} \tag{24}$$

where, x_i represents the original data, x_i' represents the normalized data, x_{max} and x_{min} respectively represent the maximum and minimum values of the variable, $x_i'{}_{max}$ and $x_i'{}_{min}$ respectively represent the maximum and minimum values of the variable after normalization. Considering that there are positive and negative changes in monitoring data, the time series is normalized to $[-1, 1]$.

2. Use ARIMA model to process time series. The variance function and genetic algorithm were used to determine the order of the ARIMA model, and then the optimized ARIMA model was used to predict. If the ARIMA prediction result of the time series $\{y_i, i = 1, 2, \cdots, N\}$ is $\hat{L}_i$, then the residual difference between the original sequence and the ARIMA prediction result sequence is e_i, that is:

$$e_i = y_i - \hat{L}_i \tag{25}$$

The residual e_i contains the nonlinear part of the original sequence and the random error, namely:

$$e_i = f(e_{t-1}, e_{t-2}, \cdots, e_{t-n}) - \varepsilon_t \tag{26}$$

where ε_t is the random error, $f(*)$ is a nonlinear mapping part function.

3. Build bisquare space base kernel function. Multivariate time series fusion starts with kernel function construction, and the monitoring data fusion model of a certain section can be defined as:

$$ST = F(x_1, x_2, \cdots, y_1, y_2, \cdots, z_1, z_2, \cdots) \tag{27}$$

where $(x_1, x_2, \cdots, y_1, y_2, \cdots, z_1, z_2, \cdots)$ is the nonlinear part of the ARIMA prediction residual of the monitoring data of the section at a certain time, and $F(*)$ is a nonlinear function. The fusion time series is constructed with $(x_1, x_2, \cdots, y_1, y_2, \cdots, z_1, z_2, \cdots)$ as the data units. In order to mine the spatial correlation between multivariate data of the residual nonlinear part of DLSSVM modeling, bisquare space basis is used to construct a kernel function based on the distance between monitoring points, and the resulting kernel function is a positive definite symmetric matrix based on the positive qualitative properties of the matrix.

4. Conduct DLSSVM model training. The residual sequence uses the bisquare spatial base kernel function for DLSSVM training, gives the initial ε, starts the training, and then adjusts the parameter a of the ε for training, so that the training stops when the input makes the model have the minimum MSE value, and calculates the ε value at this time.

5. Use the DLSSVM model for modeling and forecasting. Let the prediction result of the residual sequence be $\hat{e}_i$, and add the prediction results of the two models to get the combined prediction result $\hat{y}_i$, that is:

$$\hat{y}_i = \hat{L}_i + \hat{e}_i \tag{28}$$

Finally, the normalized inverse operation is used to restore the final prediction result $\hat{y}_i$, and the final prediction result is obtained.

3 Real Experiment for Monitoring Data

3.1 Monitoring Data

This paper selects a complete section monitoring data time series of a tunnel in Central Yunnan water diversion Project, including 84 periods of data from 44 instruments, including 3 compressive stress gauges, 2 no strain gauges, 4 osmometers, 10 anchor stress gauges, 6 steel reinforcement gauges, 3 steel plate gauges, 9 multi-point displacement gauges, 4 strain gauges, and 3 joint gauges.

The data from periods 1–64 were used as training data, and the data from the last 20 periods were used as true values to compare with the predicted results. The 44 monitoring sequences after normalization were shown in Fig. 4. Among them, there are no strain gauge values+3osmometer values+6, anchor stress gauge values+9, steel reinforcement gauge values+12, steel plate gauge values+15, and multi-point displacement gauge values+18, The strain gauge value+21 and the joint gauge value+24 are displayed. Considering the display effect, select an odd number of data for display.

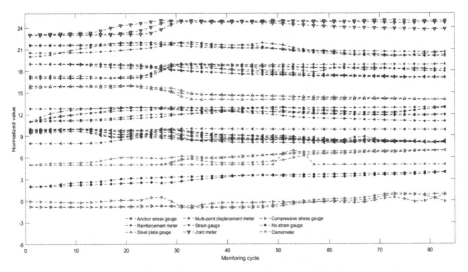

Fig. 4. Time series of 44 monitoring data after normalization processing

3.2 Data Processing

3.2.1 ARIMA Modeling

It can be seen from Fig. 4 that most of the monitoring series have significant nonlinear characteristics. The variance function of each data series is calculated, and it is found that the autocorrelation of each monitoring data series is very high, and most of them are unsteady time series. The difference order of ARIMA model of each time series is determined by variance function.

Genetic algorithm is used to optimize regression and moving coefficient, and the parameters that make ARIMA model fit best can be obtained, and then the time series can be stabilized by differential processing. After differential processing by ARIMA model, all the data have been basically stabilized, and the ARIMA prediction results can reflect the general trend of time series, but it is obvious that the longer the prediction time is, the larger the error will be. This is because the traditional time series model can only reflect the trend law of time series changes, and the short-term prediction accuracy is high, but the long-term prediction accuracy will rapidly decline. Then, the residual part of ARIMA model prediction, that is, the nonlinear part of residual time series, is obtained by the difference between the predicted result and the actual value.

3.2.2 Build Kernel Function

The residual sequence modeled by ARIMA also contains unused spatial correlation information. In order to make full use of the spatial correlation in multivariate time series, the spatial correlation among residual sequences is analyzed by calculating the variance function among all residual sequences. When calculating, the spatial lag distance h of the variance function adopts the Euclidean distance of each monitoring point in the design drawing, then the variable r determined by the variance function is the variable of the bisquare spatial base kernel function. The bisquare space kernel function of DLSSVM model can be calculated by determining the range r of all variance functions. It is found that most of the spatial variation can be obtained by selecting 373-order spatial basis, among which the first scale is 49 order and the second scale is 324 order.

3.2.3 Modeling DLSSVM

The residual of ARIMA prediction results is a one-dimensional time series. In order to take into account the spatial correlation among multiple data, multiple data fusion is necessary for long-term prediction of time series. The DLSSVM model uses the combination of residual sequences predicted by the ARIMA model to obtain the input vector, and the difference between the real data and the ARIMA predicted data is used as the output vector to learn. Bisquare spatial base kernel function is used to establish spatial correlation, and the risk function is constantly adjusted by the adjustment and optimization of parameter ε to improve the prediction effect of the model.

3.2.4 ARIMA-b-DLSSVM Model Prediction

The ARIMA-b-DLSSVM model completed with the above time series were used to make long-term prediction of the training data, and the prediction results of the ARIMA model and DLSSVM model were added together, and then normalized and reduced by the normalized parameters to obtain the final prediction results. In order to verify the effect of ARIMA-b-DLSSVM model, 44 monitoring time series were respectively predicted by ARIMA, SVM, DLSSVM and ARIMA-SVM, and the prediction results were analyzed and compared.

4   Results and Analysis

4.1   Prediction Effect of ARIMA-b-DLSSVM

As shown in Fig. 5, ARIMA-b-DLSSVM model can predict multivariate time series well. The predicted results are in good agreement with the actual values, but the longer the forecast time, the greater the error, which is an inevitable rule of long-term forecasting.

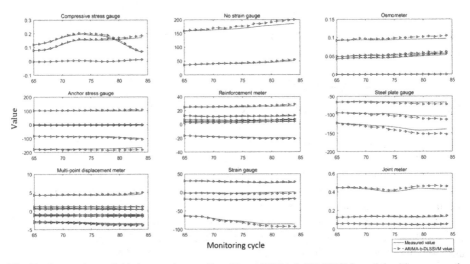

Fig. 5. Comparison of 44 time series predicted by ARIMA-b-DLSSVM model with measured values.

4.2   Comparison of Prediction Effect of Several Models

The ARIMA, SVM, DLSSVM and ARIMA-SVM models were simultaneously adopted to make long-term prediction of the above data. The long-term prediction results of all monitoring instruments are shown in Table 1. The prediction results of the ARIMA-b-DLSSVM model are superior to those of other models. The RMSE value of Compressive stress gauge and Osmometer results is too small, which is caused by the small scale of data. In order to better display the prediction results of several models, The prediction results of two monitoring data, Steel plate gauges and Strain gauges, are shown in Fig. 6 and Fig. 7.

Table 1. Comparison of RMSE values of predicted values of each model

Monitoring data	ARIMA	SVM	DLSSVM	ARIMA- SVM	ARIMA-b-DLSSVM
Compressive stress gauge	0.04	0.04	0.03	0.04	0.02
No strain gauge	10.20	9.94	9.75	9.91	9.47
Osmometer	0.03	0.03	0.02	0.03	0.01
Anchor stress gauge	10.13	9.74	9.11	9.56	8.72
Reinforcement meter	6.43	6.22	6.04	6.19	5.78
Steel plate gauge	18.82	16.73	12.17	15.33	10.26
Multi-point displacement meter	1.93	1.73	1.59	1.70	1.36
Strain gauge	11.53	10.02	8.49	9.32	7.62
Joint meter	1.78	1.65	1.37	1.51	1.04

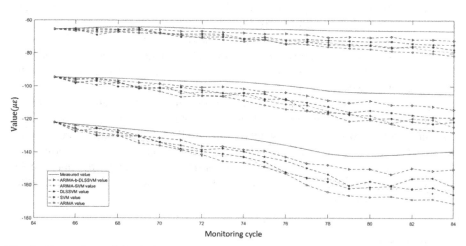

Fig. 6. Comparison of Steel plate gauges predicted by ARMIA-b-DLSSVM model and other models

As can be seen from Fig. 6, Fig. 7 and Table 1, neither ARIMA model nor SVM model has good forecasting effect, because they can only reflect linear or non-linear features of the series, and cannot fully capture the complex laws of time series. Compared with DLSSVM, ARIMA-b-DLSSVM model has much higher prediction accuracy. It is shown that the ARIMA-b-DLSSVM model, which combines linear and nonlinear information prediction methods and takes into account the spatial correlation between nonlinear information, can make better use of the useful information in the original time series and avoid the limitation of a single model. The prediction effect of DLSSVM model is better than that of ARIMA, SVM and ARIMA-SVM model, mainly because the dynamic

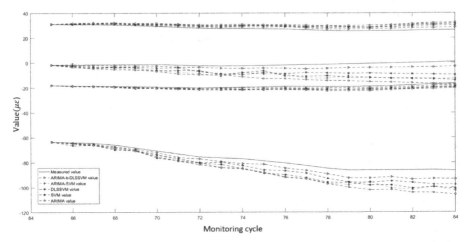

Fig. 7. Comparison of Strain gauges prediction results of ARMIA-b-DLSSVM model and other models

adjustment of noise sensitivity parameter ε changes the weight of the data in the time series, so as to make better use of the time correlation of the series.

As can be seen from Table 1, the RMSE value of the ARIMA-b-DLSSVM model is lower than that of the ARIMA-SVM and DLSSVM models, because the ARIMA-b-DLSSVM model takes into account the temporal correlation of time series and the spatial correlation between series, makes use of more implicit information, and makes ε change with time. The recent data weights are dynamically adjusted to optimize the traditional LSSVM model, and the excellent linear prediction ability of ARIMA model is also taken into account. The parameter ε of the ARIMA-SVM model is fixed, which makes the prediction of the SVM model lack of time correlation and spatial correlation. Although the DLSSVM model makes good use of time correlation, it does not have the accurate linear relationship capture of the spatial correlation and ARIMA model, so the prediction accuracy is not high.

5   Conclusion

Combining ARIMA, bisquare spatial basis, DLS and LSSVM, a spatio-temporal prediction method with multivariate time series is proposed in this paper. The model takes into account the temporal and spatial correlations, as well as the linear and nonlinear relationships in time series, and makes up for the shortcomings of a single model through the combination of traditional prediction models and machine learning. The model uses variation function and machine learning to obtain parameters, which reduces manual intervention and reduces the dependence of model accuracy on the initial value. The analysis and prediction results of a tunnel section monitoring data of the central Yunnan water diversion project show that the proposed ARIMA-b-DLSSVM model can perform the long-term prediction of multiple time series well, and has obvious advantages compared with the traditional time series prediction model and the single model.

References

1. Rossi, A., Gallo, G.M.: Volatility estimation via hidden Markov models. J. Empir. Financ. **13**(2), 203–230 (2006)
2. Dilli, R.A., Wang, Y.W.: Time-series analysis with a hybrid box-Jenkins ARIMA and neural networks model. J. Harbin Inst. Technol. **11**(4), 413–421 (2004)
3. Li, C., Andersen, S.V.: Efficient blind system identification of non-Gaussian autoregressive models with HMM modeling of the excitation. IEEE Trans. Signal Process. **55**(6), 2432–2445 (2007)
4. Brooks, E.B., et al.: Fitting the multitemporal curve: a fourier series approach to the missing data problem in remote sensing analysis. IEEE Trans. Geosci. Remote Sens. **50**(9), 3340–3353 (2012)
5. Sinap, A., Assche, W.V.: Polynomial interpolation and Gaussian quadrature for matrix valued functions. Linear Algebra Appl. **207**(94), 71–114 (2012)
6. Schoellhamer, D.H.: Singular spectrum analysis for time series with missing data. Geophys. Res. Lett. **28**(16), 1499–1512 (2001)
7. Du, P., et al.: Advances of four machine learning methods for spatial data handling: a review. J. Geovis. Spat. Anal. **4**(1), 1–25 (2020)
8. Chen, Y., et al.: Mapping croplands, cropping patterns, and crop types using MODIS time-series data. Int. Appl. Earth Observ. Geoinf **69**, 133–147 (2018)
9. Sharma, A., Liu, X., Yang, X.: Land cover classification from multi-temporal, multi-spectral remotely sensed imagery using patch based recurrent neural networks. Neural Netw. **105**, 346–355 (2018)
10. Scholkopf, B., Smola, A.: Learning with Kernels: Support Vector Machines, Regularization, and Beyond. MIT Press, Cambridge (2002)
11. Bai, S., Kolter, J.Z., Koltun, V.: An empirical evaluation of generic convolutional and recurrent networks for sequence modeling (2018)
12. Ahmed, N.K., Ativa, A.F., Gavar, N.E., El-Shishiny, H.: An empirical comparison of machine learning models for time series forecasting. Econ. Rev. **29**, 594–621 (2010)
13. Suykens, J.A.K., Vandewalle, J.: Weighted least squares support vector machines: robustness and sparse approximation. Neurocomputing **48**, 85–105 (2002)
14. Li, Y.M., Gong, S.G., Sherrah, J., Liddel, H.: Support vector machine based multi-view face detection and recognition. Image Vision Comput. **22**(5), 413–427 (2004)
15. Yuxiang, H.: Thousands of Lu. Study on the model matching of ARIMA and adaptive SVM in stock price index prediction. J. Electron. Commer. **10**(4), 1041–1066 (2008)
16. Ghaderi, A., Sanandaji, B.M., Ghaderi, F.: Deep forecast: deep learning-based spatio-temporal forecasting. In: ICML Time Series Workshop, Sydney, Australia (2017)
17. Liu, P., Zang, W.: Incentive-based modeling and inference of attacker intent, objectives and strategies. ACM Trans. Inf. Syst. Secur. **56**(3), 283–298 (2005)
18. Cressie, N., Shi, T., Kang, E.L.: Fixed rank filtering for spatio-temporal data. J. Comput. Graph. Stat. **19**(3), 724–745 (2010)
19. Kang, E.L., Cressie, N., Shi, T.: Using temporal variability to improve spatial mapping with application to satellite data. Can. J. Stat. **38**(2), 271–289 (2010)

DyAdapTransformer: Dynamic Adaptive Spatial-Temporal Graph Transformer for Traffic Prediction

Hui Dong[1], Xiao Pan[2(✉)], Xiao Chen[3], Jing Sun[2], and Shuhai Wang[4]

[1] School of Management, Shijiazhuang Tiedao University, Shijiazhuang 050043, China
[2] School of Information Science and Technology, Shijiazhuang Tiedao University, Shijiazhuang 050043, China
`smallpx@stdu.edu.cn`
[3] Hebei Key Laboratory of Ocean Dynamics, Resources and Environments, Qinhuangdao 066004, China
[4] Department of Science and Technology, Shijiazhuang Tiedao University, Shijiazhuang 050043, China

Abstract. The transformer-based method is a popular choice for medium and long-term traffic prediction. However, it still suffers from some problems. The first is that spatial position embedding has poor interpretability. Additionally, the spatial-temporal correlation learning can struggle to reflect the actual complexity of traffic networks relationships. To address the above problems, we propose a traffic prediction framework for dynamic adaptive spatial-temporal graph transformer (DyAdapTransformer). Our method uses the method of random walk to embed the spatial position. The analyzability between transition probability and spatial position representation enhances the interpretability of the model. When learning spatial-temporal correlation, a method of dynamic adaptive graph attention network is proposed. We compared with our framework with four baselines on three datasets. The results show that DyAdapTransformer has a better predictive performance.

Keywords: Traffic Prediction · Random Walk · Dynamic Adaptive Mechanism · Graph Attention Network

1 Introduction

Traffic prediction aims to predict the actual traffic state information through spatial units (such as road segments or traffic sensors) in a certain period of time in the future by modeling the historical traffic state data of the traffic network. Accurate traffic prediction can be applied in areas such as improving traffic congestion, signal light control, etc., and contribute to efficient urban traffic planning and management. However, the traffic

---

Hui Dong is currently pursuing the Ph.D. degree in the School of Management, Shijiazhuang Tiedao University.

network presents complex spatial-temporal relationships due to the constraints of the road network and the influence of various factors (such as entity attributes, surroundings, etc.). Therefore, accurate traffic prediction is a challenging problem. Fortunately, advances in spatial-temporal graph neural networks (STGNNs) in deep learning provide opportunities for modeling complex spatial-temporal relationships in multi-source traffic data.

The core of existing traffic prediction research is based on STGNNs to model spatial-temporal correlation under the influence of complex traffic patterns. The graph convolutional network (GCN) [1–4] is commonly employed to model spatial correlations in traffic networks. The recurrent neural network (RNN) and its variants [5–12], or temporal convolutional network (TCN) [13–17] have been used to model temporal correlation of time series. However, the weights assigned by GCN to adjacent nodes remain fixed post-training, which is unfriendly for traffic prediction tasks where the spatial correlation change over time. Furthermore, RNN may have difficulties capturing long-term dependencies due to gradient disappearance. Additionally, RNN lacks parallelizability during the training process, which hinders its efficiency. Although TCN can capture long-term dependencies and be parallelized, its performance is constrained by the size of the convolution kernel.

To address the above problems, researchers have developed the traffic prediction framework based on the transformer [18, 19]. In such frameworks, the attention mechanism can dynamically determine the weights of the central node and its corresponding neighbor nodes in the traffic network. This allows it to focus on each temporal position in the time series, effectively learning long-term dependencies and enabling parallelization. Since the attention mechanism overlooks the spatial-temporal position of elements in the time series. Therefore, the challenge of transformer-based traffic prediction lies in spatial-temporal position embedding and spatial-temporal correlation learning:

(1) When embedding the spatial position, existing researches usually apply the deep learning [20] or Laplacian Eigenmaps (LE) [21] methods. However, the interpretability of deep learning methods is poor, as it heavily relies on the training process, making it challenging to verify if the representation accurately reflects the traffic network's topological relationships. The LE method primarily utilizes adjacency relationship modeling, However, nodes with similar functions in the traffic network have similar traffic patterns, despite there are non-adjacency relationships. For instance, urban roads serving similar purposes (e.g., educational, commercial, residential areas, etc.) often demonstrate similar traffic patterns even without direct adjacency. Therefore, constructing spatial position embedding models based on functional similarity presents a challenge.

(2) Existing researches on spatial-temporal correlation modeling primarily rely on predefined explicit graph structures, whose topology remains static once defined [18, 19]. However, this method fails to reflect the temporary changes of the implicit traffic network structure caused by special circumstances (e.g. road construction, traffic events, concerts, etc.) and the corresponding implicit spatial-temporal correlation. Therefore, capturing the implicit graph structure over time with input data and obtaining the corresponding implicit spatial-temporal correlations pose significant challenges.

To tackle the above issues, we propose a traffic prediction framework for dynamic adaptive spatial-temporal graph transformer (DyAdapTransformer). The main contributions of this paper are summarized as follows:

- We build a random walk-based spatial position embedding model from the perspective of enhancing model interpretability. This model integrates both adjacency and non-adjacency relationships of the traffic network structure to construct the transition probabilities, which analyzable modeling process and results enable improve model interpretability.
- We propose a dynamic adaptive spatial-temporal correlation learning model. The model learns the implicit graph structure of each temporal interval in a data-driven way through a dynamic adaptive mechanism, and uses the attention mechanism to build a model from two dimensions of spatial-temporal to learn the corresponding implicit spatial-temporal correlation. By doing so, it can adjust for the absence of key implicit information or the addition of useless explicit information when the graph structure is constructed by human experience to learn the spatial-temporal correlation.
- The validity of the proposed DyAdapTransformer is verified by experiments on three real datasets. The results show that our framework significantly outperforms the state-of-the-art traffic prediction baselines.

2 Related Work

2.1 Transformer-Based Traffic Forecasting

Transformer [22] was first used in traffic prediction in 2020, i.e., STTNs [23] and TSE-SC [24]. In STTNs, both spatial and temporal Transformer are proposed. Specifically, spatial transformer is a variant of graph neural network (GNN). It captures real-time traffic conditions and directionality of traffic flow by dynamically modeling directed spatial correlations with self-attention mechanisms. Temporal transformer is primarily used to model bidirectional temporal correlations across multiple time steps. Finally, they are combined into a block to jointly model the spatial-temporal correlation for accurate traffic prediction. In TSE-SC, a hybrid encoder-decoder architecture called Traffic Transformer is proposed. The architecture uses end-to-end training to model the consistency of spatial and temporal correlations of traffic data. Among them, Transformer is leveraged to model temporal correlations and GCN contribute to the modeling of spatial correlations. The ASTGNN [18] designs a self-attention mechanism that can make use of local context when modeling temporal correlations. When modeling spatial correlation, GCN is integrated into the self-attention mechanism to realize the capture of spatial correlations in a dynamic way. MGT [19] exploits spatial-temporal heterogeneity to improve the ability of temporal modeling when modeling temporal correlations. In modeling spatial correlations, a spatial attention mechanism under multiple graphs is proposed to better capture different types of spatial correlation. ST-TIS [25] extends the canonical transformer with information fusion and region sampling. It improves efficiency and prediction accuracy while capturing the complex spatial-temporal correlations between regions. NAST [26] has first proposed a Non-Autoregressive Transformer model for time series prediction. The model generates total decoder queries within one step and implements parallel prediction. It greatly avoids cumulative errors and make more efficient use of the attention mechanism.

The transformer-based modeling not only captures the long-term dependencies between historical data and forecast data in the temporal dimension, but also realizes parallelization in the training process compared with some RNN-based prediction frameworks [5–8, 5–8, 27]. However, most of the existing such prediction frameworks rely on human experience when modeling graph structures, which hardly reflects the actual complexity of traffic networks relationships.

2.2 Adaptive GNN-Based Traffic Forecasting

The principle of the adaptive mechanism is end-to-end learning by stochastic gradient descent of the model itself to construct and update an adaptive matrix without any prior knowledge. Graph WaveNet [14] first introduced an adaptive mechanism into GNN-based traffic prediction modeling. The model adopts the GCN in the learning of spatial dependencies, and adds a network completion method (i.e. adaptively learning a new adjacency matrix according to the data). AGCRN [8] achieves automatic capture of node-specific spatial and temporal correlations in time series data without the need for a pre-defined graph by integrating adaptive GCN into gated recurrent unit (GRU).

This type of traffic prediction framework learns the implicit spatial structure through an adaptive mechanism. Traffic flow belongs to spatial-temporal dynamic data, and the implied spatial structure driven by dynamic data should change dynamically. However, only a shared adjacency matrix reflecting the implicit spatial structure was learned in the above work, limiting its ability to accurately capture evolving traffic network relationship. Additionally, the framework heavily relies on the training process and lacks interpretability.

Drawing from the above analysis, we propose a novel approach that integrates that the random walk method [28, 29] and dynamic adaptive mechanism. This not only enhances the interpretability of the modeling process but also learns the intricate relationships in traffic network driven by dynamic traffic state data. We research focuses on the field of traffic prediction through the development of a dynamic adaptive spatial-temporal transformer.

3 Preliminaries

3.1 Definitions

Definition 1. Traffic network. The traffic network is defined as a directed/undirected graph $G = (V, E)$, where $V = \{v_1, v_2, ..., v_N\}$ represents the node set, which can be any transportation entity (such as sensors deployed on the road segments, the intersections, or metro station etc.). E is an edge set, where each item (v_i, v_j) denotes a directed/undirected edge from node v_i to node v_j. In reality, each edge represents the connection between two transportation entities.

Definition 2. Traffic signal matrix. A traffic network signal matrix is defined as the traffic flow values at different temporal interval t_n (divided by a fixed period t) for each node in the traffic network, which can be expressed as $tms_{t_n} =$

$[tsm_{(t_n,v_1)}, tsm_{(t_n,v_2)}, ..., tsm_{(t_n,v_N)}] \in R^{N \times C}$. Among them, $t_n \in T = \{t_1, t_2, ..., t_H\}$ is a certain temporal interval n of a fixed period, $tsm_{(t_n,v_i)}$ is the feature vector of node v_i at a certain temporal interval t_n, $N = |V|$ is the number of nodes in the traffic network, C is the number of features in the feature vector, where $C = 1$ or 2 (i.e., distinguish between inflow and outflow compared to the former).

Definition 3. Temporal position indicators. The temporal location indicator S^G refers to adding an indicator of all temporal intervals in a day based on actual features (e.g., all temporal intervals in a day are added to indicate the day in a week.). The temporal position indicators at t_n are denoted as $TPI_{t_n} \in R^{S^G}$.

3.2 Problem Formulation

Given the traffic network $G = (V, E)$, Traffic signal matrix (TSM) composed of historical traffic data in H temporal intervals, the temporal position indicators over the past H (TPI_H) and the next F temporal intervals (TPI_F). We aim to forecast the traffic flow in F temporal intervals in the future. In particular, we formulize the problem as Eq. (1).

$$\begin{cases} TSM = [tsm_{t_1}, tsm_{t_2}, ..., tsm_{t_H}] \in R^{H \times N \times C} \\ TPI = TPI_H \in R^{H \times 1 \times S^G} \text{ and } TPI_F \in R^{F \times 1 \times S^G} \end{cases} \tag{1}$$
$$\Rightarrow TSM = [tsm_{t_{H+1}}, tsm_{t_{H+2}}, ..., tsm_{t_{H+F}}] \in R^{F \times N \times C}$$

4 The Proposed Model

Figure 1 shows the overall architecture DyAdapTransformer. It's adopting an encoder-decoder structure and autoregressive prediction method. The encoder and decoder components are stacked by several DASCL (Dynamic adaptive spatial-temporal correlations learning) layers. Each DASCL block consists of a temporal self-attention and a dynamic adaptive GAT, which together capture the dynamic adaptive spatial-temporal correlation in the traffic network. The attention mechanism ignores the order of nodes in the input spatial-temporal series. Therefore, we constructed a random walk-based spatial position embedding model respectively by combining the factors that actually affect the spatial-temporal position. In this way, a more accurate spatial-temporal position feature representation can be obtained. Similar to the transformer [22] framework, in order that each position in the decoder can respond to all positions in the input sequence in time, an encoder-decoder temporal attention module is established in each layer of the decoder; in order to ensure that the model deeply and effectively learns the dynamic adaptive spatial-temporal correlation, residual connections [30] and layer normalization [31] are used inside the spatial-temporal attention module of each layer of the encoder and decoder.

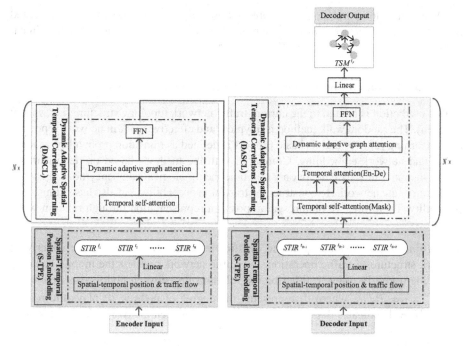

Fig. 1. DyAdapTransformer architecture

5   S-TPE: Spatial-Temporal Position Embedding

5.1   Temporal Position Embedding (TPE)

Traffic flow belongs to spatial-temporal dynamic data, which has the nature of proximity, periodicity and trend. One of the prerequisites for accurately describing the typical feature of traffic flow is the need to accurately locate the temporal position. Existing methods [18, 19] mainly represent the temporal position from two aspects: additional time attributes (e.g., time of day, day of the week, and day off indicators, etc.) and relative positions of a clear temporal interval t_n.

The temporal position embedding mainly includes the temporal indicators and temporal interval t_n representation. The temporal indicators are represented by one-hot encoding. Specifically, the number of temporal position indicators is S^G, so each temporal interval t_n can be represented as an S^G-dimensional vector according to the actual situation. Then, the learnable matrix $M \in R^{S^G \times d_{\text{mod}\,el}}$ linear transformation is used to d_{mode}-dimensional vector. The representation of the temporal interval t_n uses the method of position embedding in transformer is represented as shown in Eq. (2).

$$\begin{cases} TPE_{(t_n, 2d)} = \sin(t_n/10000^{2d/d_{\text{mod}\,el}}) \\ TPE_{(t_n, 2d+1)} = \cos(t_n/10000^{2d/d_{\text{mod}\,el}}) \end{cases} \tag{2}$$

where t_n represents the position of the temporal interval and $1 \leq d \leq d_{\text{mod}\,el}$ represents the dimension of the vector.

Above, the temporal position representation of the same dimension is obtained from the two aspects, and the final temporal position after concatenation and linear transformation is expressed as $TPE_{t_n} \in R^{d \bmod el}$.

5.2 Spatial Position Embedding (SPE) Based on Random Walk

Traffic prediction is related to the current traffic network topology structure (i.e., spatial position). The random walk method is a typical and effective work in network representation learning [28, 29] and its basic process is defined as transition probability, random walks and network embedding. Compared with the methods based on deep learning or LE, the random walk can not only combine the topological adjacency/non-adjacency modeling of the networks to construct the transition probability, but also has strong interpretability. Therefore, we obtain spatial position representation through random walk, as follows.

The Adjacency Relationship of the Traffic Network Structure. As the underlying network structure of traffic operation, the traffic network restricts the mobile behavior of mobile users. In order to describe the relationship between nodes, it is defined as $Conn_{v_i \to v_j}^{adj} = P/d_i$, where d_i represents the degree of node v_i, P plays the role of marker, $P = 1$ indicates that there is an adjacency between the two nodes, otherwise $P = 0$.

The Non-adjacency Relationship of the Traffic Network Structure. Typically, nodes with similar functions have similar traffic patterns. Therefore, in addition to the adjacency relationship between nodes in the above transportation network, there are also some non-adjacency relationships due to functional similarity (such as commercial areas, residential areas, etc.), denoted as $Conn_{v_i \to v_j}^{fun\_sim}$.

To sum up, the equation of transition probability $(v_i \to v_j)$ is shown in Eq. (3). Use this equation for random walk to obtain random walk sequences. Finally, the spatial position embedding of the traffic network $SPE \in R^{N \times d \bmod el}$ is obtained by training random walk sequences.

$$P_{v_i \to v_j} = Norm(Conn_{v_i \to v_j}^{adj} + Conn_{v_i \to v_j}^{fun\_sim}) \tag{3}$$

The traffic flow corresponds to the division of temporal intervals, and the traffic flow in each temporal interval is used as a signal of the traffic network, i.e., $TSM \in R^{H \times N \times C}$. In order to be fused with temporal and spatial position embeddings, it is made into the d_{model} dimension by linear mapping (i.e., $TSM \in R^{H \times N \times C} \xrightarrow{Linear} TSME \in R^{H \times N \times d \bmod el}$). In summary, the spatial-temporal information representation obtained fusion of temporal position embedding, spatial position embedding and traffic signal embedding is used as the input of the DASCL layer (i.e., $DASCL_{input} = STIR = Linear(TPE + SPE + TSME) \in R^{H \times N \times d \bmod el}$).

6 DASCL: Dynamic Adaptive Spatial-Temporal Correlations Learning

6.1 Encoder

It can be seen from Fig. 1 that the spatial-temporal encoder is stacked by a set of identical layers (i.e., N layers of DASCL in total). The core module of each layer is a spatial-temporal block that learns dynamic adaptive spatial-temporal correlation. This black is composed of temporal self-attention and dynamic adaptive GAT, and the involved attention mechanisms are all multi-head structures. Specifically, the former aims to learn the temporal correlation between nodes in temporal sequences based on the self-attention mechanism. The latter aims to learn explicit and implicit spatial correlation at each temporal interval based on the dynamic adaptive GAT.

Temporal Self-attention. The specific process of learning temporal correlation by the temporal self-attention mechanism is as follows. First, the attention scores are calculated between elements in the temporal sequence. For the mth $\in \{1, 2, ..., M\}$ head, node v_i and attention score at intervals t_s and t_e, are shown in Eq. (4). Then, the softmax function is used to normalize the attention score to the input vector $STIR_{v_i}^{t_n}$ (i.e., representation of the spatial-temporal information of node v_i at temporal interval t_n) at different temporal interval with node v_i weighted sum, as shown in Eq. (6). Finally, the results of multi-head attention are concatenated, as shown in Eq. (7).

$$atten_m(v_i^{t_s}, v_i^{t_e}) = \frac{(STIR_{v_i}^{t_s} \cdot W_{Q_m}) \cdot (STIR_{v_i}^{t_e} \cdot W_{K_m})^T}{\sqrt{d}} \tag{4}$$

$$\alpha_m(v_i^{t_s}, v_i^{t_e}) = soft\max(atten_m(v_i^{t_s}, v_i^{t_e})) = \frac{\exp(atten_m(v_i^{t_s}, v_i^{t_e}))}{\sum_{t_n \in T} \exp(atten_m(v_i^{t_s}, v_i^{t_n}))} \tag{5}$$

$$R_{v_i,m} = (\sum_{t_n \in T} \alpha_m(v_{v_i}^{t_s}, v_{v_i}^{t_n}) \cdot STIR_{v_i}^{t_n}) W_{V_m} \tag{6}$$

$$\hat{R}_{v_i} = Concat(R_{v_i,1}, R_{v_i,2}, ..., R_{v_i,M}) W^O \tag{7}$$

Dynamic Adaptive Graph Attention Network. GAT is to apply the self-attention mechanism to the graph structure. Its core idea is to calculate the attention between a node and each of its adjacent nodes in the graph, and to combine the features of the node itself and the attention features of its neighbor nodes are concatenated to update the feature of this node. In order to enable self-attention to obtain stable nodes representation, a multi-head attention mechanism is usually used to improve the representation ability of the model. The core operation of multi-head graph attention is to use M, W to calculate self-attention, and then concatenate the results obtained by each self-attention to obtain the output vector, as shown in Eq. (8).

$$\overrightarrow{x'}_{v_i} = \Big\|_{m=1}^{M} \sigma \Big(\sum_{v_j \in N_{v_i}} \alpha_{v_{ij}}^m W^m \overrightarrow{x}_{v_j} \Big) \tag{8}$$

where $\alpha_{v_{ij}}$ denotes the normalized attention score of the current node and each of its neighbors.

Existing researches [18, 19, 25] are mainly based on explicit graph modeling to learn spatial correlation abstracted by human experience. However, in the process of abstracting graphs based on human experience, the absence of key information or the addition of useless information will affect the traffic flow prediction. Therefore, a dynamic adaptive GAT is proposed to solve these problems. Specifically, first, we learn the dynamic implicit graph by driving the dynamic traffic data, constructing an adaptive matrix for each temporal interval (i.e., a dynamic adaptive matrix), as shown in Eq. (9). Then, a predefined explicit graph and a dynamic implicit graph are modeled based on the GAT to learn the explicit and implicit spatial correlations, as shown in Eq. (10).

$$\tilde{A}_{t_n \in T} = soft \max(\mathrm{ReLU}(E_1 \cdot E_2^T)) \tag{9}$$

$$\vec{x'}_{v_i^{t_n}} = \Big\|_{m=1}^{M} \sigma \Big(\sum_{v_j \in N_{v_i}^{t_n}} \alpha_{v_{ij}^{t_n}}^{m} W^m \vec{x}_{v_j} + \tilde{A}_{v_{ij}^{t_n}}^{m} W^m \vec{x}_{v_j} \Big) \tag{10}$$

where $v_j \in N_{v_i}$ represents the neighbor nodes of the node v_i. Its neighbor nodes include neighbor nodes in predefined explicit graphs and dynamic adaptive implicit graphs (in the experiment, the threshold is set as 0.1 to shield some weakly connected graphs).

6.2 Decoder

Temporal Self-attention (Mask). The principle of temporal self-attention with masking mechanism in dynamic adaptive spatial-temporal correlation decoding is similar to that without encoding. The difference is mainly reflected in the addition of masking mechanism to decoding temporal self-attention, as shown in Eq. (11). Among them, t_s represents the current temporal interval, and when calculating the attention value of the temporal sequences, add mask $= -\infty$ to the attention value after the current temporal interval t_s obtained, and add mask $= 0$ to the rest. During dynamic adaptive spatial-temporal decoding, the output sequence is generated in an autoregressive manner. In order to maintain the autoregressive feature, the future time step input is masked through a masking mechanism. The rest of the calculation process is the same as the temporal self-attention during encoding.

$$mask = \begin{cases} 0 & , t_s \text{ before } t_e \\ -\infty, & t_s \text{ after } t_e \end{cases} \tag{11}$$

Temporal Attention (Encoder-Decoder). In order to enable the input of each temporal interval to participate in the encoder's spatial-temporal sequence encoding feature process during dynamic adaptive spatial-temporal correlation decoding, the encoder-decoder temporal attention is added. This layer extracts features from the output of the encoder (as key (K) and value (V)) and the output of the attention layer with masking mechanism in the decoder (as query (Q)) to establish correlation between encoder and decoder input sections. That is, the K

and V are $\{K_{t,i}^m | t \in (1, 2, ..., H), i \in (v_1, v_2, ..., v_N), m \in (1, 2, ..., M)\}$ and $\{V_{t,i}^m | t \in (1, 2, ..., H), i \in (v_1, v_2, ..., v_N), m \in (1, 2, ..., M)\}$ respectively, and the Q is $\{Q_{t,i}^m | t \in (H + 1, H + 2, ..., H + F), i \in (v_1, v_2, ..., v_N), m \in (1, 2, ..., M)\}$.

The above modules are used to build the same N-layer spatial-temporal block in dynamic adaptive spatial-temporal correlation decoding. Finally, the future traffic flow is predicted by linear layer mapping autoregression, and the metric Mean Absolute Error (MAE), is used as the loss function.

7 Experimental Analysis

7.1 Datasets

We conducted experiment analysis on three traffic datasets, HZMetro [32], SHMetro [32] and PEMS08 [33]. The division ratios of training, validation and testing sets for the three datasets are shown in Table 1.

Table 1. The division ratios of training, validation and testing sets for three datasets.

Datasets	Nodes	Edges	Training: Validation: Testing
HZMetro	80	248	18:2:5
SHMetro	288	958	62:9:21
PEMS08	170	295	3:1:1

7.2 Baseline Methods

To comprehensively evaluate the performance of DyAdapTransformer, we consider four classic baselines for comparison: DCRNN [9], Graph-WaveNet [14], ASTGNN [18], and MGT [19]. In the experiment, the baselines are based on the code provided in the corresponding paper.

To evaluate the forecast results, the predicted values are retransformed to actual values and compared with the actual true values. Mean Absolute Error (MAE), Root Mean Square Error (RMSE) and Mean Absolute Percentage Error (MAPE) were used as metrics.

7.3 Experimental Settings

In the experimental stage, the forecast is based on the traffic states of the past hour (4 steps for HZMetro and SHMetro, 12 steps for PEMS08) to predict the traffic states of the next hour. Among them, the input feature size of the two datasets HZMetro and SHMetro is 2 (i.e., The inflow and outflow of human), and PEMS08 is 1 (i.e., the traffic flow). The code of the DyAdapTransformer framework is based on the code modifications provided by the

MGT framework, which is implemented in general using the PyTorch [34] framework. The Adam optimization method [35] is used for training, the initial learning rate is 0.001, and the weight decay is 0.0002. The framework involves hyperparameters in RW and DASCL spatial-temporal correlation learning, whose settings are shown in Table 2.

Table 2. Hyperparameter setting for DyAdapTransformer prediction framework.

Parameters (RW)	size	Parameters (DASCL)	size
Dimension vector d	64	Input dimension d_{model}	64
Number of times as starting node n	10	Head of attention h	8
Path length L	40	Encoder layers N	4
Context window size w	5	Decoder layers N'	4

7.4 Experimental Results and Analysis

In order to evaluate the effectiveness of the proposed DyAdapTransformer framework, a comparative experimental analysis was conducted on three datasets with four baseline methods. The prediction results of different traffic prediction frameworks on the three traffic flow datasets are shown in Table 3. In order to obtain relatively stable and accurate prediction results, each prediction framework is run 5 times to take the average value as the final prediction result. The results in this table are the average of all temporal intervals. It can be seen from the table that the proposed DyAdapTransformer framework gets better prediction results (bold font) than the baseline methods. In the three datasets, compared with the sub-optimal results (with an asterisk label) MAE, RMSE and MAPE were respectively improved by: HZMetro: 1.60%, 1.71%, 0.14%; SHMetro: 2.15%, 1.23%, 6.36%; PEMS08: 4.15%, 3.22%, 5.21%.

Table 3. Comparison of prediction results of different traffic prediction frameworks on three datasets.

Datasets	Metrics	DCRNN	GWN	ASTGNN	MGT	DyAdapTransformer
HZMetro	MAE	26.15	24.67	26.24	23.69*	**23.31**
	RMSE	44.22	41.63	45.47	39.25*	**38.58**
	MAPE	15.60	15.38	16.51	14.34*	**14.32**
SHMetro	MAE	28.62	25.69	27.38	24.24*	**23.72**
	RMSE	58.76	51.46	55.82	47.32*	**46.74**
	MAPE	21.62	18.71	19.99	17.90*	**16.83**
PEMS08	MAE	18.56	14.61	14.86	13.74*	**13.17**
	RMSE	28.71	23.86	24.32	23.61*	**22.85**
	MAPE	12.11	9.33	9.53	9.21*	**8.73**

7.5 Interpretability Analysis

In order to show that the spatial position embedding method based on random walk above in section IV has strong interpretability, we take the part of HZMetro dataset as an example to analyze. In this method, the transition probability represents the relative spatial proximity relationship between nodes in the traffic network. After the spatial position embedding the obtained representation should maintain this proximity relationship.

For clarity, only the relationship between one node and the remaining 79 nodes as an example for visualization. Figure 2 shows the comparison of the transition probability between nodes of metro station and the similarity after the spatial position representation. The reason for choosing two similarity measures is to eliminate chance. By comparing the trend lines of No. ① and No. ② in Fig. 2, it can be found that the trends of the two are basically the same, while the trend line of No. ③ is basically opposite to the two. This is due to the fact that between nodes with greater similarity in spatial have relatively small distances (near), and large (far) on the contrary.

Above, the random walk has procedural data reflecting the actual network in the process of spatial position embedding, which improves the interpretability of the model.

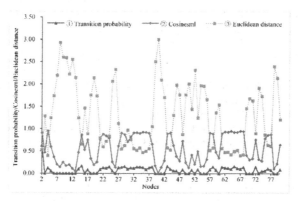

Fig. 2. Comparison of the transition probability and the similarity between nodes after spatial position embedding.

8 Conclusion

In this paper, we proposed a traffic prediction framework with the dynamic adaptive spatial-temporal graph transformer, denoted as DyAdapTransformer. Our framework not only improves model interpretability, but also explores implicit spatial-temporal relationships in traffic networks. First, we propose a random walk method that integrates adjacency and non-adjacency of traffic network structures to represent spatial position. Then, a dynamic adaptive spatial-temporal correlation learning model is proposed to mine the implicit spatial-temporal correlation in the traffic network. Finally, we perform comparative experimental analysis with four classical baselines on three datasets, and the results show that DyAdapTransformer is superior to the state-of-the-art baselines.

Acknowledgments. This work was supported in part by the Natural Science Foundation of Hebei Province under Grant F2021210005 and F2023407003; in part by the Outstanding Youth Foundation of Hebei Education Department under Grant BJ2021085; in part by the Postgraduate Innovation Foundation of Hebei under Grant CXZZBS2022117; in part by the Key Laboratory of Marine Dynamic Process and Resources and Environment Open Course of Hebei Province under Grant HBHY02.

References

1. Wang, Y., Jing, C.: Spatiotemporal graph convolutional network for multi-scale traffic forecasting. ISPRS Int. J. Geo Inf. **11**(2), 102 (2022)
2. Shin, Y., Yoon, Y.: PGCN: progressive graph convolutional networks for spatial-temporal traffic forecasting. arXiv preprint arXiv:2202.08982 (2022)
3. Djenouri, Y., Belhadi, A., Srivastava, G., et al.: Hybrid graph convolution neural network and branch-and-bound optimization for traffic flow forecasting. Futur. Gener. Comput. Syst. **139**, 100–108 (2023)
4. Ali, A., Zhu, Y., Zakarya, M.: Exploiting dynamic spatio-temporal graph convolutional neural networks for citywide traffic flows prediction. Neural Netw. **145**, 233–247 (2022)
5. Zhao, L., Song, Y., Zhang, C., et al.: T-GCN: a temporal graph convolutional network for traffic prediction. IEEE Trans. Intell. Transp. Syst. **21**(9), 3848–3858 (2019)
6. Chen, C., Li, K., Teo, S.G., et al.: Gated residual recurrent graph neural networks for traffic prediction. In: Proceedings of the AAAI Conference on Artificial Intelligence, vol. 33, no. 01, pp. 485–492 (2019)
7. Ye, J., Zhao, J., Ye, K., et al.: Multi-STGCnet: a graph convolution based spatial-temporal framework for subway passenger flow forecasting. In: 2020 International Joint Conference on Neural Networks (IJCNN), pp. 1–8. IEEE (2020)
8. Bai, L., Yao, L., Li, C., et al.: Adaptive graph convolutional recurrent network for traffic forecasting. Adv. Neural. Inf. Process. Syst. **33**, 17804–17815 (2020)
9. Li, Y., Yu, R., Shahabi, C., et al.: Diffusion convolutional recurrent neural network: Data-driven traffic forecasting. arXiv preprint arXiv:1707.01926 (2017)
10. Huang, R., Huang, C., Liu, Y., et al.: LSGCN: long short-term traffic prediction with graph convolutional networks. In: IJCAI, vol. 7, pp. 2355–2361 (2020)
11. Khaled, A., Elsir, A.M.T., Shen, Y.: TFGAN: Traffic forecasting using generative adversarial network with multi-graph convolutional network. Knowl.-Based Syst. **249**, 108990 (2022)
12. Chen, L., Shao, W., Lv, M., et al.: AARGNN: an attentive attributed recurrent graph neural network for traffic flow prediction considering multiple dynamic factors. IEEE Trans. Intell. Transp. Syst. **23**(10), 17201–17211 (2022)
13. Li, M., Zhu, Z.: Spatial-temporal fusion graph neural networks for traffic flow forecasting. In: Proceedings of the AAAI conference on artificial intelligence, vol. 35, no. 5, pp. 4189–4196 (2021)
14. Wu, Z., Pan, S., Long, G., et al.: Graph wavenet for deep spatial-temporal graph modeling. arXiv preprint arXiv:1906.00121 (2019)
15. Song, C., Lin, Y., Guo, S., et al.: Spatial-temporal synchronous graph convolutional networks: A new framework for spatial-temporal network data forecasting. In: Proceedings of the AAAI Conference on Artificial Intelligence, vol. 34, no. 01, pp. 914–921 (2020)
16. Wang, Y., Fang, S., Zhang, C., et al.: TVGCN: Time-variant graph convolutional network for traffic forecasting. Neurocomputing **471**, 118–129 (2022)
17. Guo, G., Yuan, W., Liu, J., et al.: Traffic forecasting via dilated temporal convolution with peak-sensitive loss. IEEE Intell. Transp. Syst. Mag. **15**(1) (2023)

18. Guo, S., Lin, Y., Wan, H., et al.: Learning dynamics and heterogeneity of spatial-temporal graph data for traffic forecasting. IEEE Trans. Knowl. Data Eng. **34**(11), 5415–5428 (2021)
19. Ye, X., Fang, S., Sun, F., et al.: Meta graph transformer: a novel framework for spatial–temporal traffic prediction. Neurocomputing **491**, 544–563 (2022)
20. Li, Q., Han, Z., Wu, X.M.: Deeper insights into graph convolutional networks for semi-supervised learning. In: Proceedings of the AAAI Conference on Artificial Intelligence, vol. 32, no. 1 (2018)
21. Belkin, M., Niyogi, P.: Laplacian eigenmaps and spectral techniques for embedding and clustering. Adv. Neural Inf. Process. Syst. **14** (2001)
22. Vaswani, A., Shazeer, N., Parmar, N., et al.: Attention is all you need. Adv. Neural Inf. Process. Syst. **30** (2017)
23. Xu, M., Dai, W., Liu, C., et al.: Spatial-temporal transformer networks for traffic flow forecasting. arXiv preprint arXiv:2001.02908 (2020)
24. Cai, L., Janowicz, K., Mai, G., et al.: Traffic transformer: capturing the continuity and periodicity of time series for traffic forecasting. Trans. GIS **24**(3), 736–755 (2020)
25. Li, G., Zhong, S., Deng, X., et al.: A lightweight and accurate spatial-temporal transformer for traffic forecasting. IEEE Trans. Knowl. Data Eng. (2022)
26. Chen, K., Chen, G., Xu, D., et al.: NAST: non-aut oregressive spatial-temporal transformer for time series forecasting. arXiv preprint arXiv:2102.05624 (2021)
27. Bogaerts, T., Masegosa, A.D., Angarita-Zapata, J.S., et al.: A graph CNN-LSTM neural network for short and long-term traffic forecasting based on trajectory data. Transp. Res. Part C: Emerg. Technol. **112**, 62–77 (2020)
28. Perozzi, B., Al-Rfou, R., Skiena, S.: DeepWalk: online learning of social representations. In: Proceedings of the 20th ACM SIGKDD International Conference on Knowledge Discovery and Data Mining, pp. 701–710 (2014)
29. Grover, A., Leskovec, J.: node2vec: scalable feature learning for networks. In: Proceedings of the 22nd ACM SIGKDD International Conference on Knowledge Discovery and Data Mining, pp. 855–864 (2016)
30. He, K., Zhang, X., Ren, S., et al.: Deep residual learning for image recognition. In: Proceedings of the IEEE Conference on Computer Vision and Pattern Recognition, pp. 770–778 (2016)
31. Ba, J.L., Kiros, J.R., Hinton, G.E.: Layer normalization. arXiv preprint arXiv:1607.06450 (2016)
32. Liu, L., Chen, J., Wu, H., et al.: Physical-virtual collaboration modeling for intra-and inter-station metro ridership prediction. IEEE Trans. Intell. Transp. Syst. **23**(4), 3377–3391 (2020)
33. Chen, C., Petty, K., Skabardonis, A., et al.: Freeway performance measurement system: mining loop detector data. Transp. Res. Rec. **1748**(1), 96–102 (2001)
34. Paszke, A., Gross, S., Massa, F., et al.: PyTorch: an imperative style, high-performance deep learning library. Adv. Neural Inf. Process. Syst. **32** (2019)
35. Kingma, D.P., Ba, J.: Adam: a method for stochastic optimization. arXiv preprint arXiv:1412.6980 (2014)

Predicting Future Spatio-Temporal States Using a Robust Causal Graph Attention Model

Peixiao Wang[1,2], Hengcai Zhang[1,2(✉)], and Feng Lu[1,2,3]

[1] State Key Laboratory of Resources and Environmental Information System, Institute of Geographic Sciences and Natural Resources Research, CAS, Beijing 100101, China
{wpx,zhanghc,luf}@lreis.ac.cn

[2] College of Resources and Environment, University of Chinese Academy of Sciences, Beijing 100049, China

[3] Fujian Collaborative Innovation Center for Big Data Applications in Governments, Fuzhou 350003, China

Abstract. Spatiotemporal prediction is a research topic in urban planning and management. Most existing spatiotemporal prediction models currently face challenges. More specifically, most prediction models are sensitive to missing data, meaning most prediction models are only tested on spatiotemporal data assuming no missing data. Although missing data can be imputed, spatiotemporal prediction models with the capability of handling missing data are needed. In this study, we propose a novel missing-data-tolerant causal graph attention model called CGATM to address the above challenges. To enable the CGATM model to be tested on spatiotemporal data with missing data, we propose a novel missing data handling mechanism that automatically handles missing data according to the probability of data missing patterns. To improve the nonlinear fitting ability of the CGATM model, we propose a novel causal graph attention method that represents geospatial heterogeneity by adjacent nodes with different weights. In addition, we design the CGTAM model as an Imputer-Predictor architecture and define a novel loss function to optimize model parameters. The proposed model was validated on three real-world spatiotemporal datasets (traffic dataset, PM2.5 dataset, and temperature dataset). Experimental results showed that the proposed model has better prediction performance under four missing scenarios, and outperforms eight existing baselines regarding prediction accuracy.

Keywords: Spatiotemporal prediction · spatiotemporal data missing · causal dilatation convolution · graph attention network

1 Introduction

With the rapid development of the Internet of Things, the spatiotemporal prediction models have been widely used in urban planning, environmental monitoring, and meteorological disaster management. The current common modeling idea for spatiotemporal prediction is to use supervised learning methods to establish a mapping function from

X. Meng et al. (Eds.): SpatialDI 2024, LNCS 14619, pp. 242–251, 2024.
https://doi.org/10.1007/978-981-97-2966-1_18

input data to output data, and then use the mapping function to predict future data (Manibardo et al., 2021; L. Xu et al., 2021). However, most existing spatiotemporal prediction models still face challenges. Specifically, most existing spatiotemporal prediction models cannot deal with missing data, meaning that most prediction models are only tested on spatiotemporal data assuming no missing data (Che et al., 2018; Cui et al., 2020; Wang et al., 2023). However, in the actual environment, data missing is a common phenomenon and presents complex missing patterns (such as random missing, and block missing), affecting the application scope and the prediction accuracy of most prediction models (Chittor Sundaram et al., 2020; Kadow et al., 2020; Wang et al., 2022).

Overall, the complex missing patterns in spatiotemporal data directly or indirectly affect the prediction accuracy of spatiotemporal prediction models (Wang et al., 2023). Therefore, we urgently need to develop missing data-tolerant spatiotemporal prediction models. In this study, we propose a novel Causal Graph ATtention model with tolerating Missing data (CGATM). Specifically, the main contributions of this study are summarized as follows:

(1) We design a novel missing data handling component (MDH) that enables the proposed CGATM model with the ability to automatically handle missing data according to missing patterns. In addition, we propose a causal graph attention mechanism (CGAT) that enhances the nonlinear fitting ability of the proposed CGATM model.
(2) To enable the CGATM model to be used for both spatiotemporal prediction tasks under missing and no-missing scenarios, we design the CGTAM model as an Imputer-Predictor architecture. Correspondingly, we define a novel loss function that considers the imputation and prediction tasks to optimize model parameters.
(3) We used the traffic dataset, PM2.5 dataset, and temperature dataset to evaluate the prediction performance of the CGATM model, and visualized the missing-data handling mechanism of CGATM.

2 Preliminaries

Definition 1 (Graph): The graph $G = <V, A>$ represents the graph structure abstracted from multiple sensors, where $V = \{v_i\}_{i=1}^n$ represents n sensors (n graph nodes), $A \in \mathcal{R}^{n \times n}$ indicates the adjacency matrix between graph nodes.

Definition 2 (Spatiotemporal State Matrix): The spatiotemporal data monitored by all sensors in all time windows can be represented as a spatiotemporal state matrix with missing data $X \in \mathcal{R}^{n \times T}$, where x_i^t indicates the spatiotemporal data of node v_i in the t th time window, and $x^t = \{x_i^t\}_{i=1}^n \in \mathcal{R}^{n \times 1}$ represents the spatial sequence of all sensors in the t th time window.

Definition 3 (Mask Matrix): The mask matrix $M \in \mathcal{R}^{n \times T}$ is a matrix used to distinguish between missing data and observed data in $X \in \mathcal{R}^{n \times T}$. When $m_i^t = 0$ indicates that the spatiotemporal data of node v_i in the t th time window is missing, and when $m_i^t = 1$ indicates that the spatiotemporal data of node v_i in the t th time window is not missing. Similarly, $m^t = \{m_i^t\}_{i=1}^n \in \mathcal{R}^{n \times 1}$ is used to distinguish between missing data and observed data in $x^t = \{x_i^t\}_{i=1}^n \in \mathcal{R}^{n \times 1}$.

Our research goal is to establish a functional model $\mathcal{M}_G$ that can mine spatiotemporal correlation patterns from the spatiotemporal state matrix $\boldsymbol{X}$ containing missing data. Specifically, given a spatiotemporal state matrix $\boldsymbol{X}_{t-p+1}^t = \{\boldsymbol{x}^\tau\}_{\tau=t-p+1}^t \in \mathcal{R}^{n \times p}$, the process is shown in Eq. (1).

$$\{\hat{\boldsymbol{x}}^{t+1}, \hat{\boldsymbol{x}}^{t+2}, \ldots \ldots, \hat{\boldsymbol{x}}^{t+q}\} = \mathcal{M}_G\left(\boldsymbol{X}_{t-p+1}^t, \boldsymbol{M}_{t-p+1}^t; \boldsymbol{W}\right) \tag{1}$$

where $\mathcal{M}_G(\cdot)$ represents the prediction model based on the graph structure G, i.e., the CGATM model; $\boldsymbol{X}_{t-p+1}^t = \{\boldsymbol{x}^\tau\}_{\tau=t-p+1}^t \in \mathcal{R}^{n \times p}$ represents the input data for the CGATM model; p represents the time dependent step; $\boldsymbol{M}_{t-p+1}^t$ represents the mask matrix corresponding to $\boldsymbol{X}_{t-p+1}^t$; $\hat{\boldsymbol{x}}^{t+q}$ represents the prediction result of the CGATM model; q represents the prediction step; $\boldsymbol{W}$ represents learnable parameters in the CGATM model.

3 Methodology

In this section, we describe the proposed CGATM model for spatiotemporal prediction. As shown in Fig. 1, the proposed CGATM model is an end-to-end Imputer-Predictor architecture. Except for the different definitions of loss function and input, the internal structures of the Imputer and Predictor are identical, with a missing data handling component (MDH) on the left and multiple causal graph attention components (CGAT) on the right. Among them, the MDH can automatically handle missing data according to missing patterns in spatiotemporal data (discussed in Sect. 3.1.1), and the CGAT can enhances the nonlinear fitting ability of the proposed model (discussed in Sect. 3.1.2).

3.1 Forward Propagation of the CGATM

In this subsection, we elaborate on the forward propagation of the CGATM model. For simplicity, we further analyze the internal composition of the CGATM model. During the forward propagation, the spatiotemporal data are used as the input of the Imputer module to obtain a temporary variable, i.e., the output of the Imputer. Then, the temporary variable is used as the input of the Predictor module to obtain the final prediction result. Due to the same internal composition of the Imputer and the Predictor, the processing of input data is similar in the Imputer and the Predictor, i.e., through one MDH component and N_I/N_P CGAT components. Specifically, taking spatiotemporal data $\boldsymbol{X}_{t-p+1}^t$ as an example, the forward propagation process of CGATM model is shown in Eqs. (2) and (3).

$$\text{Imputer:} \begin{cases} \overline{\boldsymbol{X}}_{t-p+1}^t = MDH\left(\boldsymbol{X}_{t-p+1}^t, \boldsymbol{X}_{t-p+1}^t, \boldsymbol{M}_{t-p+1}^t; \boldsymbol{W}\right) \\ \mathcal{O}_{1:t-p+1}^{l:t} = \begin{cases} CGAT\left(\overline{\boldsymbol{X}}_{t-p+1}^t; \boldsymbol{W}\right) & l = 1 \\ CGAT\left(\mathcal{O}_{l-1:t-p+1}^{l-1:t}; \boldsymbol{W}\right) & l < N_I \end{cases} \\ \hat{\boldsymbol{X}}_{\text{Imputer}:t-p+1}^{\text{Imputer}:t} = F * \mathcal{O}_{N_I:t-p+1}^{N_I:t} \end{cases} \tag{2}$$

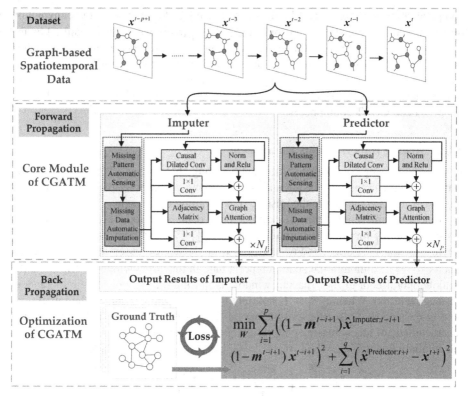

Fig. 1. Workflow of the CGATM model.

$$\text{Predictor:} \begin{cases} \overline{X}^t_{t-p+1} = MDH\left(X^t_{t-p+1}, X^{\text{Imputer}:t}_{\text{Imputer}:t-p+1}, M^t_{t-p+1}; W\right) \\ \mathcal{O}^{l:t}_{1:t-p+1} = \begin{cases} CGAT\left(\overline{X}^t_{t-p+1}; W\right) & l = 1 \\ CGAT\left(\mathcal{O}^{l-1:t}_{l-1:t-p+1}; W\right) & l < N_P \end{cases} \\ \widehat{X}^{\text{Predictor}:t+q}_{\text{Predictor}:t+1} = F * \mathcal{O}^{N_P:t}_{N_P:t-p+1} \end{cases} \tag{3}$$

where $X^t_{t-p+1} = \{x^\tau\}^t_{\tau=t-p+1} \in \mathcal{R}^{n \times p}$ represents the input spatiotemporal data for the CGATM model; p represents the time dependent step; M^t_{t-p+1} represents the mask matrix corresponding to X^t_{t-p+1}; $\widehat{X}^{\text{Imputer}:t}_{\text{Imputer}:t-p+1} = \left\{\widehat{x}^{\text{Imputer}:\tau}\right\}^t_{\tau=t-p+1} \in \mathcal{R}^{n \times p}$ is the output of the Imputer and the input of the Predictor; $\widehat{X}^{\text{Predictor}:t+q}_{\text{Predictor}:t+1} = \left\{\widehat{x}^{\text{Predictor}:\tau}\right\}^{t+q}_{\tau=t+1} \in \mathcal{R}^{n \times q}$ is the output of the Predictor, and the final prediction result of the CGATM model; q represents the prediction step; $\overline{X}^t_{t-p+1} \in \mathcal{R}^{n \times p}$ indicates the output of the *MDH* component in the Imputer or Predictor; $\mathcal{O}^{l:t}_{l:t-p+1} \in \mathcal{R}^{n \times p \times e}$ indicates the output of the lth CGAT component in the Imputer or Predictor, where e represents the dimension of spatiotemporal data in the CGAT component; N_I and N_P represent the number of CGAT components in the Imputer and Predictor, respectively; $F*$ represents the convolution operation that converts the dimensions of $O_{Np:t-p+1}^{Np:t}$ to the dimensions required by the Imputer or the Predictor (i.e., dimension alignment); W represents learnable parameters in the CGATM model. Equations (2) and (3) further show that the difference between the Imputer and the Predictor is mainly the difference between the input and the output. Furthermore, it is clear from Eqs. (2) and (3) that the core of the Imputer or Predictor is the MDH and CGAT components.

3.1.1 Missing Data Handling Component

In general, missing data requires different handling strategies under different missing patterns (such as random missing and block missing). Therefore, the identification of missing patterns is the key to the missing data handling component.

To identify missing patterns in spatiotemporal data, we introduce an auxiliary quantity $c^t = \{c_i^t\}_{i=1}^n$ for spatiotemporal data $x^t = \{x_i^t\}_{i=1}^n$ under a specific time window, where c_i^t denotes the time window size of x_i^t from the nearest observation. Specifically, when $c_i^{t-1} = 1$, although the spatiotemporal data in the target window is missing, the spatiotemporal data in the adjacent window is not missing (characteristic of random missing patterns). When $c_i^{t-1} > 1$, not only the spatiotemporal data in the target window is missing, but also the spatiotemporal data in the adjacent window is missing (characteristic of block missing patterns). Equation (4) shows the calculation method of the auxiliary quantity $c^t = \{c_i^t\}_{i=1}^n$.

$$c_i^t = \begin{cases} 1 + c_i^{t-1} & t > 1, m_i^{t-1} = 0 \\ 1 & t > 1, m_i^{t-1} = 1 \\ 0 & t = 1 \end{cases} \tag{4}$$

where c_i^t denotes the time window size of x_i^t from the nearest observation; m_i^{t-1} is used to distinguish whether the data of node v_i is missing in the $(t-1)$th time window. When $m_i^{t-1} = 0$, the data of node v_i in the $(t-1)$th time window is missing. When $m_i^{t-1} = 1$, the data of node v_i in the $(t-1)$th time window is not missing.

It can be seen from the above that c^t represents the missing pattern of missing data to some extent. Therefore, we further define the process of MDH component to automatically handle missing data based on c^t. The estimated value of missing data can be expressed as the weighted sum of the most similar observation in the spatial dimension and the closest observation in the temporal dimension. Specifically, we first convert c^t into the probability of missing patterns, and then estimate the missing data based on the probability weighting, as shown in Eq. (5).

$$\text{MDH:} \begin{cases} \bar{x}^t = m^t \odot x^t + \left(1 - m^t\right) \odot \left(\delta^t \odot x^{t:tm} + \left(1 - \delta^t\right) \odot x^{t:sm}\right) \\ \delta^t = \exp\{-\max(0, W_\delta c^t + b_\delta)\} \end{cases} \tag{5}$$

where $\bar{x}^t$ denotes the spatiotemporal data processed by the MDH component, and the spatiotemporal data under all time windows comprise $\overline{X}_{t-p+1}^t = \{\bar{x}^\tau\}_{\tau=t-p+1}^t \in \mathcal{R}^{n \times p}$; $x^{t:tm} \in \mathcal{R}^{n \times 1}$ denotes the closest observations of all nodes in the time dimension; $x^{t:sm} \in \mathcal{R}^{n \times 1}$ denotes the most similar observations of all nodes in the temporal dimension; δ^t

denotes the probability (or weight) of missing pattern calculated by c^t; when δ^t tends to 1, the pattern of missing data tends to be random missing, and when δ^t tends to 0, the pattern of missing data tends to be block missing; exp denotes the exponential function; max denotes the maximum function; $W_\delta \in \mathcal{R}^{1 \times 1}$ denotes the learnable parameters in the MDH component. **Note:** The specific value of δ^t will be determined autonomously based on the final spatiotemporal prediction task, i.e. autonomously determining the processing strategy for the missing data.

3.1.2 Causal Graph Attention Component

After the input data is passed through the MDH component, the spatiotemporal relationships are further captured by the CGAT component. In this subsection, we detail the forward propagation process of the CGAT component. The CGAT component mainly contains causal dilation convolution operator and the graph attention operator, which respectively mine spatial and temporal correlations in spatiotemporal data. Taking spatiotemporal data $\overline{X}^t_{t-p+1} = \{\overline{x}^\tau\}^t_{\tau=t-p+1}$ as an example, the forward propagation process of the CGAT component is shown in Eq. (6).

$$
\text{CGAT:} \begin{cases}
\mathcal{H} = CDC\left(\overline{X}^t_{t-p+1}\right) = F *_d \overline{X}^t_{t-p+1} \\
\mathcal{H}' = Relu(Norm(\mathcal{H})) \\
\mathcal{H}'' = Relu\left(Norm(CDC(\mathcal{H}'))\right) + F * \overline{X}^t_{t-p+1} \\
\mathcal{O} = GAT\left(\mathcal{H}''\right)
\end{cases} \tag{6}
$$

where $\mathcal{H}$, $\mathcal{H}'$, and $\mathcal{H}'' \in \mathcal{R}^{n \times p \times e}$ indicate the intermediate state; Taking $\mathcal{H}$ as an example, $\mathcal{H}$ can be expanded as $\{H_i\}^n_{i=1}$ along the spatial dimension, expanded as $\{H^\tau\}^t_{\tau=t-p+1}$ along the temporal dimension. Among them, $\{H_i\}^n_{i=1}$ can be used for spatial modeling, and $\{H^\tau\}^t_{\tau=t-p+1}$ can be used for temporal modeling. $\mathcal{O}$ represents the output result of CGAT; CDC represents causal dilation convolution operator; GAT represents graph attention operator; $F * \overline{X}^t_{t-p+1}$ denotes performing convolution operations on spatiotemporal data $\overline{X}^t_{t-p+1}$; $Norm$ represents the parameter regularization function; $Relu$ represents the activation function.

3.2 Optimization of the CGATM

In this study, the loss function mainly consists of two parts: the loss of prediction task (i.e., loss of the Predictor) and the loss of imputation task (loss of the Imputer). Among them, the prediction task loss is mainly used to ensure the accuracy of the prediction results, and the imputation task loss mainly considers the impact of missing data on the prediction results. The designed loss function is shown in Eq. (7).

$$
\mathcal{L}(W) = \min_W \left(\begin{aligned} &\sum_{i=1}^p \left((1 - m^{t-i+1})\hat{x}^{\text{Imputer}:t-i+1} - (1 - m^{t-i+1})x^{t-i+1} \right)^2 \\ &+ \sum_{i=1}^q \left(\hat{x}^{\text{Predictor}:t+i} - x^{t+i} \right)^2 \end{aligned} \right) \tag{7}
$$

where $\sum_{i=1}^{p} \left(\left(1 - \boldsymbol{m}^{t-i+1}\right)\hat{\boldsymbol{x}}^{\text{Imputer}:t-i+1} - \left(1 - \boldsymbol{m}^{t-i+1}\right)\boldsymbol{x}^{t-i+1} \right)^{2}$ denotes the loss function for the Imputer; $\sum_{i=1}^{q} \left(\hat{\boldsymbol{x}}^{\text{Predictor}:t+i} - \boldsymbol{x}^{t+i} \right)^{2}$ denotes the loss function for the Predictor. In this study, the loss of the prediction task is equally weighted with the loss of the imputation task.

4 Experimental Results and Analysis

4.1 Data Preparation

In this study, we used three spatiotemporal datasets to evaluate the performance of the CGATM model, i.e., traffic dataset, PM$_{2.5}$ dataset, and temperature dataset (Wang et al., 2023).

To support this study, we preprocessed three spatiotemporal datasets as follows: (1) There are natural missing values in the collected spatiotemporal data. Considering the impact of natural missing values on subsequent modeling, we used the BTTF model to estimate the natural missing values in spatiotemporal data (Chen & Sun, 2022); (2) Referring to Cui et al. (2020) and Wang et al. (2023), we randomly deleted some spatiotemporal data with a missing rate of 20% and 40%; (3) We constructed the adjacency matrices for three spatiotemporal datasets. In this study, the adjacency matrix is constructed by a similarity matrix, and we use the ten most similar spatial objects as the neighbors of the target spatial object.

4.2 Comparison with Baselines

In this study, Root Mean Square Error (RMSE) and Mean Absolute Percentage Error (MAPE) are used as quantitative indicators to verify the prediction accuracy of the proposed model. Since the predictive performance of classical statistical models on spatiotemporal forecasting tasks is often lower than that of data-driven models, we mainly compare CGATM models with popular data-driven methods. The baseline methods used can be roughly divided into four categories. The first category is prediction models that do not tolerate missing data and do not consider geospatial heterogeneity, including the ST-KNN model (Yu et al., 2016), and the T-GCN model(Zhao et al., 2020). The second category is prediction models that do not tolerate missing data and consider geospatial heterogeneity, including the ASTGCN model (Guo et al., 2019), and the GDGCN model(Y. Xu et al., 2023). The third category is prediction models that tolerate missing data and do not consider geospatial heterogeneity, including the BTMF model (Chen & Sun, 2022), and the LSTM-M model (Tian et al., 2018). The fourth category is prediction models that tolerate missing data and consider geospatial heterogeneity, including the SGMN model (Cui et al., 2020), and the D-TGNM model (Wang et al., 2023).

In the missing scenario, we use the Imputer-Predictor architecture (i.e., CGATM model) to complete the spatiotemporal prediction task. Table 1 show the comparison results of prediction accuracy between CGATM and baselines under missing scenarios. The results show that the four categories of models exhibit significant differences under missing scenarios. Among them, the prediction accuracy of the third-category model is better than that of the first-category model and the second-category model, and the prediction accuracy of the fourth-category model is better than that of the third-category model. Specifically, the missing-data-tolerant prediction models are significantly superior to the missing-data-intolerant prediction models. Compared to baselines, the prediction accuracy of the proposed CGATM model is better than that of ST-KNN, T-GCN, ASTGCN, GDGCN, BTMF, LSTM-M, and SGMN models, and approaches the prediction accuracy of the D-TGNM model.

Table 1. Comparison results (in RMSE/MAPE) of prediction accuracy between CGATM and baselines under random missing scenario

Model	MR	Traffic Volume		$PM_{2.5}$		Temperature	
		1-step	3-steps	1-step	3-steps	1-step	3-steps
ST-KNN	20%	19.40/37.51	19.68/38.36	29.34/44.70	31.64/51.97	7.94/20.66	8.04/21.13
	40%	30.02/50.37	30.28/51.37	42.72/58.74	44.14/63.78	13.01/38.97	13.17/39.54
T-GCN	20%	13.20/34.70	14.72/37.36	18.83/37.10	24.48/44.90	2.12/5.76	3.31/9.58
	40%	14.11/35.70	15.50/39.08	19.68/39.01	25.06/49.53	2.21/6.03	3.32/9.60
ASTGCN	20%	10.34/31.66	11.93/33.67	16.68/28.62	22.27/46.02	1.33/3.54	1.71/4.81
	40%	11.29/32.87	12.48/35.48	17.64/32.03	23.42/46.39	1.50/4.34	1.84/5.16
GDGCN	20%	8.35/29.17	9.04/31.02	14.17/25.04	20.91/45.35	1.03/2.81	1.31/3.45
	40%	9.43/31.64	10.68/35.91	15.34/29.68	21.09/46.35	1.05/2.85	1.38/3.78
BTMF	20%	7.28/26.00	8.41/28.43	12.86/24.03	19.01/35.65	0.84/2.11	1.03/2.79
	40%	7.89/27.61	8.92/30.19	14.22/26.54	20.65/38.98	0.91/2.62	1.18/3.27
LSTM-M	20%	7.43/24.91	8.53/27.79	14.87/26.88	20.68/39.61	0.54/1.86	0.95/2.35
	40%	8.06/28.42	9.08/29.63	17.52/32.01	22.20/44.46	0.63/2.23	1.15/2.88
SGMN	20%	7.31/26.35	8.34/28.63	14.62/25.32	19.31/38.32	0.55/1.43	0.84/2.23
	40%	7.86/27.63	8.93/31.97	15.56/27.10	21.36/41.65	0.58/1.47	0.86/2.26
D-TGNM	20%	7.16/24.43	8.16/27.63	12.76/23.36	18.97/36.15	0.54/1.40	0.78/2.09
	40%	7.83/26.98	8.86/30.39	14.10/25.87	20.34/39.13	0.59/1.49	0.81/2.21
CGATM	**20%**	**6.96/24.37**	**7.99/27.69**	**12.21/22.35**	**18.31/34.06**	**0.52/1.34**	**0.74/1.91**
	40%	**7.71/26.72**	**8.62/29.22**	**13.56/25.05**	**19.19/36.76**	**0.55/1.44**	**0.76/1.95**

4.3 Qualitative Analysis of CGATM Model

In this subsection, we analyzed the ability of the CGATM model to automatically handle missing data from a qualitative perspective. More specifically, we analyze the ability of the CGATM model to automatically handle missing data by visualizing the relationship between c^t and δ^t. As shown in Fig. 2, the red curve reflects the relationship between c^t and δ^t, and the blue curve reflects the relationship between c^t and $1 - \delta^t$. The results show significant differences in the missing data handling strategies for the three spatiotemporal datasets. For example, when the missing pattern tends to random missing, the traffic and $PM_{2.5}$ datasets use the temporal dimension observations to impute the missing data, while the temperature dataset uses spatial dimension observations to impute the missing data. When the missing pattern tends to block missing, the traffic and PM$_{2.5}$ datasets use spatial dimension observations to impute the missing data, while the temperature dataset uses temporal dimension observations to impute the missing data. The reasons for these differences are as follows. The proposed CGATM model can autonomously determine the missing data handling strategies under different missing patterns according to the characteristics of the spatiotemporal datasets, which explains the superior prediction accuracy of the CGATM model under missing scenarios.

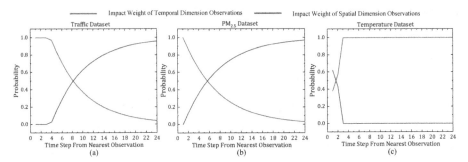

Fig. 2. Illustration of missing patterns in spatiotemporal data:(a) traffic dataset, (b)PM$_{2.5}$ dataset, and (c) temperature dataset.

5   Conclusion

In this study, we proposed a missing data-tolerant spatiotemporal prediction model, i.e., the CGATM model. In the experimental section, three real spatiotemporal datasets (traffic dataset, PM$_{2.5}$ dataset, and temperature dataset) are used to verify the prediction performance of the CGATM model. First, we compared eight existing baselines, including ST-KNN, T-GCN, ASTGCN, GDGCN, BTMF, LSTM-M, SGMN, and D-TGNM models. Experimental results show that the proposed CGATM model has good prediction performance under two missing scenarios (20% random missing and 40% random missing), and outperforms eight existing baselines in prediction accuracy. Second, we visualized the missing-data handling mechanism of CGATM, which helped justify the superior prediction accuracy of the proposed CGATM model.

Funding. This project was supported by National Key Research and Development Program of China [Grant No. 2022YFB3904102], China National Postdoctoral Support Program for Innovative Talents [Grant No. BX20230360], China Postdoctoral Science Foundation [Grant No. 2023M743454].

References

Che, Z., Purushotham, S., Cho, K., Sontag, D., Liu, Y.: Recurrent neural networks for multivariate time series with missing values. Sci. Rep. **8**(1), 6085 (2018). https://doi.org/10.1038/s41598-018-24271-9

Chen, X., Sun, L.: Bayesian temporal factorization for multidimensional time series prediction. IEEE Trans. Pattern Anal. Mach. Intell. **44**, 4659–4673 (2022). https://doi.org/10.1109/TPAMI. 2021.3066551

Chittor Sundaram, R., Naghizade, E., Borovica-Gajic, R., Tomko, M.: Harnessing spatio-temporal patterns in data for nominal attribute imputation. Trans. GIS **24**(4), 1001–1032 (2020). https://doi.org/10.1111/tgis.12617

Cui, Z., Lin, L., Pu, Z., Wang, Y.: Graph Markov network for traffic forecasting with missing data. Transp. Res. Part C: Emerg. Technol. **117**, 102671 (2020). https://doi.org/10.1016/j.trc.2020.102671

Guo, S., Lin, Y., Feng, N., Song, C., Wan, H.: Attention based spatial-temporal graph convolutional networks for traffic flow forecasting. In: Proceedings of the AAAI Conference on Artificial Intelligence, vol. 33, pp. 922–929 (2019). https://doi.org/10.1609/aaai.v33i01.3301922

Kadow, C., Hall, D.M., Ulbrich, U.: Artificial intelligence reconstructs missing climate information. Nat. Geosci. **13**(6), 408–413 (2020). https://doi.org/10.1038/s41561-020-0582-5

Manibardo, E.L., Lana, I., Ser, J.D.: Deep learning for road traffic forecasting: does it make a difference? IEEE Trans. Intell. Transp. Syst. 1–25 (2021). https://doi.org/10.1109/TITS.2021.3083957

Tian, Y., Zhang, K., Li, J., Lin, X., Yang, B.: LSTM-based traffic flow prediction with missing data. Neurocomputing **318**, 297–305 (2018). https://doi.org/10.1016/j.neucom.2018.08.067

Wang, P., Hu, T., Gao, F., Wu, R., Guo, W., Zhu, X.: A hybrid data-driven framework for spatiotemporal traffic flow data imputation. IEEE Internet Things J. **9**(17), 16343–16352 (2022). https://doi.org/10.1109/JIOT.2022.3151238

Wang, P., Zhang, Y., Hu, T., Zhang, T.: Urban traffic flow prediction: a dynamic temporal graph network considering missing values. Int. J. Geogr. Inf. Sci. **37**(4), 885–912 (2023). https://doi.org/10.1080/13658816.2022.2146120

Xu, L., Chen, N., Chen, Z., Zhang, C., Yu, H.: Spatiotemporal forecasting in earth system science: methods, uncertainties, predictability and future directions. Earth Sci. Rev. **222**, 103828 (2021). https://doi.org/10.1016/j.earscirev.2021.103828

Xu, Y., Han, L., Zhu, T., Sun, L., Du, B., Lv, W.: Generic dynamic graph convolutional network for traffic flow forecasting. Inf. Fusion 101946 (2023). https://doi.org/10.1016/j.inffus.2023.101946

Yu, B., Song, X., Guan, F., Yang, Z., Yao, B.: K-nearest neighbor model for multiple-time-step prediction of short-term traffic condition. J. Transp. Eng. **142**(6), 04016018 (2016). https://doi.org/10.1061/(ASCE)TE.1943-5436.0000816

Zhao, L., et al.: T-GCN: a temporal graph convolutional network for traffic prediction. IEEE Trans. Intell. Transp. Syst. **21**(9), 3848–3858 (2020). https://doi.org/10.1109/TITS.2019.2935152

Remote Sensing Data Classification

MADB-RemdNet for Few-Shot Learning in Remote Sensing Classification

Kun Wang[1], Yingying Wang[1], and Zhiming Ding[2(✉)]

[1] Beijing University of Technology, Beijing 100124, China
`wangyingying@emails.bjut.edu.cn`
[2] Institute of Software, Chinese Academy of Sciences, Beijing 100190, China
`zhiming@iscas.ac.cn`

Abstract. The problem of small sample classification is to identify image categories that have not appeared in the training concentration when marking the scarce sample samples of the training data set. Such tasks are of great significance in the recognition of remote sensing scenarios. It is a problem worth studying in this field. As we all know, training a deep learning model for classification requires a considerable labeling data set, which makes the production of training data sets huge. In this article, we propose a MADB feature extraction model based on Mixed Attention Module as a base model to extract features. Using RccaEMD module as the measurement algorithm to distinguish the classification of remote sensing scenarios. In NWPU-RESISC45 dataset, AID dataset, and UC-Merced dataset, it proves that our method has achieved higher accuracy than the current advanced methods of this field.

Keywords: few-shot learning · remote sensing classification · EMD algorithm

1 Introduction

Remote sensing image scene classification is the process of analyzing remote sensing data, such as satellite or aerial imagery, to classify or categorize the land cover or land use of a specific area on the Earth's surface. Owing to the development of new satellite and sensor technologies [1,2], improvements in data storage and processing capabilities have led to a significant increase in the volume of remote sensing images being collected and made available. In recent years, driven by the availability of data, computing power, and advanced algorithms, deep learning has made significant progress in the field of image classification.

Under this trend, researchers in the field of remote sensing scene classification have also transitioned from using traditional methods to utilizing deep learning methods and models to study this problem. They have achieved significant breakthroughs, such as the work of Hu [3], Chaib [4], and Li [5], who

This work is supported by the National Key R&D Program of China under Grant 2022YFF0503900.

have proposed a series of deep CNN models that possess strong characteristic representation and recognition abilities. However, training a deep learning model typically requires a large amount of labeled datasets. Deep learning models are designed to learn complex patterns and features directly from data. The more data they are trained on, the better they are able to generalize to new, unseen examples. Compared to natural images, acquiring and annotating remote sensing images is more challenging. Some remote sensing datasets even require expert-level skills in this field to complete the labeling.

In contrast to machine vision algorithms, humans can quickly and efficiently learn new concepts with very few examples. This ability is often referred to as "one-shot" or "few-shot" learning. Few-shot learning is inspired by the human ability to learn new concepts from very few examples, and researchers are actively working on developing machine learning algorithms that can replicate this capability. The goal of few-shot learning is to enable machines to quickly and efficiently learn new concepts, even with very limited labeled data. Few-shot learning has been successfully applied in a wide range of fields, including computer vision and natural language processing (NLP).

Generally speaking, few-shot learning can be divided into the following three methods: transfer learning-based methods, metric learning-based methods, and meta-learning-based methods. Transfer learning-based methods are typically built upon model transfer learning. This approach involves transferring knowledge from a model that has been trained on a source task to the target task, by reusing the source task model. Metric learning-based methods [8–10] encode samples as low-dimensional feature vectors by training feature embedding networks, then compare the similarity of samples in the metric space to achieve the goal of classification. Meta-learning-based methods [6,7] can train meta-models that are applicable to multiple tasks and have the characteristics of rapid adaptation. The three methods mentioned above employ the episodic training strategy for model training. This training strategy was first used by Vinyals [20] and his colleagues in the matching network.

In recent research on this issue, the focus is typically on the classification performance of the model and its ability to generalize to new class recognition with a small number of sample sets. However, this often overlooks the significance of a well-designed feature encoder. However, due to the following characteristics of remote sensing images:

1. There is a significant intraclass diversity.
2. High interclass similarity
3. Large variance in object/scene scales
4. Coexistence of multiple ground objects:

As shown in Fig. 1, due to the above characteristics, previous studies such as ProtoNet [8], and MatchingNet [20]. The approach of obtaining the distance between images by some metric algorithm and training a classifier based on this metric leads to most of the scenarios being misclassified, resulting in a trained model that often performs poorly. Therefore, we can find that it is very important to design a feature encoder with favorable performance. To address this issue, we propose MADB(Mixed Attention Dense Block), a feature encoder architecture that incorporates a hybrid attention mechanism, which enables the model to capture feature regions of variability among remote sensing image classes while enhancing the extraction of their high-level scene semantic features. In addition, unlike the previous models in which ResNet is used as the base model, this paper uses Dense Block as the base model. According to the experiments in Simpleshot [28], using Dense Block as the feature encoder of the small-sample model can make the model performance better.

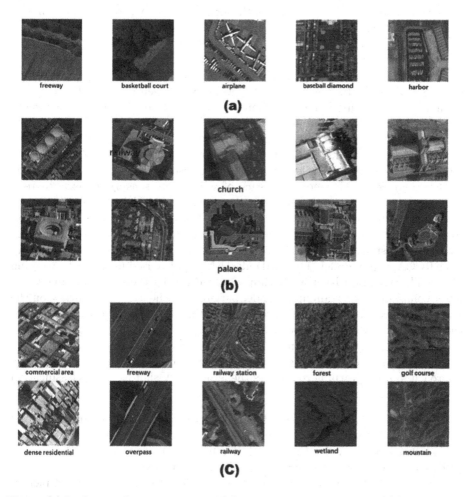

Fig. 1. (a) Irrelevant object interference. (b) Large intraclass variances. (c) Large interclass similarity.

In this paper, we not only design a new feature encoder architecture called MADB by combining the hybrid attention mechanism, but we also design a new classifier by combining the attention mechanism RCCA [26] (Recurrent Criss-Cross Attention) and the metric algorithm EMD. This classifier first corrects the globally encoded remote sensing image features using the RCCA attention mechanism. It then extracts these features into local features of multiple image blocks, which are trained through meta-training. Finally, it calculates the sum of distances between similar image blocks to discriminate the classes of remote sensing images. Compared to the cosine distance and cross entropy used in previous related research, this learnable metric algorithm utilizes the principle of optimal matching flow of local features. It also enhances the capture ability of advanced scene semantic features through the RCCA attention mechanism. This algorithm is able to solve the cluttered background of remote sensing scene images and the large factor of intraclass differences. Additionally, it can more accurately measure the probability of two images belonging to the same class.

With the similarity to previous research methods, we also adopt a two-stage training approach. In the base model, we selected Dense Block. For the pre-training stage, we used the migration learning method and selected a remote sensing training dataset. We used the parameters from training Densenet on the ImageNet dataset for pre-training, and fine-tuned the MADB feature encoder parameters. After completing the pre-training, we used the episodes training strategy to enter the meta-learning training phase. This phase helps train the model to construct the semantic space of the remote sensing dataset, thereby improving the discriminative performance of the model. Additionally, we incorporated the idea of metric learning and introduced the EMD metric algorithm to measure the distance between remote sensing dataset pictures in the semantic space. This distance serves as the basis for discriminating the classes. Finally, we used RCCA in the model. The EMD algorithm is also used in the meta-learning phase. The attention layer is also implemented during the meta-learning stage. After completing the training of model parameters, the average accuracy on the evaluation dataset, organized based on episodes, is tested to verify the classification performance of the model.

To summarize the key points of this paper's contribution:

We propose the MADB-RemdNet model, which utilizes the metric learning approach in meta-learning to address the issue of few-shot learning classification in remote sensing scenes.

1. In order to enhance the hierarchy and effectiveness of the features extracted by the feature encoder, a hybrid attention mechanism is introduced into the feature encoder architecture called MADB. This mechanism enables the feature encoder to extract more representative scene features.
2. This study introduces EMD algorithm to calculate the similarity of picture scenes. Additionally, the RCCA attention mechanism is incorporated into the EMD algorithm. This mechanism allows the metric algorithm to focus on the foreground region of the scene and prioritize the weighting of picture regions in the EMD algorithm. This mechanism can enhance the performance of the model by making the metric algorithm focus more on the foreground region

of the scene. It also makes the EMD algorithm more reasonable and accurate in assigning weights to the image regions.

3. Compared with other modelling approaches in the field, we conducted extensive experiments on three large-scale scene classification datasets: NWPU-RESISC45 [13], Aid [15], and UC-Merced [14]. Experiments prove that our model performs better in 5way-1shot and 5way-5shot few-shot learning classification tasks.

ARTICLE REVIEW: The organizational framework of this thesis is as follows. In the second part, we introduce some previous studies in the research area of this paper and discuss the related research contents on the problem of remote sensing few-shot scene classification. In the third part, this paper introduces the overall architecture of the model and the design of the hybrid attention feature extractor. The fourth section focuses on the datasets used for the experiments, as well as the experimental setup and the results obtained from these experiments. Finally, the conclusion and summary are presented in Section five.

2   Related Work

2.1   Few-Shot Remoting Scene Classification

Few-shot remote scene classification is an active area of research in both machine learning and remote sensing, and there have been several recent developments in this field. In the research area of Few-Shot Remote Sensing Scene Classification, it can be broadly divided into two schools of thought: transfer learning and meta-learning. The problem of migrating from the source domain to the target domain can be solved using migration learning. This involves training a feature extractor in the base class using the cross-entropy loss function. Afterward, the linear classification head is fine-tuned through a novel small-sample learning task based on the episode strategy [16]. Such a learning approach can significantly reduce the time spent on pre-training the neural network, and the fine-tuning of the classification head can be more effectively tailored to the target dataset. Revised 2: In addition to the architectural approach mentioned above, there are several ways to improve the classification head. One approach is to train nearest neighbour classifiers to make category predictions [17]. Another approach is to incorporate auxiliary techniques into the feature representation model layer to enhance its capability. For instance, the self-supervision technique of S2M2 mechanism [18] is added to enhance the model's ability to accurately capture small changes in data distribution. Additionally, the self-supervision technique of S2M2 mechanism is used to accurately capture the data distribution [19]. Accurately capturing spatial contrastive learning (SCL) [19] is also proposed to solve the problem of missing categories and anomalous missing samples.

In recent years, meta-learning has become the dominant strategy. There have been several related studies, including SPNet [29], which proposes a promising approach for scene classification of shot-less remote sensing images. This app-roach utilizes a concatenated network architecture and prototype learning. SCL-MLNet [19] employs a self-supervised adversarial learning approach to train bet-ter feature extractors. LCPT-AMP's [30] proposed approach leverages calibrated pretext tasks to improve feature representations in few-shot scene classification. Meanwhile, the AMN Network [31] introduces a novel architecture for the AMN model, which consists of an attention module, feature extractor, and metric mod-ule. Although all of the mentioned models use meta-learning as a foundational strategy, each model has its own distinct architecture built upon it.

2.2 Meta Learning

The goal of meta-learning is to enable the fast and efficient application of learning algorithms to new tasks by learning a generalized learning algorithm or strategy from a set of related tasks. The core idea is to learn a metric function that maps input samples into a low-dimensional embedding space in order to distinguish or cluster query samples. There are two main approaches: metric-based and gradient-based.

The metric-learning-based approaches involve learning a distance metric between the query set and support set. This approach has been widely applied in many research studies in the field, such as matching networks (MatchingNet) [20], prototypical networks (ProtoNet) [8], and relation networks (RelationNet) [10]. Three types of networks are described in detail: MatchingNet introduces an attention mechanism and a similarity measure function to enhance its fast learn-ing ability. ProtoNet trains a model using prototype learning and measures the similarity between input samples and prototypes by calculating the Euclidean or cosine distances. RelationNet proposes a unique neural network structure that computes the relational representation of input samples using a relational network. It distinguishes the samples through relational reasoning and feature fusion.

In addition, there are some gradient-based methods, such as MAML [6], Meta-SGD [7], and LLSR [32]. MAML does not rely on a specific model struc-ture, but mainly focuses on how to quickly adapt the model parameters to new tasks. It achieves this by iteratively updating the model on a set of related tasks to learn an initial parameterized model, which can then be quickly adapted to new tasks. The model to converge quickly on a new task. Meta-SGD allows the model to adapt and optimize efficiently on multiple tasks by learning the hyper-parameters of the optimization algorithm. It also helps the model to converge on a new task by dynamically adjusting the learning rate. Additionally, LLSR enhances the generalization performance of the model by introducing supervised regularization.

2.3 Attention Mechanism

The attention mechanism aims to allocate varying weights to different segments of the input data, allowing the model to prioritize important information for the desired output. Attention mechanisms have been successfully implemented in the field of image processing.

These mechanisms can be classified into three categories when used for this purpose: Spatial Attention, also known as Spatial Attention Pooling, is commonly used for tasks such as image classification, target detection, and image segmentation. The performance and accuracy of the model are improved by calculating the importance of different regions in the image. This is done by taking a weighted average of the pixels in each channel or spatial location. Additionally, the channel attention mechanism is used to enhance image classification and target detection. The model's performance and accuracy are enhanced by weighing different parts of it based on the mean and standard deviation calculations of each channel's significance. One example of this is SENet [33], which utilizes global average pooling to dynamically learn inter-channel dependencies and, as a result, achieve more efficient feature representation. Additionally, self-attention used utilized. The self-attention mechanism, also referred to as multi-head attention, is primarily used for tasks such as image segmentation and image generation. By calculating the similarity between different regions in an image, the system determines their significance and assigns weights to various parts of the model in order to improve its performance and accuracy.

Of course, there are also attention mechanisms that combine both spatial and channel attention. These combined attention mechanisms consume more computational resources but result in better performance improvements. Examples of such mechanisms include the CBAM attention mechanism [34] and the Dual attention mechanism [35].

In recent years, many papers in the field of remote sensing scene classification have integrated the attention mechanism into the feature extractor of the model. This enhances the semantic features of the extracted feature map to be richer and more advanced [21]. Additionally, some researchers have employed the pure attention mechanism to develop the feature extraction network, leading to advancements in image recognition [22], semantic segmentation [25], target detection [23], remote sensing image scene classification [24], and other related tasks. Attention networks can achieve remarkable performance at a reasonable computational cost compared to traditional networks, such as convolutional and recurrent neural networks.

3 Methodology

In this section, we will present a thorough introduction to the overall architecture of MADB-RemdNet, a few-shot classification model designed for remote sensing scenes.

3.1 Overall Architecture

The model proposed in this paper is called MADB-RemdNet, which consists of two main parts: the MADB (Mixed Attention Dense Block) feature encoder and the RccaEMD (RCCA-Attention EMD) metric module. The overall architectural framework of the two sectors is depicted in Fig. 2 and Fig. 3.

In our model architecture, we initially randomly select episodic subtasks from the dataset to learn the metric space through meta-learning. Then, we utilize the MADB feature encoder in conjunction with the Mixed Attention mechanism to generate feature vectors for the samples. Finally, the RccaEMD module measures the feature vectors of the samples and calculates the distances in the feature space to discriminate between sample categories.

We apply the MADB-RemdNet model to the task of classifying small samples in 5way-1shot and 5way-5shot remote sensing scenes.

The pre-training process of this model is based on the episodic-training strategy. Randomly selected from the training dataset are 5-way-1-shot and 5-way-5-shot episodic tasks. Each task contains randomly selected images from five categories of the training (support) dataset. In the 1-shot task, one image is randomly selected for each category, while in the 5-shot task, five images are randomly selected for each category as the validation set. The 5-shot task randomly selects 5 images from each category. Additionally, 15 query set images are included in each category as the validation set.

The meta-training process of this model involves extracting 5 labeled images from the support dataset and 75 query set images from the feature map using the MADB feature encoder. These images are then passed into the REMD (Rcca-Attention EMD) module, which measures the embedding features of the 75 query samples and 5 query set images. Embedding features of 75 query samples and embedding features of 5 support samples in the metric space. Each query will ultimately receive a similarity measure result with 5 categories of support samples. Based on this outcome, the predicted label will be determined.

The evaluation process of this model involves randomly selecting 2000 episodic tasks from the test dataset during the testing phase. The average accuracy of these tasks is then calculated and taken as the final result. It is important to note that the scenario categories in the test dataset should also appear in both the training and validation datasets.

3.2   Problems Definition and Notations

Few-shot learning defines a task as a K-way N-shot learning problem, where the objective is to classify K classes given N examples per class. The task is divided into a support set and a query set. The support set contains a small number of labeled examples for each of the K classes, while the query set comprises unlabeled examples for the same K classes. Formally, the support set is denoted by $S = (x_1, y_1), (x_2, y_2), ..., (x_{K*N}, y_{K*N})$, where x_i is an example from class y_i, and $K * N$ is the total number of examples in the support set. The query set can be defined as $Q = x_1, x_2, ..., x_Q$, where x_q is an unlabeled example from one of the K classes, and Q is the total number of examples in the query set. The goal of few-shot learning is to use the support set to learn a model that can accurately classify the examples in the query set. This involves learning a function f that maps an input example x to a predicted label $y : y = f(x)$. Various machine learning techniques, such as neural networks or decision trees, can be used to learn the function f. The performance of the model is typically evaluated based on its accuracy in classifying the examples in the query set.

We divide the dataset D, which totals N categories, into a training set D_{train}, a validation set D_{val}, and a test set D_{test} according to the following Table 1. This division covers all the data categories in the dataset and ensures that the categories in the three sets do not intersect each other, this means that $L_{\text{train}} \cap L_{\text{val}} = \emptyset$, $L_{\text{train}} \cap L_{\text{test}} = \emptyset$, $L_{\text{val}} \cap L_{\text{test}} = \emptyset$, and $|L_{\text{total}}| = |L_{\text{train}} \cup L_{\text{val}} \cup L_{\text{test}}|$.

Table 1. Exact Splits on Three Data Sets

Datasets	Training	Validation	Testing
NWPU-RESISC45	Cloud; Ship; Palace; Sea Ice; Mountain; Harbor; Roundbout; Sparse Residential; Snowberg; Basketball Court; Wetland; Industrial Area; Circular Farmland; Storage Tank; Forest; Meadow; Beach; Railway Station; Intersection; Rectangular Farmland; River; Baseball Diamond; Mobile Home Park; Ground Track Field; Overpass	Commercial Area; Parking Lot; Church; Stadium; Golf Course; Bridge; Dense Residential; Tennis Court; Terrace; Thermal Power Station	Runway; Chaparral; Island; Airplane; Railway; Freeway; Medium Residential; Desert; Airport; Lake
Aid	Bare Land; Baseball Field; Bridge Church; Dense Residential; Desert; Forest; Industrial; Meadow; Mountain; Park; Pond; Railway Station; Resort; River; School; Stadium; Storage Tanks	Beach; Center; Farmland; Medium Residential; Playground; Port	Airport; Commercial; Parking; Square; Sparse Residential; Viaduct
UC-Merced	Chaparral; Forest; Buildings; Tennis Court; Dense Residential; Parking Lot; River; Freeway; Airplane; Mobile Home Park; Medium Residential	Baseball Diamond; Harbor; Golf Course; Overpass; Runway	Sparse Residential; Intersection; Beach; Storage Tanks; Agricultural

3.3 Mixed Attention Dense Block Feature Extractor

The backbone of the model in this paper is different from the classical network structures used in other studies, such as ConvNet and ResNet. We have chosen to use the dense block layer, which is the most important architecture in Densenet, as the backbone of the feature encoder. The dense block layer is designed to ensure that each layer in the network receives inputs from all previous layers and passes the feature mapping of that layer to the convolutional layer behind it. These short connections ensure that valid features can be passed to the end, enabling the network to extract accurate global features. It can enhance the ability to extract both texture features and high-level features from remote sensing scene images, which can then be used as input for the metric algorithm used in classification.

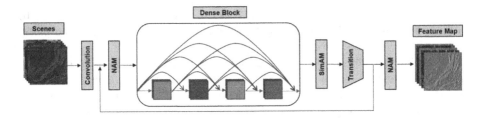

Fig. 2. Mixed Attention Dense Block Architecture

Each of these Dense Blocks contains multiple sets of $1*1$ and $3*3$ convolutional layers, which are used for concatenation operations. Although it is structured in a dense concatenation pattern, it requires fewer parameters compared to a traditional convolutional network.

As shown in Fig. 2, the feature encoder's body is composed of multiple Dense Block modules. Additionally, the SimAM attention mechanism is connected before the Transition layer in the Dense Block module, and the Nam attention mechanism is connected at the head and tail of the Dense Block. We combine the Nam and SimAM attention mechanisms in the Dense Block module, defining it as MADB. In our paper, the input image size is $3 \times 128 \times 128$, and the shape of the output embedding features of MADB is $64 \times 8 \times 8$.

The hybrid attention mechanism in the MADB module consists of two attention mechanisms, namely Nam and SimAM. Nam is a lightweight and efficient attention mechanism that redesigns the spatial attention module and channel attention module. For the channel attention module, Nam utilizes a scaling factor γ from Batch Normalization, as shown in the following Eq. (1). The scaling factor represents the variance in BN, which reflects the size of change in each channel feature. The larger the variance, the more feature information is contained in the channel, making it more important. That is, it can play a role in enriching relevant information while suppressing irrelevant features. Where μ_B and σ_B are the mean and standard deviation of the small batch $\mathcal{B}$, respectively, and γ and β are the trainable affine transformation parameters (scale and displacement).

$$B_{out} = BN(B_{in}) = \gamma \frac{B_{in} - \mu_\mathcal{B}}{\sqrt{\sigma_\mathcal{B}^2 + \epsilon}} + \beta \tag{1}$$

The output characteristics of the channel attention sub-module in Nam are shown in Eq. (2), where $W_\gamma = \frac{\gamma_i}{\Sigma_{j=0}\gamma_j}$ represents the weights. The scale factor of Batch Normalization is applied to the spatial dimension, which Nam mechanism refers to as pixel normalization. The output feature of the corresponding Spatial Attention Module in NAM is shown in Eq. (3), where $W_\lambda = \frac{\lambda_i}{\Sigma_{j=0}\lambda_j}$ represents the weights.

$$\mathbf{M}_c = sigmoid(W_\gamma(BN(\mathbf{F}_1))) \tag{2}$$

$$\mathbf{M}_s = sigmoid(W_\lambda(BN_s(\mathbf{F}_2))) \tag{3}$$

The Nam attention mechanism can be embedded at the end of the residual structure. We placed it after the first convolutional layer as well as after the transition layer. The purpose of doing so is to allow any layer in the Dense Block module to receive the output of the convolutional layer behind it. Therefore, including the Nam attention mechanism in the header and the tailer can serve as an overall suppression of the features of the unimportant regions and channels. This makes the features encoded by the MADB module more tangible and distinguishable.

SimAM attention mechanism is an attention module with unified weights. Attention mechanisms, such as BAM and CBAM, combine spatial attention and channel attention either in serial or parallel. However, in the human brain, these two types of attention usually work together. For these reasons, Yang [27] proposed the attention module called SimAM. This attention mechanism is inspired by the phenomenon of null-space inhibition, where active neurons can suppress the activity of neighboring neurons. On the premise that neurons with pronounced inhibitory effects in the null-space can be assigned higher priority in visual processing, active neurons are identified by measuring the linear separability between a target neuron and other neurons. For this purpose, it is necessary to evaluate the importance of each neuron, and neuronal activity is assessed by defining the following energy Eq. (4), where $\hat{t} = w_t t + b_t, \hat{x}_i = w_t x_i + b_t$.

$$e_t(w_t, b_t, \mathbf{y}, x_i) = (y_t - \hat{t})^2 + \frac{1}{M-1}\sum_{i=1}^{M-1}(\gamma_o - \hat{x}_i)^2 \tag{4}$$

Linear separability between the target neuron t and all other neurons in the same channel can be determined by minimizing the above functions. In this paper, the SimAM attention mechanism is inserted after the Dense block convolutional layer and before entering the transitional layer. This placement offers the advantage of enhancing the salient features without introducing additional parameters.

By combining the Dense Block with the two attention mechanisms mentioned above, the feature capture ability of the entire feature encoder for remote sensing scene images is significantly enhanced. The performance of the module is verified in the experimental section.

3.4   Cross-Reference with RCCA Module EMD Metric Network

The RccaEMD metric module proposed in this study is a component of the MADB-RemdNet model and is depicted in Fig. 3.

After the image is encoded by the feature extractor, the feature map undergoes correction through the RCCA attention mechanism. The corrected feature map is then partitioned into block regions of $H * W$, and their weights are computed by cross-referencing the EMD module. Dynamic planning matching is

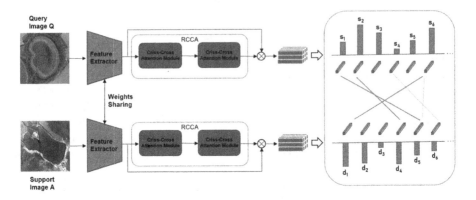

Fig. 3. RCCA EMD Metric Module Architecture

subsequently executed, and the minimum matching cost for the regions of both feature maps is computed. This provides the criterion for determining whether the two images belong to the same class.

The EMD algorithm, initially applied in the field of image restoration, essentially represents a technique for optimal transportation. Zhang et al. [36] proposed the DeepEMD few-shot learning model and first applied this algorithm to calculate the similarity between images in the field of small sample learning. The overall process is roughly as follows: the two sample images in the support and query sets are encoded using a feature encoder. The local embedding feature vectors of the two images are then extracted, and the corresponding distances between them are calculated using the EMD algorithm. Assuming that there are $H * W$ vectors in each set, and the embedding nodes of any two images are ui and vj, the Eq. (5) for calculating the cost of each unit is shown below, where $c(i, j)$ represents the distance between the two nodes in the vector space, the more similar the nodes are, the smaller the resulting cost, which is the distance.

$$c(i, j) = 1 - \frac{\mathbf{u}_i^T \mathbf{v}_j}{\| \mathbf{u}_i \| \| \mathbf{v}_j \|} \qquad (5)$$

And to determine the similarity between the two images, the optimal transportation matrix $\tilde{\chi}$ needs to be further computed using the Eq. (6), where $\tilde{x}_{ij}$ is an entry in the matrix $\tilde{\chi}$ and $s(U, V)$ represents the similarity between two images.

$$s(\mathbf{U}, \mathbf{V}) = \sum_{i=1}^{HW} \sum_{j=1}^{HW} (1 - c_{ij}) \tilde{x}_{ij} \qquad (6)$$

In this paper, we utilize the aforementioned method as the metric algorithm to optimize the generation of embedding nodes through the RCCA cross-attention mechanism. RCCA attention mechanism is used for the feature encoder MADB to encode X. It utilizes a $1 * 1$ convolution operation to obtain a reduced dimensional feature mapping W. After a series of calculations, a new feature mapping H' is generated, which gathers information from the vertical and horizontal directions for each pixel. The Eq. (7) is shown below, where Q, K, V are obtained by applying the $Conv_{1 \cdot 1}$ operation on X, and $*$ represents the Affinity operation.

$$H' = X + Aggregation(V, Softmax(Q * K)) \tag{7}$$

H'' is obtained by performing the above operation again, and each pixel can gather the contextual information of all pixels simultaneously. Finally, Finally, the concatenation operation of W'' and X can enhance the ability of X to capture the global semantics while maintaining the local feature recognition capability.

We do this for two reasons. Firstly, the residual sense block module is based on the convolution operation on pixels within the sensing field. Secondly, the EMD algorithm provides local features for global optimal matching, both of which inherently have local module defects. Secondly, certain remote sensing scenarios require the model to be capable of detecting global features such as deserts, lakes, and other landscapes.

The cross-attention mechanism is a type of attention mechanism that exhibits non-local characteristics. The classical non-local module can capture semantic information from the context and globally featured images. However, it assigns unique weight values to each pixel point, which in turn weights the feature map and significantly increases computation. The RCCA attention mechanism optimizes computational complexity while preserving the advantages of the non-local module. A single CCA module can only capture cross-path features on the feature map. Therefore, this paper utilizes a two-stage serial CCA attention mechanism to achieve global feature fusion on the map. This is undertaken between the MADB feature encoder and the EMD metric module and serves as a neutralization.

By combining the RCCA attention mechanism with the EMD metric algorithm, the MADB-RemdNet model gains a stronger capability to identify images of remote sensing scenes.

4   Experiment

In this section, we mainly introduce the related experiments of this paper and analyze the experimental results. Firstly, we introduce the three public datasets used in the experiments of this paper and the parameter settings of the experiments; then we will compare the performance of the model in this paper with other small-sample classification models; finally, we will analyze the effectiveness of the MADB module and the effectiveness of the RccaEMD module on the performance improvement of the model.

4.1   Data Sets

In order to validate the effectiveness of our small-sample classification model for this remote sensing scene, we tested it on three public datasets commonly used in the field. The datasets used in this study include the North-western Polytechnical University (NWPU)-RESISC45 (NWPU) [13] dataset, the University of California Merced (UCM) dataset [14], and the aerial image data (AID) dataset [15]. We divide the datasets mentioned above into training set, validation set, and test set. The specific division results are shown in Table 1.

4.2   Implementation Details

The first step is to establish the hyperparameters. In this paper, the training size of remote sensing scene images is consistently scaled to $128 * 128$. During the training phase, we employ the standard method for image classification training. In this method, the images in the training set are trained using a batch size of 128 and the cross-entropy loss function. The validation and testing stages, on the other hand, follow the episodes method as previously described. We utilize 100 randomly generated episodes for validation and 2000 for testing. In the validation and testing stages, the episodes are randomly generated. We use 2000 episodes for testing. Each episode consists of five categories of support and query images, with each category containing either one or five sample images. For the 5-way-1-shot task, one sample image is randomly chosen from each of the five categories. On the other hand, for the 5-way-5-shot task, five images are randomly selected from each category. Additionally, each query set includes 15 randomly selected sample images from the categories. Using additional sample images in the query set during loss computation and model training can enhance the stability and robustness of the model. Moreover, for the sake of fairness in comparison, this paper has set the number of samples in the query set to 15, which aligns with the majority of the other models being compared.

Our feature encoder consists of four Dense Blocks, with the initial convolutional layer using a $7 * 7$ convolutional kernel. The Dense Block incorporates a bottleneck structure, which is composed of $BN - RELU - Conv_{1*1} - BN - RELU - Conv_{3*3}$. The Transition layer acts as a connecting layer between the Dense Blocks and is composed of $BN - RELU - Conv_{1*1} - AvgPool_{2*2}$. The hybrid attention mechanism is integrated at the beginning and end of each Dense Block, as well as before the Transition layer.

In this study, we utilized the SGD optimizer to enhance the feature extractor. Specifically, we set the initial learning rate to 0.001, the momentum to 0.9, and the weight decay to $1 * 10^{-4}$. Additionally, we utilized the Cosine Learning Rate Decay method to update the learning rate, where the lrf parameter was set to 0.1. Our experiments were conducted on the following hardware platform: Intel Xeon Silver 4210 10-Core processor 2.2 GHz, 64 GB of Magnesium DDR4 2666 MHz RAM, and the GPU NVIDIA GeForce RTX 2080ti with 11 GB of memory.

4.3   Comparison with Other Few-Shot Classification Methods

In this paper, we analyze the experimental performance of the model by comparing it with small-sample classification methods that have been used in recent years for remote sensing scenes. Table 2 and Table 3 display the experimental performance of our model in comparison to other models across the three datasets. These methods include gradient descent-based approaches, such as MAML [6], Meta-SGD [37], and LLSR [38]. MAML and Meta-SGD enable easy fine-tuning by using meta-learning training to determine the optimal decision point for training with small samples. The only difference between the two is that the latter is an enhanced version of the former gradient descent method. LLSR is an incremental learning method specifically designed for remote sensing scene classification.

Metric-based learning methods, such as classical metrics, MatchingNet [20], ProtoNet [8], and RelationNet [10], are available. MatchingNet and ProtoNet utilize predefined and fixed metrics, but the specific metrics they use differ. MatchingNet implements predefined and fixed metrics. The approach of MatchingNet and ProtoNet is similar, as both utilize predefined and fixed metrics. However, the specific metrics employed differ. MatchingNet applies cosine distance, ProtoNet employs Euclidean distance measured using Bregman's dispersion, and RelationNet incorporates a nonlinear model with learning capabilities as the metric.

These methods utilize Conv-4-64 as the feature extraction module. Each convolution module consists of a $3*3$ convolution with 64 convolution kernels, a BN layer, a ReLU nonlinear activation layer, and a $2*2$ maximum pooling layer. Technical abbreviations will be explained upon their first use. We conducted experimental comparisons with recent metric learning methods, including DLA-MatchNet [39], SCL-MLNet [40], and LCPT-AMP [41]. DLA-MatchNet utilizes Conv-256 for feature extraction. Its embedding layer consists of 5 convolutional blocks. Additionally, it employs a learnable MLP layer as a matcher, which classifies samples based on similarity scores. SCL-MLNet utilizes a feature extractor comprising six convolutional layers, in addition to the self-supervised comparison algorithm SCL, to efficiently classify remote sensing samples. LCPT-AMP, on the other hand, employs ResNet12 as its feature extractor and introduces the AMP regularization technique and pretext for enhanced performance. Both approaches resize their input images to $128*128$, which is also the case for our model.

The metrics for evaluating model performance are defined as follows: during the testing phase, an episode consists of a C-way K-shot task, and the overall accuracy is calculated by averaging the results of 2000 episode tasks. The difference in performance between different models is assessed using the average accuracy mentioned above.

As shown in Table 2, our model achieves the best experimental results in the two datasets NWPU-RESISC45 and AID for the 5-way-1shot and 5-way-5shot tasks, respectively. This demonstrates that our model not only outperforms previous models in the field but also exhibits exceptional generalization capabilities. Furthermore, the experimental accuracy for both datasets shows significant improvement. Furthermore, the accuracy of the model's performance is influenced by the MADB feature extractor. It shows an improvement in performance

Table 2. Few-Shot Classification Global Average Accuracies on NWPU-RESISC45 and UC-Merced.

Model	Backbone	NWPU-RESISC45		AID	
		5way-1shot	5way-5shot	5way-1shot	5way-5shot
S2M2	ResNet12	63.24 ± 0.47	83.23 ± 0.28	66.22 ± 0.45	82.87 ± 0.29
MAML	Conv-4-64	58.99 ± 0.45	72.67 ± 0.38	60.11 ± 0.50	70.28 ± 0.41
LLSR	Conv-4-64	51.43	72.90	–	–
Meta-SGD	ResNet12	60.63 ± 0.90	75.75 ± 0.65	53.14 ± 1.46	66.94 ± 1.20
MatchingNet	Conv-4-64	60.21 ± 0.77	71.66 ± 0.45	63.31 ± 0.46	73.35 ± 0.35
MatchingNet	ResNet12	61.57 ± 0.49	76.02 ± 0.34	64.30 ± 0.46	74.49 ± 0.35
ProtoNet	Conv-4-64	52.77 ± 0.44	75.32 ± 0.35	55.14 ± 0.44	75.77 ± 0.35
ProtoNet	ResNet12	64.52 ± 0.48	81.95 ± 0.30	67.08 ± 0.47	82.44 ± 0.29
SCL-MLNet	Conv-256	62.21 ± 1.12	80.86 ± 0.76	59.49 ± 0.96	76.31 ± 0.68
DLA-MatchNet	Conv-256	68.80 ± 0.70	81.63 ± 0.46	57.21 ± 0.82	73.45 ± 0.61
DLA-MatchNet	ResNet12	71.56 ± 0.30	83.77 ± 0.64	–	–
LCPT-AMP	Conv-4-256	64.79 ± 0.49	81.40 ± 0.30	66.73 ± 0.49	81.71 ± 0.29
LCPT-AMP	ResNet12	76.70 ± 0.44	89.87 ± 0.21	72.67 ± 0.43	87.33 ± 0.23
Ours	ResNet12	$\mathbf{80.12 \pm 0.39}$	91.82 ± 0.19	73.84 ± 0.23	89.91 ± 0.12
Ours	MADB	80.03 ± 0.40	$\mathbf{92.42 \pm 0.19}$	$\mathbf{74.48 \pm 0.39}$	$\mathbf{90.73 \pm 0.21}$

ranging from 0.60% to 0.82% on the 5-way 5-shot task on NWPU-RESISC45 dataset, as well as on the 5-way 1-shot and 5-way 5-shot tasks on the AID dataset, when compared to the experimental results obtained using Resnet12. This improvement in performance provides strong evidence of the effectiveness of the MADB feature extraction module.

Table 3 validates the accuracy comparison between this model and other models using the baseline metric algorithm, EMD. Ablation experiments were conducted primarily on the AID and UC-Merced datasets to compare the performance of the DeepEMD and Multi-Attention DeepEMD models. According to the experimental results, when using Resnet12 as the feature extractor, the accuracies of the four tasks increased by 3.04% to 25% compared to the Deep-EMD model. Furthermore, the Multi-Attention DeepEMD model resulted in a minimum of 3% improvement in accuracy for all four tasks. A minimum improvement of 4% and a maximum improvement of 25% were achieved compared to the Multi-Attention DeepEMD model. The AID dataset for the 5-way-1-shot task showed a slightly lower improvement of 0.04% compared to the Multi-Attention DeepEMD model. However, all other tasks exhibited an accuracy increase ranging from 1% to 16%. Furthermore, switching to MADB as the feature extractor results in a 0.57%–0.82% increase in accuracy for the entire model, confirming the effectiveness of the MADB feature extraction module.

Table 3. Few-Shot Classification Global Average Accuracies on AID and UC-Merced.

Model	Backbone	AID		UC-Merced	
		5way-1shot	5way-5shot	5way-1shot	5way-5shot
DeepEMD	ResNet12	70.80 ± 0.53	83.22 ± 0.67	52.28 ± 0.25	77.82 ± 0.66
Mattn DeepEMD	ResNet12	$\mathbf{74.52 \pm 0.25}$	88.91 ± 0.62	61.16 ± 0.31	80.39 ± 0.71
Ours	ResNet12	73.84 ± 0.23	89.91 ± 0.12	77.35 ± 0.31	92.59 ± 0.14
Ours	MADB	73.84 ± 0.23	$\mathbf{90.73 \pm 0.21}$	$\mathbf{78.14 \pm 0.30}$	$\mathbf{93.16 \pm 0.14}$

5   Conclusion

In this paper, we present a new architecture model called MADB-RemdNet for classifying small sample remote sensing scene images. The model consists of a feature encoder and a metric algorithm module. To enhance the feature aggregation capability of MADB-RemdNet, the feature encoder incorporates a hybrid attention mechanism called MADB. Moreover, the RCCA-EMD metric module combines the RCCA attention mechanism with the EMD algorithm to enhance the model's discriminative capability. Finally, the rationality and effectiveness of the MADB-RemdNet model architecture were validated through comparison experiments with other models on three remote sensing scene datasets.

However, there are some issues with the suggested model architecture in this paper. Despite the high performance of the MADB-RemdNet model, its computational complexity exceeds that of other models due to the inherent drawbacks of the EMD algorithm. Therefore, our future objective is to reduce the time complexity of the EMD algorithm in order to reduce the computational cost of the model, while still maintaining excellent performance.

References

1. Hu, Q., et al.: Exploring the use of Google Earth imagery and object-based methods in land use/cover mapping. Remote Sens. **5**(11), 6026–6042 (2013)
2. Gómez-Chova, L., Tuia, D., Moser, G., Camps-Valls, G.: Multimodal classification of remote sensing images: a review and future directions. Proc. IEEE **103**(9), 1560–1584 (2015)
3. Hu, F., Xia, G.S., Hu, J., Zhang, L.: Transferring deep convolutional neural networks for the scene classification of high-resolution remote sensing imagery. Remote Sens. **7**(11), 14680–14707 (2015)
4. Chaib, S., Liu, H., Gu, Y., Yao, H.: Deep feature fusion for VHR remote sensing scene classification. IEEE Trans. Geosci. Remote Sens. **55**(8), 4775–4784 (2017)
5. Li, E., Xia, J., Du, P., Lin, C., Samat, A.: Integrating multilayer features of convolutional neural networks for remote sensing scene classification. IEEE Trans. Geosci. Remote Sens. **55**(10), 5653–5665 (2017)
6. Finn, C., Abbeel, P., Levine, S.: Model-agnostic meta-learning for fast adaptation of deep networks. In: Proceedings of the International Conference on Machine Learning, Sydney, Australia, 6–11 August 2017 (2017)
7. Li, Z., Zhou, F., Chen, F., Li, H.: Meta-SGD: learning to learn quickly for few shot learning. arXiv (2017). arXiv:1707.09835

8. Snell, J., Swersky, K., Zemel, R.S.: Prototypical networks for few-shot learning. In: Proceedings of the International Conference on Neural Information Processing Systems, Long Beach, CA, USA, pp. 4077–4087 (2017)

9. Koch, G., Zemel, R., Salakhutdinov, R.: Siamese neural networks for one-shot image recognition. In: Proceedings of the International Conference on Machine Learning, Lille, France, 6–11 July 2015, vol. 2 (2015)

10. Sung, F., Yang, Y., Zhang, L., Xiang, T., Torr, P., Hospedales, T.M.: Learning to compare: relation network for few-shot learning. In: Proceedings of the IEEE Conference on Computer Vision and Pattern Recognition, Salt Lake City, UT, USA 18–23 June 2018, pp. 1199–1208 (2018)

11. Sharma, S., Roscher, R., Riedel, M., Memon, S., Cavallaro, G.: Improving generalization for few-shot remote sensing classification with meta-learning. In: 2022 IEEE International Geoscience and Remote Sensing Symposium, IGARSS 2022, Kuala Lumpur, Malaysia, pp. 5061–5064 (2022). https://doi.org/10.1109/IGARSS46834.2022.9884699.

12. Yang, Q., Yang, X., Ji, X.: NAM net: meta-network with normalization-based attention for few-shot learning. In: 2022 2nd International Conference on Computer Science, Electronic Information Engineering and Intelligent Control Technology (CEI), Nanjing, China, pp. 473–476 (2022). https://doi.org/10.1109/CEI57409.2022.9950152

13. Cheng, G., Han, J., Lu, X.: Remote sensing image scene classification: benchmark and state of the art. Proc. IEEE **105**(10), 1865–1883 (2017)

14. Yang, Y., Newsam, S.: Bag-of-visual-words and spatial extensions for land-use classification. In: Proceedings of the 18th SIGSPATIAL International Conference on Advances in Geographic Information Systems (GIS), pp. 270–279 (2010)

15. Xia, G.-S., et al.: AID: a benchmark data set for performance evaluation of aerial scene classification. IEEE Trans. Geosci. Remote Sens. **55**(7), 3965–3981 (2017)

16. Chen, W.-Y., Liu, Y.-C., Kira, Z., Wang, Y.-C., Huang, J.-B.: A closer look at few-shot classification. In: Proceedings of the International Conference on Learning Representations, pp. 1–16 (2019)

17. Chen, Y., Liu, Z., Xu, H., Darrell, T., Wang, X.: Meta-baseline: exploring simple meta-learning for few-shot learning. In: Proceedings of the IEEE/CVF International Conference on Computer Vision (ICCV), pp. 9062–9071 (2021)

18. Mangla, P., Singh, M., Sinha, A., Kumari, N., Balasubramanian, V.N., Krishnamurthy, B.: Charting the right manifold: manifold mixup for few-shot learning. In: Proceedings of the IEEE Winter Conference on Applications of Computer Vision (WACV), pp. 2218–2227 (2020)

19. Ouali, Y., Hudelot, C., Tami, M.: Spatial contrastive learning for few-shot classification. In: Oliver, N., Pérez-Cruz, F., Kramer, S., Read, J., Lozano, J.A. (eds.) ECML PKDD 2021. LNCS, vol. 12975, pp. 671–686. Springer, Cham (2021). https://doi.org/10.1007/978-3-030-86486-6_41

20. Vinyals, O., Blundell, C., Lillicrap, T., et al.: Matching networks for one shot learning. In: Advances in Neural Information Processing Systems, vol. 29 (2016)

21. Pan, X., et al.: Dynamic refinement network for oriented and densely packed object detection. In: Proceedings of the IEEE/CVF Conference on Computer Vision and Pattern Recognition, Seattle, WA, USA, 13–19 June 2020, pp. 11207–11216 (2020)

22. Dosovitskiy, A., et al.: An image is worth 16×16 words: transformers for image recognition at scale. arXiv (2020). arXiv:2010.11929

23. Zhu, X., Su, W., Lu, L., Li, B., Wang, X., Dai, J.: Deformable DETR: deformable transformers for end-to-end object detection. arXiv (2020). arXiv:2010.04159

24. Cao, R., Fang, L., Lu, T., He, N.: Self-attention-based deep feature fusion for remote sensing scene classification. IEEE Geosci. Remote Sens. Lett. **18**, 43–47 (2021)

25. Tao, A., Sapra, K., Catanzaro, B.: Hierarchical multi-scale attention for semantic segmentation. arXiv (2020). arXiv:2005.10821

26. Huang, Z., Wang, X., Huang, L., et al.: CCNet: criss-cross attention for semantic segmentation. In: Proceedings of the IEEE/CVF International Conference on Computer Vision, pp. 603–612 (2019)

27. Yang, L., Zhang, R.Y., Li, L., et al.: SimAM: a simple, parameter-free attention module for convolutional neural networks. In: International Conference on Machine Learning, pp. 11863–11874. PMLR (2021)

28. Wang, Y., Chao, W.L., Weinberger, K.Q., et al.: Simpleshot: revisiting nearest-neighbor classification for few-shot learning. arXiv preprint arXiv:1911.04623 (2019)

29. Cheng, G., et al.: SPNet: Siamese-prototype network for few-shot remote sensing image scene classification. IEEE Trans. Geosci. Remote Sens. **60**, 1–11 (2022)

30. Ji, H., Gao, Z., Zhang, Y., Wan, Y., Li, C., Mei, T.: Few-shot scene classification of optical remote sensing images leveraging calibrated pretext tasks. IEEE Trans. Geosci. Remote Sens. **60**, 1–13, Article no. 5625513 (2022). https://doi.org/10.1109/TGRS.2022.3184080

31. Li, X., Pu, F., Yang, R., et al.: AMN: attention metric network for one-shot remote sensing image scene classification. Remote Sens. **12**(24), 4046 (2020)

32. Zhai, M., Liu, H., Sun, F.: Lifelong learning for scene recognition in remote sensing images. IEEE Geosci. Remote Sens. Lett. **16**(9), 1472–1476 (2019). https://doi.org/10.1109/LGRS.2019.2897652

33. Hu, J., Shen, L., Sun, G.: Squeeze-and-excitation networks. In: Proceedings of the IEEE Conference on Computer Vision and Pattern Recognition, pp. 7132–7141 (2018)

34. Woo, S., Park, J., Lee, J.Y., Kweon, I.S.: CBAM: convolutional block attention module. In: Ferrari, V., Hebert, M., Sminchisescu, C., Weiss, Y. (eds.) ECCV 2018. LNCS, vol. 11211, pp. 3–19. Springer, Cham (2018). https://doi.org/10.1007/978-3-030-01234-2_1

35. Fu, J., Liu, J., Tian, H., et al.: Dual attention network for scene segmentation. In: Proceedings of the IEEE/CVF Conference on Computer Vision and Pattern Recognition, pp. 3146–3154 (2019)

36. Zhang, C., Cai, Y., Lin, G., et al.: DeepEMD: differentiable earth mover's distance for few-shot learning. IEEE Trans. Pattern Anal. Mach. Intell. **45**(5), 5632–5648 (2022)

37. Li, Z., Zhou, F., Chen, F., et al.: Meta-SGD: learning to learn quickly for few-shot learning. arXiv preprint arXiv:1707.09835 (2017)

38. Zhai, M., Liu, H., Sun, F.: Lifelong learning for scene recognition in remote sensing images. IEEE Geosci. Remote Sens. Lett. **16**(9), 1472–1476 (2019)

39. Li, L., Han, J., Yao, X., et al.: DLA-MatchNet for few-shot remote sensing image scene classification. IEEE Trans. Geosci. Remote Sens. **59**(9), 7844–7853 (2020)

40. Li, X., Shi, D., Diao, X., et al.: SCL-MLNet: boosting few-shot remote sensing scene classification via self-supervised contrastive learning. IEEE Trans. Geosci. Remote Sens. **60**, 1–12 (2021)

41. Ji, H., Gao, Z., Zhang, Y., et al.: Few-shot scene classification of optical remote sensing images leveraging calibrated pretext tasks. IEEE Trans. Geosci. Remote Sens. **60**, 1–13 (2022)

Convolutional Neural Network Based on Multiple Attention Mechanisms for Hyperspectral and LiDAR Classification

Yingying Wang[1], Kun Wang[1], and Zhiming Ding[2]([⊠])

[1] Beijing University of Technology, Beijing 100124, China
wangyingying@emails.bjut.edu.cn
[2] Institute of Software, Chinese Academy of Sciences, Beijing100190, China
zhiming@iscas.ac.cn

Abstract. With the emergence of a large number of remote sensing data sources, how to effectively use the useful information in multi-source data for better earth observation has become an interesting but challenging problem. In this paper, the deep learning method is used to study the joint classification of hyperspectral imagery (HSI) and light detection and ranging (LiDAR) data. The network proposed in this paper is named convolutional neural network based on multiple attention mechanisms (MatNet). Specifically, a convolutional neural network (CNN) with an attention mechanism is used to extract the deep features of HSI and LiDAR respectively. Then the obtained features are introduced into the dual-branch cross-attention fusion module (DCFM) to fuse the information in HSI and LiDAR data effectively. Finally, the obtained features are introduced into the classification module to obtain the final classification results. Experimental results show that our proposed network can achieve better classification performance than existing methods.

Keywords: Convolutional neural network (CNN) · deep learning · hyperspectral imagery (HSI) · data fusion · feature extraction

1 Introduction

In recent years, with the rapid development of satellite sensor technology and artificial intelligence deep learning, people can obtain more and more remote sensing (RS) images every day, such as synthetic aperture radar (SAR) [9], light detection and ranging (LiDAR) [8], hyperspectral imagery (HSI) [13], multispectral imagery (MSI) and so on. Remote sensing images have also been applied to various Earth observation(EO) tasks, such as land cover classification [2,20], scene classification [4,12], environmental monitoring [15], and biodiversity conservation [14]. All these tasks are explored using data from a single EO sensor

This work is supported by the National Key R&D Program of China under Grant 2022YFF0503900.

(i.e., hyperspectral imaging instrument). The HSI data obtained by the EO sensor can provide rich spectral and spatial information simultaneously. However, the data obtained by using a single sensor often cannot achieve high classification accuracy of ground objects. To solve this problem, many scholars have proposed to use of multimodal data for HSI classification tasks. Since the data collected by different sensors are often complementary, they are often used cumulatively in the field of remote sensing for a wide range of multimodal learning applications [5,22].

Since the sensors collecting HSI and LiDAR data are very different in terms of imaging mechanism, spatial resolution, and coverage, this results in the two being able to capture different object information and attributes [22]. HSIs provide detailed spectral information for ground object identification and LiDAR provides elevation information for ground objects [16]. Therefore many researches are devoted to joint classification using HSI and LiDAR data. One of the keys to this research topic is how to carry out information interaction and fusion between the two modes, that is, how to choose the fusion strategy.

Feature fusion is the primary information fusion technique. It may be categorized into three phases based on the fusion phase: early, moderate, and late. Early fusion and late fusion have been shown to exacerbate overfitting by suppressing the information interaction of inner modality or intermodality, as demonstrated by Hong et al. [7] and Wang et al. [17]. Because of its versatility in deep learning techniques, intermediate fusion is the approach utilized in the majority of studies [1]. Reconstructing multimodal pictures allows for improved neuronal activation across modalities, which is how feature fusion was accomplished in [6] and [22].

Prior to information fusion, cross-modality interaction [21] is typically conducted, and it can facilitate the interpretation of content across different modalities. Feature fusion and feature interaction are frequently intertwined in hyperspectral and LiDAR data categorization techniques. Stated differently, feature fusion is thought to be the exclusive process for intermodality interaction. Recent research has demonstrated that explicit feature interaction helps to increase the number of subsequent features and the classifier's capacity for discrimination. Weight sharing approach was applied for feature interaction during feature extraction in [7]. LiDAR features were taken into consideration as the weight of HSI features' spatial attention in [11]. By using octave convolution [3], Zhao et al. [23] carefully divided low-frequency and high-frequency characteristics and interacted.

These newly developed methods have proven to be effective in fusing multiple remote sensing data sources, but these existing methods are still limited in their ability to handle multimodal data, especially heterogeneous data. This may be due to the lack of more advanced fusion strategies to better bridge the gap between different modalities and obtain diagnostic features. To get around this problem, we created a brand-new dual-branch cross-attention fusion module (DCFM) and paired it with CNN feature extraction to fuse the two modalities' deeper information, increasing the classification accuracy. The following are the specific contributions made by this paper:

1. We introduce the attention module in the process of feature extraction using CNN, which alleviates the drawbacks of traditional CNN ignoring global information to some extent and enhances the feature expression ability of the model.
2. We propose a dual-branch cross-attention fusion module, which can adequately fuse features from HSI and LiDAR data. The fused features obtained using this module are used to guide the classification task, which effectively improves the classification accuracy.

The rest of this article is arranged as follows. In the second section, the details of the proposed classification network are described. In the third section, experiments are conducted on the two most representative multimodal datasets, i.e., the Houston2013 dataset and the Trento dataset, to compare with the existing state-of-the-art multimodal classification methods, and ablation experiments are conducted on the DCMF. Finally, the fourth section draws a conclusion.

2   Methodology

As shown in Fig. 1, our proposed model is mainly composed of four stages: data preprocessing, deep feature extraction, dual-branch cross-attention fusion, and classification. Next, these four modules are introduced respectively.

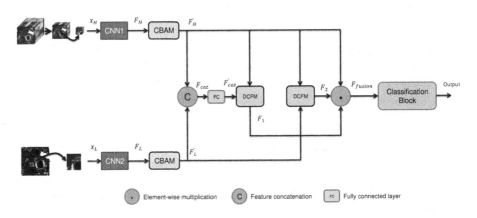

Fig. 1. Flowchart of the proposed model.

2.1   Data Preprocessing

Given a hyperspectral image, $X_h \in \mathbb{R}^{m \times n \times l}$, and a corresponding LiDAR image $X_l \in \mathbb{R}^{m \times n}$ covers the same area on the Earth's surface. Here, m and n represent the height and width, respectively, of the two images, and l refers to the number of spectral bands of the hyperspectral image. Our goal is to sufficiently fuse the information from X_h and X_l to improve the classification performance. HSI data contains a large number of spectral bands to transmit valuable information, but this also leads to a sharp increase in the amount of calculation. Therefore, we choose to use principal component analysis (PCA) to extract the first b principal components of X_h and reduce the number of spectral bands of HSI data from l to b. In this way, the spatial dimension of the data is maintained and the computational cost is reduced. The HSI data X_h after PCA dimensionality reduction is transformed into $X_H^{pca} \in \mathbb{R}^{m \times n \times b}$.

Next, for each pixel, 3-D and 2-D patch extraction is performed to obtain a small patch cube $x_H \in \mathbb{R}^{k \times k \times b}$ and a small patch $x_L \in \mathbb{R}^{k \times k}$, respectively, where $k \times k$ is the patch size. The indices of the center pixel are used to label each patch. For edge pixels, a padding operation on these pixels is performed-the width of padding is $(k-1)/2$. Thus, the number of small patch cubes of the HSI data and small patches of the LiDAR data are both $m \times n$. Then x_H and x_L are sent to the depth feature extraction module for feature extraction. Based on the experimental results in Sect. 3.4, we set the local space window size k to 11.

2.2 Deep Feature Extraction

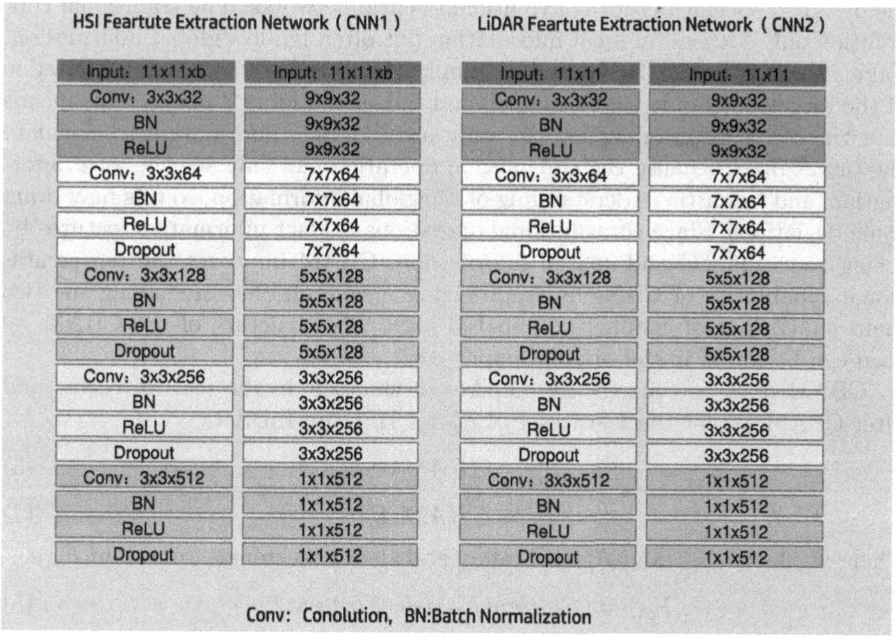

HSI Feartute Extraction Network (CNN1)		LiDAR Feartute Extraction Network (CNN2)	
Input: 11x11xb	Input: 11x11xb	Input: 11x11	Input: 11x11
Conv: 3x3x32	9x9x32	Conv: 3x3x32	9x9x32
BN	9x9x32	BN	9x9x32
ReLU	9x9x32	ReLU	9x9x32
Conv: 3x3x64	7x7x64	Conv: 3x3x64	7x7x64
BN	7x7x64	BN	7x7x64
ReLU	7x7x64	ReLU	7x7x64
Dropout	7x7x64	Dropout	7x7x64
Conv: 3x3x128	5x5x128	Conv: 3x3x128	5x5x128
BN	5x5x128	BN	5x5x128
ReLU	5x5x128	ReLU	5x5x128
Dropout	5x5x128	Dropout	5x5x128
Conv: 3x3x256	3x3x256	Conv: 3x3x256	3x3x256
BN	3x3x256	BN	3x3x256
ReLU	3x3x256	ReLU	3x3x256
Dropout	3x3x256	Dropout	3x3x256
Conv: 3x3x512	1x1x512	Conv: 3x3x512	1x1x512
BN	1x1x512	BN	1x1x512
ReLU	1x1x512	ReLU	1x1x512
Dropout	1x1x512	Dropout	1x1x512

Conv: Conolution, BN:Batch Normalization

Fig. 2. Detailed structure of CNN1 and CNN2.

Many studies have shown that CNN for image feature extraction has good performance. In this paper, in order to obtain the deep features of HSI and LiDAR data, we first use two convolutional neural networks to extract the features of HSI data and the features of LiDAR data, which are denoted as CNN1 and CNN2, respectively, and then use CBAM [18] to make the model pay more attention to the important features and improve the feature extraction ability of the model. The detailed structure of the CNN1 and CNN2 is shown in Fig. 2, where the size (e.g., 3×3) and number (e.g., 32, 64) of the convolutional kernels for each convolutional layer are shown on the left side, and the size of the output (e.g., $9 \times 9 \times 32$) for each operator is shown on the right side.

For CNN1 and CNN2, after some convolutional layers, we use the batch normalization (BN) layer to solve the overfitting problem caused by the small number of training samples, and also to accelerate the training performance; the rectified linear unit (ReLU) layer is used to achieve efficient smooth propagation of the loss gradient by introducing an nonlinear term into the output feature map. The Dropout layer is used to reduce the complexity of the model and improve the generalization ability of the model. The extracted features are denoted as F_H, F_L:

$$F_H = CNN1(x_H) \tag{1}$$

$$F_L = CNN2(x_L) \tag{2}$$

For obtaining, CBAM [18] is used to enhance the feature expression ability of the model. The reason for choosing CBAM is that CBAM is an attention module designed specifically for convolutional neural networks. The traditional convolution only focuses on local information but often ignores global information. Taking the 3×3 convolution as an example, the filter has 9 pixels, and the value of the target pixel only refers to itself and the surrounding 8 pixels. This means that the convolution operation can only use the local information to calculate the target pixel because the convolution operation can only see the local information, and has little understanding of the global information, so this may bring some deviations. Since convolutional operations extract informative features by fusing cross-channel and spatial information, CBAM improves the representational capabilities of CNNs by emphasizing meaningful features along the two main dimensions of channel and spatial axes. The structure of the CBAM we used can be found in the original paper [18].

CBAM does not change the number of channels in the feature vector and after CBAM we get the features F'_H, F'_L for HSI and LiDAR:

$$F'_H = CBAM(F_H) \tag{3}$$

$$F'_L = CBAM(F_L) \tag{4}$$

Then, we flatten F'_H and F'_L separately and then concatenate to obtain F_{cat}:

$$F_{cat} = (Flatten(F'_H)) \oplus (Flatten(F'_L)) \tag{5}$$

where $\oplus$ is for concatenating.

In order to keep the dimension of F_{cat} consistent with the other feature vectors, we finally use a fully connected layer to adjust the dimension of F_{cat}:

$$F'_{cat} = FC(F_{cat}) \tag{6}$$

where FC denotes a fully connected layer.

2.3   Dual-Branch Cross-Attention Fusion

How to effectively fuse the obtained features is the key to the problem we want to study. Recently, more and more scholars have applied the attention mechanism to deep neural networks, made many valuable breakthroughs, and successfully applied them to cross-modal tasks (e.g., visual quizzing, image description, and graphic matching). This has also led to a growing number of recent approaches that use attentional mechanisms to enhance the fusion between multimodal remote sensing data. Inspired by this, this paper proposes a dual-branch cross-attention fusion module (DCFM) to adequately and efficiently fuse information from HSI and LiDAR data. We use the obtained fused features for guiding the classification task. The structure of DCFM is shown in Fig. 3. DCFM can be defined as:

$$F_{fusion} = CrossAttention(F_H^\backslash, F_L^\backslash) \odot CrossAttention(F_H^\backslash, F_{cat}^\backslash) \qquad (7)$$

where CrossAttention denotes cross-attention fusion and $\odot$ denotes an element-wise multiplication.

For each CrossAttention, the input feature maps are first fed into the fully connected layer separately, then element-wise addition is performed, and the resulting result is again subjected to fully connected operations, and a sigmoid function is performed to obtain F_1, F_2 :

$$F_1 = \sigma(FC(FC(F_H^\backslash) + FC(F_L^\backslash))) \qquad (8)$$

$$F_2 = \sigma(FC(FC(F_H^\backslash) + FC(F_{cat}^\backslash))) \qquad (9)$$

where $\sigma(\cdot)$ is the sigmoid function, FC is the fully connected layer used to map the channel features, and the purpose of this operation is to realize the feature interaction between HSI and LiDAR data, and + denotes an element-wise addition.

After that, in order to exchange the feature information of different modes more efficiently, we multiply the first half of the channels of F_1 with $F_H^\backslash$, and the second half with $F_L^\backslash$, and splice the obtained results, and perform softmax for activation after splicing. The same operation is proformed for F_2, $F_H^\backslash$, $F_{cat}^\backslash$. Finally, we get F_{11}, F_{22}:

$$F_{11} = softmax((F_H^1 \odot F_H^\backslash) \oplus (F_L^1 \odot F_L^\backslash)) \qquad (10)$$

$$F_{22} = softmax((F_H^2 \odot F_H^\backslash) \oplus (F_{cat}^2 \odot F_{cat}^\backslash)) \qquad (11)$$

where F_H^1 denotes the first half of the channel of F_1, F_L^1 denotes the second half of the channel of F_1, F_H^2 denotes the first half of the channel of F_2, and F_{cat}^2 denotes the second half of the channel of F_2, $\odot$ denotes an element-wise multiplication , $\oplus$ is for concatenating.

Finally, the F_{11} and F_{22} are multiplied to obtain the final F_{fusion}:

$$F_{fusion} = F_{11} \odot F_{22} \qquad (12)$$

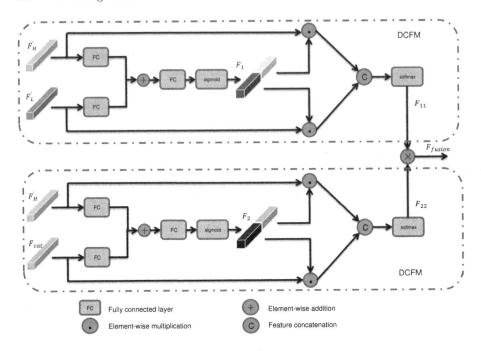

Fig. 3. The structure of DCFM

2.4   Classification

In order to make more effective use of the information of each modality, we refer to the decision-level fusion method while performing feature fusion. We input the HSI features $F_H^{\backslash}$, LiDAR features $F_L^{\backslash}$ and fusion features F_{fusion} into three output layers respectively to generate three classification results. We use three fully connected layers as output layers to obtain three classification results:

$$R_1 = FC(F_H^{\backslash}) \tag{13}$$

$$R_2 = FC(F_L^{\backslash}) \tag{14}$$

$$R_3 = FC(F_{fusion}) \tag{15}$$

After that, these three classification results are weighted to get the final classification result. The weight of each classification result is determined by its classification accuracy:

$$R = w_1 \odot R_1 + w_2 \odot R_2 + w_3 \odot R_3 \tag{16}$$

where $R \in \mathbb{R}^{c \times 1}$ denotes the final classification output, where c denotes the number of categories to be discriminated, and $w_1 \in \mathbb{R}^{c \times 1}$, $w_2 \in \mathbb{R}^{c \times 1}$ and $w_3 \in \mathbb{R}^{c \times 1}$ denote the weights.

3 Experiments

3.1 Data Description

Table 1. Number of training and testing samples for the Houston2013 data

No.	Class Name	Training Set	Testing Set
Class 1	Healthy Grass	198	1053
Class 2	Stressed Grass	190	1064
Class 3	Synthetic grass	192	505
Class 4	Trees	188	1056
Class 5	Soil	186	1056
Class 6	Water	182	143
Class 7	Residential	196	1072
Class 8	Commercial	191	1053
Class 9	Road	193	1059
Class 10	Highway	191	1036
Class 11	Railway	181	1054
Class 12	Parking Lot1	192	1041
Class 13	Parking Lot2	184	285
Class 14	Tennis Court	181	247
Class 15	Running Track	187	473
	Total	2832	12197

Table 2. Number of training and testing samples for the Trento data

No.	Class Name	Training Set	Testing Set
Class 1	Apple trees	129	3905
Class 2	Buildings	125	2778
Class 3	Ground	105	374
Class 4	Woods	154	8969
Class 5	Vineyard	184	10317
Class 6	Road	122	3525
	Total	819	29595

Houston2013 Dataset: The dataset was captured by the National Airborne Center for Laser Mapping, and it was used as a challenge in the 2013 GRSS Data Fusion Contest. The HSI was captured by the CASI sensor (144 spectral bands at a resolution of 2.5 m). Coregistered LiDAR data with the same resolution are available. A total of 15029 ground-truth samples are distributed in 15 classes. They are divided into train and test sets containing 2832 and 12197 pixels, respectively. Table 1 details the scenario information for the Houston2013 dataset, including class names and the number of training and test samples.

Trento Dataset: The dataset was collected in a rural region south of Trento, Italy. The HSI image consists of 63 bands with a wavelength range of 0.42–0.99 μm. The size of the dataset is 166 × 660 pixels, and the spatial resolution of the dataset is 1.0 m. A total of 30214 ground-truth samples are distributed in six classes. Table 2 lists the distribution of training and test samples for the Trento dataset.

3.2 Implementation Details

We implemented MatNet using the PyTorch framework. Raw HSI and LiDAR data were fed into MatNet and trained end-to-end. In the training phase, Adam is used as the optimizer. The training batch was set to 200, the batch size was set to 64, and the initial learning rate was set to 0.0001. The experiments were implemented on a personal computer with an Inter i5-13500HX, 2.50 GHz processor, 16 GB RAM, and an NVIDIA GeForce RTX 4060 graphics card.

3.3 Objective Function

Using a particular training set $(x_h^{(i)}, x_l^{(i)}, y^{(i)})|i = 1, 2, \cdots, N$, where N is the number of training samples and $y^{(i)}$ is the groundtruth for the ith sample, the whole network in Fig. 1 is trained end-to-end. For every sample, we can get three outputs by a feed-forward procedure. A cross-entropy loss function can be used to calculate their loss values. For example, the formula for the loss value between the groundtruth y and the first output $\hat{y}_1$ is as follows:

$$L_1 = -\frac{1}{N}\sum_{i=1}^{N}[y^{(i)}log(\hat{y}_1^{(i)}) + (1 - y^{(i)})log(1 - \hat{y}_1^{(i)})] \tag{17}$$

Similarly, we can also derive $L^{(2)}$ and $L^{(3)}$ for the other two outputs. $L^{(3)}$ is designed to supervise the learning process of the fused feature between hyperspectral and LiDAR data, whereas $L^{(1)}$ and $L^{(2)}$ are responsible for the hyperspectral and LiDAR features, respectively. The final loss value L is represented as the combination of $L^{(1)}$, $L^{(2)}$, and $L^{(3)}$:

$$L = \lambda_1 L_1 + \lambda_2 L_2 + \lambda_3 L_3 \tag{18}$$

where λ_1 and λ_2 denote the weight parameters of $L^{(1)}$ and $L^{(2)}$, respectively. In our experiments, we empirically set them to 0.01 as it gives satisfactory performance. Their effects on the classification performance will be analyzed in Sect. 3.4.

3.4 Parameter Settings

We analyze several hyperparameters that may affect the classification performance and the training process, including the reduced spectral dimension b, the block size k of the input data blocks, and the analysis of the weighting parameters. The following experimental results were all obtained on the Houston2013 dataset.

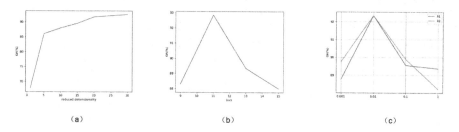

(a)   (b)   (c)

Fig. 4. Overall accuracy (%) achieved by the proposed MatNet model with different parameters for the Houston data sets. (a) Number b of principal components. (b) Size of the local spatial window. (c) Weight parameters λ_1 and λ_2.

1. Analysis on the Reduced Dimensionality: For the proposed model, we have two hyperparameters that need to be predetermined. The first one is the number b of dimensionality reduction of the hyperspectral data using PCA, and the second one is the neighborhood size $k \times k$ extracted from the hyperspectral and LiDAR data. To evaluate the impact of b, fix k and choose b from the candidate set $\{1, 5, 10, 15, 20, 25, 30\}$. Figure 4(a) shows the performance (i.e., OA) of MatNet on the Houston dataset. From the figure, we can observe that as b increases, OA first increases and then tends to a stable state. Considering the computational complexity and classification performance, b can be set to 20.
2. Analysis on the Neighboring Size: Similar to the analysis of b, we can also evaluate the impact of k by fixing b and selecting k from the candidate set $\{9, 11, 13, 15\}$. Figure 4(b) shows the variation of OA values corresponding to different sizes of k. It can be seen that the highest OA value can be obtained when k is taken to be 11, therefore, k can be set to 11.
3. Analysis on the Weight Parameters: The loss function of the proposed model in 18 contains two hyper-parameters (i.e., λ_1 and λ_2). In order to test their effects on the classification performance, we firstly fix λ_1 and change λ_2 from a candidate set $\{0.001, 0.01, 0.1, 1\}$. Then, we set λ_2 to the optimal value and change λ_1 from the same set $0.001, 0.01, 0.1, 1$. Figure 4(c) illustrates the OA obtained by our proposed model on the Houston data for different values of λ_1 and λ_2. It is shown that as λ_2 increases, the OA will first increase and then decrease. The highest OA value appears when $\lambda_2 = 0.01$. Similar conclusions can be observed for λ_1. Therefore, the optimal values for λ_1 and λ_2 are 0.01.

3.5   Experiment Results

We selected several representative deep learning-based methods for joint classification of HSI and LiDAR data to compare with our proposed method. Two-branch CNN [19] is a typical two-branch model; EndNet [6] is an encoder-decoder architecture that uses a reconstruction strategy for feature fusion; A^3CLNN [10] developed a new dual-channel spatial, spectral and multiscale attentional convolutional long- and short-term memory neural network for feature extraction and classification of multi-source remote sensing data.

Table 3. Classification accuracies (%) and Kappa coefficients of different models on the Houston2013 data. The best accuracies are shown with the bold type face.

Method	C1	C2	C3	C4	C5	C6	C7	C8	C9
Two-branch CNN	**83.10**	84.10	**100**	93.09	**100**	**99.30**	92.82	82.34	84.70
EndNet	81.58	83.65	**100**	93.09	99.91	95.10	82.65	81.29	88.29
A^3CLNN	81.73	84.43	91.49	96.72	99.97	97.9	87.06	**96.93**	87.88
MatNet	83.00	**93.70**	99.00	**98.20**	99.91	**99.30**	94.21	95.15	**90.93**
	C10	C11	C12	C13	C14	C15	OA	AA	Kappa
Two-branch CNN	65.44	88.24	89.53	92.28	96.76	**99.79**	87.98	90.11	0.8698
EndNet	**89.00**	83.78	90.39	82.46	**100**	98.10	88.52	89.95	0.8759
A^3CLNN	70.82	98.13	**94.65**	**96.02**	97.30	96.05	90.55	91.81	0.8975
MatNet	80.98	**93.55**	93.37	92.63	**100**	96.19	**93.00**	**94.01**	**0.9240**

The classification performance of each model is evaluated by the OA, the average accuracy (AA), the per-class accuracy, and the Kappa coefficient. OA defines the ratio between the number of correctly classified pixels to the total number of pixels in the test set, AA refers to the average of accuracies in all classes, and Kappa is the percentage of agreement corrected by the number of agreements that would be expected purely by chance.

Quantitative comparisons on the Houston 2013 dataset are shown in Table 3 and on the Trento dataset in Table 4. From the results on the two datasets, it can be seen that the MatNet proposed in this paper achieves the best performance on OA, AA, and Kappa compared to other methods. It is shown that our model effectively models the correlation between multivariate samples and has superiority and great potential in multimodal feature fusion. Meanwhile, we can see that MatNet largely improves the classification accuracy of the Houston2013 dataset for the categories "Trees" (C4), "Residential" (C7), and "Railway" (C11), which is due to the fact that there is a more obvious change in the height of these categories compared to their surroundings, and this also shows that the proposed deep feature extraction module can extract the elevation information in LiDAR images more effectively.

Table 4. Classification accuracies(%) and Kappa coefficients of different models on the Trento data. The best accuracies are shown with the bold type face.

Method	C1	C2	C3	C4	C5	C6	OA	AA	Kappa
Two-branch CNN	98.70	95.21	93.32	99.93	98.78	89.98	97.92	96.19	0.9681
EndNet	88.19	98.49	95.19	99.30	91.96	90.14	94.17	93.88	0.9222
A^3CLNN	98.92	99.14	98.12	**100**	**99.95**	90.57	98.73	97.78	0.9831
MatNet	**99.92**	**99.34**	**98.99**	99.92	99.94	**92.91**	**98.80**	**98.50**	**0.9897**

3.6 Ablation Studies

In order to highlight the effectiveness of DCFM in MatNet, a detailed ablation study is conducted in this paper to understand their contribution to the classification performance. A^3CLNN [10] was used as a baseline for experiments on the Houston2013 dataset. For convenience, those containing DCFM are denoted as (with) and those without DCFM are denoted as (without).

In order to fully utilize the information in the HSI and LiDAR data and fuse them with sufficient information, we take advantage of the attention mechanism and propose the DCFM module. To demonstrate its effectiveness, we analyze the impact of DCFM by adding and removing DCFM in our MatNet, after removing DCFM, we directly use the result of feature splicing,F_{cat}, as the fusion result for classification, and the results are reported in Table 5. Compared with A^3CLNN, our proposed model gains 0.54% and 0.52% on OA and AA without DCFM, respectively; and then gains 1.91% and 1.63% on OA and AA with DCFM, respectively, which indicates that DCFM can fuse the data features of the two modalities more effectively, thus improving the whole model's classification performance.

Table 5. Impact of the proposed DCFM.

Model	OA	AA	Kappa
A^3CLNN	90.55	91.81	0.8975
Propoesd(without)	91.09	92.33	0.9034
Proposed(with)	**93.00**	**94.01**	**0.9240**

4 Conclusion

In this paper, a new convolutional neural network based on multiple attention mechanisms is proposed for HSI and LiDAR classification. The proposed network mainly contains a deep feature extraction module and a feature fusion module, where deep feature extraction is realized using a CNN containing an attention mechanism, and feature fusion is realized using a dual-branch cross-attention fusion module. The proposed method can effectively alleviate the drawbacks of CNN in feature extraction, and can effectively fuse the feature information of two modalities. Experimental results show that MatNet outperforms existing HSI and LiDAR classification methods on the same dataset.

References

1. Baltrušaitis, T., Ahuja, C., Morency, L.P.: Multimodal machine learning: a survey and taxonomy. IEEE Trans. Pattern Anal. Mach. Intell. **41**(2), 423–443 (2019). https://doi.org/10.1109/TPAMI.2018.2798607
2. Bartholomé, E., Belward, A.: GLC 2000: a new approach to global land cover mapping from earth observation data. Int. J. Remote Sens. **26**, 1959–1977 (2005). https://doi.org/10.1080/01431160412331291297

3. Chen, Y., et al.: Drop an octave: Reducing spatial redundancy in convolutional neural networks with octave convolution. In: 2019 IEEE/CVF International Conference on Computer Vision (ICCV), pp. 3434–3443 (2019). https://doi.org/10.1109/ICCV.2019.00353

4. Cheng, G., Yang, C., Yao, X., Guo, L., Han, J.: When deep learning meets metric learning: Remote sensing image scene classification via learning discriminative CNNs. IEEE Trans. Geosci. Remote Sens. **56**(5), 2811–2821 (2018). https://doi.org/10.1109/TGRS.2017.2783902

5. Debes, C., et al.: Hyperspectral and lidar data fusion: Outcome of the 2013 GRSS data fusion contest. IEEE J. Sel. Top. Appl. Earth Observ. Remote Sens. **7** (2014). https://doi.org/10.1109/JSTARS.2014.2305441

6. Hong, D., Gao, L., Hang, R., Zhang, B., Chanussot, J.: Deep encoder-decoder networks for classification of hyperspectral and lidar data. IEEE Geosci. Remote Sens. Lett. **19**, 1–5 (2022). https://doi.org/10.1109/LGRS.2020.3017414

7. Hong, D., et al.: More diverse means better: multimodal deep learning meets remote-sensing imagery classification. IEEE Trans. Geosci. Remote Sens. **59**(5), 4340–4354 (2021). https://doi.org/10.1109/TGRS.2020.3016820

8. Huang, R., Hong, D., Xu, Y., Yao, W., Stilla, U.: Multi-scale local context embedding for lidar point cloud classification. IEEE Geosci. Remote Sens. Lett. **17**(4), 721–725 (2020). https://doi.org/10.1109/LGRS.2019.2927779

9. Kang, J., Hong, D., Liu, J., Baier, G., Yokoya, N., Demir, B.: Learning convolutional sparse coding on complex domain for interferometric phase restoration. IEEE Trans. Neural Netw. Learn. Syst. **32**(2), 826–840 (2021). https://doi.org/10.1109/TNNLS.2020.2979546

10. Li, H.C., Hu, W.S., Li, W., Li, J., Du, Q., Plaza, A.: A3 CLNN: spatial, spectral and multiscale attention ConvLSTM neural network for multisource remote sensing data classification. IEEE Trans. Neural Netw. Learn. Syst. **33**(2), 747–761 (2022). https://doi.org/10.1109/TNNLS.2020.3028945

11. Mohla, S., Pande, S., Banerjee, B., Chaudhuri, S.: FusAtNet: dual attention based spectrospatial multimodal fusion network for hyperspectral and lidar classification. In: 2020 IEEE/CVF Conference on Computer Vision and Pattern Recognition Workshops (CVPRW), pp. 416–425 (2020). https://doi.org/10.1109/CVPRW50498.2020.00054

12. Qian, X., et al.: Generating and sifting pseudolabeled samples for improving the performance of remote sensing image scene classification. IEEE J. Sel. Top. Appl. Earth Observ. Remote Sens. **13**, 4925–4933 (2020). https://doi.org/10.1109/JSTARS.2020.3019582

13. Rasti, B., et al.: Feature extraction for hyperspectral imagery: the evolution from shallow to deep: Overview and toolbox. IEEE Geosci. Remote Sens. Mag. **8**(4), 60–88 (2020). https://doi.org/10.1109/MGRS.2020.2979764

14. Turner, W., Spector, S., Gardiner, E., Fladeland, M., Sterling, E., Steininger, M.: Remote sensing for biodiversity science and conservation. Trends Ecol. Evol. **18**, 306–314 (2003). https://doi.org/10.1016/S0169-5347(03)00070-3

15. Ustin, S.: Manual of Remote Sensing/Remote Sensing for Natural Resource Management and Environmental Monitoring (2004)

16. Wang, M., Gao, F., Dong, J., Li, H.C., Du, Q.: Nearest neighbor-based contrastive learning for hyperspectral and lidar data classification. IEEE Trans. Geosci. Remote Sens. **61**, 1–16 (2023). https://doi.org/10.1109/TGRS.2023.3236154

17. Wang, W., Tran, D., Feiszli, M.: What makes training multi-modal classification networks hard? In: 2020 IEEE/CVF Conference on Computer Vision and

Pattern Recognition (CVPR), pp. 12692–12702 (2020). https://doi.org/10.1109/CVPR42600.2020.01271

18. Woo, S., Park, J., Lee, J.Y., Kweon, I.S.: CBAM: convolutional block attention module. ArXiv abs/1807.06521 (2018). https://api.semanticscholar.org/CorpusID:49867180

19. Xu, X., Li, W., Ran, Q., Du, Q., Gao, L., Zhang, B.: Multisource remote sensing data classification based on convolutional neural network. IEEE Trans. Geosci. Remote Sens. 56(2), 937–949 (2018). https://doi.org/10.1109/TGRS.2017.2756851

20. Zhang, B., Li, S., Jia, X., Gao, L., Peng, M.: Adaptive Markov random field approach for classification of hyperspectral imagery. IEEE Geosci. Remote Sens. Lett. 8(5), 973–977 (2011). https://doi.org/10.1109/LGRS.2011.2145353

21. Zhang, C., Yang, Z., He, X., Deng, L.: Multimodal intelligence: representation learning, information fusion, and applications. IEEE J. Sel. Top. Signal Process. 14(3), 478–493 (2020). https://doi.org/10.1109/JSTSP.2020.2987728

22. Zhang, M., Li, W., Du, Q., Gao, L., Zhang, B.: Feature extraction for classification of hyperspectral and lidar data using patch-to-patch CNN. IEEE Trans. Cybern. 50(1), 100–111 (2020). https://doi.org/10.1109/TCYB.2018.2864670

23. Zhao, X., Tao, R., Li, W., Philips, W., Liao, W.: Fractional Gabor convolutional network for multisource remote sensing data classification. IEEE Trans. Geosci. Remote Sens. 60, 1–18 (2022). https://doi.org/10.1109/TGRS.2021.3065507

Few-Shot Learning Remote Scene Classification Based on DC-2DEC

Ziyuan Wang[1], Zhiming Ding[2](✉), and Yingying Wang[1]

[1] Beijing University of Technology, Beijing 100124, China
{S202274147,wangyingying}@emails.bjut.edu.cn
[2] Institute of Software, Chinese Academy of Sciences, Beijing 100190, China
zhiming@iscas.ac.cn

Abstract. Few-shot learning image classification (FSLIC) is a task that has gained enhanced focus in recent years, the cost of collecting and annotating large number of data samples in some specialised domains is expensive, Few-shot remote scene classification (FRSSC) is of great utility in scenarios where sample is scarce and labelling is extremely costly, the core problem of this task is how to identify new classes with scarce and expensive few-shot samples. However, existing work prefers complicated feature extraction in various ways and the enhancement results are not satisfactory, this paper aims to improve the effectiveness of FSLIC not only through complicated feature extraction but also by exploring alternative approaches. Here are multiple avenues to improve the performance of few-shot classifiers. Training with a scarce data in a few-shot learning (FSL) task often results in a biased feature distribution. In this paper, we propose a method to address this issue by calibrating the support set data feature using sufficient base class data. (Our data distribution calibration method (DC) is on top of feature extractor), requiring no additional parameters. And the feature extraction model is further optimised and the feature extractor of DC-2DEC is optimised with the task of dealing with the spatial context structure of the image i.e. rotation prediction pretext, specifically rotation prediction. We refer to the proposed method as DC-2DEC, and we apply it to few-shot learning classification in RS image (RS image) scene recognition. Through experiments conducted on traditional few-shot datasets and RS image datasets, we validate the algorithm and present corresponding experimental results. These results demonstrate the competitiveness of DC-2DEC, highlighting its efficacy in few-shot learning classification for RS images.

Keywords: few-shot remote scene classification · distribution calibration · remote sensing image · pretext task · few-shot learning

1 Introduction

In the past few years, there has been rapid development in deep neural networks for image-related tasks, leading to significant breakthroughs. However, when

This work is supported by the National Key R&D Program of China under Grant 2022YFF0503900.

image data are scarce and expensive, obtaining a large amount of labeled training data becomes challenging. The data-driven nature of deep learning frameworks often faces difficulties and is prone to overfitting under such circumstances. To address this issue, researchers have turned to meta-learning, specifically FSL tasks, inspired by the human capacity to learn rapidly through knowledge transfer.

Meta-learning is designed to facilitate rapid generalization to new domains, even with limited computational resources and data availability, by leveraging adaptation techniques. In essence, it entails training a network architecture with exceptional learning capabilities. FSL is currently a challenging field that is anticipated to thrive in the future [1]. In the realm of RS, where data acquisition can be costly and expensive, FRSSC has emerged as a valuable task, captivating the interest of numerous researchers in the field of RS image processing.

RS image scene classification is a crucial task in RS image understanding, playing a significant role in applications such as traffic analysis, disaster warning, land use assessment, urban planning, and more. The objective of FRSSC is to associate descriptive labels with image regions based on visual features extracted from the image [2]. As an essential component of RS image analysis, this task has garnered extensive attention from researchers.

FSLIC methods are typically selected from three methods: 1) learning fine-tuning, 2) recurrent neural networks with memory function, and 3) metric-based learning methods. In recent years, many researchers have explored various FSLIC with better performance based on metric learning. However, these proposed methods often overlook the differences between RS images and other few-shot images, such as intrinsic features and insensitivity to spatial rotation. They also fail to fully exploit the feature information between rotated images. To address these issues, an image supervised context-informed task module called Pretext-Task-Based Representation Learning is added to the network for fine-tuning intra-class image classification evaluation [3].

Furthermore, many existing FSLIC learning frameworks do not effectively handle data distribution calibration [4]. Given the constrained amount of data in the support set, a skewed distribution can easily occur. Deep learning frameworks, which are designed for large-scale data, assume a large amount of data and rely on the true distribution of data. However, the task-heavy support set data in FSLIC is limited, exacerbating the distribution problem. To mitigate this issue, the network architecture in this paper attempts to correct the support set data using base class data to align it with the true data distribution [5].

Our proposed DC-2DEC implementation of FSLIC, after feature extraction, data distribution calibration is applied to the query level using the base class dataset to ensure the robustness of the model training, after that the image context structure is calibrated using the image context structure to identify the 2D rotations of the image to guide the intra-class consistency versus intra-class differences, Finally cosine distance metric function with data distribution correction module is used as the final evaluation classification layer.

In summary, the primary contributions of our devised DC-2DEC can be summarised as follows:

1) After performing feature extraction, this paper proposes the use of a query set to correct the data distribution in the support set. This approach aims to address the issue of limited data at the query level. By calibrating the data distribution in the support set, the scarcity of few-shot data queries can be mitigated.

2) In the feature extraction layer of DC-2DEC, an additional task called the pretext task is introduced. The pretext task is performed in conjunction with the rotation prediction task. By incorporating the pretext task, the paper successfully tackles the Few-shot Recognition with FRSSC problem, achieving promising results.

3) We proposed DC-2DEC model is evaluated through experiments conducted on three publicly accessible FSL datasets. The results demonstrate the effectiveness and competitiveness of DC-2DEC in addressing the FRSSC problem. The model achieves good performance, highlighting its potential in the field of FSL.

2 · Related Works

The following section will provide a comprehensive review of the relevant aspects closely associated with our few-shot image classification (FSLIC) approach.

2.1 Few-Shot Learning Image Classification

FSL aims to classify new classes with limited examples. In the field of learning with FSLIC, two main approaches have been explored: metric learning-based methods and optimization-based methods.

Optimization-based approaches focus on efficiently adapting model parameters to novel mission in the FSL context. There are many applications of metric learning in FSLIC [1,6,7]. In metric-based approaches, the primary objective is to represent data in a suitable feature space, differentiating data from different classes based on a distance metric. The distance metric is designed to minimize the intra-class distances while maximizing the inter-class distances

In addition to the metric learning-based and optimization-based approaches, several alternative effective approaches have been suggested to tackle the challenge of FSLIC. These include graph-theory based methods [8], knowledge distillation, reinforcement learning [10], differentiable support vector machines [9], and more [11]. Furthermore, FSL has also been investigated in the context of image semantic segmentation [12,13] and image recognition target detection tasks [14]. Prior work related to the techniques used in this paper has also been studied.

In [15], an adaptive matching network (DLA-MatchNet) based on a meta-learning framework was proposed for discriminative learning.DLA-MatchNet leverages attention mechanisms and an adaptive distance matcher to acquire discriminative features from few-shot labeled data for the FRSSC task. An additional meta-learning-based model was introduced in for task-level feature learning [15], which combined with the Balance loss function to achieve classification results.

In [16]implicit, the Siam Prototype Network was developed to tackle FRSSC tasks with few-shot samples. SPNet improves the traditional prototype generation scheme to accommodate the characteristics of remote sensing scenarios. The results of this method in FRSSC are highly encouraging. Cui et al. [17] proposed the Meta Kernel Network (MKN) for FRSSC, which embeds the kernel technique into a meta-learning framework.

Multi-scale multi-angle networks and class-level prototype guided learning algorithms were advanced for FRSSC in the literature [18]. These methods aim to capture the complex land cover in a remote sensing scene based on a limited number of labels and have achieved satisfactory results.

Furthermore, [7] mentions the availability of aerial image datasets with diverse data distributions, which can be used to comprehensively evaluate FSL algorithms. Additionally, the authors propose the DC-DML model, which addresses the FRSSC task by adjusting the distances between intra- and inter-class samples.

Many notable meta-learning algorithms do not incorporate local feature matching between samples, yet local features can significantly benefit the training network, especially in few-shot scenarios. In this paper, we utilize a simple feature extraction layer for feature matching. For FSLIC, data scarcity is a common challenge. To mitigate this problem, we propose an enhancement technique based on image context structure. By leveraging the image context structure, we can extract more information about image features, thereby improving the classification performance.

2.2 Distribution Calibration

MatchingNet [19] and ProtoNet [1] are learning algorithms that classify samples by comparing the distance between them and representatives of each category. The data distribution calibration feature sampling process proposed in this paper does not involve any learnable parameters. Another algorithm for categories is to make up for the lack of the number of available samples by generating them. Some researchers have proposed the idea of using GAN [20] or autoencoders [21] to generate samples to enhance the learning of the network. Researchers have proposed to synthesise data by introducing task-conditional adversarial generators. [22]attempted to train variational autoencoders for approximating distributions and predict labels based on predicted statistical samples. Autoencoders can also enhance data by projecting between visual semantics to increase sample speed and semantic space [22].

Data augmentation is a well-established and effective approach for increasing the number of training data. [23] and [24] proposed to use traditional data augmentation techniques to construct an pretext task for unsupervised FSL. [25]

and [23] used the broader idea of data calibration to design illusionary models to generate augmented versions of images. The inputs to these models have different options, such as images and noise [25], or a concatenation of multiple features [26] attempted to enhance feature representation by utilising within-class variance. These methods estimate class-level distributions by learning to calibrate from the original data or their feature representations, which can reduce the imputation bias of individual data and provide more varied synthesis from calibrated distributions.

2.3 Pretext-Task-Based Representation Learning

The pretext task was originally designed to learn effective visual representations without annotations. Typically, this task involves training the network to generate embeddings, where similar images are grouped together and dissimilar images are separated. To achieve this, the input X of the model is first transformed into X', and the outputs Y and Y' should be close in Euclidean space. Examples of such pairs $\{X, X'\}$ include different channels of an image [27], color blocks [28], rotated copies [29], or applying contrast learning techniques like SimCLR [3] to transform different frames of an image or video [3]. Among these methods, image rotation prediction [30] is a representative approach that leverages the spatial context structure of the image.

In our research, we propose a combination of a self-supervised rotation prediction task and an image semantic classification task for FRSSC. By calibrating the task and facilitating model training, our work aims to enhance the performance of FRSSC in the absence of sufficient training samples.

2.4 Few-Shot Remote Sensing Scene Classification

With the rapid advancement of satellite technology, RS image processing has gained significant attention. Deep learning and FSLIC have witnessed remarkable progress in extracting feature information from RS image samples, addressing the challenges of limited availability and high cost. Few-shot learning techniques offer a promising solution for RS image scene recognition.

Existing FSLIC techniques can be broadly categorized into transfer learning and meta-learning, with the latter being the prevailing approach for lensless FRSSC of optical RS images. Inspired by metric learning, some researchers have proposed concatenated prototype networks to enhance the performance of prototype-based classification. These approaches incorporate strategies for prototype self-calibration and inter-calibration [31]. Additionally, methods utilizing scaled cosine similarity have been employed to measure the distance between query data and supporting data [32]. Other distance metrics, such as CNN relational modules [33] and Euclidean distances [34], have also been utilized to train multiple frameworks for metric-based learning. However, the potential and effectiveness of data distribution correction using pretext tasks have not been fully explored. Thus, this paper aims to shed new light on the positive impact of pretext tasks.

3 Method

In this section, details of our proposed method are presented, including data distribution calibration, full objective, Few-Shot Classification, and rotation prediction task (image context-based pretext task).

3.1 Full Objective

The few-shot task divides the dataset into D_{base}, D_{val}, and D_{novel}, using the D_{base} dataset for scene recognition network training, after which the D_{val} data is used to learn the best parameter θ from the feature extractor to get the optimal network architecture f_θ, and finally the algorithm is elaborated by performing classification prediction in the well-divided support set and query set in D_{novel} to get the final result:

Algorithm 1. Pipeline of the Proposed Method

Input: $Datasets : D_{base}, D_{val}, and D_{novel}$
Output: $Feature\ extractor\ f_\theta$
$\triangleright Training$
for
while $\theta\ not\ converged$ **do**
   for $(x, y)\ \in\ D_{base}$ **do**
      Optimize θ
   end for
   Select best θ using D_{val}
end while
Output f_θ
$\triangleright Inference$
for $(S, Q)\ \in\ D_{novel}$ **do**
   Perform classification
end for

---

c_b is the feature extraction architecture semantic category prediction, α is the hyperparameters, c_r is the rotation prediction task and the final result is as follows:

$$c_{full} = c_b + \alpha c_r \qquad (1)$$

We propose the DC-2DEC model, which encompasses the following components. The feature extraction layer of DC-2DEC comprises two parts: a pretext task module that leverages the image context structure to rectify semantic category prediction. The DC layer, also known as the data distribution calibration layer, is responsible for performing data calibration on the support set. Lastly, the cosine distance metric is utilized to derive the final results. The model architecture of DC-2DEC is illustrated as Fig. 1.

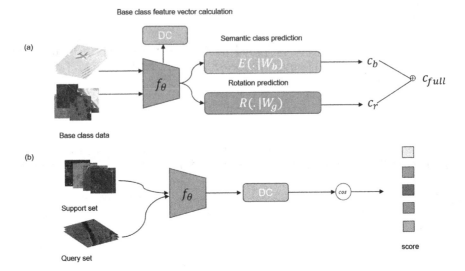

Base class feature vector calculation

Fig. 1. This figure depicts the overall framework idea of our approach.

3.2 Distribution Calibration

The base class typically contains a substantial amount of data, while the evaluation task involves sampling from a new class with a limited number of labeled samples. Predictions based on the distributional statistics of the base class tend to be more accurate than those based on a smaller sample size. When assuming a Gaussian distribution for the sample features, the mean and variance of each category exhibit a strong correlation with the category's semantics. Motivated by this observation, we can compute the degree of similarity between two classes and transfer the statistics from the base class to the new class if they exhibit a high degree of similarity.

In this paper, we propose a distribution calibration method that operates at the feature level and can be integrated into any feature extractor. Assuming Gaussian distribution for the features of the base class, the average of the feature vector for base class i corresponds to the average of each dimension of the computed vector [4] (Fig. 2).

$$\mu_i = \frac{\sum_{i=1}^{n_i} x_j}{n_i} \tag{2}$$

The feature vector of the jth input image in the base class i is x_j, and the total number of samples in class i is n_i. Because the sample feature vector x_j is multi-dimensional, this paper adopts the covariance to appropriately represent the variance between any pair of elements in the feature vector. The covariance matrix $\sum_i$ of the features of class i is calculated as follows:

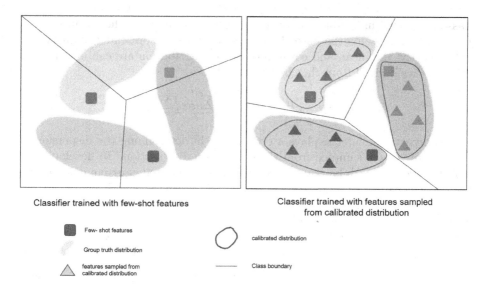

Classifier trained with few-shot features

Classifier trained with features sampled from calibrated distribution

- Few-shot features
- Group truth distribution
- features sampled from calibrated distribution
- calibrated distribution
- Class boundary

Fig. 2. Figure of the comparison between no data distribution correction and data distribution correction after feature extraction.

$$\sum_i = \frac{1}{n_i - 1} \sum_{j=1}^{n} (x_j - \mu_i)(x_j - \mu_i)^T. \tag{3}$$

To promote a feature distribution that closely resembles a Gaussian distribution, the following formulaic approach is employed to modify the features of the query level and support set in the target assignment. This transformation aims to reduce skewness and bring the distribution closer to Gaussian:

$$\widehat{x} = \begin{cases} x^\lambda & if \lambda \neq 0 \\ \log(x) & if \lambda = 0 \end{cases} \tag{4}$$

In our approach, we introduce the hyperparameter λ to adjust the correction distribution. When λ is set to 1, the samples retain their original features. By decreasing λ, we effectively reduce the positive skewness of the distribution, and vice versa. For our specific study, we have chosen to use a value of 0.5 for λ. Furthermore, we adopt a algorithm to select the top K base classes based on their proximity to the features derived from the support set data. The selection process involves using similarity or proximity measures to identify the base classes that are closest to the support set features.

$$S_d = \{-||\mu_i - \widehat{x}||^2 | i \in C_b\} \tag{5}$$

$$S_N = \{i| - ||\mu_i - \widehat{x}||^2 \in topk(S_d)\} \tag{6}$$

The function topK($\cdot$) is utilized to select the top element from the set of input distances, denoted as S_d. Within our methodology, S_N stores the k closest base classes, with the indicator of closeness determined based on the feature vector x. Here, C_b represents the base class, and support set represents the query set. Subsequently, the mean and covariance of the distribution are calibrated using the statistics derived from the closest base classes.

$$\mu' = \frac{\sum_{i \in S_N} \mu_i + \widehat{x}}{k+1}, \sum' = \frac{\sum_{i \in S_N} \sum_i}{k} + \alpha \tag{7}$$

The hyperparameter α plays a crucial role in determining the dispersion of the feature vectors sampled from the calibration distribution. To develop a set of feature vectors with label y, we sample from a corrected gaussian distribution using a specific set of calibration statistics, S_y, associated with class y in the target assignment. The dispersion of the sampled features is controlled by the value of the hyperparameter α.

$$D_y = \{(x,y) | x \sim N(\mu, \textstyle\sum), \forall(\mu, \textstyle\sum) \in S^y\} \tag{8}$$

To ensure a consistent number of features for each class, the hyperparameters determine the overall quantity of features generated. These features are evenly distributed within each calibration distribution in S_y. The fabricated features, combined with the original support set features from multiple tasks, are employed as training sample for the task-specific classifier. The classifier is trained by decreasing the cross-entropy loss between the support set features S and the developed features D_y.

$$\ell = \sum_{(x,y) \sim \overrightarrow{S} \cup D_{y}, y \in Y^T} - \log Pr(y|x; \theta), \tag{9}$$

where Y_T is the set of task T. S represents the support set of features converted by TLP (Turkey's Ladder of Powers) transformation, and the classifier model is parameterised by θ.

3.3   Rotation Prediction Task(Pretext Tasks Based on Image Context Structure)

The purpose of the rotation pretext assignment is to represent which of diverse rotations angles of rotation [41]. For example: $[0°, 90°, 180°, 270°]$, a given image has undergone, thus representing it as a four-way classification task. Formally, we define a set of rotation operators as $G = \{g_r\}_{r=1}^{R}$, $x_r = g_r(x)$ where denotes the number of degrees of rotation the image is transformed by and R refers to the quantity of rotations. In the experiments, the amount and size of the recognised rotations are not fixed, thus giving the network different rotations to extract features for the recognition task. With the rotation classifier parameters being given $W_b = [w_1, w_2, ..., w_c]$, the likelihood of input x_i is (Fig. 3):

Fig. 3. Visualization of images rotated by different rotation degree

The loss function for the rotation prediction task based on the image context structure can be expressed in the following form:

$$L_r = -\sum_{i=1}^{B}\sum_{i=1}^{R} II(y_i^g = r)\log(p(\widehat{y}_i^g = r|x_i)). \tag{10}$$

$$p(\widehat{y}_i^g = r|x_i) = \frac{exp(w_r^T f_\theta(g_r(x_i)))}{\sum_{r=1}^{n} exp(w_r^T f_\theta(g_r(x_i)))} \tag{11}$$

Unlike semantic category labelling, the monitoring signals employed here are also independent across categories, which greatly facilitates information sharing across categories. More important is the understanding behind the rotation monitoring signals that the neural network should have recognised the category and learnt the object part of the sample before performing the rotation recognition task effectively. In [35], quantitative results show a strong linear correlation between the accuracy of the rotational prediction task and semantic categorisation (i.e., category determination) when both tasks are trained simultaneously. This imagery may imply that this rotationally supervised signal positively affects category classification, i.e., semantic categorisation. However, the authors did not observe a notable improvement in semantic categorization accuracy when employing a multi-task framework.

Conversely, our study revealed that the rotational prediction task positively impacted the accuracy of FRSSC. We hypothesise that this is due to task differences: We hypothesise that this is due to task differences: 1) the overall classification task involves tasks where the training and test sets have the same categories, in line with the generic definition of generalisation, and 2) the few-shot classification task involves tasks where the training and test sets do not have intersecting categories. Since the distributional difference between the training and test sets in few-shot classification is much larger than that in holistic classification, it is more important to share cross-category information in few-shot settings. This universal information typically encompasses certain inherent features. As a result, FSLIC can gain advantages from the rotation prediction task.

In addition, during training, the rotation prediction pretext task network receives all rotated copies of a sample at the same time. Since each image that undergoes this change has not only a rotation label in addition to a semantic category label, We anticipate that these rotated copies are likely to share certain rotation-independent features. Therefore, we need to retrain the category (semantic) classifier to recognise the input transformed data and the category semantic information of their sources. The effect of the classifier is then evaluated by formulating the semantic classification loss with the following formula:

$$L_b = - \sum_{i=1}^{BR} \sum_{c=1}^{c} II(y_i = c) \log(p(\widehat{y}_i = c|x_i)) \tag{12}$$

The likelihood is calculated as follows:

$$p(\widehat{y}_i = c|x_i) = \frac{exp(w_c^T f_\theta(g_r(x_i)))}{\sum_{c=1}^{C} exp(w_c^T f_\theta(g_r(x_i)))}. \tag{13}$$

4 Experiments

In this section, we construct standard FSL tasks to evaluate the methods in this paper, and we conduct rich experiments to corroborate and validate the effectiveness of our few-shot meta-learning task framework.

4.1 Datasets

We perform experiments on three publicly available and challenging datasets to validate our ideas. The datasets: miniImageNet , NWPU-RESISC45, WHU-RS-19.

4.2 Implementation Details

In order to make a reasonable comparison with previous FSLIC tasks, in this paper we use ResNet12 as our backbone, by which we use WideResNet [40] as a simple feature extractor, which is widely used in the FSLIC literature. The model generates feature maps of size $5 \times 5 \times 512$, i.e., 25–512 dimensional vectors. In this paper, we use feature pre-training and train the network using meta-learning. We will perform a 1-shot 5-way versus a 5-shot 5-way task on the selected dataset. We rotate the image by $0°, 90°, 180°, 270°$ ($0°$ is the image itself) to construct the rotation prediction task. The λ parameter is set to 0.5 for the DC layer.Select vector cosine distance metric as metric function.We use Adam as our optimizer. The initial learning rate is 0.001.

4.3 Analysis of Experimental Results and Comparison to the State-of-the-Art

We utilized DC-2DEC to obtain results on traditional few-shot datasets and remote sensing datasets, respectively in Table 1, Table 2, and Table 3.

Table 1. Results on **MiniImageNet** dataset

Method	Backbone	1-shot	5-shot
ProtoNet [7]	Resnet12	60.12 ± 0.77	77.46 ± 0.52
MatchNet [19]	Resnet12	62.29 ± 0.83	74.89 ± 0.58
TADAM [7]	Resnet12	57.42 ± 0.33	74.22 ± 0.28
MTL [36]	Resnet12	61.20 ± 1.80	75.50 ± 0.80
DC-2DEC (ours)	Resnet12	66.67 ± 0.84	83.85 ± 0.51

Table 2. Results on **NWPU-RESISC45** dataset

Method	Backbone	1-shot	5-shot
ProtoNet [7]	Resnet12	64.52 ± 0.48	81.95 ± 0.30
MatchNet [19]	Resnet12	61.57 ± 0.49	76.02 ± 0.34
RelationNet [37]	Conv-4-64	60.77 ± 0.47	76.08 ± 0.34
ProtoNet [1]	Conv-4-64	52.77 ± 0.44	75.32 ± 0.55
MAML [38]	Conv-4-64	48.62 ± 0.70	63.31 ± 0.52
DC-2DEC (ours)	Resnet12	72.89 ± 0.55	84.92 ± 0.47

Table 3. Results on **WHU-RS-19** dataset

Method	Backbone	1-shot	5-shot
MAML [38]	Conv-4-64	59.92 ± 0.35	82.30 ± 0.23
MetaSGD [39]	Conv-4-64	51.54 ± 2.31	61.74 ± 2.02
RelationNet [37]	Resnet12	70.02 ± 0.38	81.22 ± 0.36
DLA-MatchNet [33]	Resnet12	71.56 ± 0.30	83.77±0.64
DC-2DEC (ours)	Resnet12	79.82 ± 0.57	86.98 ± 0.21

We utilized DC-2DEC to obtain results on traditional few-shot datasets and remote sensing datasets, respectively in Table 1, Table 2, and Table 3. We compared DC-2DEC with popular network methods. Our results, particularly in the 1-shot 5-way tasks, outperformed the popular models. Additionally, we observed a performance gap between Conv-4-256 and ResNet12. In the NWPU-RESISC45 dataset, ProtoNet employed Conv-4-64 and ResNet12 as backbones, respectively. During the experiments, ResNet12 demonstrated better performance as a backbone. Based on the results from the three experimental tables, ResNet12 usually outperformed Conv-4-64 as a backbone, and its performance on remote sensing datasets significantly improved compared to few-shot datasets. Furthermore, we conducted experiments on the simple WHU-RS-19 dataset and found that the 1-shot task exhibited good performance. However, on the NWPU-RESISC45 dataset, which is larger and more complex, the network model's sensitivity was higher, resulting in relatively poorer performance in the 1-shot tasks. DC-

2DEC not only exhibited strong performance on remote sensing datasets but also achieved excellent results on traditional few-shot datasets, showcasing its robust generalization ability.

4.4 Ablation Study

To demonstrate the validity of the different components of the model proposed in this paper, we conducted ablation experiments to assess the influence that each module has on the overall approach.

Table 4. Results on Ablation Study

DC	Pretext Task	miniImageNet 1-shot	miniImageNet 5-shot	WHU-RS-19 1-shot	WHU-RS-19 5-shot
✓	✗	60.62 ± 0.56	80.82 ± 0.43	71.87 ± 0.32	79.92 ± 0.45
✗	✗	59.89 ± 0.19	76.19 ± 0.87	66.82 ± 0.47	75.90 ± 0.27
✗	✓	62.37 ± 0.22	79.66 ± 0.45	70.15 ± 0.31	82.33 ± 0.39
✓	✓	66.67 ± 0.84	83.85 ± 0.51	79.82 ± 0.57	86.98 ± 0.21

As can be seen from Table 4, in this paper, ablation experiments are done in two datasets, miniImageNet and WHU-RS-19, and we find that if the rotation prediction task is now added to the RS dataset the accuracy improves more in the RS dataset. The speculation is because the RS dataset has spatial rotation insensitivity compared to other natural optical images, and the orientation information of RS images is not clear, while the natural images have obvious orientation information, and different angles are different poses. Instead, the FSL classifier should consistently generate category probability distributions for the same RS image at various rotation angles. In addition, since the view content in diverse rotation angles of each RS image has essentially the same positive effect on the labels for semantic classification, the deep shared information between RS images is discriminative and plays an important role in querying the category and centre matching of samples. Scenes containing the same semantic content, i.e., the same category, in RS images differ due to factors such as background, illumination, and distribution differences. Furthermore, the dense presence of scenes from various categories may encompass similar objects, resulting in diminished inter-class discrimination differences. Due to the common occurrence of high intra-class variance and low inter-class discrimination in RS images, certain support set data tend to reside in the category-ambiguous region of the feature space (referred to as hard samples). This phenomenon can have a detrimental effect on the model's decision boundary and weaken its generalization capability. As a result, in order to make the model's discriminative power of the decision boundary more accurate, the use of a targeted rotation prediction task will effectively improve the performance of the scene classification task. And the results of the ablation experiments prove exactly that. As for the DC architecture, the performance of backbone algorithm with DC architecture is significantly improved, DC architecture can effectively calibrate the support set features by using the base class data features, and it is found that the performance of DC architecture in the 5-shot task is obvious in the experiments, and in the field of small samples, the DC architecture is easy to join other models to improve the performance. the addition of DC architecture does not make the model performance decline, which proves the effectiveness of the DC architecture. This proves the effectiveness of DC architecture. In conclusion, the whole architecture of DC-2DEC is reasonable and effective (Figs. 4, 5 and 6).

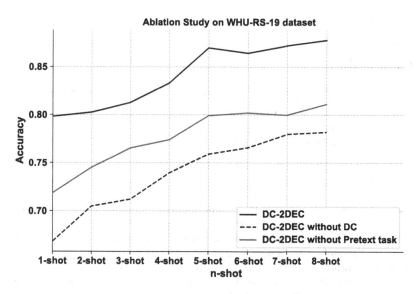

Fig. 4. This figure shows the changes of DC-2DEC in n-shot ablation experiments.

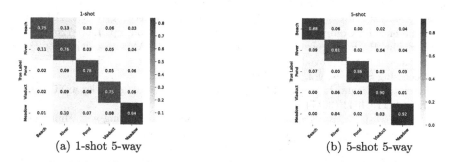

Fig. 5. Confusion matrix for DC-2DEC on the WHU-RS-19 dataset.

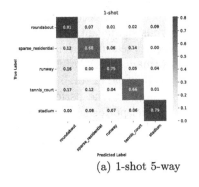
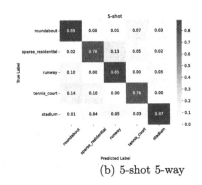

(a) 1-shot 5-way   (b) 5-shot 5-way

Fig. 6. Confusion matrix for DC-2DEC on the NWPU-RESISC45 dataset.

5   Conclusion

In this paper, we introduce a novel FSLIC model called DC-2DEC. Our model presents a unique and improved approach compared to existing FSL methods. Competitive results compared to popular network models are obtained on mini-ImageNet, NWPU-RESISC45, WHU-RS-19 datasets.

References

1. Snell, J., Swersky, K., Zemel, R.: Prototypical networks for few-shot learning. In: Advances in Neural Information Processing Systems, vol. 30 (2017)
2. Yuan, Q., et al.: Deep learning in environmental remote sensing: achievements and challenges. Remote Sens. Environ. **241**, 111716 (2020)
3. Chen, T., Kornblith, S., Norouzi, M., Hinton, G.: A simple framework for contrastive learning of visual representations. In: International Conference on Machine Learning, pp. 1597–1607. PMLR (2020)
4. Yang, S., Liu, L., Xu, M.: Free lunch for few-shot learning: distribution calibration. arXiv preprint arXiv:2101.06395 (2021)
5. Tukey, J.W., et al.: Exploratory Data Analysis, vol. 2. Reading (1977)
6. Li, W., Wang, L., Xu, J., Huo, J., Gao, Y., Luo, J.: Revisiting local descriptor based image-to-class measure for few-shot learning. In: Proceedings of the IEEE/CVF Conference on Computer Vision and Pattern Recognition, pp. 7260–7268 (2019)
7. Oreshkin, B., Rodríguez López, P., Lacoste, A.: TADAM: task dependent adaptive metric for improved few-shot learning. In: Advances in Neural Information Processing Systems, vol. 31 (2018)
8. Garcia, V., Bruna, J.: Few-shot learning with graph neural networks. arXiv preprint arXiv:1711.04043 (2017)
9. Lee, K., Maji, S., Ravichandran, A., Soatto, S.: Meta-learning with differentiable convex optimization. In: Proceedings of the IEEE/CVF Conference on Computer Vision and Pattern Recognition, pp. 10 657–10 665 (2019)
10. Chu, W.-H., Li, Y.-J., Chang, J.-C., Wang, Y.-C.F.: Spot and learn: a maximum-entropy patch sampler for few-shot image classification. In: Proceedings of the IEEE/CVF Conference on Computer Vision and Pattern Recognition, pp. 6251–6260 (2019)

11. Bartunov, S., Vetrov, D.: Few-shot generative modelling with generative matching networks. In: International Conference on Artificial Intelligence and Statistics, pp. 670–678. PMLR (2018)
12. Liu, W., Zhang, C., Lin, G., Liu, F.: CRNet: cross-reference networks for few-shot segmentation. In: Proceedings of the IEEE/CVF Conference on Computer Vision and Pattern Recognition, pp. 4165–4173 (2020)
13. Zhang, C., Lin, G., Liu, F., Guo, J., Wu, Q., Yao, R.: Pyramid graph networks with connection attentions for region-based one-shot semantic segmentation. In: Proceedings of the IEEE/CVF International Conference on Computer Vision, pp. 9587–9595 (2019)
14. Yang, Z., Wang, Y., Chen, X., Liu, J., Qiao, Y.: Context-transformer: tackling object confusion for few-shot detection. In: Proceedings of the AAAI Conference on Artificial Intelligence, vol. 34, no. 07, pp. 12 653–12 660 (2020)
15. Keshari, R., Vatsa, M., Singh, R., Noore, A.: Learning structure and strength of CNN filters for small sample size training. In: Proceedings of the IEEE Conference on Computer Vision and Pattern Recognition, pp. 9349–9358 (2018)
16. Krantz, S.G., Parks, H.R.: The Implicit Function Theorem: History, Theory, and Applications. Springer, Cham (2002). https://doi.org/10.1007/978-1-4612-0059-8
17. Munkhdalai, T., Yuan, X., Mehri, S., Trischler, A.: Rapid adaptation with conditionally shifted neurons. In: International Conference on Machine Learning, pp. 3664–3673. PMLR (2018)
18. Naik, D.K., Mammone, R.J.: Meta-neural networks that learn by learning. In: Proceedings 1992 IJCNN International Joint Conference on Neural Networks, vol. 1, pp. 437–442. IEEE (1992)
19. Vinyals, O., Blundell, C., Lillicrap, T., Wierstra D., et al.: Matching networks for one shot learning. In: Advances in Neural Information Processing Systems, vol. 29 (2016)
20. Goodfellow, I., et al.: Generative adversarial nets. In: Advances in Neural Information Processing Systems, vol. 27 (2014)
21. Rumelhart, D.E., Hinton, G.E., Williams, R.J.: Learning representations by back-propagating errors. Nature **323**(6088), 533–536 (1986)
22. Zhang, J., Zhao, C., Ni, B., Xu, M., Yang, X.: Variational few-shot learning. In: Proceedings of the IEEE/CVF International Conference on Computer Vision, pp. 1685–1694 (2019)
23. Qin, T., Li, W., Shi, Y., Gao, Y.: Diversity helps: unsupervised few-shot learning via distribution shift-based data augmentation. arXiv preprint arXiv:2004.05805 (2020)
24. Antoniou, A., Storkey, A.: Assume, augment and learn: unsupervised few-shot meta-learning via random labels and data augmentation. arXiv preprint arXiv:1902.09884 (2019)
25. Wang, Y.-X., Girshick, R., Hebert, M., Hariharan, B.: Low-shot learning from imaginary data. In: Proceedings of the IEEE Conference on Computer Vision and Pattern Recognition, pp. 7278–7286 (2018)
26. Hariharan, B., Girshick, R.: Low-shot visual recognition by shrinking and hallucinating features. In: Proceedings of the IEEE International Conference on Computer Vision, pp. 3018–3027 (2017)
27. Tian, Y., Krishnan, D., Isola, P.: Contrastive multiview coding. In: Vedaldi, A., Bischof, H., Brox, T., Frahm, J.-M. (eds.) ECCV 2020. LNCS, vol. 12356, pp. 776–794. Springer, Cham (2020). https://doi.org/10.1007/978-3-030-58621-8_45

28. Noroozi, M., Favaro, P.: Unsupervised learning of visual representations by solving jigsaw puzzles. In: Leibe, B., Matas, J., Sebe, N., Welling, M. (eds.) ECCV 2016. LNCS, vol. 9910, pp. 69–84. Springer, Cham (2016). https://doi.org/10.1007/978-3-319-46466-4_5

29. Gidaris, S., Singh, P., Komodakis, N.: Unsupervised representation learning by predicting image rotations. arXiv preprint arXiv:1803.07728 (2018)

30. Wang, X., Gupta, A.: Unsupervised learning of visual representations using videos. In: Proceedings of the IEEE International Conference on Computer Vision, pp. 2794–2802 (2015)

31. Cheng, G., et al.: SPNet: siamese-prototype network for few-shot remote sensing image scene classification. IEEE Trans. Geosci. Remote Sens. **60**, 1–11 (2021)

32. Zhang, P., Bai, Y., Wang, D., Bai, B., Li, Y.: Few-shot classification of aerial scene images via meta-learning. Remote Sens. **13**(1), 108 (2020)

33. Li, L., Han, J., Yao, X., Cheng, G., Guo, L.: DLA-MatchNet for few-shot remote sensing image scene classification. IEEE Trans. Geosci. Remote Sens. **59**(9), 7844–7853 (2020)

34. Liu, B., Yu, X., Yu, A., Zhang, P., Wan, G., Wang, R.: Deep few-shot learning for hyperspectral image classification. IEEE Trans. Geosci. Remote Sens. **57**(4), 2290–2304 (2018)

35. Deng, W., Gould, S., Zheng, L.: What does rotation prediction tell us about classifier accuracy under varying testing environments? In: International Conference on Machine Learning, pp. 2579–2589. PMLR (2021)

36. Sun, Q., Liu, Y., Chua, T.-S., Schiele, B.: Meta-transfer learning for few-shot learning. In: Proceedings of the IEEE/CVF Conference on Computer Vision and Pattern Recognition, pp. 403–412 (2019)

37. Sung, F., Yang, Y., Zhang, L., Xiang, T., Torr, P.H., Hospedales, T.M.: Learning to compare: relation network for few-shot learning. In: Proceedings of the IEEE Conference on Computer Vision and Pattern Recognition, pp. 1199–1208 (2018)

38. Finn, C., Abbeel, P., Levine, S.: Model-agnostic meta-learning for fast adaptation of deep networks. In: International Conference on Machine Learning, pp. 1126–1135. PMLR (2017)

39. LiZ., Z., Zhou, F., Chen, F., Li, H.: Meta-SGD: learning to learn quickly for few-shot learning. arXiv preprint arXiv:1707.09835 (2017)

40. Zagoruyko, S., Komodakis, N.: Wide residual networks. arXiv preprint arXiv:1605.07146 (2016)

41. Ji, H., Gao, Z., Zhang, Y., Wan, Y., Li, C., Mei, T.: Few-shot scene classification of optical remote sensing images leveraging calibrated pretext tasks. IEEE Trans. Geosci. Remote Sens. **60**, 1–13 (2022)

Applications of Spatiotemporal Data Mining

Neural HD Map Generation
from Multiple Vectorized Tiles Locally
Produced by Autonomous Vehicles

Miao Fan[✉], Yi Yao, Jianping Zhang, Xiangbo Song, and Daihui Wu

NavInfo Co., Ltd., Beijing 100094, China
miao.fan@ieee.org
https://en.navinfo.com/

Abstract. High-definition (HD) map is a fundamental component of autonomous driving systems, as it can provide precise environmental information about driving scenes. Recent work on vectorized map generation could produce merely 65% local map elements around the ego-vehicle at runtime by one tour with onboard sensors, leaving a puzzle of how to construct a global HD map projected in the world coordinate system under high-quality standards. To address the issue, we present **GNMap** as an end-to-end generative neural network to automatically construct HD maps with multiple vectorized tiles which are locally produced by autonomous vehicles through several tours. It leverages a multi-layer and attention-based autoencoder as the shared network, of which parameters are learned from two different tasks (i.e., pretraining and fine-tuning, respectively) to ensure both the completeness of generated maps and the correctness of element categories. Abundant qualitative evaluations are conducted on a real-world dataset and experimental results show that GNMap can surpass the SOTA method by more than 5% F1 score, reaching the level of industrial usage with a small amount of manual modification. We have already deployed it at Navinfo Co., Ltd., serving as an indispensable software to automatically build HD maps for autonomous driving systems.

Keywords: HD map · Autonomous driving · Vectorized tile · Multiple tours

1 Introduction

High-definition (HD) map [7] plays a pivotal role in autonomous driving [4,11]. Illustrated by Fig. 1, it provides high-precision vectorized elements (including pedestrian crossings, lane dividers, road boundaries, etc.) about road topologies and traffic rules, which are quite essential for the navigation of self-driving

This work is supported by the National Natural Science Foundation of China under Grant No. U22A20104. For more details about our recent studies, please visit corresponding author's website: https://godfanmiao.github.io/homepage-en/.

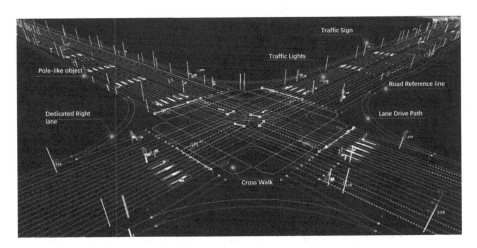

Fig. 1. Illustration of a snapshot of vectorized HD map. It is composed of static map elements, such as pedestrian crossings, lane dividers, road boundaries, etc., which are geometrically discretized into polylines or polygons.

vehicles. Vectorized map elements are geometrically discretized into polylines or polygons, and conventionally produced offline by SLAM-based methods [17,20] with heavy reliance on human labor of annotation, facing both scalability and up-to-date issues.

To address the issues, recent studies [6,9,10,12,14,18] focus on developing online approaches for vectorized map construction. These methods aim at devising vehicle-mounted models that learn to generate local elements around the ego-vehicle at runtime with onboard sensors such as LiDARs [16] and cameras. Learning-based approaches have drawn ever-increasing attention as they can alleviate human efforts to some extent. However, even the SOTA methods [6,10] among them could merely produce 65% vehicle-around map elements by one tour, leaving a puzzle of how to construct a global HD map projected in the world coordinate system under high-quality standards.

As the first attempt to solve the puzzle, we present **GNMap** in this paper. It is an end-to-end generative neural network which takes vehicle-produced vectorized tiles through multiple tours as inputs and automatically generates a globalized HD map under the world coordinates as the output. Specifically, GNMap adopts a multi-layer and attention-based autoencoder as the shared network, of which parameters are learned from two different tasks (i.e., pretraining and finetuning, respectively). At pretraining phase, the shared autoencoder is responsible for completing the masked vectorized tiles. The pretrained parameters are further leveraged as the initial weights for finetuning, which aims at assigning each pixel of map elements to the correct category. In this way, we ensure both the completeness of generated maps and the correctness of element categories.

Additionally, we build a real-world dataset to conduct qualitative assessments offline. Each instance of the data belongs to a vectorized tile mainly composed of three kinds of map elements, i.e., pedestrian crossings, lane dividers, and road boundaries. Besides that, a tile is passed through multiple tours by autonomous vehicles with a street view for each tour. Ablation studies demonstrate that it is vital to conduct pretraining on GNMap for the sake of achieving the best performance. Experimental results of abundant evaluations also show that it can surpass the SOTA method by more than 5% F1 score. So far, GNMap has already been deployed at Navinfo Co., Ltd. for industrial usage, serving as an indispensable software to automatically build HD maps of Mainland China for autonomous driving.

2 Related Work

2.1 SLAM-Based Methods (Offline)

HD maps are conventionally annotated manually on LiDAR point clouds of the environment. These point clouds are collected from LiDAR scans of survey vehicles with GPS [8] and IMU [3]. In order to fuse LiDAR scans into an accurate and consistent point cloud, SLAM methods [17,20] are mostly used, and they generally adopt a decoupled pipeline as follows. Pairwise alignment algorithms like ICP [1] and NDT [2] are firstly employed to match LiDAR data between two nearby timestamps. And for the purpose of constructing a globally consistent map, it is critical to estimate the accurate pose of ego-vehicle by GTSAM [5]. Although several machine learning methods [13] are further devised to extract static map elements such as pedestrian crossings, lane dividers and road boundaries from fused LiDAR point clouds, it is still laborious and costly to maintain a scalable HD map since it requires timely update for autonomous driving.

2.2 Learning-Based Approaches (Online)

To get rid of offline human efforts, learning-based HD map construction has attracted ever-increasing interests. These approaches [6,9,10,12,14,18] propose to build local maps at runtime based on surround-view images captured by vehicle-mounted cameras. Specifically, HDMapNet [9] first produces semantic map and then groups pixel-wise semantic segmentation results in the post-processing. VectorMapNet [12] adopts a two-stage coarse-to-fine framework and utilizes auto-regressive decoder to predict points sequentially, leading to long inference time and the ambiguity about permutation. To alleviate the problem, BeMapNet [14] adopts a unified piece-wise Bezier curve to describe the geometrical shape of map elements. InstaGraM [18] proposes a novel graph modeling for vectorized polylines of map elements that models geometric, semantic and instance-level information as graph representations. MapTR [10] uses a fixed number of points to represent a map element, regardless of its shape complexity. PivotNet [6] models map elements through pivot-based representation in a set prediction framework. However, even the SOTA methods among them could merely produce 65% vehicle-around map elements by one tour, leaving a puzzle of how to build a global HD map projected under the world coordinates.

3   Model

3.1   Problem Formulation

The objective of GNMap is to generate a globalized HD map under the world coordinates from several vehicle-produced tiles. The vehicle-produced tiles are represented by RGB images, and we use $\mathcal{X}$ to denote the set of the images as inputs. As shown by Eq. 1, GNMap is formulated as $\mathcal{F}(\mathcal{X};\Theta)$ which learns to fuse the images $\mathcal{X}$ and to generate a globalized HD map as the output denoted by $\mathcal{Y}$:

$$\mathcal{Y} = \mathcal{F}(\mathcal{X};\Theta), \tag{1}$$

where Θ represents the set of best parameters that GNMap needs to explore.

3.2   Shared Autoencoder

To realize $\mathcal{F}(\Theta)$, we devise an autoencoder that is structured into two parts: a neural encoder $E(\mathcal{X};\theta_e)$ and a neural decoder $D(\mathcal{Z};\theta_d)$. The relationship between the encoder and the decoder is shown by Eq. 2 and Eq. 3:

$$\mathcal{Z} = E(\mathcal{X};\theta_e) \tag{2}$$

and

$$\mathcal{Y} = D(\mathcal{Z};\theta_d), \tag{3}$$

where $E(\mathcal{X};\theta_e)$ takes $\mathcal{X}$ as inputs to produce the intermediate feature representation $\mathcal{Z}$ by means of the parameters θ_e of encoder, and $D(\mathcal{Z};\theta_d)$ takes intermediate feature $\mathcal{Z}$ as the input to generate the output $\mathcal{Y}$ by means of the parameters θ_d of decoder. Both θ_e and θ_d belong to Θ:

$$\Theta = (\theta_e, \theta_d). \tag{4}$$

Illustrated by Fig. 2, both the encoder $E(\mathcal{X};\theta_e)$ and the decoder $D(\mathcal{Z};\theta_d)$ are multi-layer networks mainly composed of multi-head self-attention functions. We will elaborate on them in the following paragraphs.

Encoder: $E(\mathcal{X};\theta_e)$ is composed of M layer neural blocks with the same structure. Each block includes a multi-head self-attention (MSA [19]), a multi-layer perceptron (MLP), and a layer normalization (LN) module. Here we use U_i to denote the intermediate output of the block at the i-th layer of encoder, and U_i is calculated by Eq. 5 and Eq. 6:

$$U_i' = MSA\left(U_{i-1}\right) + U_{i-1}, \quad i \in \{1, 2, ..., M\} \tag{5}$$

and

$$U_i = LN\left(MLP\left(U_i'\right) + U_i'\right), \quad i \in \{1, 2, ..., M\}, \tag{6}$$

where $\mathcal{X} = U_0$ and $\mathcal{Z} = U_M$.

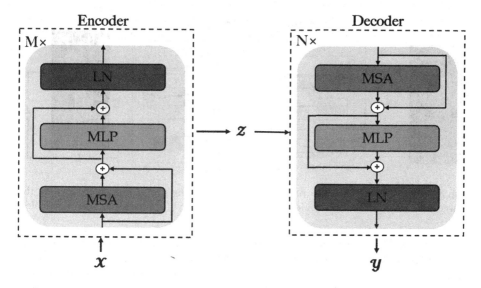

Fig. 2. The architecture of shared autoencoder employed by GNMap. It is a multi-layer generative neural network mainly composed of multi-head self-attention functions.

Decoder: $D(\mathcal{Z}; \theta_d)$ has N stacked blocks with the same structure. Each block is composed of includes a multi-head self-attention (MSA [19]), a multi-layer perceptron (MLP), and a layer normalization (LN) function as well. If we use V_j to denote the intermediate output of the block at the j-th layer of decoder, V_j is calculated by Eq. 7 and Eq. 8:

$$V_j^{'} = MSA\left(V_{j-1}\right) + V_{j-1}, \quad j \in \{1, 2, ..., N\} \tag{7}$$

and

$$V_j = LN\left(MLP\left(V_j^{'}\right) + V_j^{'}\right), \quad j \in \{1, 2, ..., N\}, \tag{8}$$

where $\mathcal{Z} = V_0$ and $\mathcal{Y} = V_N$.

In order to obtain the best parameters of both θ_e and θ_e, we propose to adopt the "pretraining & finetuning" manner which divides the training procedure into two phases, corresponding to different tasks and learning objectives. Details about the two phases will be elaborated by Sect. 3.3 and Sect. 3.4.

3.3 Pretraining Phase

At the pretraining phase, the learning objective of the shared autoencoder is to complete masked vectorized tiles, and the pretrained parameters are further leveraged as the initial weights for finetuning. Illustrated by Fig. 3, we will elaborate pretraining phase from the perspectives of input, output, ground truth, and loss function in the following paragraphs.

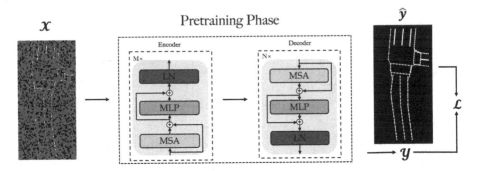

Fig. 3. Illustration of the data processing pipeline at the pretraining phase, where the shared autoencoder is responsible for completing masked (gray-scaled) vectorized tiles.

Input: We split the manually annotated HD maps into multiple vectorized tiles. Each of the vectorized tiles can be transferred into a gray-scaled image denoted by $\mathcal{X} \in \mathbb{R}^{h \times w \times 1}$, where h and w represent the height and the width of the image respectively. In $\mathcal{X}$, each pixel of any may elements is set to 255 and the background's pixel is set to 0. Then the image is divided into non-overlapping patches with the shape of $k \times l$. As a result, $\frac{h \times w}{k \times l}$ patches (each $p \in \mathbb{R}^{k \times l}$) can be obtained. We sample a subset of patches and mask (i.e., remove) the remaining ones. Our strategy is straightforward: sampling random patches without replacement, following a uniform distribution with a high masking ratio (i.e., the ratio of removed patches). In this way, we have created a task that cannot be easily solved by extrapolation from visible neighboring patches.

Output: We expect to obtain a completed gray-scale tile as the output through the shared autoencoder which takes the masked patches as inputs. The completed image is denoted by $\mathcal{Y} \in \mathbb{R}^{h \times w \times 1}$, where h and w represent the height and the width of the completed image, respectively. The value of each predicted pixel y_i where $i \in \{1, 2, ..., h \times w\}$ ranges from 0.0 to 1.0 since it is scaled by the softmax function.

Ground Truth: Correspondingly, the ground-truth image is the unsliced one (i.e., $\mathcal{X}$) used as the input. We denoted it by $\hat{y} \in \mathbb{R}^{h \times w \times 1}$ since each pixel of $\hat{y}$ is set by either 0 or 1 to indicate whether it belongs to the background or vectorized map elements.

Loss Function: We employ the mean squared error (MSE) as the loss function (denoted by $\mathcal{L}$) for pretraining.

$$\mathcal{L} = \frac{1}{h \times w} \sum_{i=1}^{h \times w} (y_i - \hat{y}_i)^2. \tag{9}$$

As shown by Eq. 9, it measures the overall difference between $\mathcal{Y}$ and $\hat{\mathcal{Y}}$, by calculating the squared errors between the predicted pixels and the ground-truth pixels at the same coordinates.

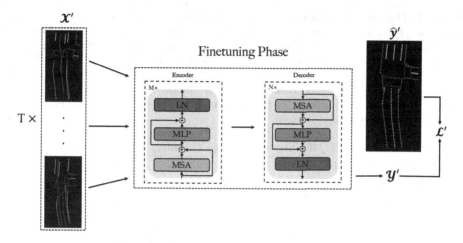

Fig. 4. Illustration of the data processing pipeline at finetuning phase, where the pretrained parameters are leveraged as initial weights of the shared autoencoder. It aims at assigning each pixel of map elements to the correct category.

3.4 Finetuning Phase

At finetuning phase, the learning objective of the shared autoencoder changes to assigning each pixel of the elements of the generated map to the correct category, leveraging the pretrained parameters as initial weights. Illustrated by Fig. 4, we will elaborate finetuning phase from the perspectives of input, output, ground truth, and loss function in the following paragraphs.

Input: In this work, a tile is passed through T times of tours by autonomous vehicles with a street view for each tour. The original street views collected by the cameras mounted on survey vehicles are usually RGB images and learning-based approaches [6,9,10,12,14,18] generally transfer them into vectorized images where each pixel belongs to a certain category such as the background or land divider, etc. As a matter of fact, we can obtain T images at the beginning of the finetuning phase. We use a shared CNN network to fetch the features from the T images and concatenate them together as the input of the shared autoencoder.

Output: We expect to achieve a fused tile from GNMap as the output at the finetuning phase. The generated image is denoted by $\mathcal{Y} \in \mathbb{R}^{h \times w \times c}$, where h and w represent the height and the width of the image, respectively, and c stands for the kinds of map elements. Each predicted pixel $\mathbf{y}_i$ is represented by a c-dimensional vector where the value at each dimension ranges from 0.0 to 1.0 to indicate the probability of the predicted category and the sum of all these values is 1.0.

Ground Truth: Correspondingly, the ground-truth image is denoted by $\hat{\mathcal{Y}} \in \mathbb{R}^{h \times w \times c}$. In addition, each pixel of $\hat{\mathcal{Y}}$ is denoted by a c-dimensional vector where only one of the values is set by 1.0 exclusively indicating that the pixel belongs to a certain category such as the background, pedestrian crossing, or etc.

Table 1. The statistics of a real-world dataset for the offline assessment of HD map generation from multiple vectorized tiles locally produced by autonomous vehicles in Mainland China. The subsets are separately leveraged for the purpose of model training (abbr. *Train*), hyper-parameter tuning (abbr. *Valid*), and performance testing (abbr. *Test*). Each instance of data belongs to a vectorized *tile* which is mainly composed of several *map elements* (such as pedestrian crossings, lane dividers and road boundaries). Besides that, autonomous vehicles passed through a tile multiple times (*tours*) and collected a *street view* for each tour.

Subset	#(Tiles)	#(Map Elements)	Avg. #(Tours)/Tile	#(Street Views)
Train	40,000	162,493	5.2	208,207
Valid	5,000	19,928	5.0	24,982
Test	5,000	20,061	5.1	25,564

Loss Function: We employ the cross-entropy (CE) function as the loss (denoted by $\mathcal{L}'$) of the finetuning phase.

$$\mathcal{L}' = -\frac{1}{h \times w} \sum_{i=1}^{h \times w} \hat{\mathbf{y}}'_i \cdot \log\left(\mathbf{y}'_i\right). \tag{10}$$

As shown by Eq. 10, it measures the divergence between $\mathcal{Y}$ and $\hat{\mathcal{Y}}$, by summing up the log-likelihood at ground-truth pixels.

4   Experiments

4.1   Dataset and Metrics

In order to conduct an offline assessment on methods of HD map generation, we build a real-world dataset that contains street views and vectorized tiles produced by autonomous vehicles through multiple tours. We randomly split the dataset into three subsets. As shown by Table 1, they are separately leveraged for the purpose of model training (abbr. *Train*), hyper-parameter tuning (abbr. *Valid*), and performance testing (abbr. *Test*). Each subset is composed of many exclusive tiles, each of which is passed through multiple *tours* by autonomous vehicles. For each tour, a *street view* is collected and a vectorized tile is produced simultaneously online by vehicle-mounted models. Following up previous work, we mainly focus on three kinds of map elements, including pedestrian crossings (abbr. as ped.), lane dividers (abbr. as div.), and road boundaries (abbr. as bou.).

For each generated tile, we use precision (P) and recall (R) to evaluate the quality of HD map reconstruction at the pixel level in one instance. Illustrated by Fig. 5, a predicted point is accepted as the positive pixel when it is located near a ground-truth (GT) point within the Euclidean distance of 0.5 m and they must belong to the same category as well. More importantly, a GT point can only accept one nearest predicted point for evaluation. Assuming that the test

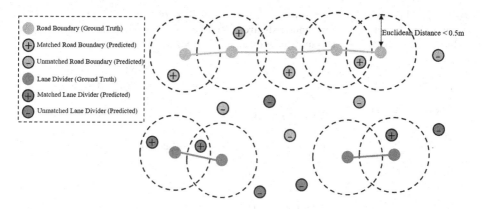

Fig. 5. An example on how to calculate *Precision* (abbr. as *P*) and *Recall* (abbr. as *R*). In this case, we have three map elements (two lane dividers and a road boundary). For lane dividers (colored by green), there are 7 predicted points/pixels and 4 ground-truth points/pixels. 3 of 7 are accepted as they locate within 0.5 m of the ground-truth pixels. Therefore, $P_{div.} = 3/7$ and $R_{div.} = 3/4$. For the road boundary (colored by yellow), there are 8 predicted points/pixels and 5 ground-truth points/pixels. 4 of 8 are accepted as they locate within 0.5 m of the ground-truth pixels. Therefore, $P_{bou.} = 4/8$ and $R_{bou.} = 4/5$. (Color figure online)

set contains n instances, average precision (AP) and average recall (AR) are formulated by Eq. 11 and Eq. 12 as follows,

$$AP = \frac{1}{n} \sum P \tag{11}$$

and

$$AR = \frac{1}{n} \sum R \tag{12}$$

Then mAP and mAR represent the mean average precision and recall over all categories (i.e., pedestrian crossing, lane divider, and road boundary), which are shown by Eq. 13 and Eq. 14.

$$mAP = \frac{AP_{ped.} + AP_{div.} + AP_{bou.}}{3} \tag{13}$$

$$mAR = \frac{AR_{ped.} + AR_{div.} + AR_{bou.}}{3} \tag{14}$$

To measure the overall performance of approaches on HD map generation, we adopt F1 score, as shown by Eq. 15, which calculates the harmonic mean of mAP and mAR.

$$F1 = \frac{2 \times mAP \times mAR}{mAP + mAR} \tag{15}$$

Table 2. The experimental results of the offline evaluations on different methods for HD map construction. All the methods are tested by the real-world dataset shown by Table 1 and measured by the metrics mentioned in Sect. 4.1

Method	mAP			mAR			F1
	$AP_{ped.}$	$AP_{div.}$	$AP_{bou.}$	$AR_{ped.}$	$AR_{div.}$	$AR_{bou.}$	
HDMapNet [9]	45.3			44.1			44.7
	42.8	47.9	45.1	41.3	47.5	43.6	
VectorMapNet [12]	62.9			61.5			62.2
	60.4	65.3	63.1	59.2	61.8	63.4	
InstaGraM [18]	53.6			62.4			57.7
	51.9	54.2	54.8	59.8	62.3	65.1	
BeMapNet [14]	62.3			66.1			64.1
	60.5	61.6	64.9	62.8	70.3	65.1	
MapTR [10]	64.5			73.2			68.6
	62.8	65.2	65.5	71.3	73.4	74.9	
PivotNet [6]	64.8			72.4			68.4
	63.1	66.5	64.8	70.3	72.8	74.1	
GMM [15]	63.4			63.2			63.3
	61.4	64.7	64.0	59.8	67.6	62.3	
GNMap (Ours)	72.5			75.6			74.0
	70.5	74.8	72.3	75.4	78.1	73.3	

4.2   Comparison Details

We mainly compare GNMap with two groups of approaches. One group contains vehicle-mounted models (including HDMapNet [9], VectorMapNet [12], InstaGraM [18], BeMapNet [14], MapTR [10], and PivotNet [6]) which infer vectorized tiles online from real-time street views captured by onsite cameras. The other group represents approaches (i.e., GMM [15] and our GNMap) on fusing the vehicle-produced tiles to construct a global HD map. Table 2 reports the experimental results of these two groups of methods for HD map construction. All the approaches are tested by the real-world dataset shown in Table 1 and measured by the metrics mentioned in Sect. 4.1. Based on our results, MapTR and PivotNet achieve comparable performance of online map learning through only one tour. Our GNMap outperforms GMM over 10.0% F1 score. Even compared with the existing SOTA method of online map learning, GNMap achieves over 5.0% higher F1, demonstrating advanced performance on HD map construction.

4.3   Ablation Study

We report ablation experiments in Table 3, to validate the effectiveness of employing the pretraining phase, and the robustness of using different vehicle-mounted models. We select MapTR [10] and PivotNet [6], as the SOTA one-tour vehicle-mounted models, to produce vectorized tiles for GMM [15] and our GNMap. Experimental results demonstrate that GNMap achieves consistent improvements over GMM regardless of the vehicle-mounted models. Moreover,

Table 3. Ablation about whether or not to conduct the pretraining phase and to adopt different onsite models that produce vectorized tiles locally.

Method	mAP $AP_{ped.}$ | $AP_{div.}$ | $AP_{bou.}$	mAR $AR_{ped.}$ | $AR_{div.}$ | $AR_{bou.}$	F1
GMM (MapTR)	62.5 61.8 | 63.2 | 62.5	66.5 65.4 | 67.3 | 66.9	64.5
GNMap (MapTR) w/o Pre.	64.2 64.3 | 63.6 | 64.8	67.3 66.3 | 67.4 | 68.3	65.7
GNMap (MapTR) w/ Pre.	72.7 70.8 | 74.8 | 72.5	75.6 73.3 | 78.1 | 75.4	74.1
GMM (PivotNet)	61.7 60.9 | 61.5 | 62.7	65.6 64.7 | 66.6 | 65.4	63.6
GNMap (PivotNet) w/o Pre.	63.8 62.8 | 63.7 | 64.9	66.5 65.2 | 66.3 | 67.9	65.1
GNMap (PivotNet) w/ Pre.	72.6 72.8 | 73.1 | 71.9	75.5 74.2 | 77.3 | 75.1	74.0

the pretrained GNMap can provide at least 8.0% higher F1 score than those without pretraining.

5 Conclusion

In this paper, we present GNMap as an end-to-end generative framework for HD map construction, which is distinguished from recent studies on producing vectorized tiles locally by autonomous vehicles with onboard sensors such as LiDARs and cameras. GNMap is an essential research to follow up those studies, as it first attempts to fuse multiple vehicle-produced tiles to automatically build a globalized HD map under the world coordinates. To be specific, it adopts a multi-layer autoencoder purely composed of multi-head self-attentions as the shared network, where the parameters are learned from two different tasks (i.e., pretraining and finetuning, respectively) to ensure both the completeness of map generation and the correctness of element categories. Ablation studies demonstrate that it is vital to conduct pretraining on GNMap for the sake of achieving the best performance for industrial usage. And experimental results of abundant evaluations on a real-world dataset show that GNMap can surpass the SOTA method by more than 5% F1 score. So far, it has already been deployed at Navinfo Co., Ltd., serving as an indispensable software to automatically build HD maps of Mainland China for autonomous driving.

References

1. Besl, P., McKay, N.D.: A method for registration of 3D shapes. IEEE Trans. Pattern Anal. Mach. Intell. **14**(2), 239–256 (1992)
2. Biber, P., Straßer, W.: The normal distributions transform: a new approach to laser scan matching. In: Proceedings 2003 IEEE/RSJ International Conference on Intelligent Robots and Systems, vol. 3, pp. 2743–2748 (2003)

3. Borodacz, K., Szczepański, C., Popowski, S.: Review and selection of commercially available IMU for a short time inertial navigation. Aircr. Eng. Aerosp. Technol. **94**, 45–59 (2021)
4. Boubakri, A., Gammar, S.M., Brahim, M.B., Filali, F.: High definition map update for autonomous and connected vehicles: a survey. In: 2022 International Wireless Communications and Mobile Computing (IWCMC), pp. 1148–1153 (2022)
5. Dellaert, F., Kaess, M.: Factor graphs for robot perception. Found. Trends Robot. **6** (2017)
6. Ding, W., Qiao, L., Qiu, X., Zhang, C.: PivotNet: vectorized pivot learning for end-to-end HD map construction. In: Proceedings of the IEEE/CVF International Conference on Computer Vision, pp. 3672–3682 (2023)
7. Elghazaly, G., Frank, R., Harvey, S., Safko, S.: High-definition maps: comprehensive survey, challenges, and future perspectives. IEEE Open J. Intell. Transp. Syst. **4**, 527–550 (2023)
8. Kaplan, E.D.: Understanding GPS: principles and applications (1996)
9. Li, Q., Wang, Y., Wang, Y., Zhao, H.: HDMapNet: An online HD map construction and evaluation framework. In: 2022 International Conference on Robotics and Automation (ICRA), pp. 4628–4634. IEEE (2022)
10. Liao, B., Chen, S., Wang, X., Cheng, T., Zhang, Q., Liu, W., Huang, C.: MapTR: structured modeling and learning for online vectorized HD map construction. In: The Eleventh International Conference on Learning Representations (2023)
11. Liu, R., Wang, J., Zhang, B.: High definition map for automated driving: overview and analysis. J. Navig. **73**, 324–341 (2020)
12. Liu, Y., Yuan, T., Wang, Y., Wang, Y., Zhao, H.: VectorMapNet: end-to-end vectorized HD map learning. In: International Conference on Machine Learning, pp. 22352–22369. PMLR (2023)
13. Mi, L., et al.: HDMapGen: a hierarchical graph generative model of high definition maps. In: 2021 IEEE/CVF Conference on Computer Vision and Pattern Recognition (CVPR), pp. 4225–4234 (2021)
14. Qiao, L., Ding, W., Qiu, X., Zhang, C.: End-to-end vectorized HD-map construction with piecewise Bezier curve. In: Proceedings of the IEEE/CVF Conference on Computer Vision and Pattern Recognition, pp. 13218–13228 (2023)
15. Reynolds, D.A., et al.: Gaussian mixture models. Encycl. Biomet. **741**(659-663) (2009)
16. Roriz, R., Cabral, J., Gomes, T.: Automotive lidar technology: a survey. IEEE Trans. Intell. Transp. Syst. **23**, 6282–6297 (2021)
17. Shan, T., Englot, B., Meyers, D., Wang, W., Ratti, C., Rus, D.: LIO-SAM: tightly-coupled lidar inertial odometry via smoothing and mapping. In: 2020 IEEE/RSJ International Conference on Intelligent Robots and Systems (IROS), pp. 5135–5142 (2020)
18. Shin, J., Rameau, F., Jeong, H., Kum, D.: Instagram: instance-level graph modeling for vectorized HD map learning. arXiv preprint arXiv:2301.04470 (2023)
19. Voita, E., Talbot, D., Moiseev, F., Sennrich, R., Titov, I.: Analyzing multi-head self-attention: specialized heads do the heavy lifting, the rest can be pruned. In: Korhonen, A., Traum, D., Màrquez, L. (eds.) Proceedings of the 57th Annual Meeting of the Association for Computational Linguistics, pp. 5797–5808. Association for Computational Linguistics, Florence (2019)
20. Zhang, J., Singh, S.: LOAM: Lidar odometry and mapping in real-time. In: Robotics: Science and Systems (2014)

Trajectory Data Semi-fragile Watermarking Algorithm Considering Spatiotemporal Features

Yuchen Hu[1,2,3], Changqing Zhu[1,2,3(✉)], Na Ren[1,2,3], and Jinjie Gu[1,2,3]

[1] Key Laboratory of Virtual Geographic Environment, Ministry of Education, Nanjing Normal University, Nanjing, China
zcq88@263.net
[2] State Key Laboratory Cultivation Base of Geographical Environment Evolution (Jiangsu Province), Nanjing, China
[3] Jiangsu Center for Collaborative Innovation in Geographical Information Resource Development and Application, Nanjing, China

Abstract. The high privacy and accuracy of trajectory data make data integrity and security critical. However, existing algorithms cannot ensure the integrity of temporal attributes and resist common operations in the normal use of data, which limits the use of data. For this reason, this paper proposes a semi-fragile water-marking algorithm for trajectory data that takes into account spatiotemporal features. The proposed algorithm utilizes the minimum area bounded rectangle (MABR) to group the trajectory data. Finally, the fragile watermarks generated from spatial and temporal attributes are embedded into an embedded domain with geometric invariance in stages using the multiple quantization index modulation (MQIM) technique. Experimental results show that the proposed algorithm is extremely robust to geometric attacks. Meanwhile, it can accurately identify whether the temporal and spatial attributes have been tampered with and the type of tampering. The proposed algorithm balances robustness and tampering detection capability, providing a feasible solution for the security protection of trajectory data.

Keywords: Trajectory Data · Integrity of Spatiotemporal Features · Semi-fragile Watermark · Multiple Quantization Index Modulation · Tampering Detection

1 Introduction

The trajectory data consists of a series of consecutive coordinates, time, and other related information, which is widely used in transportation, urban planning, environment, and other fields due to its rich spatiotemporal characteristics [1, 2]. The high privacy and high-precision characteristics of trajectory data determine the importance of its data security [3]. With the broadening of the usage scenarios, data owners and users gradually pay more attention to the integrity of the content of trajectory data. It is crucial to ensure the integrity of trajectory data during transmission, storage, and processing for the data to be trustworthy and useful [4].

X. Meng et al. (Eds.): SpatialDI 2024, LNCS 14619, pp. 319–332, 2024.
https://doi.org/10.1007/978-981-97-2966-1_23

The fragile watermark is a type of digital watermarking technology, which embeds the identification code of data or information generated by data features into the data to prevent data tampering [5]. It can identify data that has been tampered with, so it plays an important role in data integrity authentication. Existing fragile watermarking techniques can be categorized into two types: fully fragile watermarking and semi-fragile watermarking.

Fully fragile watermarking means that small changes to watermark-containing data can produce extremely sensitive reactions. Works [6] group linear entities based on vector graphics and embed fragile watermarks within these groups for data integrity protection. Works [7] group vector maps and embed localization bits by simulated annealing algorithm. Further, literature [8] uses optimized k-mean clustering for grouping to achieve more stable tampering localization. The mentioned algorithm achieves integrity authentication of trajectory data and localization of tampering but does not allow any manipulation of the trajectory data, which contradicts the background of the extensive use of trajectory data.

Semi-fragile watermarking allows data to perform certain permitted operations but remains vulnerable to other operations. Semi-fragile watermarking is more robust and has more usage scenarios than fully fragile watermarking. Works [9] embeds the watermark in the middle-frequency region of the DCT coefficients, which can resist common geometric attacks (translation, rotation, and scaling). Literature [10] uses the Douglas Peucker algorithm to extract feature points, and then embed the watermark generated from the point coordinates into the feature points, which enhances robustness to compression attacks. Semi-fragile watermarks legalize some operations, and these legal operations can not destroy the integrity of the data. However, the above algorithms only use spatial features to construct fragile watermarks.

In summary, the fully fragile watermarking of trajectory data has a good performance in terms of accurate authentication of data, but it does not allow some common operations on the data, which restricts the use of the data. The semi-fragile watermark increases resistance to common operations based on the fully fragile watermark, achieving partial legitimacy of certain operations. However, all existing semi-fragile watermarks focus only on the spatial features of trajectory data, ignoring the importance of temporal characteristics, and cannot ensure the integrity of the temporal attributes of the data.

To solve the mentioned problems, this paper proposes a semi-fragile watermarking algorithm that takes into account spatiotemporal features. The proposed algorithm utilizes distance ratio to construct the embedding domain against geometric attacks, and groups trajectory points based on the Minimum area bounded rectangle (MABR) of the points. Then, the fragile watermarks generated by trajectory data spatial and temporal information are embedded separately into distance ratios using multiple quantization index modulation (MQIM). The proposed algorithm takes into account both data integrity authentication and algorithm robustness. The paper is organized as follows: Sect. 2 describes the idea of the proposed algorithm, Sect. 3 gives the algorithm and implementation, Sect. 4 gives the experimental results and analysis of the paper and Sect. 5 concludes.

2 Basic Idea and Preliminaries

2.1 Basic Idea

The core of the semi-fragile watermarking technique proposed in this study is to maintain the integrity of spatiotemporal attributes of trajectory data while allowing common operations on trajectory data. The paper proposes watermark embedding based on the geometric domain, which enhances resistance against geometric attacks. At the same time, we also ensure the stability of semi-fragile watermark tampering localization by group-based processing using MABR.

Following the above ideas, the paper proposes an algorithm that uses trajectory points to construct MABR and perform group partitioning through MABR. Furthermore, using MQIM, spatial fragile watermarks, and temporal fragile watermarks are embedded into the distance ratios generated by the geometric domain based on the points in each subgroup. The algorithm considers both robustness and spatiotemporal tampering detection capability. The proposed algorithm in this study consists of two parts: embedding and detection, as shown in Fig. 1.

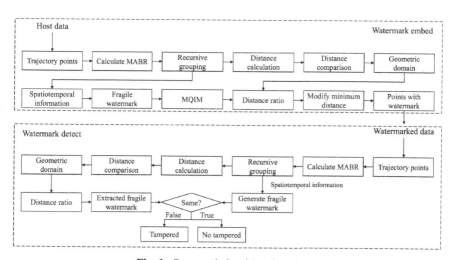

Fig. 1. Proposed algorithm flowchart.

2.2 Trajectory Data Grouping

The trajectory data grouping mechanism plays an important role in locating tampered positions and improving watermark embedding efficiency [11]. It is one of the important steps in semi-fragile watermark algorithms. In order to enhance the robustness of semi-fragile watermark algorithms against common attacks, the results of partitioning should also resist common attacks. The trajectory data grouping mechanism proposed in this paper is shown in Fig. 2, and the specific steps are as follows:

Step1: Calculate the MABR formed by the trajectory points;

Step2: Connect the midpoints of the two long sides of the MABR to divide it into two equal parts, H_1 and H_2. If the number of trajectory points in one of the equal parts is greater than three, keep this partitioning result; otherwise, cancel this partitioning;

Step3: Connect the midpoints of the two long sides of H_1 and divide it into two equal parts, H_{11} and H_{12}. If the number of trajectory points in one of the equal parts is greater than three, keep this partitioning result; otherwise, cancel this partitioning;

Step4: Connect the midpoints of the two longer sides of H_2, dividing it into two equal parts H_{21} and H_{22}. If the number of trajectory points in one of the equal parts is greater than three, keep this partitioning result; otherwise, cancel this partitioning;

Step5: Repeat steps 2 to step 4 until all trajectory points are grouped.

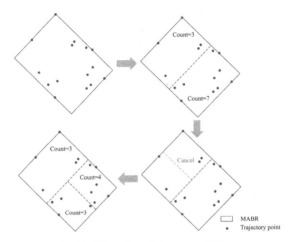

Fig. 2. Trajectory data segmentation.

2.3 Geometric Domain

The geometric domain is used in robust watermark algorithms for vector map data due to Its good geometric variance [12, 13]. Therefore, the paper chooses geometric features as the embedding domain. The process of constructing the geometric domain is introduced below:

Step1: Given a point to be embedded, $p = (x_k, y_k)$, calculate the distances l_1, l_2, l_3, and l_4 from point p to the four sides of the sub-group it belongs to.

Step2: Compare l_1, l_2, l_3, l_4 and obtain the lengths of the longest and shortest distances l_{max}, l_{min}:

$$\begin{cases} l_{max} = Max(l_1, l_2, l_3, l_4) \\ l_{max} = Min(l_1, l_2, l_3, l_4) \end{cases} \tag{1}$$

where *Max* and *Min* respectively represent the maximum value function and the minimum value function.

Step3: Calculate the ratio of l_{min} to l_{max}. The ratio can be described as follows:

$$r_{dis} = \frac{l_{min}}{l_{max}} \tag{2}$$

where the ratio r_{dis} is the geometric embedding domain constructed.

2.4 Multiple Quantization Index Modulation

Quantized index modulation technology embeds watermarks by quantizing carrier information. It has strong anti-interference capability and stability, which makes it a popular embedding method in the field of digital watermarking [14]. The coordinate axis is divided into multiple equally spaced intervals, and the length of each interval is called the step size. The carrier information is quantized into different intervals by the quantizer, thereby embedding watermark bits corresponding to each interval. Typically, only one watermark bit can correspond to one interval. Multiple quantization achieves the purpose of embedding multiple watermarks by secondary partitioning of intervals based on the original quantization index. Figure 3 shows the embedding method of MQIM, and the embedding rule is shown in Eq. (3).

$$\begin{cases} \alpha\prime = \alpha + \frac{s}{2^k}, \text{ if } \left(\left(\left(\alpha\%\frac{s}{2^{k-1}}\right) < \frac{s}{2^k}\right) \& (bit == 1)\right) \\ \alpha\prime = \alpha - \frac{s}{2^k}, \text{ if } \left(\left(\left(\alpha\%\frac{s}{2^{k-1}}\right) >= \frac{s}{2^k}\right) \& (bit == 0)\right) \end{cases} \tag{3}$$

where α is the original data, $\alpha\prime$ is the embedded data, k is the number of embeddings, s is the quantization step size, and bit is the watermark bit to be embedded. Correspondingly, the detection rules for MQIM are as follows:

$$\begin{cases} \hat{bit} = 0, \text{ if } \left(\hat{\alpha}\%\frac{s}{2^{k-1}}\right) < \frac{s}{2^k} \\ \hat{bit} = 1, \text{ if } \left(\hat{\alpha}\%\frac{s}{2^{k-1}}\right) >= \frac{s}{2^k} \end{cases} \tag{4}$$

where $\hat{\alpha}$ is the detection data, $\hat{bit}$ is the detected watermark bit.

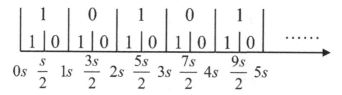

Fig. 3. MQIM embedded mechanism.

3 Methodology

3.1 Fragile Watermark Generation

Fragile watermark is usually composed of important features of the carrier data itself. Due to the rich spatiotemporal information of trajectory data, the proposed algorithm uses the spatiotemporal information of trajectory data to construct a fragile watermark. The specific steps are as follows:

Step1: Based on the trajectory data grouping results, sort the trajectory points within each sub-group from nearest to farthest based on their distance from the center point of the MABR;

Step2: According to the sorted results, calculate the distance sequence of adjacent points in order $d = \{d_1, d_2, \ldots, d_{n-1}\}$. Then calculate r which is the sum of ratios of adjacent distance sequences one by one:

$$r = \sum_{i=1}^{n-2} \frac{d_{i+1}}{d_i} \tag{5}$$

where n is the number of points.

Step3: Encrypt the temporal attribute of the point according to Eq. (6), resulting in an integer I;

$$I = HE\left(\frac{\sum_{i=1}^{n-1} Y_i + M_i + D_i}{\sum_{i=1}^{n-1} h_i + m_i + s_i}\right) \tag{6}$$

where, HE represents the hash encryption algorithm, Y, M, D, h, m, s respectively represent the year, month, day, hour, minute, and second attributes of time.

Step4: Construct the fragile watermark corresponding to the group spatial and time attributes by using the ratio sum r and the encrypted time attribute I as parameters for the hash function:

$$\begin{cases} FW_s = Hash(r) mod 2 \\ FW_t = Hash(I) mod 2 \end{cases} \tag{7}$$

where, $Hash()$ represents a hash function, FW_s and FW_t respectively refer to spatial fragile watermark and temporal fragile watermark.

3.2 Fragile Watermark Embedding

The embedding of fragile watermarking first requires calculating the MABR of trajectory points. Then, the trajectory points are divided into groups, and the geometric domain is used to embed the fragile watermark generated by the spatiotemporal features of these groups into each point within the groups. The detailed steps are as follows:

Step1: Given a trajectory dataset, use the trajectory grouping method to segment the trajectory points in the dataset and obtain several sub-groups of trajectory points;

Step2: Traverse the trajectory point sub-groups. If the number of trajectory points in this sub-group, excluding those on MABR, is greater than or equal to three, perform subsequent operations on it; otherwise, skip this sub-group;

Step3: Generate the fragile watermark fw_s and fw_t for the trajectory points in the sub-groups according to the method of generating fragile watermarks;

Step4: Traverse each point in the sub-group and construct the geometric domain of that point. Then use MQIM technology to embed the fragile watermarks fw_s and fw_t into it;

Step5: After embedding, keep l_{max} unchanged, obtain the new shortest distance value l_{min}', and thus obtain the trajectory points after watermark embedding.

3.3 Fragile Watermark Detection

The detection of fragile watermarks first requires the extraction of MABR from the trajectory dataset to divide them into groups. Then, use the constructed distance ratio to obtain the embedded domain, and extract the embedded fragile watermark using MQIM. Finally, it is compared with the fragile watermark generated by the spatiotemporal attributes of that group to determine whether the sub-group has been tampered with. The detailed steps are described below:

Step1: Given a trajectory dataset, use the trajectory grouping method to group it and obtain several sub-groups of trajectory points;

Step2: Traverse the trajectory point sub-groups. If the number of trajectory points in this sub-group is greater than or equal to three, perform subsequent operations on it; otherwise, skip this sub-group;

Step3: Generate the fragile watermark fw_s' and fw_t' for the trajectory points in the sub-groups according to the method of generating fragile watermarks;

Step4: Traverse each point in the sub-group and construct the geometric domain of that point. Then, use MQIM technology to extract the embedded fragile watermarks $\widehat{fw_s}'$ and $\widehat{fw_t}'$;

Step5: Compare fw_s' with $\widehat{fw_s}'$, fw_t' with $\widehat{fw_t}'$ to see if they are consistent. If they are consistent, it means that the sub-group has not been tampered with. Otherwise, it means that the spatial or temporal attributes of the sub-group have been tampered with.

4 Experiment and Result

4.1 Experimental Data

The experimental data used are from a publicly available trajectory dataset: Geolife, a trajectory dataset released by Microsoft Research, which contains trajectory data recorded by users using GPS devices in Beijing and its surrounding areas [15]. Data numbered 026 to 030 in the Geolife dataset are selected, which included 453 trajectories and 987,539 trajectory points. The example data are shown in Fig. 4.

Fig. 4. Experimental data sample.

Table 1. Experiment design.

Category	Subcategory	Brief Introduction
Invisibility	Invisibility evaluation	Evaluate whether data changes significantly after watermark embedding
Robustness	Geometric attack	Rotate, scale, and translate attacks on trajectory data respectively
Tampering Detection	Spatial tampering	Modify the coordinates of the trajectory in the original groups
	Temporal tampering	Modify the time attribute of the trajectory in the original groups

4.2 Experimental Design

We design experiments of different types and strengths to verify the performance of the proposed algorithm. The experiment consists of three major categories and five subcategories. The experimental design is shown in Table 1.

In addition, we selected two semi-fragile watermarking algorithms designed for trajectory data to use as a basis for comparison. The first algorithm involves grouping points through coordinate sorting, followed by embedding watermarks into the DCT transform domain of each point group [9]. The second algorithm employs the Douglas Peucker algorithm to extract feature points, followed by embedding fragile watermarks into both the extracted feature points and non-feature points separately [10]. For convenience, the two algorithms are denoted as Alg.A and Alg.B in the following.

4.3 Evaluation Indicators

The point coordinate error(Er) and the root mean square error($RMSE$) are employed to evaluate the invisibility [16]. Equation (8) shows the mathematical equation for Er, Eq. (9) shows the mathematical equation for $RMSE$.

$$Er = \frac{\sqrt{(x_i - \hat{x}_i)^2 + (y_i - \hat{y}_i)^2}}{n} \tag{8}$$

$$RMSE = \sqrt{\frac{\sum_{i=1}^{n}\sqrt{(x_i - \hat{x}_i)^2 + (y_i - \hat{y}_i)^2}}{n}} \tag{9}$$

where n represents the number of points, (x_i, y_i) and $(\hat{x}_i, \hat{y}_i)$ represent the coordinates of the i th original point and the coordinates after watermark embedding. The values of Er and $RMSE$ are smaller, and the error between the two datasets is smaller, i.e., the watermark embedding is less destructive to the data accuracy.

The normalized correlation (NC) value is employed to evaluate the robustness of watermarking [17, 18]. The mathematical equation of NC is as follows:

$$NC = \frac{\sum_{i=1}^{n} W[i] \times \widehat{W}[i]}{\sqrt{\sum_{i=1}^{n} W[i]^2}\sqrt{\sum_{i=1}^{n} \widehat{W}[i]^2}} \tag{10}$$

where n represents the number of groups, $W[i]$ and $\widehat{W}[i]$ represent the fragile watermark embedded and extracted in the i th group. A larger value of NC means that the two are more similar, which also implies better robustness of the algorithm. Based on research experience [12, 19], a threshold value of 0.75 is usually chosen.

Additionally, to quantitatively evaluate the algorithm's capability for detecting tampering location, we employ the true detection rate (TDR) for evaluation. The mathematical equation of TDR is as follows:

$$TDR = \frac{DC}{RC} \times 100\% \tag{11}$$

where DC represents the number of correctly detected tampered groups and RC represents the actual number of tampered groups. If TDR is below 100%, it indicates the presence of undetected tampering. The closer TDR is to 100%, implies the stronger capability for detecting tampered locations.

4.4 Invisibility Experiments

The damage to data accuracy after watermark embedding should be as small as possible, and invisibility is an important evaluation index for semi-fragile watermarking algorithms. To evaluate the invisibility of the algorithms, we embedded fragile watermarks on the experimental data using each of the three algorithms and then computed the maximum Er, minimum Er and $RMSE$ of the point coordinates before and after embedding. The calculation results are shown in Table 2.

Table 2. Results of invisibility experiments.

Evaluation indicators	Proposed algorithm	Alg.A	Alg.B
$Max(Er)$	4.67E−9	8.56E−10	1.32E−04
$Min(Er)$	8.85E−12	1.65E−12	2.93E−06
$RMSE$	2.61E−11	3.24E−12	2.43E−06

As can be seen from Table 2, although the proposed algorithm performs two embeddings, the damage to the coordinate accuracy is still small and has not affected the further use of the data. In contrast, Alg.B has the largest embedded error due to its direct modification of the lowest valid bit of the coordinates, with $Max(Er)$ reaching 1.32E−04. Alg.A embeds watermarks in the low-energy DCT mid-frequency coefficients, which have the least impact on data accuracy. In summary, the proposed algorithm has limited damage to the data accuracy and has good invisibility.

4.5 Robustness Experiments

Geometric attacks usually consist of rotation, scaling, and translation, and it is also the most common manipulation of trajectory data during usage. The semi-fragile watermarking algorithm should be robust to geometric attacks. Therefore, we design different attack strengths to test the robustness of the algorithm to geometric attacks. Figure 5 shows the performance of different algorithms under geometric attacks.

Under the three geometric attacks, both the proposed algorithm and Alg.A are not affected, and their NC values are maintained at 1.00. The reason for this result is that both the proposed algorithm and Alg.A is designed to correspond to the geometric attacks. In the proposed algorithm, a geometric domain that can resist geometric attacks is chosen as the embedding domain, and also the robustness of the grouping mechanism to geometric attacks is increased by MABR. Alg.A, on the other hand, removes geometric distortions by employing a hypercurve algorithm. In contrast, Alg.B chooses to embed directly in the coordinates, hence its robustness to geometric attacks is poor.

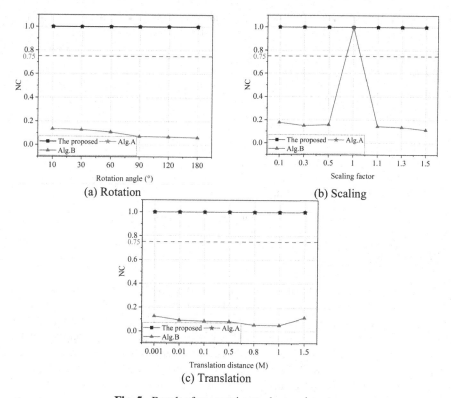

Fig. 5. Result of geometric attack experiment.

4.6 Tampering Detection Experiments

As spatiotemporal data, the biggest difference between trajectory data and common vector geographic data is that it has spatiotemporal attributes at the same time. Data tamperers often modify the spatiotemporal attributes of trajectory data to evade copyright detection. Therefore, tamper detection experiments are designed to verify the ability of semi-fragile watermarking algorithms to authenticate the integrity of spatiotemporal attributes. We modify the temporal and spatial attributes of some groups of data from known groups, and then use *TDR* as an indicator by evaluating the actual detection ability of the algorithm.

Figure 6 shows the experimental results of tamper detection. It is obvious that the proposed algorithm has 100% in both temporal and spatial tampering detection. While Alg.A and Alg.B does not use the temporal attribute as a parameter for constructing the vulnerable watermark. Therefore, both are undetectable for temporal tampering. In addition, the proposed algorithm also embeds the temporal and spatial generated fragile watermarks separately, which ensures independence, and can effectively distinguish whether it is temporal tampering or spatial tampering.

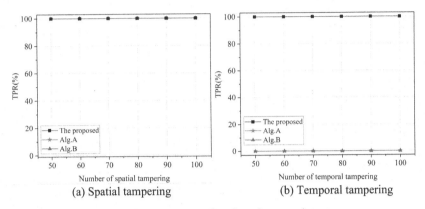

Fig. 6. Result of tampering detection experiment.

5   Conclusion

In this paper, we propose a semi-fragile watermarking algorithm for trajectory data that takes into account spatiotemporal features. The proposed algorithm solves the problem that existing algorithms are unable to authenticate the integrity of temporal attributes and have poor robustness. It uses the MABR of trajectory points for grouping, making the results of grouping more stable. Then, embed fragile watermarks, generated from temporal and spatial features of trajectory points, into the distance ratio with geometric invariance. Experimental results demonstrate that the proposed algorithm exhibits greater robustness against typical attacks and superior invisibility compared to existing algorithms. The algorithm utilizes MQIM to embed spatial and temporal fragile watermarks in multiple stages, enabling it to identify spatiotemporal tampering and easily distinguish the types of tampering. Furthermore, the proposed watermarking algorithm can still be improved in terms of tampering type recognition to improve the detection ability of the algorithm, which is also a future research direction.

Acknowledgments. This work was supported by the National Key Research and Development Program of China (Grant No. 2022YFC3803600), the National Nature Science Foundation of China (Grant Nos. 41971338 and 42071362), and the Postgraduate Research & Practice Innovation Program of Jiangsu Province (Grant No. KYCX22_1584).

Disclosure of Interests. No conflict of interest exists relating to this article, which is approved by all authors for publication. The work described is original research that has not been published previously and is not under consideration for publication elsewhere, in whole or in part.

References

1. Bao, L., et al.: Spatiotemporal clustering analysis of shared electric vehicles based on trajectory data for sustainable urban governance. J. Clean. Prod. **412**, 137373 (2023). https://doi.org/10.1016/j.jclepro.2023.137373

2. Xia, X., et al.: An automated driving systems data acquisition and analytics platform. Transp. Res. Part C Emerging Technol. **151**, 104120 (2023). https://doi.org/10.1016/j.trc.2023.104120

3. Wu, L., Qin, C., Xu, Z., Guan, Y., Lu, R.: TCPP: achieving privacy-preserving trajectory correlation with differential privacy. IEEE Trans. Inf. Forensics Secur. **18**, 4006–4020 (2023). https://doi.org/10.1109/TIFS.2023.3290486

4. Pan, Z.Y., Bao, J., Zhang, W.N., Yu, Y., Zheng, Y.: TrajGuard: a comprehensive trajectory copyright protection scheme. In: Proceedings of the 25th ACM SIGKDD International Conference on Knowledge Discovery & Data Mining, Anchorage, AK, USA, pp. 3060–3070. ACM (2019). https://doi.org/10.1145/3292500.3330685

5. Peng, F., Long, B., Long, M.: A semi-fragile reversible watermarking for authenticating 3D models based on virtual polygon projection and double modulation strategy. IEEE Trans. Multimedia **25**, 892–906 (2023). https://doi.org/10.1109/TMM.2021.3134159

6. Zheng, L.B., Li, Y., Feng, L.P., Liu, H.Q.: Research and implementation of fragile watermark for vector graphics. In: 2010 2nd International Conference on Computer Engineering and Technology, pp. V1-522–V1-525 (2010). https://doi.org/10.1109/ICCET.2010.5485995

7. Wang, N., Kankanhalli, M.: 2D vector map fragile watermarking with region location. ACM Trans. Spatial Algorithms Syst. **4**, 12.1–12.25 (2018). https://doi.org/10.1145/3239163

8. Hou, X., Min, L., Tang, L.: Fragile watermarking algorithm for locating tampered entity groups in vector map data. Geomat. Inf. Sci. Wuhan Univ. **45**, 309–316 (2020). https://doi.org/10.13203/j.whugis20170404

9. Zhang, H.L., Gao, M.: A semi-fragile digital watermarking algorithm for 2D vector graphics tamper localization. In: 2009 International Conference on Multimedia Information Networking and Security, Wuhan, China, pp. 549–552. IEEE (2009). https://doi.org/10.1109/MINES.2009.224

10. Ren, N., Wang, Q.S., Zhu, C.Q.: Selective authentication algorithm based on semi-fragile watermarking for vector geographical data. In: 2014 22nd International Conference on Geoinformatics, Kaohsiung, Taiwan, pp. 1–6. IEEE (2014). https://doi.org/10.1109/GEOINFORMATICS.2014.6950830

11. Hou, X., Min, L., Yang, H.: A fragile watermarking scheme for vector map data using geographic graticule block-wise method. J. Comput.-Aided Des. Comput. Graph. **30**, 2042–2048 (2018)

12. Ren, N., Guo, S., Zhu, C., Hu, Y.: A zero-watermarking scheme based on spatial topological relations for vector dataset. Expert Syst. Appl. **226**, 120217 (2023). https://doi.org/10.1016/j.eswa.2023.120217

13. Ren, N., Zhao, M., Zhu, C., Sun, X., Zhao, Y.: Commutative encryption and watermarking based on SVD for secure GIS vector data. Earth Sci. Inf. **14**, 2249–2263 (2021). https://doi.org/10.1007/s12145-021-00684-5

14. Wang, Y., Yang, C., Ding, K.: Multiple watermarking algorithms for vector geographic data based on multiple quantization index modulation. Appl. Sci. **13**, 12390 (2023). https://doi.org/10.3390/app132212390

15. Zheng, Y., Xie, X., Ma, W.-Y.: GeoLife: a collaborative social networking service among user, location and trajectory. IEEE Data Eng. Bull. **33**, 32–40 (2010)

16. Guo, S., Zhu, S., Zhu, C., Ren, N., Tang, W., Xu, D.: A robust and lossless commutative encryption and watermarking algorithm for vector geographic data. J. Inf. Secur. Appl. **75**, 103503 (2023). https://doi.org/10.1016/j.jisa.2023.103503

17. Zhou, Q., Zhu, C., Na Ren, Chen, W., Gong, W.: Zero watermarking algorithm for vector geographic data based on the number of neighboring features. Symmetry **13**, 208 (2021). https://doi.org/10.3390/sym13020208
18. Abubahia, A., Cocea, M.: Advancements in GIS map copyright protection schemes - a critical review. Multimed. Tools Appl. **76**, 12205–12231 (2017). https://doi.org/10.1007/s11042-016-3441-z
19. Ren, N., Zhou, Q., Zhu, C., Zhu, A.-X., Chen, W.: A lossless watermarking algorithm based on line pairs for vector data. IEEE Access **8**, 156727–156739 (2020). https://doi.org/10.1109/ACCESS.2020.3017700

HPO-LGBM-DRI: Dynamic Recognition Interval Estimation for Imbalanced Fraud Call via HPO-LGBM

Xiliang Liu[1], Xiaoying Zhi[1(✉)], Qiang Mei[2], Peng Wang[3], Haoru Su[1], and Jiayi Wang[1]

[1] Information Technology, Beijing University of Technology, Beijing 100124, China
{liuxl,suhaoru}@bjut.edu.cn, s202375050@emails.bjut.edu.cn
[2] Navigation Institute, Jimei University, Xiamen 361000, China
meiqiang@jmu.edu.cn
[3] Key Laboratory of the Ministry of Education, Hainan Normal University, Hainan 570203, China

Abstract. The prevention and crackdown of fraud calls have been paid more and more attention by industrial and academic societies. Most current researches based on machine learning ignore the imbalanced data distribution characteristic between normal and fraudulent call users, and the outputs neglect the probability fluctuation range of the suspected fraudulent calls. To overcome these limitations, we first construct user behavioral feature vector by a random forest method. Secondly, we propose a novel hierarchical sampling method to overcome the class imbalance problem. Thirdly, we propose a novel fraud call recognition method based on HPO-LGBM (the Bayesian hyper parameter optimization based on random forest and Light Gradient Boosting Machine). Finally, we further evaluate the method's performance with a DRI (dynamic recognition interval) model. Experimental results on public datsets show that the proposed HPO-LGBM holds a 92.90% F1 value, a 91.90% AUC, a 92.92% G-means, and a 92.37% MCC in fraud call recognition. In addition, the proposed HPO-LGBM model can further give the dynamic recognition interval of the output result, behaving more robust than other models (i.e., LR, RF, MLP, GBDT, XGBOOST, LGBM).

Keywords: Fraud call · Imbalanced data · Feature selection · Hierarchical sampling · Dynamic recognition interval

1 Introduction

With the rapid development of information and communication technology, fraud call is more and more rampant [1]. As the encumbrance for a telecommunication operator, fraud call befalls a serious international problem for various network service providers, causing enormous losses. In China, this situation gets even worse. At the beginning of 2020, affected by the COVID-19, the user scale of most online applications such as online payment and online education has increased significantly. At present, network monitoring is the main way to prevent and crackdown on fraud calls in China, but this technology lags far behind the changing forms of fraud calls. The most effective method is shielding based on manual labelling, which greatly reduces the efficiency of monitoring work [2]. In traditional machine learning for fraud call detection, low accuracy stems from inadequate feature selection. Selecting many features for comprehensive data can impair computational efficiency and performance. Hence, reducing dimensions is vital for large-scale fraud call models.

Current solutions often ignore the impact of imbalanced data, resulting in unsatisfactory outcomes. Standard evaluation metrics like accuracy, precision, and recall don't indicate the likelihood of fraud or prediction variability, hindering fraud detection.

The main contributions of this paper are as follows:

- We construct user behavioral feature vector by a random forest feature selection method based on the parcel model.
- We propose a novel hierarchical rebalancing method to overcome the class imbalance problem.
- We propose a new fraud call recognition method based on HPO-LGBM.
- We establish a dynamic recognition interval model to detect the fraudulent calls.

2 Related Works

Fraud call refers to the misuse of telecommunication services to gain money from telecommunication customers and companies, causing huge personal and business losses.

With the development of information technology, various advanced technologies such as artificial intelligence and machine learning, (i.e., Logistic Regression [3], Random Forest [4], Multilayer Perceptron [5], Gradient Boosting tree [6], Extreme Gradient Boosting [7], Light Gradient Boosting Machine [8], etc.), have been widely used in telecom fraud detection research. Research on fraud call recognition has achieved high accuracy, offering valuable insights for our study [9]. However, existing methods tend to focus on accuracy and recall rather than comprehensive metrics like F1-score and G-means, neglecting the predicted probability range of suspected fraud calls.

The rebalancing process of fraud call data sets is to change the distribution of imbalanced datasets through some mechanism to obtain relatively balanced datasets. For the data level means, the imbalanced data processing methods contain oversampling, undersampling, and hybrid sampling methods. An undersampling method, for example, ENN [10], Balance Cascade [11], NearMiss [12], SPE [13], and so on. is a simple method to adjust the data distribution balance by deleting majority class samples from the original data set. An oversampling method, (i.e., EasyEnsemble [11], SMOTE [14], ADASYN [15], etc.) is to synthesize the minority samples according to a certain rule so as to achieve data rebalancing. A hybrid sampling algorithm, (i.e., SMOTE-TOMEK [16], SMOTE-ENN [17], iForest-SMOTE [18] etc.) is a sampling method that combines the advantages of under-sampling and over-sampling. These methods have shown better performance in recent years. At the algorithm level, there are cost-sensitive learning [19], transfer learning [20], and self-supervised imbalanced learning for data rebalancing. Most researchers adopt various sampling methods to sample and rebalance data in specific fields, which can relief the ratio of positive and negative samples in imbalanced data to some extent, but these methods do not consider the distribution characteristics of samples near the classification boundary.

The generalized confidence level refers to the correct possibility. Confidence is a measure of evaluation probability, which indicates the reliability of an event [21]. The forms of fraud calls are complex and diverse, which greatly increases the difficulty of modeling fraud call recognition. Most of the current fraud call recognition methods which are based on machine learning have poor recognition results. Therefore, this paper introduces a dynamic recognition interval into the modeling of fraud call recognition, which is shown in Fig. 1.

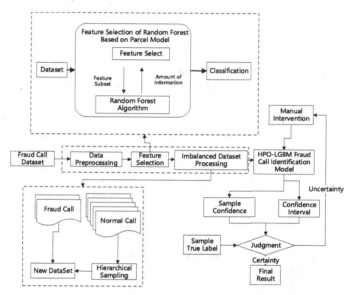

Fig. 1. Flow chart of the overall framework of fraud call recognition.

3 Methodology

3.1 Preliminary Notations

The training dataset S with n examples is defined as:

$$S = \{(x_i, y_i)\}, i = 1, 2, \ldots, n \tag{1}$$

Here, $x_i \in X$ is defined as an instance from the feature space $X = \{v_1, v_2, \ldots, v_m\}$, and $y_i \in Y = \{1, 2, \ldots, C\}$ stands for the class label in corresponding to x_i. For binary classification, $C = 2$. $S_{min} \in S$ and $S_{maj} \subset S$ are the minority subset and majority subset from the original dataset, and $S_{min} \subset S$, $S_{maj} \subset S$, $S_{min} \cup S_{maj} = S$, $S_{min} \cap S_{maj} = \varnothing$.

3.2   Feature Selection

In this paper, there are 39 dimensions in the user behavior data of fraud calls. In order to alleviate data dimension disaster, we should eliminate redundant and irrelevant characteristics. To this end, we employ a random forest feature selection method based on parcel forest on select the data features of fraudulent call user behavior.

A random forest-based feature selection method for fraudulent call user behavior is to calculate the importance of each dimension feature and common factor variance in the fraudulent call user behavior dataset, and to select the first n features with common factor variance greater than 80%. According to the forward search algorithm combined with the feature importance of the random forest algorithm output, the optimal feature subset is found, and the behavior feature vector of fraudulent call users is constructed.

3.3   Rebalancing

In the task of identifying fraud calls, the data of fraud call user behavior is far less than normal user behavior data, and there are noise points and sample points near the classification boundary that are difficult to classify in the fraudulent call user behavior data. To this end, in this paper, a rebalancing method for imbalanced data based on hierarchical sampling is proposed, which can not only better distinguish the samples that are easily misclassified at the classification boundary, but also improve the classification performance of the fraudulent call recognition model. The architecture diagram of rebalancing method for imbalanced data based on hierarchical sampling is shown in Fig. 2.

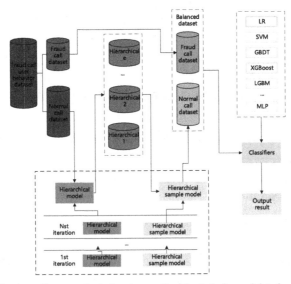

Fig. 2. The architecture diagram of rebalancing method for imbalanced data based on hierarchical sampling.

The specific design idea of hierarchical sampling is to divide the majority sample points into different classification difficulty levels according to the classification difficulty. It sets the level weight for each level according to different classification difficulty levels and sets the sample activation function according to the grade weight. And then this method undersamples each level based on the level of difficulty. These samples that are closer to the classification boundary and are more likely to be classified into the wrong class will be selected as the representative samples of the majority. Finally, this method combines the samples obtained by undersampling as the representative of the majority class samples and the minority class samples into a new data set.

3.4 HPO-LGBM Based Fraud Call Recognition Model

The LGBM algorithm [8], which generates leaves with depth limits, speeds up computation using histograms and improves efficiency through parallel processing. However, its many hyperparameters pose a challenge due to the uncertainty in their optimal selection, impacting performance. The HPO-LGBM model integrates Bayesian optimization with random forest to refine LGBM's hyperparameters. This method selects parameters based on a specified input data model, aiming to optimize the learning algorithm by refining the chosen number of parameters. We set the base classifier as $f(x)$, x represents the input feature value of the sample. The LGBM algorithm is composed of M base classifier models superimposed and can be expressed as $F(X) = \sum_{t=1}^{m} f_t(x_i)$, where f_t represents the t-th basis model. The loss function is set as

$$\ell(Y, F(X)) = \frac{1}{m} \sum_{i=0}^{m} (y_i - F_m(x_i))^2 \tag{2}$$

The classifier function can be expressed as:

$$F_m(X) = \sum_{t=1}^{m} f_t(x_i) = F_{m-1}(X) + f_m(X) \tag{3}$$

Find the first-order partial derivative of the loss function to get:

$$\frac{\partial \ell}{\partial F(X)} = \ell'(Y, F(X)) = -\frac{2}{n} \sum_{i=0}^{m} (y_i - F_m(x_i)) \tag{4}$$

$$\ell'(Y, F_m(X)) = \ell'(Y, F_{m-1}(X)) + f_m(X) \tag{5}$$

Find the second-order partial derivative of the loss function to get:

$$\ell''(Y, F(X)) \tag{6}$$

According to Taylor's expansion formula, we can get:

$$\ell'(Y, F_m(X)) = \ell'(Y, F_{m-1}(X)) + \ell''(Y, F_{m-1}(X)) * f_m(X) \tag{7}$$

Converted and solved:

$$f_m(X) = -\frac{\ell'(Y, F_{m-1}(X))}{\ell''(Y, F_{m-1}(X))} \tag{8}$$

Taking the first-order partial derivative and the second-order partial derivative of the loss function into the solution, we get:

$$f_m(X) = \frac{1}{n} \sum_{i=0}^{m} (y_i - F_{m-1}(x_i)) \tag{9}$$

The $f(x)$ function is obtained by calculating the mean value of the residuals for $m-1$ rounds. The Bayesian hyper parameter optimization algorithm based on random forest uses the Bayesian model as the surrogate objective function $x' = \underset{x \in X}{argmin} f(x)$, selects the hyper parameters with the best performance on the surrogate objective function and applies the hyper parameters to the objective function to achieve parameter optimization.

3.5 The Confidence Level of Fraud Call Recognition

The confidence level of fraud call recognition is a method to evaluate the probability whether a sample is a fraud call. The value of this function represents the probability that a sample is a fraud call. It can be defined as a function $C(Y)$, Y is an element in the event space $\{Y_1, Y_2, Y_3, ..., Y_K, ...\}$, if $Y_1 > Y_2, C(Y_1) > C(Y_2)$ and $0 \le C(Y) \le 1$. The fraud call recognition model is defined as FM. The confidence of the sample is $C(S|FM)$. The pseudo code of Dynamic recognition interval method is shown in Algorithm 1.

Algorithm 1: Dynamic recognition interval method
___

Input: Training set
$S=(s_1, s_2, s_3, ... s_n)$, $s_i = (x, y), i = 1,2,3,... n$, Model FM
1. Calculate sample confidence $C(S|FM)$
2.

If $1 \ge C(s_i|FM) \ge \alpha$, $1 > \alpha \ge 0$;
  then s_i is a fraud call;

  end if;
If $\chi < C(s_i|FM) < \delta$, $\beta \le \chi$ && $\chi < \delta$ && $\delta \le \alpha$;
  then s_i requires manual intervention judgment;
  end if;
If $0 \le C(s_i|FM) \le \beta$, $0 \le \beta \le \chi$;
  then s_i is a normal call;
end if;
  3.print result;
4.return;
___

Thus, a dynamic interval of fraud call recognition is built based on the confidence level of the sample recognition by the HPO-LGBM model. And then the potential recognition results are analyzed through interval estimation.

4 Experiments

4.1 Dataset and Evaluation Metrics

The experimental dataset[1] is public datasets provide by Liu, including desensitized call records from a specific area within a week. This dataset contains three call types. The first one is fraud call, the second one is courier call, and the third one is normal call. Both couriers and fraud users need to frequently call strangers' phone numbers. It is specified that the data label of fraud call sample is set to 1, and the data label of the normal call sample is set to 0. The calling detail records (CDRs) contain 40 dimensions.

Commonly, classifiers are evaluated using accuracy or precision, but these metrics don't fully represent performance with imbalanced data. Traditional evaluation relies on single criteria like overall accuracy, insufficient for imbalanced learning contexts. For practical fraud call recognition, we adopt F1 score, G-means, AUC, and MCC as additional metrics. Accuracy and precision indicate algorithm correctness, while recall shows completeness in detection. Experiment & result analysis.

Data Preprocessing
In data preprocessing step, we first delete CDRs with missing value and the outliers from the original dataset, and then normalize all the features into the same span $[-1, 1]$ so as to eliminate the scaling affect. After processing, 116,383 pieces of data remained. These include 107,935 pieces of normal call user behavior data and 8,448 pieces of fraudulent call user behavior data.

Feature Selection
We first select the first 12 features with common factor variance greater than 0.8 according to the common factor variance bar graph of each dimension of user behavior data. Secondly, we construct new features based on the importance of the user behavior feature output based on the random forest feature selection method and the forward search algorithm. Specifically, we add the features with high importance to the previous feature subset one by one according to feature importance calculated by the random forest algorithm which is shown in Fig. 3.

Finally, we use the LGBM model to experimentally verify each feature subset. Experimental results are shown in Fig. 4 below.

After removing feature v_8, the model's performance significantly drops, confirming the efficacy of using 0.8 as a threshold for Sub1 (11 features). Sub2 to Sub12 show results from adding ranked features based on random forest importance and forward search. Model performance improves with more features but declines post-Sub11. Hence, Sub9, which performs best, is chosen for the fraudulent call user behavior feature vector in formula (10).

$$V = \left\{ \begin{array}{l} v_{18}, v_2, v_{19}, v_3, v_{25}, v_{20}, v_{15}, v_1, v_5, v_{16}, v_{13}, v_8, \\ v_6, v_{10}, v_{11}, v_9, v_{14}, v_{22}, v_{17}, v_4, v_{12}, v_{1label} \end{array} \right\} \tag{10}$$

---

[1] https://github.com/khznxn/TF-Dataset.

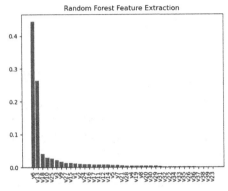

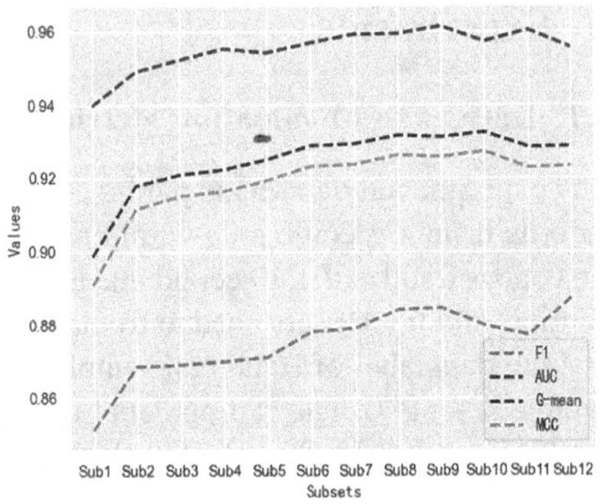

Fig. 3. Feature importance map based on random forest. (left)

Fig. 4. Feature subset running result graph. (right)

Hierarchical Sampling

In order to reduce the impact of the imbalanced data set on the model and the effectiveness of the rebalancing method for imbalanced data based on hierarchical sampling, 5 commonly used public data sets of imbalanced data classification(BankMarketing[2], Credit Card Data[3],Haberman-Survival Data[4], German-Credit Data[5] and Pima-Indians Diabetes[6]) are downloaded from UCI and Kaggle for comparative experiments.

In this paper, the commonly used rebalance data processing methods (i.e., RandomOverSample(ROS), RandomUnderSample (RUS), SMOTETOMEK(ST), ENN, SMOTEENN(SE), EasyEnsemble(EE), SMOTE, ADASYN, BalancedBagging(BB) etc.) are used to compare experiments with the methods proposed in this study. In the experiments, LGBM is selected as the classification model, and the result that the F1 value of each method through 10-fold cross-validation is obtained. The experimental results are shown in Table 1 below.

It can be seen that the seven rebalancing methods of ROS, SMOTE, ENN, ADASYN, ROS, ST, and SE get the same results as the experimental results on the original data set, and they do not improve the performance of model recognition. Compared with the above methods, EE and BB have effectively improved the recognition performance of the model. The Hierarchical sampling method proposed in this study outperforms the other nine rebalancing methods on multiple imbalanced public data sets.

Fraud Call Recognition Based on HPO-LGBM

According to the current literature review, in this paper, 7 commonly used fraudulent call recognition algorithms are used as the basic algorithm, including LR, RF, MLP, GDBT, XGBoost, LGBM, and HPO-LGBM to conduct experiments on the new sample

---

[2] https://www.kaggle.com/janiobachmann/bank-marketing-dataset.

[3] http://archive.ics.uci.edu/ml/datasets/default+of+credit+card+clients.

[4] http://archive.ics.uci.edu/ml/datasets/Haberman%27s+Survival.

[5] http://archive.ics.uci.edu/ml/datasets/Statlog+%28German+Credit+Data%29.

[6] https://storage.googleapis.com/kagglesdsdata/datasets/14370/19291/pima-indians-diabetes. csv.

Table 1. Comparison of experimental results of different rebalancing methods.

Methods	BankMarketing	Credit Card	Haberman	German Credit	Pima
Original	0.5972	0.4765	0.2781	0.5797	0.6062
ROS	0.5972	0.4765	0.2781	0.5797	0.6062
SMOTE	0.5972	0.4765	0.2781	0.5797	0.6062
ADASYN	0.5972	0.4765	0.2781	0.5797	0.6062
ENN	0.5972	0.4765	0.2781	0.5797	0.6062
RUS	0.5972	0.4765	0.2781	0.5797	0.6062
ST	0.5972	0.4765	0.2781	0.5797	0.6062
SE	0.5972	0.4765	0.2781	0.5797	0.6062
EE	0.6018	0.5311	0.4170	0.6106	0.6845
BB	0.6121	0.4989	0.3819	0.5760	0.6485
HS	**0.6782**	**0.5528**	**0.4444**	**0.7648**	**0.8293**

set formed after processing. For model evaluation, 10-fold cross-validation is employed. The final results come from the averaging of all the iterations, which is shown in Table 2.

Table 2. Comparison of experimental results of different fraudulent call recognition methods.

Models	F1	AUC	G-mean	MCC	Time(s)
LR	0.7832	0.7630	0.7857	0.7703	**0.931**
RF	0.9304	0.9126	0.9305	0.9251	9.807
MLP	0.3391	0.2469	0.4315	0.2606	9.476
GBDT	0.9043	0.8856	0.9047	0.8971	1.204
XGBoost	0.9215	0.9110	0.9218	0.9158	3.851
LSTM	**0.9255**	**0.9175**	**0.9258**	**0.9202**	3.476

The LGBM model achieves the best experimental results in F1 value, AUC value, G-mean, and MCC value, and the efficiency of the algorithm is second only to LR and GBDT, and better than RF, MLP, and XGBoost. Therefore, the LGBM algorithm is chosen to conduct subsequent experiments to build a fraudulent call recognition model.

The HPO-LGBM model uses the Bayesian hyper parameter optimization algorithm based on the random forest to optimize the parameters of the LGBM model and uses cross-validation to evaluate the performance. The final optimal parameters are shown in Table 3.

The HPO-LGBM results are shown in Table 4. The comparison chart of the multi-model experimental results is shown in Fig. 5. Figure 6 shows the results of the multi-model running time.

Table 3. HPO-LGBM model parameters.

Parameters	Values
max_depth	21
num_leaves	163
learning_rate	0.095
num_trees	210
feature_fraction	0.9

Table 4. HPO-LGBM model experimental results.

	F1	AUC	G-mean	MCC	Time(s)
HPO-LGBM	0.9290	0.9190	0.9292	0.9237	8.023

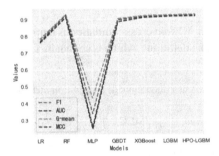
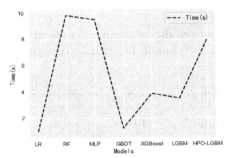

Fig. 5. Comparison of experimental results of multiple models. (left)

Fig. 6. Multiple models running time comparison. (right)

From the above chart, it can be seen that the HPO-LGBM model achieves the best experimental results in F1 value, AUC value, G-mean, and MCC value, and the recognition performance of the LGBM model is also significantly improved. It proves the superiority of the method proposed in this paper.

Dynamic Recognition Interval

The HPO-LGBM fraudulent call recognition model is used to output the confidence level of each sample. The confidence scatters diagram of the sample points of fraudulent call user behavior data is drawing as shown in Fig. 7. The orange dots represent fraudulent calls, and the blue dots represent normal calls. In this paper, statistical analysis of sample confidence is carried out based on the experimental results.

Table 5 shows the statistical ratio of the confidence level of the fraudulent call samples. We analyze the confidence of normal call samples in detail and draws a statistical table. The statistical table of normal calls with sample confidence is shown in Table 6.

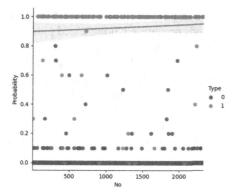

Fig. 7. Confidence scatter plot of sample points of fraud call user behavior data. (Color figure online)

Table 5. Fraud call statistical table of sample confidence ratio.

Probability	Sample Sizes	Ratio
C(X) ≥ 0.9	146	85.89%
C(X) ≥ 0.8	147	86.47%
C(X) ≥ 0.7	148	87.06%
C(X) ≥ 0.6	150	88.24%

Table 6. Normal call statistical table of sample confidence ratio.

Probability	Sample Sizes	Ratio
C(X) ≥ 0.9	8	0.27%
0.9 > C(X) > 0.2	12	0.56%
C(X) ≤ 0.2	2142	99.17%
C(X) ≤ 0.1	2137	98.94%

5   Conclusions

In this paper, we propose a novel HPO-LGBM-DRI fraud call recognition method.

We first construct user behavioral feature vector by a random forest method. The feature selection method of fraudulent call user behavior data based on a random forest of parcel model proposed in this paper is better than PCA, RF, and the original data set. The LGBM model is better than other methods in F1, AUC, G-mean, and MCC.

Secondly, we design a novel hierarchical sampling method to overcome the class imbalance problem. We compared the rebalancing method performance of the proposed hierarchical sampling method with nine well-known methods. The results show that, in most cases, the hierarchical sampling method proposed in this paper outperforms the other nine rebalancing methods on multiple imbalanced public data sets.

Thirdly, we propose a novel fraud call recognition method based on HPO-LGBM. Using public data set provided by Liu Ming, we compared the fraud call recognition method performance of the proposed HPO-LGBM method with LR, RF, MLP, GBDT, XGBOOST, and LGBM. The results show that the proposed HPO-LGBM method holds a 92.90% F1 value, a 91.90% AUC, a 92.92% G-means, and a 92.37% MCC in fraud call recognition. In addition, the proposed HPO-LGBM-DRI model can further give the dynamic recognition interval of the output result, behaving more superior and robust than other models.

In the future, we plan to combine user behavior data from multiple operators to research through federated learning.

References

1. An, M.: Fraud telephone characteristics analysis and prevention. China Inf. Secur. **5**, 86–89 (2014)
2. Zhou, C., Lin, Z.: Study on fraud detection of telecom industry based on rough set. In: Proceedings of the IEEE Annual Computing and Communication Workshop and Conference, Las Vegas, United states, pp. 15–19, January 2018
3. Naveen, P., Dlwan, B.: Relative analysis of ML algorithm QDA, LR and SVM for credit card fraud detection dataset. In: Proceedings of the International Conference on IoT in Social, Mobile, Analytics and Cloud, Palladam, India, pp. 976–981, October 2020
4. Wu, S., Li, J.: IDD fraud detection model based on decision tree and random forest. Commun. Technol. **51**(12), (2018)
5. Pehlivanli, D., Eken, S., Ayan, E.: Detection of fraud risks in retailing sector using MLP and SVM techniques. Turk. J. Electr. Eng. Comput. Sci. **27**, 3633–3647 (2019)
6. Lenka, S.R., Pant, M., Barik, R.K., Patra, S.S., Dubey, H.: Investigation into the efficacy of various machine learning techniques for mitigation in credit card fraud detection. In: Bhateja, V., Peng, S.L., Satapathy, S.C., Zhang, Y.D. (eds.) Evolution in Computational Intelligence. Advances in Intelligent Systems and Computing, vol. 1176. Springer, Singapore (2021). https://doi.org/10.1007/978-981-15-5788-0_24
7. Chen, T., Guestrin, C.: XGBoost: a scalable tree boosting system. In: Proceedings of the ACM SIGKDD International Conference on Knowledge Discovery and Data Mining, San Francisco, United States, pp. 785–794, August 2016
8. Ke, G., Meng, Q., Finley, T., et al.: LightGBM: a highly efficient gradient boosting decision tree. In: Proceedings of the Advances in Neural Information Processing Systems, Long Beach, United States, pp. 3147–3155, December 2017
9. Olszewski, D.: A probabilistic approach to fraud detection in telecommunications. Knowl. Based Syst. **26**, 246–258 (2012)
10. Tomek, I.: An experiment with the edited nearest-neighbor rule. IEEE Trans. Syst. Man Cybern. **06**(06), 448–452 (1976)
11. Liu, X., Wu, J., Zhou, Z.: Exploratory undersampling for class-imbalance learning. IEEE Trans. Syst. Man Cybern. Part B Cybern. **39**, 539–550 (2009)
12. Mani, I., Zhang, I.: KNN approach to unbalanced data distributions: a case study involving information extraction. In: Proceedings of the Workshop on Learning from Imbalanced Datasets, vol. 126 (2003)

13. Liu, Z., Cao, W., Gao, Z., et al.: Self-paced ensemble for highly imbalanced massive data classification. In: Proceedings of the International Conference on Data Engineering, pp. 841–852, April 2020
14. Chawla, N.V., Bowyer, K.W., Hall, L.O., Kegelmeyer, W.P.: SMOTE: synthetic minority over-sampling technique. J. Artif. Intell. Res. **16**, 321–357 (2002)
15. He, H., Bai, Y., Garcia, E.A., et al.: ADASYN: adaptive synthetic sampling approach for imbalanced learning. In: Proceedings of the International Joint Conference on Neural Networks, Hongkong, pp. 1322–1328, June 2008
16. Batista, G.E., Bazzan, A.L., Monard, M.C.: Balancing training data for automated annotation of keywords: a case study. In: WOB, pp. 10–18 (2003)
17. Batista, G.E., Prati, R.C., Monard, M.C.: A study of the behavior of several methods for balancing machine learning training data. ACM SIGKDD Explor. Newslett. **6**(1), 20–29 (2004)
18. Zheng, Y., Li, G., Zhang, T.: An improved over-sampling algorithm based on iForest and SMOTE. In: Proceedings of the ACM International Conference on Software and Computer Applications, Penang, Malaysia, pp. 75–80, February 2019
19. Zhou, Z.-H.: Cost-sensitive learning. In: Torra, V., Narakawa, Y., Yin, J., Long, J. (eds.) MDAI 2011. LNCS (LNAI), vol. 6820, pp. 17–18. Springer, Heidelberg (2011). https://doi.org/10.1007/978-3-642-22589-5_2
20. Yin, X., Yu, X., Sohn, K., et al.: Feature transfer learning for face recognition with under-represented data. In: Proceedings of IEEE Computer Society Conference on Computer Vision and Pattern Recognition, Long Beach, CA, pp. 5697–5706, June 2019
21. Fayoll, J., Moreau, F., Raymond, C., et al.: CRF-based combination of contextual features to improve a posteriori word-level confidence measures. In: Proceedings of the Annual Conference of the International Speech Communication Association, Makuhari, Japan, pp. 1942–1945 (2010)

A Review on Urban Modelling for Future Smart Cities

Han Zhang[1,2], Zhaoya Gong[1,2(✉)], and Jean-Claude Thill[3]

[1] School of Urban Planning and Design, Peking University Shenzhen Graduate School, Shenzhen, Guangdong, China
z.gong@pku.edu.cn
[2] Key Laboratory of Earth Surface System and Human-Earth Relations of Ministry of Natural Resources of China, Peking University Shenzhen Graduate School, Shenzhen, Guangdong, China
[3] Department of Geography and Earth Sciences, University of North Carolina at Charlotte, Charlotte, USA
Jean-Claude.Thill@uncc.edu

Abstract. The rapid development of information technology has brought about the emergence of urban multi-source big data and the improvement of computing power, and promoted the emergence of new technologies such as artificial intelligence, making the study paradigm of urban modelling face change. Based on the concept of smart city, this paper sorts out the types of urban big data in the information age, and puts forward new opportunities and challenges brought by big data to urban modelling research; Secondly, this paper lists a number of cases for reference on how big data can provide services to the public in the form of network and infrastructure; Finally, the latest progress in the innovation of new technologies such as artificial intelligence, deep learning, data mining, etc. caused by the improvement of computing power is discussed.

Keywords: Smart city · Urban modelling · Urban informatics · Big data

1 Introduction

Over the past 20 years, "smart cities" have been promoted globally as urban planning and development strategy. In the construction of smart cities in Japan, cooperation between government and enterprise is advocated, and there are many commendable aspects in the construction of real estate development, infrastructure, smart infrastructure, life service, life lifestyle and culture (Shen Zhenjiang, Li Miao-ai, Lin Xinyi, & Hu Feiyu, 2017). In order to better respect and conform to the self-organization law of urban development, Xiongan New Area pioneered the concept of "digital twin cities" (Zhou Yu & Liu Chuncheng, 2018).

X. Meng et al. (Eds.): SpatialDI 2024, LNCS 14619, pp. 346–355, 2024.
https://doi.org/10.1007/978-981-97-2966-1_25

The integration of technology and city is often referred to as "smart city" (Yigitcanlar et al., 2018). The six key areas in the US Report on Technology and Future Cities show that the construction of smart cities is guided by information and communication technologies, which are constantly applied and developed in different areas of the city (Wang Bo, Zhen Feng, & Lu Peiying, 2018). The technologies required for smart cities include but are not limited to: Deep Learning (DL), Machine learning (ML), Internet of Things (IoT), Mobile Computing, Big Data, Block Chain, Sixth Generation (6G) networks, WiFi-7, Industry 5.0, Robotics Systems, Heating Ventilation and Air Conditioning (HVAC), Digital Certification, Industrial Control Systems, Connected and Automated Vehicles (CAVs), Electric Vehicles, Product Recycling, flying cars, pantry backups, disaster backups, and cybersecurity... (Javed et al., 2022) In summary, four kinds of urban intelligent planning technologies: computer-aided design technology, urban quantitative analysis technology, urban dynamic simulation technology and urban intelligent interaction technology (Ganwei, 2018).

2   Generational Change of Urban Model

2.1   First Generation

In the first half of the 20th century, influenced by regional science (empiricism) and urban (spatial) economics, the study of the spatial organization of urban systems in the first generation was rooted in location theory, which proposed what economic activities were located where and why in a market with a given external location. The central place theory (CPT), the new urban economics (NUE), Von Thunen's agricultural location theory, Lowry model, and other theories emerged successively, and more and more theoretical models were applied to practice. However, due to the mismatch between urban model theory and reality, the era of the first generation of urban models ended in the mid-1970s. This mismatch can be attributed to two aspects: first, the lack of a theoretical foundation that can reflect the reality of the spatial organization of urban systems. Although the central place theory is fundamental and intuitive for understanding the organization of urban spatial economics, it is largely descriptive and does not explain why central locations should appear where they do. Second, as urbanization rapidly suburbanized from 1950 to 1970, the spatial organization of cities became increasingly detached from the classical single-center model represented by CPT. The first generation of urban models was essentially static models based on general equilibrium or local equilibrium mechanisms, lacking the ability to explain dynamics, and gradually evolved into the second generation.

2.2   Second Generation

From the early 1970s to the 1980s, the focus of planning practice shifted from broader urban-regional areas to individual cities, and the invention of large-scale computers led to the emergence of second-generation urban models. In urban studies, behavioral methods played a role in the empirical paradigm, focusing on the spatial behavior of households and firms at the micro level, and how their decisions shape the entire urban system (Batty, 1994). Spatial interaction models derived from entropy maximization, microeconomic land market models based on utility maximization, path search based on cost minimization, and discrete choice analysis of travel behavior based on stochastic utility maximization all appeared in this stage. After Forrester's (1969) early attempt to introduce dynamics into urban system theory, the theoretical development of non-equilibrium models focused on the dynamic process of nonlinear growth in urban systems, which not only produces continuous changes but also produces discontinuities and catastrophes (Forrester, 1969). Allen and Sanglier (1979, 1981) developed a dynamic model of central place systems and demonstrated how it generates bifurcations (Allen & Michèle, 2010). To explain the multi-center and suburbanization within cities, multi-center models were developed, assuming the existence of multiple exogenously designated centers (Sullivan, 1986; White, 1976) and non-monocentric models formed endogenously within city centers and sub-centers (Fujita, 1988b; Fujita & Ogawa, 1982; Ogawa & Fujita, 2006). Both types of models were constructed using general or partial equilibrium methods. Although multi-center models allow for the analysis of economic activity under a multi-center spatial structure, the reasons for the existence of these centers remain unexplained. On the other hand, urban system theory began to develop in urban economics (Henderson, 1972, 1974) at the inter-city scale (e.g., large metropolitan areas containing multiple cities), but the spatial structure of cities described in CPT remains unexplained.

2.3   Third Generation

Since the 1990s, advances in urban systems theory and modeling have been promoted within three main schools of thought. The multi-center network paradigm has been introduced into urban and regional planning to enhance territorial cohesion and regional economic strength and competitiveness. The approaches of NUE (New Urban Economics) and NEG (New Economic Geography) complement each other. In the institutional mechanisms of urban formation, the atomistic agent approach adopted by NEG contrasts with the macro agent approach of NUE, which involves city developers or local governments coordinating the actions of businesses and workers to create new cities. In NEG, the emergence of cities is the result of countless individual economic decisions made by economic agents seeking their own interests. In other words, "the city is shown as a complex system, the result of a self-organizing process" [62] (Fujita and Thisse, 2002, p. 354).

Third generation urban-regional modeling is deeply influenced by complexity science, where increasing complexity represents more time scales, more opportunities, and more diversity. This method emphasizes a new bottom-up paradigm, rather than the previous top-down aggregate urban models. Manuel Castells' theory of space of flows has moved from the "space of place" to "flow of space," while Michael Batty's urban dynamics explores how countless processes and elements can be combined into an organic whole within the framework of complexity theory. Cellular automata (CA) are typical urban models of this paradigm, simulating urban development and land use changes as diffusion processes. Quantitative urban models represented by CA and agent-based models (ABM) have been widely used in urban simulation research.

Activity-based methods, as a typical implementation method of transportation planning, belong to a broader concept of microsimulation. Microsimulation simulates the decision-making process and complex interactions between individual actors in an open system at the micro level, such as TRANSIMS (Nagel et al., 1999), UrbanSim (Waddell, 2002), and ILUTE (Miller et al., 2004), which are actual applied urban simulation models.

3   Development Trend of Urban Modelling

3.1   Intelligent Transformation Driven by Multi-source Big Data

Big data generally has three dimensions, known as the "three Vs": (1) Volume - the amount of data that can be collected and stored; (2) Velocity – the speed at which data is captured; (3) Variety – including structured (organized and stored in tables and relationships) and unstructured (text, images) data (De Mauro, Greco, & Grimaldi, 2014). Urban sensing is regarded as a collection of technologies that perceive and acquire information about physical space and human activities in urban areas. Technological progress brings information explosion and massive data. Urban sensing is to use the opportunity of multi-source big data to conduct more detailed urban research and reproduction the multiple dynamic relationship between urban systems.

Urban big data can be roughly divided into data about objects (Earth observation, that is, data collected by air and ground sensors) and human activities (geospatial and cyberspace). Object data mainly comes from remote sensing and mapping. Such as optical satellites, laser radar, photogrammetry, ground-penetrating radar, mobile maps based on sensors embedded in mobile platforms, surveillance cameras and so on; Data related to human activity comes from indoor location technology, wearable device, the Internet of Things, social sensing data, and more.

Our physical world is being projected into cyberspace at an unprecedented rate. The availability of large amounts of social sensing data provides a unique opportunity to understand urban space in a data-driven way and to improve many urban computing application, from urban planning and transportation planning to disaster control and travel planning. Zhang (2021) and others used multimodal embedding technology based on social media data to construct vector representations of different modes to simulate people's space-time activities (Zhang & Han, 2021). It is noteworthy that Voluntary Geographic Information (VGI) and User-Generated Content (UGC), which are unique characteristics of information sharing and public participation in the information age, have been fully displayed. Voluntary Geographic Information (VGI) is geographic information created voluntarily by citizens. VGI data is very useful in mapping time-critical events (such as disasters) with very fine detail and immediacy; User-Generated Content (UGC), which includes geotagged photos, social network posts, street view images, and crowdsourced GPS tracks (Tu, Li, Zhang, & Yue, 2021), creates unprecedented opportunities to perceive what was previously hidden on the surface of the physical space of the city, mapping out the interactions between infrastructure, geographic information and people. Open Street Map (OSM) is generally considered a successful crowdsourced mapping project: people have mapped many of the world's cities on a voluntary basis with remarkable accuracy.

The emergence of multi-source big data provides new opportunities for the study of urban dynamics. The urban system model has a mature theoretical basis and rigorous causal inference, and the rise of multi-source data also makes up the data gap in its application, enabling it to reveal the dynamic game relationship between the development of urban subsystems according to local conditions (Yang Tianren, Jinying, & Fangzhou, 2021). Ubiquitous, continuous streams of data are a great thing because they allow us to capture space-time dynamics directly (rather than extrapolating them from snapshots) and at multiple scales (Miller & Goodchild, 2015), Provides opportunities for better understanding of human behaviour, urban dynamics, human-environment interactions, and many more fundamentally important issues (X. Liu et al., 2022). Multi-source data provides a new perspective for the study of polycentric urban form. In a study on the new urban form of Shanghai, scholars used multi-source data to build a dynamic spatial balance model and explore possible polycentric development scenarios (Yang, Jin, Yan, & Pei, 2019).

However, with the popularity of big data, geospatial big data is faced with challenges brought by high dimension, lack of data standards, privacy and security, multiple IP addresses, false information, and fake data. Problems such as heterogeneity and noise in big data itself make the problem of multi-source big data fusion increasingly serious. Therefore, a group of scholars have devoted themselves to optimizing models based on multi-source big data, among which Yuan et al. devoted themselves to the research of environmental remote sensing data fusion and discussed various fusion methods of multi-source remote sensing big data, spatio-temporal information and deep learning models. For example, spatial-spectral information fusion and multi-temporal information fusion based on regression model, spatial-spectral information fusion and multi-temporal information fusion based on data-driven and deep residual model (Yuan, Zhang, Li, Shen, & Zhang, 2018). Then they made a comprehensive summary of the deep learning methods and deep neural network models in the field of environmental remote sensing, including the prediction and estimation of land cover, vegetation parameters, agricultural production, land surface temperature and humidity, aerosol and particle content, precipitation, snow cover, evaporation, radiation and ocean color parameters, etc. (Yuan et al., 2020).

3.2   Web-Service Oriented Urban Big Data Infrastructure

The concept of infrastructure refers to ubiquitous available resources such as electricity, and one does not need to be an expert in electricity to use it simply by plugging in a power source (Xiao & Miller, 2021). For example, a geographic portal (Tait, 2005) provides users with the ability to discover geospatial data based on data catalogs maintained in the geological portal, view and map the data sets discovered, and provide data using various data query techniques such as REST, GeoRSS, and KML. The nature of urban big data infrastructure should include not only the big data itself, but also the software needed to process the data, the people with the necessary skills and the public and decision makers who can enjoy the services of urban big data, with a focus on how data is provided to the public in the form of infrastructure. In the past, the goal of smart cities was to build urban infrastructure. However, the focus is now on providing smart city services. Thus, the operation and maintenance of smart city services is becoming more important than their construction (Kim, 2022).

Technologies supported by urban big data include but are not limited to 3D digital modelling technology (L. Li et al., 2021), building information modelling (BIM), spatial search technology, CityEngine, CyberGIS (network geographic information system), Internet of Things (loT), etc. Among them, BIM provides completed information about building infrastructure and usage to multiple stakeholders such as owners, architects and engineers, contractors, subcontractors and manufacturers, and there is a growing need to combine semantic 3D city models and BIM representations (Kolbe & Donaubauer, 2021). CityEngine was developed as a multi-purpose planning tool capable of enforcing regulations, providing vision visualization of plans, processing 2D city map Geographic Information System (GIS) data to create detailed 3D city models, and supporting many functions of city government (Kelly, 2021). Based on the CyberGIS-Jupyter, CyberGIS uses high-performance computing to extend the scope of traditional GIS utilizing large-scale computing by integrating CyberGIS and real-time city sensing (Shaowen Wang et al., 2021). While the value, quantity, velocity and variety of data collected from devices make the opportunities for urban Internet of Things almost limitless, the investment of urban Internet of Things devices in urban modelling opens up a new era of simulation and prediction of the environment (Hudson-Smith, Wilson, Gray, & Dawkins, 2021).

The QUANT model developed by the Batty team builds all modelling capabilities into the server as a set of web services, which constitute a "model-view-controller" architecture and are seen as the basis for "urban modelling as a service" (Batty & Milton, 2021). In addition, Batty and Goodchild proposed the concept of smart city based on real-time GIS, which elaborated the technical realization of real-time city simulation, real-time urban data visualization and real-time GIS processing (W. Li, Batty, & Goodchild, 2020). Agent-based modelling (ABM), cellular automata (CA), microsimulation and network modelling are popular techniques to simulate urban dynamics from the perspective of complex systems science (Batty, 2007; Lomax & Smith, 2017; Sengupta, 2017), it is the emergence of new digital technologies and urban big data infrastructure that provides unlimited opportunities for real-time GIS and visualization.

New disruptive technologies, including blockchain and digital twin, are also being used to improve urban environments and governance. Citizens' easy access to local public services, such as bicycle use and local food distribution, is a positive innovation for city dwellers (Clifton & Pal, 2022). The concept of geoscientific knowledge atlas has also been increasingly promoted. As an important tool for the expression, extraction and management of geographical knowledge, it integrates the representation of multiple information carriers such as map, text and number to provide open and extensible geospatial knowledge services to the public (Zhou Chenghu et al., 2021).

However, attention should also be paid to issues related to geographic privacy during the construction of urban big data infrastructure. Dobson et al. studied the current trend of technology, data collection, legislation and public acceptance and found that if there is no extensive specific regulations to restrict the collection and use of location data, including the pursuit of the universal protection right of anonymity by individuals, governments, commercial enterprises, employers and individuals will increasingly use tracking technology at the expense of geographical privacy (Dobson & Herbert, 2021). In addition, the fundamental challenge of developing urban big data infrastructure goes beyond the technical field: the relationship between data, data providers, data users, software developers and suppliers is often unclear, which makes it difficult for such infrastructure to operate effectively. According to the study of Xiao et al., self-organized and self-organizing agile methods are promising to help solve this problem (Xiao & Miller, 2021).

3.3 Improvement of Computility Supports Urban Computing

The late 1960s and early 1970s triggered a quantitative revolution in geography, and the late 1970s and early 1980s witnessed the rise of databases, improvements in computing performance and the development of massively parallel architectures that allowed previously intractable analytical problems to be solved by deterministic methods. What was once GeoComputation faced a number of major challenges, including but not limited to: developing robust clustering algorithms that could operate across spatio-temporal scales, obtaining computability that were too complex for the hardware and software of the time, visualizing and virtual reality paradigms that enabled exploration, understanding, and communication of geographic phenomena... Now, in the age of information technology, there has been another sea change in data availability and computing power, both hardware and software. We have a powerful platform to use this new data and computability to "make the best of what we have" (Wilson, 2018). Taking deep learning model as an example, with the deepening of neural network and the increase of parameters, the complexity of the model also increases, and the required number of training samples also increases simultaneously, so the required data storage and processing capabilities are more demanding (Zhang Yongsheng et al., 2021). Whereas past models took months to build and often days to run, today's models of the same size can be built in hours, run in minutes, or even seconds (Batty & Milton, 2021).

Urban computing is based on being able to perform highly scalable, fast, reliable, and flexible computing. Advances in supercomputing (high-performance computing), GPU (graphics processing units), cloud, mobile, and edge computing have greatly enhanced the computing power of urban applications. High performance computer (HPC) solves today's super-large, ultra-high and ultra-complex computing tasks. After entering the era of HPC, China has developed a series of machines such as Yinhe, Sunway and Shuguang (Zhou Xingming, 2011). GPU computing uses the GPU (graphics processing unit) as a coprocessor to speed up the CPU to speed up the running speed of scientific, analytical, engineering, consumer and enterprise applications (Wu Enhua & Liu Kuo, 2004). Cloud computing brings scalability and on-demand computing capabilities to urban system simulation for timely prediction. Mobile computing brings portability and social interaction for citizens to report instant information, thus better integrating knowledge. Edge computing allows data generated by field devices to be processed and analyzed at the edge of the network, thus reducing it to central storage (Q. Liu et al., 2021).

The increase in computability has foreshadowed the emergence of new methods of urban computing, and artificial intelligence technology has mushroomed. AI techniques widely used in urban computing, including supervised learning, semi-supervised learning, unsupervised learning, matrix decomposition, graphical modelling, etc. AI technology also plays a role in urban computing in the fields of urban planning, urban transportation, location-based social networking (LBSNs), urban security and urban environmental monitoring (Senzhang Wang & Cao, 2021). At present, researchers have tried to integrate artificial intelligence technology (data-driven) into the framework of traditional urban model (theory-driven), for example, through land use development data to reveal the space-time interaction rules between the development of different functional plots and extrapolate the trend. Artificial intelligence is also difficult to use sometimes, and one of the key problems in terms of systems that generate big data in real time is thinking of these systems as black boxes that are not easily explained by modal models. As we know, the model that can produce good prediction only depends on the data used for training and prediction, which may produce very unpredictable results at any point in time (Batty, 2022). Urban simulation and prediction need to avoid its potential "black box" attribute, and more clearly reveal the interaction between the development of different spatial scales and different urban departments, and rely on the change of empirical data to constantly test the simulation results and challenge the model prediction.

Deep learning is a machine learning method. In addition to the powerful learning ability from big data, another significant difference and advantage between deep learning and traditional machine learning is that deep learning does not need to manually make features, but can automatically learn features from the input raw data. Deep learning architectures such as deep neural network (DNN), recurrent neural network (RNN), deep belief network (DBN) and convolutional neural network (CNN) have been widely used. Reinforcement learning is more common than supervised/unsupervised learning (Sutton & Barto, 2005). Intuitively, reinforcement learning attempts to mimic human stress responses in an attempt to solve general problems about how best to match states and actions to get the maximum long-term accumulated reward.

Data mining is the key for geographic big data to generate "great value". The dual improvement of data and methods broadens the dimension of data mining technology and engenders four important urban analysis tasks: urban pattern discovery, urban activity modelling, urban mobility modelling and urban event detection, with new depth and breadth (Zhang & Han, 2021). Geographical big data mining methods have also been improved in cluster analysis, anomaly detection, correlation mining, predictive modelling and other aspects, especially predictive modelling. The statistics-based methods are mainly based on spatial-temporal correlation modelling of historical data to achieve prediction. The machine-learning method has gradually been paid attention to in the task of geographic big data prediction modeling, including the spatial-temporal coupling method of geographic big data prediction modeling and the spatial-temporal heterogeneity modeling of geographic big data (Liu Yaolin, Liu Qiliang, Deng Min, & Shi Yan, 2022).

4   Concluding Remarks

This paper first outlines the development of smart cities of different countries, then expounds the concept and key points of smart cities, and puts forward that data-driven smart cities is the core concept throughout the test. This paper discusses the formation of the fourth paradigm of urban modelling from three aspects: 1) From urban planning and traffic scheduling to disaster control and travel planning, the availability of a large amount of social sensing data provides a unique opportunity to understand urban space in a data-driven manner and improve many urban computing applications; 2) The construction of network service-oriented urban big data infrastructure provides convenient geographic information services to the public; 3) The enhancement of computing power represented by cloud, mobile, edge and high performance computing solves the outstanding problems of the third phase of urban modelling (before 2000). Urban modeling has also gradually entered other fields, such as national defense and security, history and archeology, trade flows of ocean and inland countries, and how cities operate and evolve. We need economics, sociology, geography, psychology, and political science to make urban modeling truly interdisciplinary.

References

Yigitcanlar, T., et al.: Understanding 'smart cities': intertwining development drivers with desired outcomes in a multidimensional framework. Cities 4(81), 145–160 (2018)

Javed, A.R., et al.: Future smart cities: requirements, emerging technologies, applications, challenges, and future aspects. Cities 6(129), 103794 (2022)

Kaluarachchi, Y.: Implementing data-driven smart city applications for future cities. Smart Cities **3**(5), 455–474 (2022)

Yuan, Q., Zhang, Q., Li, J., Shen, H., Zhang, L.: Hyperspectral image denoising employing a spatial-spectral deep residual convolutional neural network. IEEE Trans. Geosci. Remote Sens. **57**(2), 1205–1218 (2019)

Yuan, Q., et al.: Deep learning in environmental remote sensing: achievements and challenges. Remote Sens. Env. **241**, 111716 (2019)

Author Index

X. Meng et al. (Eds.): SpatialDI 2024, LNCS 14619, pp. 357–358, 2024.
https://doi.org/10.1007/978-981-97-2966-1

Printed in the United States
by Baker & Taylor Publisher Services